'This third edition of *Investigative Journalism* confronts a profoundly changed media landscape. Reports of the death of investigative journalism as watchdog and custodian of conscience are way premature, as this book reveals. Essential.'
— **Dominic Ziegler,** *The Economist*

'Investigative journalism makes crucial contributions to the development of society and the improvement of institutions all over the world. This third edition of *Investigative Journalism* is a much-needed guide to investigative journalism in a new era of global uncertainty and upheaval.'
— **Zhang Lifen, Professor of Journalism, Fudan University and Associate Editor,** *Financial Times*

'This new edition, rich with case studies and best practice, illustrates a fresh encouraging wave of investigative journalism around the globe. Essential reading for students, academics and journalists who believe in holding the powerful to account.'
— **Richard Sambrook, Professor of Journalism, Cardiff University and Former Director,** *BBC News*

'Investigative journalism is seeing a huge transformation and this book tells you about the most important developments — from the growing power of international collaboration over the new importance of open source investigations to the emerging role played by NGOs. It turns an eye not only to the countries of the English-speaking world but also to Asia, Africa and Latin America.'
— **Hans-Martin Tillack,** *Stern*

'This book tracks the emergence of new tools and techniques for holding power to account and describes emerging models for cross-border collaboration and protection. The journalism of exposure can no longer be confined to nation states. It has also become even more urgent and necessary.'
— **Sheila S. Coronel, Director, Stabile Center for Investigative Journalism, Columbia University**

# INVESTIGATIVE JOURNALISM

This third edition maps the new world of investigative journalism, where technology and globalisation have connected and energised journalists, whistle-blowers and the latest players, with far-reaching consequences for politics and business worldwide.

In this new edition, expert contributors demonstrate how crowdsourcing, big data, globalisation of information, and changes in media ownership and funding have escalated the impact of investigative journalists. The book includes case studies of investigative journalism from around the world, including the exposure of EU corruption, the destruction of the Malaysian environment and investigations in China, Poland and Turkey. From Latin America to Nigeria, India to the Arab world, investigative journalists intensify their countries' evolution by inquisition and revelation.

This new edition reveals how investigative journalism has gone digital and global. *Investigative Journalism* is essential for all those intending to master global politics, international relations, media and justice in the 21st century.

**Hugo de Burgh** is Professor of Journalism at the University of Westminster, where he set up the China Media Centre in 2005. He is also Professor in the School of Media & Communications at Tsinghua University. Previously he worked for Scottish Television, the BBC and (the UK's) Channel 4. Recent books include *China's Media Go Global* (2018, with Daya Thussu and Shi Anbin) and *China's Media in the Emerging World Order, Second Edition* (2020). Previous publications include *Investigative Journalism* (three editions); *Democracy in England: Possible & Necessary*; *The Chinese Journalist*; *Making Journalists*; *China, Friend or Foe?*; *China's Environment and Chinese Environment Journalists*; *China and Britain: The Potential Impact of China's Development*; *Facing Western Media* 应对西方媒体; *The West You Really Don't Know* 你所不了解的西方故事 and *Can the Prizes Still Glitter? The Future of British Universities in a Changing World*.

**Paul Lashmar** is Head of the Department of Journalism at City University of London as well as Reader in the Department of Journalism. He has written extensively about the world of intelligence agencies for four decades. His research interests include investigative journalism, intelligence–media relations and organised crime. Lashmar has been an investigative journalist in television and print and on the staff of *The Observer*, Granada Television's *World in Action* current affairs series and *The Independent*. Books authored or co-authored by him include *Online Journalism: The Essential Guide* (2014, with Steve Hill). *Spies, Spin and the Fourth Estate* was published in September 2020.

# INVESTIGATIVE JOURNALISM

## Third edition

*Edited by Hugo de Burgh
and Paul Lashmar*

LONDON AND NEW YORK

Third edition published 2021
by Routledge
2 Park Square, Milton Park, Abingdon, Oxon, OX14 4RN

and by Routledge
52 Vanderbilt Avenue, New York, NY 10017

*Routledge is an imprint of the Taylor & Francis Group, an informa business*

© 2021 selection and editorial matter, Hugo de Burgh and Paul Lashmar; individual chapters, the contributors

The right of Hugo de Burgh and Paul Lashmar to be identified as the authors of the editorial material, and of the authors for their individual chapters, has been asserted in accordance with sections 77 and 78 of the Copyright, Designs and Patents Act 1988.

All rights reserved. No part of this book may be reprinted or reproduced or utilised in any form or by any electronic, mechanical, or other means, now known or hereafter invented, including photocopying and recording, or in any information storage or retrieval system, without permission in writing from the publishers.

*Trademark notice*: Product or corporate names may be trademarks or registered trademarks, and are used only for identification and explanation without intent to infringe.

First edition published by Routledge 2000
Second edition published by Routledge 2008

*British Library Cataloguing-in-Publication Data*
A catalogue record for this book is available from the British Library

*Library of Congress Cataloging-in-Publication Data*
A catalog record for this book has been requested

ISBN: 978-0-367-18246-5 (hbk)
ISBN: 978-0-367-18248-9 (pbk)
ISBN: 978-0-429-06028-1 (ebk)

Typeset in Bembo
by Apex CoVantage, LLC

# CONTENTS

| | |
|---|---|
| *Notes on contributors* | x |
| *Acknowledgements* | xvi |

**Introduction**     1
HUGO DE BURGH

**PART I**
**Context**     15

1 **Data journalism in a time of epic data leaks**     17
HAMISH BOLAND-RUDDER AND WILL FITZGIBBON

2 **National security**     30
PAUL LASHMAR

3 **New models of funding and executing**     44
GLENDA COOPER

4 **Digital sleuthing**     57
FÉLIM McMAHON

5 **Kill one and a dozen return**     73
STEPHEN GREY

6 **Legal threats in the United Kingdom**     87
SARAH KAVANAGH

CONTENTS

7 **Mission-driven journalism** 100
RACHEL OLDROYD

8 **Grassroots operations** 111
RACHEL HAMADA

PART II
**Places** 123

9 **China and the digital era** 125
WANG HAIYAN AND FAN JICHEN

10 **Syria: the war and before** 137
SABA BEBAWI

11 **Survival in Turkey** 149
SELIN BUCAK

12 **Poland since 1989** 162
MAREK PALCZEWSKI

13 **India's paradox** 175
PRASUN SONWALKAR

14 **Malaysia: a case study in global corruption** 187
CLARE REWCASTLE BROWN

15 **Ten years in Nigeria** 203
EMEKA UMEJEI AND SULEIMAN A. SULEIMAN

16 **The European Union and the rise of collaboration** 217
BRIGITTE ALFTER

17 **Investigative journalism in Latin America today** 230
MAGDALENA SALDAÑA AND SILVIO WAISBORD

18 **How the United Kingdom's tabloids go about it** 243
ROY GREENSLADE

viii

CONTENTS

19 **United Kingdom: reporting of the far-right** 257
PAUL JACKSON

20 **The United Kingdom's *Private Eye*: the 'club'
the powerful fear** 269
PATRICK WARD

**Afterword: manifesto for investigative journalism
in the 21st century** 280
PAUL LASHMAR

*Index* 284

# CONTRIBUTORS

## Investigative Journalism Goes Global

### *Editors' biographies*

**Hugo de Burgh** is Professor of Journalism at the University of Westminster, where he set up the China Media Centre in 2005. He is also Professor in the School of Media & Communications at Tsinghua University. Previously he worked for Scottish Television, BBC and (the UK's) Channel 4. Recent books are (the second edition of) *China's Media in the Emerging World Order* (2020) and (with Daya Thussu and Shi Anbin) *China's Media Go Global* (2018). Previous publications include *Investigative Journalism* (three editions); *Democracy in England: Possible & Necessary*; *The Chinese Journalist*; *Making Journalists*; *China, Friend or Foe?*; *China's Environment and Chinese Environment Journalists*; *China and Britain: The Potential Impact of China's Development*; *Facing Western Media* 应对西方媒体; *The West You Really Don't Know* 你所不了解的西方故事 and *Can the Prizes Still Glitter? The Future of British Universities in a Changing World.*

**Paul Lashmar** is Head of the Department of Journalism at City University of London and Reader in Journalism. He has written extensively about the world of intelligence agencies for four decades. His research interests include investigative journalism, intelligence-media relations and organised crime. Lashmar has been an investigative journalist in television and print and on the staff of *The Observer*, Granada Television's *World in Action* current affairs series and *The Independent*. Books authored or co-authored by him include (with Steve Hill) *Online Journalism: The Essential Guide* (2014). *Spies, Spin and the Fourth Estate* (2020) published in September 2020.

### *Authors' biographies*

**Brigitte Alfter** is Director of Arena for Journalism in Europe, the organisation behind the annual EIJC & Dataharvest conference. Earlier she was Managing

# CONTRIBUTORS

Editor of Journalismfund.eu, a support structure for in-depth, innovative and independent journalism in Europe. Alfter has been EU-correspondent for *Dagbladet Information* (*Danish Daily Information*) and worked freelance with the International Consortium of Investigative Journalists (ICIJ), developing the European activities of Journalismfund.eu. From 2012–2016, she taught postgraduate students of journalism at the University of Roskilde. Alfter is author of the first handbook on cross-border collaborative journalism, published in Danish as *Journalistik over grænser – håndbog i crossborder journalistik* (2015), German as *Grenzüberschreitender Journalismus – Handbuch zum Cross-Border-Journalismus Deutsch* (2017) and English (2019).

**Saba Bebawi** is currently an Australian Research Council (ARC) DECRA Fellow (2018–2020) for a project on 'Developing an Arab Culture of Investigative Journalism'. She is also Chief Investigator of an ARC Discovery Project (2018–2020), 'Media Pluralism and Online News'. Earlier, Bebawi was a broadcaster/producer for Radio Jordan English service and has worked for CNN, World New Events (USA) and Dubai TV. Bebawi is author of *Media Power and Global Television News: The Role of Al Jazeera English* (2016) and *Investigative Journalism in the Arab World: Issues and Challenges* (2016) and co-author with Mark Evans of *The Future Foreign Correspondent* (2019). She is co-editor of *Social Media and the Politics of Reportage: The 'Arab Spring'* (2014) and *Data Journalism in the Global South* (2019).

**Hamish Boland-Rudder** is online editor for the International Consortium of Investigative Journalists. He has worked on more than a dozen major ICIJ investigations, including the Pulitzer Prize-winning Panama Papers and, more recently, the FinCEN Files. He formerly worked for *The Canberra Times* in Australia, where he coordinated the newspaper's digital breaking news coverage and instituted new digital reporting rounds for the daily newsroom. Boland-Rudder has written for *The Canberra Times*, *The Sydney Morning Herald*, *The Korea Herald* and various other publications. In addition to his work for ICIJ, he also teaches journalism at the University of Technology Sydney.

**Selin Bucak** is editor of *Private Equity News* at Dow Jones. Bucak studied critical and visual studies at the Pratt Institute in New York and has an MA from SOAS, where she wrote her thesis on the relationship between President Recep Tayyip Erdoğan's ruling party and the religious organisation of exiled cleric Fethullah Gülen and its impact on the Gezi protests of 2013. Bucak has published in Reuters and the *Financial Times*, inter alia, particularly on Turkish politics and freedom of expression. She edited *Censorship in the Park: Turkish Media Trapped by Politics and Corruption*, published by the *Ethical Journalism Network*. She is an established translator of factual and literary texts from Turkish to English.

CONTRIBUTORS

**Glenda Cooper** is Senior Lecturer in Journalism at City University of London. She has published extensively on the relationship between journalists and NGOs and is the author of *Reporting Humanitarian Disasters in a Social Media Age* (2018) and co-editor of *Humanitarianism, Communications and Change* (2015). She was a Guardian Research Fellow at Nuffield College, Oxford. She has worked as a staff reporter and editor at many leading media organisations, including *The Independent, Sunday Times, Washington Post, Daily Telegraph* and BBC Radio 4.

**Will Fitzgibbon** is a Senior Reporter for the International Consortium of Investigative Journalists (ICIJ). He is also ICIJ's Africa and Middle East partnership coordinator. His reporting focuses on countries in Africa and the Middle East, and he has led regional collaborations, including *West Africa Leaks* and *Mauritius Leaks*. Fitzgibbon joined ICIJ in 2014 and has reported on major ICIJ investigations, including *the Panama Papers, Paradise Papers* and *Luanda Leaks*.

**Roy Greenslade** is Honorary Visiting and Emeritus Professor of Journalism at City, University of London. Earlier, he was editor of the *Daily Mirror*, assistant editor of *The Sun,* and managing editor (News) at the *Sunday Times*. Since From 1992 until 2020, he has been a media commentator, especially for *The Guardian*. He wrote a daily blog on *The Guardian* media site from 2006 until 2019 and a column for the *London Evening Standard* from 2006 to 2016. He is on the board of the academic quarterly the *British Journalism Review* and is a trustee of the media ethics charity MediaWise. He is the author of *Goodbye to the Working Class* (1976), *Maxwell's Fall* (1992) and *Press Gang: How Newspapers Make Profits from Propaganda* (2003).

**Stephen Grey** is a Special Correspondent on the Global Enterprise Team at Reuters News Agency. After the *Eastern Daily Press* he worked for the *Sunday Times*. He went on to report for the *New York Times, The Guardian* and *Le Monde Diplomatique*, BBC 'Newsnight,' BBC Radio 4, Channel 4 'Dispatches', and PBS and ABC News in the USA. Grey is best known for his exclusive revelations of 'extraordinary rendition' and fraud and mismanagement at the European Commission, as well as investigations in the conflict zones of Iraq and Afghanistan. He is author of *Ghost Plane, Operation Snakebite* and *The New Spymasters*. His most recent film was *Kill/Capture* for PBS Frontline. His awards include the Amnesty International Media Award (2015), from the Overseas Press Club (2006) and (2015), the Kurt Schork Award (2010) and the New York Press Club (2017).

**Wang Haiyan** is Professor in the School of Journalism and Communication at Jinan University. She is the author of *The Transformation of Investigative Journalism in China: From Journalists to Activists* (2016). Earlier, she was an investigative journalist at the *Southern City Daily* in Guangzhou. She was a Journalist Fellow at the Reuters Institute for the Study of Journalism in Oxford in 2008 and an Endeavour Research Fellow at the University of

xii

Sydney in 2012. Her research interests include investigative journalism, professionalism in journalism, role perception and performance of journalists and women in the newsrooms. Her current focus is on the impact of digitalisation on journalism with regard to the changing journalistic culture.

**Rachel Hamada** is one of the founders of the Scottish Investigative Journalism Cooperative, *The Ferret*, where she is Head of Engagement and is also part of the Bureau Local team of the Bureau of Investigative Journalism. Based in Edinburgh, Hamada has worked as a journalist for 16 years, with a particular interest in social justice and marginalised communities. Hamada has worked as an investigative journalist, as a community organiser and in journalism engagement. She designed the *New Models of Journalism* course delivered for the National Union of Journalists as well as running the Change the Story project for Bureau Local looking at reimagining the future of local news.

**Paul Jackson** is Associate Professor in History at the University of Northampton, where he specialises in the history of Fascism and the extreme right, especially in Britain after 1945. He is also the curator of the Searchlight Archive at the university, one of the United Kingdom's largest collections of material related to the recent history of extreme right groups. He is editor of Bloomsbury's book series *A Modern History of Politics and Violence*, and his most recent book is *Colin Jordan and Britain's Neo-Nazi Movement: Hitler's Echo* (2017).

**Fan Jichen** is a PhD researcher at the Chinese University of Hong Kong. He studied journalism at Renmin University (BA) and Sun Yat-sen University (MA). He has been a journalist intern at *People's Daily* and *Guangming Daily*. His research focuses on the career choices of media professionals and transformation of journalism in the digital age.

**Sarah Kavanagh** works in the campaigns and communications department at the National Union of Journalists in the United Kingdom and Ireland. She is also the staff member responsible for the union's Ethics Council. Her employment history spans almost 20 years of advocacy, policy, campaigns and communications work.

**Félim McMahon** is an investigator and strategic thinker about investigation processes who has worked in both news and philanthropic organisations. McMahon started out as a news journalist in Ireland before joining the small team which built the Dublin-based social media company, Storyful. Storyful developed verification practices as part of its news agency operations and pioneered new methods for using and authenticating citizen-generated content and other information shared online, sourcing news for outlets such as Reuters, ABC, BBC, Al Jazeera English and France24. In 2018–2019, McMahon lectured in the School of Law at the University of California, Berkeley and was Director of its Technology and Human Rights Program and of the Human Rights Investigations Lab.

# CONTRIBUTORS

**Rachel Oldroyd** joined the Bureau of Investigative Journalism in London as Deputy Editor shortly after its launch in 2010 and has led many of the organisation's key projects. Before joining the Bureau, she spent 13 years at the *Mail on Sunday*, where she ran the award-winning Reportage section in *Live* magazine. The section focused heavily on human rights violations and, under her editorship, won more than a dozen media awards. She started her career as a financial reporter working in the trade press. She became the Bureau's managing editor in October 2014. She is a trustee of the Public Benefit Journalism Research Centre.

**Marek Palczewski** is Associate Professor at the University of Social Sciences and Humanities in Warsaw in the Department of Journalism and Social Communication. He spent 18 years working at Polish Television (TVP) as a journalist and reporter and was also the Editor-In-Chief of the Polish Journalists Association (SDP) website. He is author and co-author of several books and articles on investigative journalism. His main areas of research are investigative reporting, theory of news, social media, the impact of fake news on public debate and journalistic ethics He is a member of the Polish Communication Association and the Polish Journalists Association.

**Clare Rewcastle Brown** is founder of the website Sarawak Report, which came to prominence for challenging wide-scale political corruption in Malaysia and the impacts on indigenous rights and the environment. Her investigations resulted in the exposure of the 1MDB Development Fund scandal, which upturned the Malaysian government, rocked the global financial community, helped put the off-shore finance industry on the run and embarrassed some of the most famous figures in Hollywood. She is a former British television reporter for the BBC World Service.

**Magdalena Saldaña** is an assistant professor in the School of Communications at Pontificia Universidad Católica de Chile and a researcher at the Millennium Institute for Foundational Research on Data (IMFD). Her research interests include digital journalism, investigative journalism techniques, social media and Latin American studies. She has published in the *International Journal of Press/Politics, Mass Communication and Society* and *Journalism Practice*.

**Prasun Sonwalkar** is a London-based journalist. He has reported extensively out of India between 1982 and 1999, particularly from the north-east and New Delhi on insurgencies, national politics, government and sports for The Times of India, Business Standard and other news organizations. He has been a Press Fellow of Wolfson College, Cambridge, and has reported out of London for the Indo-Asian News Service, Press Trust of India, Hindustan Times and others since 1999, when he moved to Leicester for a PhD on a Commonwealth Scholarship. He has taught in universities in Bristol and Bournemouth and his research has been published in journals and edited collections. He is a visiting research fellow in the School of Journalism, Media and Culture, Cardiff University.

**Suleiman A. Suleiman** is Assistant Professor in Communication and Multimedia Design at the American University of Nigeria. He holds a PhD from the University of East Anglia (UEA), where he has taught courses in communication and media. His research interests are in the areas of political communication in developing democracies, investigative journalism in Africa, corruption scandals and the media, digital politics, communication programme design and political public relations.

**Emeka Umejei** is a Visiting Assistant Professor in Communication and Multimedia Design at the American University of Nigeria. He holds a PhD Witwatersrand. A former journalist, Umejei is the author of *The Nigerian Media Landscape*, sponsored by the European Journalism Centre. His areas of research include journalism studies, digital journalism, global media, Chinese media, science and environmental journalism.

**Silvio Waisbord** is Professor in the School of Media and Public Affairs at George Washington University. He is the author and editor of 17 books, including more recently *Communication: A Post-Discipline* (2019), *Routledge Companion to Media and Scandals* (edited with Howard Tumber, 2019) and *A Communication Manifesto* (2019). He is the former Editor-in-Chief of the *Journal of Communication* and the *International Journal of Press/Politics*. He has lectured and worked in more than 30 countries in the Americas, Europe, Asia and Africa. He is a fellow of the International Communication Association.

**Patrick Ward** is a freelance journalist, editor and academic. His primary focus is on issues relating to humanitarian crises, international politics, the media and social movements. He has worked from Egypt, Palestine, Vietnam, India and Nepal and across Europe. He is the former editor of the English edition of the *Lens Post* and started out as editor of the *London Student* newspaper. Ward worked on *Aftershock Nepal*, a collaborative journalism project investigating and reporting on marginalised voices after the 2015 earthquake, and on *Project India*, a multimedia venture in collaboration with India's Rediff.com that covered the 2014 general election. He has contributed to books including *Voices from Nepal* and *India Elections 2014: First Reflections*. He has also written for *Private Eye, Huffington Post, Times Higher Education, Culture Trip, Bookwitty, Azhimukham, CESRAN, Gate 37, Socialist Worker, Socialist Review* and *RS21*.

# ACKNOWLEDGEMENTS

The first person to deserve thanks is the Commissioning Editor, Margaret Farrelly, who raised the idea of this third edition of IJ without realising how very patient she would have to be. Finding writers able and willing to cover our chosen areas was not easy, because investigators put investigation first, before memorialising, and there are not many academics prepared to contribute to an edited volume when their universities would prefer they spend time on journal articles. The onset of the coronavirus epidemic slowed publication even further. But we got there in the end.

We thank those who helped us find the right writers: Dominik Symonowicz, who navigated Poland for us; Ambrose Evans-Pritchard of the *Daily Telegraph*; Professor Dawn Chatty of Oxford University; Hans-Martin Tillack of *Stern* magazine; Rachel Oldroyd of *The Bureau of Investigative Journalism*; Professor Daya Thussu of Hong Kong Baptist University.

As ever, Hugo de Burgh appreciates the support of the staff of the China Media Centre, Alja Kranjec and Chang Yiru. Their colleague and mine, Guo Xu, managed the accumulation of mss and the administrative aspects with great aplomb, and we are very grateful to her.

Paul Lashmar would like to thank his team at the Department of Journalism at City University of London and also the collaborative spirit of investigative journalists whom he contacted while co-editing this edition. In particular, he would like to thank Dr Richard Danbury as Programme Director of City's MA Investigative Journalism course and the now-retired Professor David Leigh for their help on the manifesto.

It is worth noting that many of the investigative journalists who have contributed to the three editions of this book have undertaken stories that placed them at great personal risk and in some cases brought them into direct conflict with the powerful.

# INTRODUCTION

*Hugo de Burgh*

*Investigative Journalism* was first published by Routledge in 2000,[1] to immediate acclaim from teachers and students around the English-speaking world; subsequently it was translated into several languages and a second edition, published in 2008, was also successful. Unlike the two earlier editions, this one is more international, since investigative journalism, while always being rooted in the particular, is now a global practice and practised globally. Many changes are taking place, as we learn from what follows; to make sure that the book truly covers the field, I asked Paul Lashmar to co-edit with me because he has more recent experience of investigation, of the new tools and indeed of running a school of journalism with courses in investigation. The earlier editions, for which he was a contributor, are not superseded but supplemented. We expect them to remain in libraries for consultation as historical resources rather than guides to current operations.

Journalism was an Anglo-American invention,[2] and it would be reasonable to expect that, as Asia starts to eclipse Anglo-America in economic development, social dynamism and political influence, so many of the institutions and values of Anglo-America will become less respected. The media which were dominant up to the end of the 20th century have been weakened by changes both technological and commercial, putting journalism under pressure and its most troublesome form, investigative journalism, often under the axe.

Nevertheless, the story we tell here, is, in many ways, one of rejuvenation. While the platforms and personnel have changed, the profession, if that is what we can call it, is renewed. Exposure and revelation have never been monopolies of professional journalists. The whistle-blower existed long before the investigative journalist. The patron saint of Anglophone investigative journalists, William Cobbett, was not a scribbler but a soldier when he first exposed peculation in the British army of North America in the 1780s–90s. Hai Rui, whom Chairman Mao Zedong could not bear to see eulogised 500 years after the heroic whistle-blower's death, unearthed maladministration as an official in 1565. In today's England, some of the most inspiring investigations are being carried out through organisations which make no claim to journalism, such as Spinwatch.[3]

Ida Tarbell and WT Stead, to mention just two of the best-known 19th-century investigative journalists of the Anglosphere, would not recognise how their successors do things, but they would warm to the motivations and the individuals. The Internet and tools of digitalisation and minimisation have given opportunities to investigators undreamed of even as recently as the 2008 edition of this book, and globalisation has connected the canaries, newshounds, moralists, harbingers and muckrakers of every continent. In the first section of this book, you will see how investigative journalism now operates; in the second, where.

Investigative journalism may be global, but it is not universal: different cultures produce different ways of telling stories and select different stories to tell. From Latin American to Nigeria, from India to Poland, courageous men and women are contributing to their countries' evolution by holding the powerful to account in their own ways. Far from dying out with the decline of the legacy press and television, investigative journalism is an actor almost everywhere.

There are new complexities. While the enthusiasm and idealism of the citizen journalists and the NGOs and charitable foundations that fund investigations are to be welcomed, they do not necessarily subscribe to the norms of impartiality and detachment to which legacy media subscribed, nor are their operatives always trained in the profession's disciplines. We all know that the tools that investigative journalists deploy can as easily be deployed by unscrupulous businesses, oppressive governments and ideological fanatics; we are increasingly aware of the dark side of New Media:

> The old media, whatever its faults, had institutional checks, including editing, fact checking and verifying pundits. If someone appeared as an expert, viewers could expect that he or she was in fact an expert, not just a random guy with an opinion. Even if channels were biased, they were obliged to have some semblance of balance. Today, however, people can spend their entire days in media ghettos where their views are not seriously challenged, and indeed become hardened. Analysis becomes propaganda and people are increasingly only exposed to the most crazed and extreme members of the opposing tribe.[4]

In this atmosphere, it is not only terrorists, fanatics and paedophiles that we have to fear. Otherwise admirable Anglo-American journalists can see their roles as a form of activism, promoting Anglo-American liberalism as a universal ideology. This is curious, since the WikiLeaks and Snowden revelations have probably ensured that few people outside the White House or the Blair Foundation now believe that the United States is an unalloyed force for good in the world. It is a matter of concern, though, that the successful condemnation of China as, in effect, a new 'Yellow Peril' in the European and Anglo-American worlds has exacerbated polarisation such that any claim that we should try to set aside our Western perspectives is treated as apostasy. We find it difficult to imagine that other societies may have different views of what constitute human rights, of the role of the media or of the relative significance of issues revealed in the investigated country's affairs. The media of most countries claim to be impartial; only the BBC actually believes it is.[5]

We must admit the limitations of this book. We have not mentioned work in Russia and Italy, to mention just two countries in which it requires abnormal courage to be an investigative journalist. In the Anglophone world alone, we should at least mention John Pilger's *The Coming War with China*, Seymour Hersh's controversial exposure of fake news on chemical warfare in Syria and revelations of callousness and cruelty in Britain's National Health Service revealed not by journalists but the relatives of victims.[6] There is a great deal of investigation going on all over the world of which we are ignorant. We note new, recurring themes that run across the chapters.

## Overview of Part I: Context

Hamish Boland-Rudder and Will FitzGibbon's chapter, 'Data Journalism in a Time of Epic Data Leaks', details the huge changes that have taken place in investigative journalism because of the rapid development of computing. They also emphasise that journalists have to treat data like any other source of information. They have to establish credibility and reliability. Data needs to be verified. Each piece of data requires assessment before it can be relied upon for a story; it must be treated with the same level of scepticism and corroborated with the same level of care as any other source. If the identity of the source is known, this makes it easier. Can the existence of this data be proven? Is it likely that that person has access to this type of data? Can they be trusted? What are their motivations?

The *Panama Papers* was a collection of 11.5 million diverse files, mostly containing unstructured information that was not easily categorised or sorted. Even rendering it searchable was a challenge because processing this much data required more power than any individual computer could muster. At its peak, the International Consortium of Investigative Journalists (ICIJ) was running more than 30 servers simultaneously to index the information contained in each file in the dataset.

But change is not just in the techniques; the very anthropology of investigative journalism has had to change. For the *Panama Papers*, the ICIJ put together a team of more than 370 reporters from 80 countries working across 25 different languages, plus coding languages. This was collaboration on a scale never previously seen.

Traditionally, investigative journalists have been lone wolves, or at least small teams competing against other small teams. In the case of the *Panama Papers*, the size and complexity of the project enticed many of the best reporters in the world. There were plenty of stories to go around, and there were clear benefits to teamwork compared to working alone. Unprecedented access to secret documents made it worthwhile to renounce independence.

The technical methods used in the Panama Papers cannot be replicated because, as the writers put it, the pace of change in data management is rapid and relentless. 'Much of the technology employed to produce the Panama Papers is already obsolete'. But the behavioural lessons are still valid. Collaboration works.

In many democracies today, Paul Lashmar argues in 'National Security', systems of surveillance that 'make the Communist East Germany's Stasi look like a tiny cottage industry' have secretly been installed in democratic nations. Too often, the target of these surveillance monoliths are journalists. There is probing fourth-estate work yet to be done as, with few exceptions, oversight agencies have proved ineffective. What has proven more effective is investigative journalism. With this chilling rejoinder, Lashmar shows us how the formal institutions of oversight have failed to reveal rendition, torture, mass surveillance and covert operations and that we must be grateful to whistle-blowers such as Julian Assange and Edward Snowden.

Snowden's revelations about the mass acquisition of telecommunications data and bulk interception of internet traffic by the US National Security Agency showed the world how technological change has developed. We saw a global surveillance apparatus, jointly run by the Five Eyes Network in close cooperation with their commercial and international partners, which ignored laws or accountability. We saw that the agencies have secretly negotiated for 'backdoors' in the security of computer programmes, social networking sites, websites and smartphones, giving an 'extraordinary capability to hoover up and store personal emails, voice contact, social networking activity and even internet searches'. Snowden's revelations have had impact on the practice of investigative journalism. Realising that the Five Eyes had the technology to snoop on journalists and their sources, a major revaluation of journalism tradecraft has begun.

In 'New Models of Funding and Executing', Glenda Cooper shows us how the difficulties caused to investigative journalism by transformations in legacy media are being assuaged through the involvement of new actors. Investigative journalism is frequently time consuming and expensive, requiring the two commodities that mainstream media have in short supply. For this reason, there has been a growing understanding that other actors may play a role in providing newsworthy investigations for public consumption. In one sense this is nothing new; NGOs such as Amnesty International and Human Rights Watch have been investigating human rights abuses for decades. However, the ability to self-publish and the increased opportunities of open-source material mean that NGOs themselves have been examining different ways to bring their investigations to light.

New technologies that could be used for verification have been taken up with enthusiasm by those working in human rights, and some have seen the possibility of collaboration with journalists. One of the most successful has been the Amnesty International Digital Verification Corps, which now operates in six universities around the world. One of the founding partners was the Digital Verification Unit at the University of Essex.

Once upon a time, as many children know, there was a group of mice which planned to neutralise the threat of a stalking cat by placing a bell around its neck. Today, according to Félim McMahon in 'Digital Sleuthing', we have the neo-journalistic organisation Bellingcat. In a series of substantive and painstaking investigations, it has broken some of the most remarkable and consequential stories of recent years, finding innovative solutions to seemingly insurmountable problems of volume and verification of data to reveal facts that were hiding in plain sight.

All of the examples cited in this chapter have in some way re-imagined open-source journalism as an all-source activity. While logic indicates that these types of skills belong at the heart of the newsroom, it is hard to imagine them delivering the kind of impact they have had elsewhere from there. The skills learned during a stint in one of these investigative units or even on a busy verification hub, however, would serve a journalist well on any beat. As Artificial Intelligence continues to transform our world and make every aspect of life more quarriable, digital investigative journalists will need new knowledge, skills and partnerships to succeed.

Stephen Grey, famous for *Ghost Plane*, in which he revealed the Bush-Blair policy of rendition,[7] here, in 'Kill One and a Dozen Return', tells the story of how journalists have come together to render the murder of their colleagues ineffective as a deterrent by ensuring that their work is shared and continued. Probably the first extensive such collaboration was the Arizona Project, the first salvo of the Investigative Reporters and Editors (IRE). Grey details this and other early collaborations for the same purpose. Reporters from the Brazilian Association of Investigative Journalism (ABRAJI), a non-profit, kept alive the work of Tim Lopes, a reporter burned to death by drug traffickers in 2002. With the Khadija Project, set up in 2015, the Organised Crime and Corruption Reporting Project (OCCRP) continued the work of Azeri journalist Khadija Ismayilova in exposing political corruption while she was in jail.

Inspired by these, French journalist Laurent Richard developed Forbidden Stories systematically to continue the work of murdered and imprisoned journalists and to provide a technical system for reporters in dangerous situations to upload their secrets as a kind of insurance. In the event of their death or imprisonment, the secrets could be released. 'Cooperation is without a doubt the best protection' says Richard.

Although journalists in the United Kingdom are very rarely faced with the violence, torture and death that can be the too-frequent reward for their services in many parts of the world, some journalists are concerned at the new laws and police activities that hamper what they regard as their legitimate work, in particular the menacing of sources. According to Sarah Kavanagh in 'Legal Threats in the United Kingdom', 82 journalists had their data seized by British police in 2015. A total of 34 police investigations concerned themselves with relationships between 105 journalists and 242 sources.

That same year, the *Conservative Party Manifesto* pledged that there would be explicit statutory protection for journalists and a commitment to ban the police from accessing their phone records. The party won the election and a new Investigatory Powers Bill was published. As Kavanagh explains, 'this Bill has been a disappointment. It has even made life more difficult for journalists'.

That this happens in England, the birthplace of relatively free journalism, where the idea of a free press is common ground among all except the far left and far right, is indicative of a worldwide trend.

Rachel Oldroyd summarises for us the crisis of journalism in the digital, globalised world. Her purpose, in 'Mission-driven Journalism', is not merely to repeat the litany of austerity, advertising collapse and audience flight but to show us how new platforms are coming about. The 'non-profit, mission-driven' sector is burgeoning, giving new hope to watchdogs and victims everywhere. At the last count, the international grouping of such entities, the Global Investigative Journalism Network, has 182 members in 77 countries. Oldroyd herself runs the UK's Bureau of Investigative Journalism.

Philanthropic support has allowed non-profit organisations to equal the legacy media's efforts. Campaign groups such as Greenpeace employ investigative journalists. To get attention for their otherwise tranquil websites, new methods and approaches are being inaugurated. Operations such as Bellingcat – discussed in Chapter 7 – have emerged. The challenges are obvious, especially that of living up to the levels of impartiality, evidence and fact checking of the best journalists of the pre-digital past. Oldroyd tells us that practitioners have recognised the risks and that their professionalism is second to none. They are, she holds, an inspiration to the coming generations of investigators who see themselves operating on platforms other than those of the past.

The crisis of local newspapers in the United Kingdom has been met by local initiatives very typical of English society, immemorially, but also of relevance elsewhere. Until the 20th century, political power and social innovation were very localised in England; as far back as the historians can be sure, well over 1000 years, the detached family system of the English has driven them to set up social and business enterprises to stand in for the family solidarity familiar in other parts of Europe. In the 18th and 19th centuries, foreign visitors identified a rich working-class culture of associations, mutual societies and businesses quite unlike other European countries. The default position of the English, it seems, is to set up an association, as British Labour politician Ernest Bevin is supposed to have said, 'as hens lay eggs'.[8]

Rachel Hamada, writing in 'Grassroots Operations', is squarely in that tradition, as Community Organiser of the Bureau Local Project, 'a network of over 1000 people across the United Kingdom – journalists, bloggers, coders, academics, lawyers, community leaders and activists – who all come together to work on investigations and commit "acts of journalism", beyond straight reporting'.

This model has proved effective and has inspired others – for example, *Correctiv* in Germany, which took on the same model to set up *Correctiv Lokal*, and *The Correspondent*, the global news features platform headquartered in Amsterdam, which has used the Bureau Local's collaboration model for its latest investigation into surveillance during the coronavirus crisis. The Bureau Local Project operates on an open-source basis wherever possible and shares open resources online, including a blueprint for its own model. Projects are emerging all over, from Greece to India. Local news is seeing a host of imaginative versions emerging, with people willingly sharing resources, technology and success stories, super-powering this movement.

## Overview of Part II: Places

Globalisation does not bundle universalism. While journalists in Asia or Africa are happy to study the techniques of their Anglo-American counterparts, they often upset their mentors when they refuse to imbibe their assumptions. Anglophone academics may, like Davos devotees, judge every country's institutions by their proximity to the Anglosphere's, but journalists in the Maghreb or Korea or Iceland, for that matter, will point to their own traditions, media history and social values as justifications for particularities.

Investigative journalism performs a set of similar functions in any polity, but the exercise of these functions varies according to the culture of that polity. This is an important point to assert, because Anglo-Americans have become inured to the idea that there are now different habits of journalism and like to claim that theirs are of universal validity. In a world dominated by Anglo-America, the 80% of the world not descended from Europeans kept quiet when they disagreed. No longer. Now that we are coming to grasp that 'The Future is Asian',[9] difference should be respected.

The harbinger is China, if only because it has the largest population combined with the most dynamic and, on many counts, already greatest, economy. Our chapter on China is by journalists turned academics who have experience of working in China's media and studying in Europe. Because of the widespread ignorance of China outside Asia and the rapid changes in society and polity that have taken place over the recent decades, in 'China and the Digital Era', Wang and Fan have to start by reassuring us that there is an indigenous tradition of investigative journalism in their country. As elsewhere, digitalisation and the Internet have profoundly affected journalists since the millennium and, indeed, so has politics. China is going through one of its periods of ideological intensification, though, to the benefit of ordinary Chinese people as to the benefit of the rest of humankind, the ideology in question is not Marxist-Leninist but a neo-Confucianism of the kind that underpins other East Asian societies.[10]

Nevertheless, this means that investigative journalism in legacy media has been more constrained out of fear of upsetting the authorities, accelerating the shift to social media and the burgeoning influence of 'we media'. Wang and Fan give examples of stories that originated with netizens, were picked up by sites both legacy and New Media and have put pressure on the authorities. They are too polite to say that revelations in China can be more influential than their counterparts in electoral democracies, because the authorities, bereft of the checks provided by national elections, take social media complaints so very seriously.

It is not only the mode of reporting that has changed but the topics. Until recently, investigative journalism particularly targeted the 'hard' topics of abuses of power and the wrongdoings of government departments and officials. Today it tends to deal with 'softer' topics such as health, environment and ordinary people's livelihoods. Wang and Fan give examples.

There are two major developments revealed in this chapter. Underlying them is another which, though not a necessary aspect of this chapter, is nevertheless deserving of mention: the emergence of the philosophy of constructive journalism. Asian journalists have long regarded Anglophone media as irresponsible, subversive (of their own societies) and naive in claiming themselves to be impartial when they are, in other eyes, carriers of propaganda. Chinese journalists are working to theorise what they consider a fairer approach to subjects and events, one which recoils from stimulating hatred or violence.[11]

Culture-specific approaches to journalism are also reflected upon in Bebawi's chapter, 'Syria: The War and Before'. Where training was provided to Syrian journalists by outside organisations, the trainers, being from non-Arab backgrounds, were ignorant of the specifics of Arab society and governance, let alone current issues, making clear the redundancy of the idea of 'universal journalism'. While the scientific method of reasoning and evidence-seeking may be universally applicable, as well as the skills of data collection and evaluation, the ways in which you deploy it and the choice of topics must be relevant to the culture.

Bebawi, like her Chinese colleagues, wants to dispel Anglo illusions about her societies. She is at pains to point out that 'the emergence of investigative journalism was not a result of the Arab Spring' but, in fact, that 'the development of investigative reporting in some Arab countries was more prominent prior to the Arab Spring'. The Arab world is varied and, in Jordan, for example, investigative journalists moved on from social and environmental issues to addressing political matters in this period. In Syria, where journalists before the war were relatively free, the war constrained them, for all the reasons we can imagine.

In Turkey there is not, thank God, a civil war, but there is certainly a violent battle of ideas. Journalists in Turkey have long been pragmatic and generally secular and sceptical. This puts them, as a profession, at odds with the revival of traditional religion promoted by the current political leadership. President

INTRODUCTION

Erdoğan rejects the Ataturk settlement by which modern Turkey was carved out of the Ottoman Empire to be a secular republic, eschewing not only its inheritance of the Islamic Caliphate but also leadership of the mystical Turkic world from Ulan Batur to Edirne. It has never been easy to be a journalist in Turkey, for Ataturk secularism was authoritarian, and Bucak's lucid history profiles courageous individuals as well as explaining the political economy of media to tell us the story. Today, the revival of religious sentiment makes it all but impossible for Turks to practise journalism. Bucak quotes a colleague as saying that 'the better a journalist is in Turkey, the more likely he or she will be fired'. The exercise of journalism as previously understood – reporting facts and supplying evidence – is likely to send the reporter to prison.

As Bucak writes, though, getting published is remarkable, but finding sources and discovering wrongdoing are equally difficult. Even daring to consider investigating corruption can incur a charge of treason. The President describes journalists as 'gardeners' of terrorism. So, why have a chapter on Turkey, where investigative journalism barely exists? Because Turkey is an important culture and Turkic civilisation, with around 170 million people, the foundation of many geopolitically significant countries. Bucak's chapter also acts as a warning and gives food for thought even as we celebrate the globalisation of journalism.

Once totalitarianism of the Marxist-Leninist variety had been overthrown in 1989, Poland's journalists began to revive the civil society which had flourished before the Soviet-Nazi invasion of 1939. Poland is a European country, sharing with the supposed Anglophone 'inventors of journalism' those Christian principles of human equality and accountability which underlie modern secularism and are the moral basis of investigative journalism.

In 'Poland since 1989', Palczewski describes the enthusiastic deployment of investigation techniques such as undercover sting operations during the 1990s, used in revelations of corruption, paedophilia and terrorism. In the early 2000s, the trend continued, with many revelations having major political repercussions, although suspicion hung over some of the stories as to whether they were politically or commercially motivated, resulting in a period of scepticism and stagnation. Palczewski reports an impressive revival over the last 4 years, however, in which property scams, paedophilia in the church, police brutality and neo-Nazis were among the momentous exposures. Traditional investigative journalism, all in all, is in rude health in Poland.

In India, Sonwalkar reminds us, there is a 'glorious tradition' of investigative journalism. 'India's Paradox' shows that journalism in any one country does not exist in isolation but is part of a complex matrix of laws, core values and practices. The Indian cases Sonwalkar adumbrates make us wonder to what extent investigative journalism can function 'when powerful political and corporate forces steer it to one partisan extreme'. Despite the improvement of the hardware of journalism and therefore improved techniques, Sonwalkar considers that investigative journalism in India is in serious decline because of the changes in its political environment.

9

From the 1970s through the 1990s, many exposures by investigative journalists 'rocked' India, testifying to the robustness of the media and the zealousness of journalists. Since then, it is the 'Murdochization', as Sonwalkar has it, of the media that has crippled journalism, elevating moneymaking far over holding power to account as the purpose of media, offline or online. 'Paid news', often as political as commercial, squeezes out honest reportage. Media organisations and personnel critical of the party in power have suffered calamity to the extent that India's leading investigative journalist has likened India's media to that of North Korea. From the journalist's point of view, that is a terrible deterioration since India inherited its liberal press laws from the British Raj.

In this chapter, Sonwalkar shows us the heights of which Indian investigative journalism is capable and the struggles which it has fought since Independence. He also tells us about the investigation of the news organisations themselves, in which they were discovered to be being paid to defame politicians, promote a particular religion and subvert the democratic processes. Leading members of the current government have attacked the media, further vilifying and disparaging journalism.

The story of how defenceless Malaysians were being robbed of their rights, their livelihoods and their identity is told in this extraordinary tale by Clare Rewcastle Brown, 'A Malaysian Odyssey'. She gives us the whole sorry saga as she reveals how she penetrated the politics, business, criminality and downright irresponsibility of many in the Malaysian elite. Aside from the exploitation and deception of human beings, that which she investigated has disastrous environmental impacts. Yet the perpetrators used every legal and illegal technique to stop her.

The lessons to be learnt are not only of the indefatigability of a lone sleuth but the way in which social media can be mobilised on the side of the victims, whether individual poor communities or society at large. Without *Sarawak Report*, the shameless behaviour of the Taib family would never have been exposed to the world and revealed to their victims, no matter how clever Rewcastle Brown might have been in tracing their millions and their deal-making or how brave the whistle-blowers she handled. The results included a political overturn. This tale is to be read for its lessons in craft but also for its vindication of the mission.

In 'Ten Years in Nigeria', Umejei and Suleiman tell us that the Nigerian press has been vigorous since its inception in 1849. Espousing liberal ideas of a free press and watchdog journalism, it often challenged the British authorities (c. 1849–1960) under whose auspices it emerged. Today, it is the most politically vibrant in Africa, and 'through watchdog journalism and investigative reporting, Nigerian newspapers have been at the forefront of democratic development in the country'. There have been ups and downs, however, and the authors discuss those, as well as particular aspects of investigative reporting in Nigeria. One consequence of digitalisation has been the increased dependence of all media on advertisers and sponsors, with concomitant conditioning of subject matter. Since 1999, the move online has accelerated. Another issue which puts in question the trustworthiness of digital investigation is anonymity and pseudonymity. All in all, Umejei and Suleiman's rather downbeat conclusion is that legacy media's proud tradition of investigative journalism is unlikely to continue and that online media have yet to provide adequate alternative spaces.

In 2003, London's *Financial Times* headlines revealed 'A vast enterprise for looting community funds' in the European commission, and subsequently *Stern* reporter Hans-Martin Tillack was arrested at the instigation of the European Union on trumped-up charges eventually dismissed by the courts. His documents and other seized items were not returned to him until 2008.

Tillack's experience was typical of that suffered by others who have dared to enquire into the opaque activities of the European Union's governing institutions. Known or suspected corruption, financial or political, has been a principal motivator of the revulsion against the EU, manifested time and time again by demonstrators and voters in Western European countries. It is not that journalists have not tried to get to grips with this, but they have been hamstrung not only by the complexity of the institutions but by the great differences in attitudes and approaches of journalists from different countries of the Union. This is the subject of Brigitte Alfter's chapter, 'The EU and the Challenges of Collaboration'.

Twenty-seven of the 44 European countries are in the EU. Even without the recalcitrant 17, that makes for a great deal of variety. Journalists from Belgium or Hungary or Portugal, say, will be familiar with the institutions of their own countries but seldom equipped to cross borders, lacking language and knowledge. Their skills, too, are rarely transferable, because what is acceptable in Slovenia may not be in Ireland, and so on. Expectations vary. 'Scandinavian and British journalists kept pushing for more transparency and Nordic style access to documents for example and even the perception of what constituted a breach of norms varied according to country', according to Alfter, discussing some of the collaborative projects. Consequently, while co-operation is difficult, it is also the only solution if investigations are to penetrate the multilingual, multicultural cabals. Alfter nevertheless describes attempts to 'follow the money' and identify nepotism in appointments.

Although cultural differences make life as complicated for journalists as for politicians, we should celebrate rather than denigrate them, because it is the very diversity of Europe that has been the secret of its successful intellectual, artistic, scientific and social advancement over the centuries. Nationalism has often wrongly been blamed for wars which were ideological and religious in motivation. It is patriotism, attachment to cultural particularities, that has been a bulwark of resistance to despotism over many centuries, so that we should rejoice in the distinctiveness of the European countries, no matter how frustrating. Investigative journalism can only benefit from it, too.

In 'Investigative journalism in Latin America today', Saldaña and Waisbord focus on the shared concerns which have stimulated cross-continental alliances. In the 1990s, in most of the constituent countries, investigative journalism was vigorous, complementing the re-emergence of democratic politics. It was not necessarily detached; journalists were often hamstrung by vested interests, or their editors were threatened by politicians. In such circumstances, sharing responsibility can be a way out. Brazilian, Argentinean, Mexican and Colombian media participated in global exposures such as the *Panama Papers* and *Paradise Papers*. As with other nationalities' journalists, Saldaña and Waisbord remind us, such collaboration 'demonstrates a paradigm shift where exclusivity and immediacy are replaced by a culture of information sharing and "slow" journalism'.

Another major development in Latin-American journalism over the past decade has been the emergence of digital sites which feature investigations. Some of these and their achievements are introduced, as are the distinctive funding models, with combinations of subscription, consulting, service provision, advertising, crowdfunding, sales to news organisations and philanthropic sources. Of the latter, how much is supplied from foreign countries and therefore might cause alarm is not clear; perhaps this needs investigation.

Saldaña and Waisbord report that data journalism has taken off in elite media and that fact-checking operations have begun to emerge in response to the spread of unverified information, rumours and conspiracies that have been a concern raised during several elections across the region. Although they are enthusiastic about progress, they warn that when political conditions change, as in Nicaragua and Venezuela, repression is not far behind, and journalists are vulnerable to violence and online harassment. Despite this, the successes of Latin-American investigative journalists in influencing public affairs and shedding light on social problems have been remarkable and are documented here.

We return to England, the progenitor of modern journalism, as Roy Greenslade picks up again from his second-edition work on tabloid papers to review how they are continuing to undertake investigations despite the changes to the industry wrought by digitalisation. 'How the United Kingdom's Tabloids Go about It' starts by reminding us of the obloquy which shook the UK industry, destroyed one of its oldest newspapers and attracted widespread condemnation for investigative journalism, the phone-hacking scandal. That which the newspapers were lambasted for was not what serious journalists would consider investigative journalism, but the British public was confused and cursed all journalists equally. The infamy and the public enquiry that followed were reported, often with delight, around the world as evidence of the malfeasance of the notoriously rude English media.

It seemed for a time that tabloid investigative journalism would never again lift up its collective head, yet, as Greenslade reassures us, business would soon be as usual because, though shocking, investigations are an important part of the marketing mix for the tabloids and a way to claim the public service accolade for all British newspapers. Revelations about the peculiar sexual proclivities of assorted politicians, stings of vain or greedy bosses by a chap who dressed up like Lawrence of Arabia were too good to pass by, but, fortunately, stories with better claims to social value were also commissioned and published: exposures of fraudsters, violence in refugee hostels, predatory landlords, unsafe tumble dryers and suicides among army recruits indeed constituted a public service. This is not investigative journalism of the scale and depth of tabloid celebrities of a generation ago – Paul Foot and John Pilger – nor of the ambition and expectation of many of the other stories told in this book. But they show that, despite the odds, the flame of investigation is still fluttering in the popular press.

There are several nasty causes in British public life, nasty because they eschew democracy or at most see it as a means to power because of their predilection for violence and because of their hatred of other groups. Since the defeat of the terrorist IRA, these characteristics are shared today by three 'causes': far right, extreme left and Islamist fanatics. The far right has traditionally attracted most attention because its adherents initially were pleased to associate themselves with the Nazi movement and because its anti-Semitism is so repulsive to most British people, particularly since the Second World War, which came to be seen in retrospect not only as a struggle to save English freedoms threatened by a totalitarian ideology but also as a war against persecution of the Jews.

Paul Jackson, in 'United Kingdom: Reporting of the Far-Right', shows us how the grass-roots platform *Searchlight* has been investigating and supplying material to the mainstream media for half a century. It has inspired other organisations and publications, notably BBC Panorama and More4 True Stories, which over several documentary reports have exposed the actual views of members of the ostensibly moderate British National Party (BNP) and revealed weaknesses that its opponents might exploit. A similar process is evident in the relationship between a *Searchlight* subsidiary, *Hope not Hate*, and the *Mirror* and *Mail on Sunday* newspapers.

The message of this chapter is that coordination between specialist research bodies and journalists can make for long-term and meticulous investigation. In exposing a vicious and violent cause, party or group, subject expertise is as important as investigatory skills.

*Private Eye* sells 40% more copies than the internationally famous *Economist* and is the best-selling current affairs magazine in the United Kingdom. As Patrick Ward tells us in 'The United Kingdom's *Private Eye*: The "Club" the Powerful Fear', it seems laughable to the uninitiated and redolent of schoolboy humour, yet its bite is worse than its bark. It has carried out, and continues to carry out, very serious investigations as well as modest revelations which can nevertheless result in great alarm. It does so with sceptical humour, lightness of touch and exemplary professionalism. Unlike its French cousin, *Charlie Hebdo*, *Private Eye* is of no evident political persuasion; bad people are bad, for *Private Eye*, whether they are left or right or nothing but bad.

Ward gives us thumbnails of some of the *Eye*'s most effective investigations, detail on a very major long-term one, *Shady Arabia and the Desert Fix*, and introduces the regular sections which probe areas of British life such as health, local government or media. Oh, and, of course, the jokes. In doing so, he illustrates the extraordinary workstyle of *Private Eye* and what makes it unique. Every country should have one.

Our final section is not a report but an assertion. In his 'Manifesto for Investigative Journalism in the 21st Century', Paul Lashmar calls upon all nations to recognise the value of revelatory journalism. It remains 'the most effective and consistent counter to corruption and complacency' and should be protected and encouraged by all political leaders who acknowledge that they are accountable for their power.

Our enthusiasm for investigative journalism has been fired up while reading these chapters, which are inspiring. Notwithstanding the powers of darkness which beset them and the changes in political economy and technology which challenge them, brave men and women all over the world are seeking to use their journalistic skills to expose chicanery and better the lives of their fellows. The following chapters tell us.

## Notes

1 de Burgh, Hugo (2000) *Investigative Journalism* London: Routledge

2 Chalaby, Jean (1998) *The Invention of Journalism* London: MacMillan. More accurately, it was an English invention, coming out of our Civil War. See also de Burgh, Hugo (2008) 'The Emergence of Investigative Journalism', chapter 2 of (2008) *Investigative Journalism* (London: Routledge)

3 www.spinwatch.org

4 West, Ed (2020) *Small Men on the Wrong Side of History* London: Constable p311

5 Many books in recent years have explored the failings of Anglophone media, but perhaps the most influential has been Davies, Nick (2008) *Flat Earth News* London: Vintage

6 www.curethenhs.co.uk/from-ward-to-whitehall/ accessed 070720

7 See Lashmar, Paul (2008) 'From Shadow Boxing aapto Ghost Plane' in de Burgh, Hugo (ed) (2008) *Investigative Journalism* London: Routledge, pp191–214

8 Irene Noel Baker, granddaughter of Labour politician Lord Noel Baker, personal communication

9 The title of a book by Parag Khanna (New York: Simon and Schuster 2019) but also a theme running through many books and articles on international affairs and economic development. See also Mahbubani, Kishore (2020): *Has China Won?* (New York: Public Affair)

10 I discuss this at much greater length, and offer recommended reading on the phenomenon, in de Burgh, Hugo *China's Media in the Emerging World Order* (UBP: 2020), Chapter 7

11 *Africa's Media Image in the 21st Century: From Heart of Darkness to Africa Rising*, edited by Melanie Bunce, Suzanne Franks and Chris Paterson (Routledge, 2016), contains an article by James Wan, 'Propaganda or Proper Journalism: China's Media Expansion in Africa', on CCTV's challenge of 'constructive journalism'. Zhang Yanqiu (2014) 'Understand China's Media in Africa from the Perspective of Constructive Journalism', paper presented at the international conference China and Africa Media, Communications and Public Diplomacy on 10 September 2014. Available from: www.cmi.no/file/2922-.pdf accessed: 030716

# Part I

# CONTEXT

# 1

# DATA JOURNALISM IN A TIME OF EPIC DATA LEAKS

*Hamish Boland-Rudder and Will Fitzgibbon*

"Interested in data?"

These three words, sent from an anonymous whistleblower to a reporter in Germany, would ultimately lead to the biggest leak of financial data the world had ever seen.

Hidden within a trove of 11.5 million documents were the financial secrets of a wide range of politicians, celebrities, businesspeople, criminals and other individuals willing to use tax havens and shell companies to launder money, hide riches and commit crime behind a veil of anonymity.

These three words would also spark the largest investigative journalism collaboration in history. When the Panama Papers broke on April 3, 2016, its impact was both global and immediate. Within hours, the Twitter hashtag was trending worldwide, and four years later, it still attracts a steady stream of tweets.

Over the course of the first 24 hours after publication, tens of thousands of protesters filled the streets in Iceland, Malta, Pakistan, the United Kingdom and beyond. Within 48 hours, the prime minister of Iceland was forced to resign over undeclared links to an offshore company. He would not be the last head of state to lose his job over the ensuing scandal.

By the end of that first week, lawmakers were raging in parliaments around the world, governments were forming committees to draft legislative recommendations and authorities began making arrests and raiding law firms and businesses to seize evidence of wrongdoing.

From investigations to resignations to criminal prosecutions to legal reforms; for almost four years (at the time of writing), this cache of secret files has produced a steady stream of impacts. At the time of writing, more than $US1.2 billion have been recouped, thousands of investigations launched and multiple laws changed. The Panama Papers remains unprecedented.

However, for many of the 376 reporters who spent 12 months producing stories from the dataset, this project was part of a much longer data journey they had embarked upon many years previously. Over the course of the past decade, technological advances have empowered whistleblowers to share ever-growing tranches of inside information with journalists. This is both a blessing and a curse: as the amount of data has grown, so too have the challenges of receiving, ingesting, processing and organising it and, ultimately, turning oceans of complex data into important, compelling stories (Reich and Barnoy 2016).

From the early days of WikiLeaks, to Edward Snowden's NSA Files, to the ongoing leaks of financial data, including Offshore Leaks, Luxembourg Leaks and the Panama Papers, journalists (and whistleblowers) have employed very different methodologies to understand these large datasets and to wring stories from them. While every dataset has its own challenges, there are certain constants common to the way they should be approached. Journalists are trained in cross-referencing to check stories, in cultivating sources and relying on experts when it comes to handling complex data. Leaks of this size demand another, more unfamiliar dimension: collaboration and trust with peers. As ICIJ's Gerard Ryle puts it:

> This is an era of big leaks, so that is a bonanza for journalists. . . . This is also an era of easy and cheap communication. It would not have been possible for us to do this investigation 5 or 10 years ago. And because this is the era of big data, there has never been a better moment to bring hundreds of reporters together to get their collective eyes on things.
>
> (2016)

Although this may appear intuitive, news organisations are competitive in nature, and such collaboration requires high-level buy-in. Taking into account the journalistic and technological foundations laid in the lead-up to the Panama Papers, this chapter will explore the recent history of data journalism and the emergence of massive data leaks and show how journalism and journalists have adapted to exploit these invaluable sources of information.

## A new paradigm

As technology expands the size of the playing field, the players too have expanded their abilities to deal with an unprecedented amount of information from various sensitive sources. Whistleblower platform WikiLeaks is a prime example. Launched in 2006 by enigmatic Australian hacker-activist Julian Assange, WikiLeaks drew heavily on the legacy of Daniel Ellsberg and the Pentagon Papers for inspiration, pitching itself as an "anonymous global avenue for disseminating documents the public should see" (WikiLeaks 2007).

WikiLeaks has since tested numerous publishing models, including high-profile partnerships with major media outlets (Leigh and Harding 2011, p. 61). Since its inception, the site has existed somewhere in a grey zone between legitimate journalistic enterprise and a home for radical transparency activists. But its role in popularising technology as a key tool for both transmitting and publishing leaks is undeniable.

It first came to global prominence in 2010 when it captured world headlines not only because of the sensational material it published but also on account of the backstory of the whistleblower at the heart of the leaks. United States Army Private Bradley Manning (now Chelsea Manning) had not yet turned 22 when she first reached out to WikiLeaks. An intelligence analyst stationed at Camp Hammer in Iraq in 2009, Manning had broad and easy access to top secret information. She increasingly believed that the way the United States was conducting its operations in Iraq was profoundly wrong. Armed with a rewritable CD (disguised as a Lady Gaga album), Manning began extracting secret files and searching for a conduit that could help put this information where she thought it belonged, that is, in the public domain.

> "It's public data. It belongs in the public domain. Information should be free," he wrote in a chat session with a confidant. "If it's out in the open, it should be a public good, rather than some slimy intel collector."
>
> (Zetter and Poulsen 2010)

WikiLeaks had caught Manning's attention when it published a leak of what was probably National Security Agency data. After making contact and verifying Assange's online identity, Manning used encryption and secure connections to transfer her collection of secret files (Leigh and Harding 2011, pp. 31,75).

Over the course of 2010, in collaboration with major news outlets, including *The Guardian*, the *New York Times*, and *Der Spiegel*, WikiLeaks would go on to publish three major releases of this information. This included a video, editorially titled "Collateral Murder", which showed U.S. forces killing 12 people, including two Reuters journalists, in Baghdad. It also contained a tranche of top-secret military logs related to the U.S. war in Afghanistan and a cache of confidential diplomatic cables, amounting to hundreds of thousands of documents.

Apart from the effect of the content, the very act of leaking brought about a new era, one in which even the most precious of state secrets could be divulged en masse for transmission and publication to the world, sometimes after careful vetting and reporting by journalists, sometimes not. Regardless of the arguments over ownership, technology enabled the collection of this data and also enabled its dissemination.

It was in this new paradigm of massive data leaks and ever-advancing technology that a whistleblower, known only as John Doe, gained access to a new cache of information from a Panama-based law firm called Mossack Fonseca.

## Offshore Leaks

After years of reporting on a massive fraud scheme that was swindling Australian investors and using tax havens to hide the proceeds, in 2011, an Irish-Australian journalist, Gerard Ryle, received a hard drive by post.

On the drive was 260 gigabytes of data – about 2.5 million files – of secret financial information from two offshore financial service providers. It was the first large-scale leak from an insider in a shadowy industry that helps clients hide money in tax havens such as the British Virgin Islands, Singapore and the Cook Islands. Rather than keep the information to himself, Ryle took the data with him to a new job: director of the International Consortium of Investigative Journalists (ICIJ) based in Washington, D.C.

ICIJ was formed in 1997 as the international arm of an American non-profit investigative media outlet, the Center for Public Integrity. The consortium was made up of invited journalists considered among the best investigative reporters from countries around the world. The idea behind the organisation was simple: through this trusted network of members, reporters would help each other chase leads across borders and collaborate on global investigations.

Through ICIJ's network, Ryle was able to have the data processed and shared with 86 journalists in 46 countries who worked together for 12 months to produce an unprecedented global investigation, published in April 2013, that quickly became known as Offshore Leaks. Offshore Leaks would be the first in a series of ground-breaking ICIJ exposés that revealed how the rich and powerful were able to buy into a secretive parallel economy – a world where financial rules could be bent, taxes dodged and shady business deals hidden from scrutiny.

In 2014, ICIJ's international team of collaborators published an investigation based on another trove of leaked documents, this time from the offices of Price Waterhouse Coopers' Luxembourg office, exposing a system that allowed multinational companies to slash their tax bills dramatically by routing money through the tiny European country. Five years after this investigation was published, Luxembourg Leaks, or LuxLeaks, is still referenced regularly in European Parliament communiqués and legislative actions related to corporate tax dodging.

In 2015, yet another leak of financial data revealed the secret account details of tax-dodging and sanction-evading customers of HSBC's private banking arm in Switzerland. This prompted numerous government inquiries as well as a full apology from the bank itself.

This truncated history of ICIJ's investigations in the years leading up to the Panama Papers is worth recounting. The leaked material at the heart of each of these investigations was the result of earned trust and increased visibility.

ICIJ had developed an enviable track record of cracking global stories and building cohesion among erstwhile competitive news organisations. Its reporting was proof that this team of journalists was trustworthy, diligent and able to produce stories that had results. Governments, companies, individuals and their enablers that chose to operate in this netherworld now had to look over their shoulders. This was an attractive proposition for would-be whistleblowers.

Among the collaborative cohort were the German reporters who would go on to receive the Panama Papers leak: Bastian Obermayer and Frederik Obermaier.

## John Doe's path to the leak – a 'concerned citizen'

We do not know how John Doe came by the data, but there was a lot of it. "More than anything you have ever seen," he would eventually tell German reporter Bastian Obermayer (Obermayer and Obermaier 2016, p. 9).

As we have seen, Obermayer and Obermaier had been part of the international team working together on ICIJ's previous leaks of financial information, but why did John Doe choose them as the best conduits for his information? The answer likely lies in one very specific story about the raid on a German bank.

On February 24, 2015, more than 150 prosecutors, tax investigators and detectives swooped on offices and bank branches across Germany as part of a massive investigation into tax evasion and money laundering focused on the country's second-largest bank: Commerzbank. The German authorities were acting on information from leaked data purchased for almost 1 million Euros two years previously. The data came from inside a Panama-based law firm, Mossack Fonseca, and related mostly to offshore companies linked to the tiny European tax haven of Luxembourg.

Obermayer and Obermaier had received an inside tip that the raids were imminent. But they also had another weapon in their armoury – they, too, had obtained a more comprehensive version of the same dataset. Following on from ICIJ's Luxembourg Leaks investigation (published in 2014), a source had reached out to the LuxLeaks team and had given a copy of the Mossack Fonseca material to ICIJ and the German reporters (Bernstein 2017, pp. 206–208).

When they learned that Commerzbank would be raided over the data, Obermayer and Obermaier used the dataset in their possession to prepare a three-page spread for their newspaper, detailing the authorities' investigations and providing background information about the Panamanian lawyers at the heart of the case.

Their initial trove of data on Mossack Fonseca was about to be rendered insignificant compared to a new source with far more to offer. Shortly after the publication of their stories on the Commerzbank raids, John Doe sent his initial messages to Obermayer, with the first tantalising snippets of what would become the 2.6 terabytes that constitute the Panama Papers (Bernstein 2017, pp. 206–208).

## Dealing with the data first

In many ways, journalists have to treat data like any other source of information. Reporters have to establish credibility and reliability. Data needs to be verified. Each piece of data requires assessment before it can be relied upon for a story; it must be treated with the same level of scepticism and corroborated with the same level of care as any other source.

If the identity of the source is known, this makes it easier. Can the existence of this type of data be proven? Is it likely that that person has access to this type of data? Can they be trusted? What are their motivations?

However, as was the case with the anonymous John Doe, how best to check? It might be possible to discern whether this sort of data exists and whether its format matches the possible origins of the data. This reveals nothing about the trustworthiness of the source and/or their access to the material. Therefore, attention must focus on the data itself.

In this case, authentication was helped by the dataset's consistency with the first set of Mossack Fonseca material obtained prior to the Commerzbank raids. Other sources were also employed, such as matching details from court records, company registries and more.

## Finding the structure

Every dataset has its clues as to where to start, and most of the time, this begins with the metadata – the data about the data. The bigger the dataset, the more important understanding the metadata becomes. Good metadata can be a guide to the data, in the same way that knowing a source's background, qualifications, position, age or language can help a reporter prepare more informed questions and better understand the answers.

The Panama Papers was a collection of diverse files, mostly containing unstructured information that could not be easily categorised or sorted. Among the 11.5 million files, there were 4.8 million emails, 2.1 million PDF files, 1.1 million images and more than 320,000 text documents. Furthermore, of the 3 million structured files (spreadsheets, databases), it quickly became clear that the dataset did not reflect Mossack Fonseca's database in its original format. The structure was a mess, but, crucially, there were some clues hidden in the metadata that could help clean it up (Cabra 2016).

Through analysing the folder structure of the leak, for instance, it became clear that the information was sorted by client codes that could be discerned from file- and folder-naming conventions. These client codes and other hints at structure made it possible to reverse-engineer the client database to create a structure around the data that could be used as a map.

The difference between structured and unstructured data, email messages, PDF files and Excel spreadsheets can be lost on even the best investigative reporters. Regardless of the size of the dataset, data needs to be presented in a way that makes it possible to compile stories.

This will always be a challenge. The format of the data itself may present obstacles, but reporters must also be constantly aware that the dataset will likely be incomplete. So, while it may present vital evidence to back up a story, traditional methods of interviewing and cross-referencing other sources must also be followed.

The first step with the Panama Papers was to make everything searchable. This might sound obvious, but with 11.5 million files, it was a monumental task. If an individual were to spend a minute reading each document, it would have taken about 22 years to go through all the files, and even with dozens of journalists, it would have taken far too long. Obviously, this was not an option.

Instead, ICIJ turned to technology. Original hard-copy files (scanned documents, images) were digitised using optical character recognition (OCR), where a computer program recognises each letter. Then each file needs to be "read" by a computer to ingest all the words. All of this information is then combined into an index that can be queried by a journalist. Again, even with the latest technology, size still mattered.

Processing this much data required more power than any individual computer could muster, so ICIJ turned to the power of the cloud. At its peak, ICIJ was running more than 30 servers simultaneously to index the information contained in each file in the dataset.

## Building and tailoring tools

The next step was to make these documents searchable by hundreds of journalists with wide disparities in technical competence.

The ICIJ data team built a Google-like search engine based on Blacklight, open-source software originally designed for librarians. Ongoing consultation with reporters allowed the team to prioritise additional functionality, such as filters to search by date and file type, for example, PDFs or Excel spreadsheets. The team then began ticking off the boxes in the reporters' wish list, executing functionality such as the ability to link files in various folders and step through email chains message by message.

In time, the data team extended the system's capability still further to executing lists of searches through the system to find certain categories of individuals, such as elected officials. In time, journalists would also be able to use a bespoke batch-searching tool to return a tailored spreadsheet of results based on input search terms.

This two-pronged assault on the dataset enabled the development of entirely new tools that would help build a deeper understanding of the data.

When chasing money flows across jurisdictions, reporters often become deeply enmeshed in labyrinthine structures comprising anonymous owners of Russian doll-like shell companies registered by a single agent. To better understand these complex relationships, the ICIJ used a unique database format, Neo4j, combined with a third-party visual enhancement tool, Linkurious, that allows journalists to search for individuals and see at a glance the companies and addresses linked to them in a network diagram. Moreover, a simple double-click expands the network and unveils other people with interests in the same companies or using the same addresses.

## Bringing the team together

Collaboration is key to the ICIJ journalism model – combining skills, experience and resources helps reporters tell better stories than they would if working alone. Large datasets spanning interests across the world crystallise this realisation (Hamilton 2015).

There are several ways to think about a collaborative journalism investigation, but a core rationale prevails. The best collaborations are mutually beneficial – there should be a clear benefit to teamwork compared to working alone (Alfter 2016, p. 304). Leaked data can be an extremely valuable piece of this equation: the most skilled and sceptical of journalists can be persuaded to put natural competitiveness aside as the price to be paid for unprecedented access to secret documents.

Of course, competitiveness can only be sacrificed temporarily and for a specific purpose – something akin to the best club players coming together to represent their countries in pursuit of a world trophy.

In the case of the Panama Papers, the prize was big enough to entice many of the best reporters in the world. Aside from the bigger picture and the kudos involved, there would also be more than enough stories to go around – stories that would likely never have been told otherwise.

The financial secrecy at the centre of the Panama Papers required journalists with specialist financial knowledge, including politics, corruption, money-laundering and tax evasion. The global nature of the dataset also made location a key consideration. Rather than parachuting foreign journalists into unfamiliar jurisdictions, the ICIJ model is based on sourcing local reporters with invaluable local knowledge (Alfter 2018, pp. 45–46).

For example, in this case, the team needed a reputable and trustworthy reporter in Iceland to help tell the story of the Icelandic Prime Minister's connections to an offshore company. Like many stories, ICIJ reporters combed through the documents with a view to providing possible interesting angles before their partners came on board.

Other promising leads had also piqued curiosity. ICIJ required reporters in Russia and Eastern Europe to help unwind Vladimir Putin's network of allies and track the money that flowed from country to country, bank to bank, between his associates' accounts and businesses.

Partners in the United Kingdom and United States would help uncover details in key secrecy jurisdictions (from Nevada to the British Virgin Islands) and ensure the story would eventually make its way to the desks of policymakers and regulators who had the authority to change the sharp practices – even if they were technically legal.

ICIJ also needed a diversity of skills to accomplish its ambitious task. Even with the most user-friendly tools, there was still a mountain of data work and detailed research necessary to penetrate the complex corporate structures and uncover patterns of company ownership that could make or break a story.

The collaboration needed reporters skilled in complex database querying, as well as journalists whose contact books and interviewing skills could provide access to key sources. The team also required linguistic assistance – who better to chase down Swiss prosecutors than seasoned Swiss court reporters? Who better to unravel the dynamics of Pakistan's ruling family than an experienced Pakistani political reporter?

In the end, ICIJ put together a team of more than 370 reporters from 80 countries working across 25 different languages (plus a handful of coding languages, too).

At a practical level, the collaborative process began with an in-person meeting hosted in Washington, D.C., in June, 2015, where a few dozen reporters traded initial findings, swapped reporting plans and, most importantly, formed or renewed relationships with each other that would form the foundation of this collaboration. These bonds would set the tone for any journalists who would join later.

Secure communication was essential to ensuring the investigation would not be compromised. ICIJ employed two-factor authentication (where users needed both a password and a time-sensitive six-digit code to log in) and protected sensitive emails using PGP encryption.

## Finding the stories inside and outside the data

The leaked data provided tantalising signposts, but it would never prove conclusive – in the end, the Panama Papers represents the marriage of data and traditional journalism.

In some cases, the documents included low-hanging fruit that almost guaranteed a story: the passport of Syrian president Bashar Al-Assad's cousin, official letterheads from Nigerian senator David Mark and a barely legible fax that referred to possible proceeds of an infamous UK gold heist.

But even these documents required significant shoe-leather reporting to unpack the full story. Individuals who choose to hide their wealth using offshore companies tend to be devious (or have devious individuals in their employ). It would be foolish to expect to find a smoking gun email that reads "I want to pay a bribe." None were found.

Journalists matched addresses on emails, contracts and corporate filings with public property and company registries, including Open Corporates. They cross-checked the names of shell companies with details from court records – both public and confidential. Journalists verified spellings and alternative surnames of clients who used multiple aliases.

To understand the "why" question at the heart of the Panama Papers, journalists called on finance, taxation and legal experts to explain the significance of complex inter-company loan agreements, consultancy contacts and other financial deals.

## The power of collaborative publishing

The days and weeks leading up to April 3, 2016, were tense for the journalists involved. Letters were sent to the targets of the investigation – including Vladimir Putin, which prompted a pre-emptive campaign to discredit the investigation. Final interviews and doorstop calls were conducted. The team held firm as a major political bribery scandal began to unfold in Brazil and as authorities started to indict FIFA officials over corruption allegations – both of which were stories that the Panama Papers held new details on but which couldn't be published until the entire investigation was ready.

The ICIJ is often asked how more than 370 reporters managed to keep the investigation secret for a year and agree to simultaneous publication across the world. The answer is simple: every reporter that agrees to join the investigation appreciates the value of unity. It is in nobody's interest to go on a solo run: working closely together builds strong bonds and a realisation that a single deadline creates maximum worldwide impact (The Listening Post 2016).

A single news organisation publishing an in-depth investigation in one country can cause a stir – but 100 media outlets publishing various, localised stories using the same dataset on the same day makes it impossible to ignore. The ICIJ had already proven this time and again.

On Sunday, April 3, 2016, at 2 p.m. Eastern Time in the United States, 100 news organisations collectively signalled to the world that the issue of financial secrecy – and the corruption and inequality that it enables – was worthy of global attention.

Simultaneous publication also provided a measure of protection for reporters operating in regions with restricted press freedoms. In the wake of the Panama Papers, journalists in Panama, Turkey, Niger and elsewhere were harassed and threatened over their stories; journalists in Venezuela and Hong Kong were sacked; media companies in Spain and Mongolia were sued; journalists in Finland were warned that their homes might be raided. Tragically, 18 months after publication, a journalist working on a related investigation in Malta, Daphne Caruana Galizia, was assassinated.

Every time a member of the Panama Papers team faced a backlash, the whole network stood up in support. It wasn't always enough to stop sackings or litigation, but it certainly ensured that no reporter could be singled out without facing the international solidarity (and publishing power) of hundreds of their colleagues.

On May 9, 2016, a little more than a month after the first stories generated headlines around the world, ICIJ was ready to make another splash – by publishing the underlying structured data from the leak.

Information on more than 214,000 offshore entities (companies, trusts, shareholders) from 21 jurisdictions were added to a revamped interactive application called the Offshore Leaks Database. The database already held data from ICIJ's Offshore Leaks and China Leaks investigations from 2013 and 2014; the addition of the Panama Papers meant users had access to more than 360,000 names of people and companies behind secret offshore structures.

The Offshore Leaks Database provides an interactive, explorable map to parts of this system and acts as a repository of downloadable data that can be compared against other datasets. The data has been used by individual investigators as well as government authorities to augment their probes into the wrongdoing enabled by offshore finance, to confront those who may have broken the law and to push for reforms.

## Maintaining integrity and ethics

The data ICIJ chose to publish included the sort of information that could typically be found in a searchable corporate register – such as Companies House in the United Kingdom. However, most of the companies in the Panama Papers were registered in secrecy jurisdictions – places where registries of information were either limited or non-existent.

Of equal importance is the data the ICIJ chose *not* to publish. ICIJ did not publish any personal information or private account details en masse: the Offshore Leaks Database does not comprise the full tranche of 11.5 million documents that formed the Panama Papers cache.

This quickly became a point of contention. On social media, some users cried hypocrisy. "If you censor more than 99% of the documents you are engaged in 1% journalism by definition," WikiLeaks tweeted, one of a string of criticisms the organisation levelled at ICIJ in the wake of the Panama Papers (WikiLeaks 2016).

For ICIJ, the equation was – and is – very different. As journalists, bound by a code of ethics that dictates responsible, fair reporting, ICIJ is only comfortable releasing documents that have been 100% verified and reported out, where subjects have been given the chance to respond, and where there's a strong public interest justification for publishing the information (Greenberg 2016; Walker Guevara 2016).

Most of the 11.5 million documents in the Panama Papers leak related to private, personal matters, issues that would not shed light on important figures or entities, documents that would not add anything to the understanding of this shadowy underworld. No organisation in the world could responsibly sift through these documents to determine which would pass a simple public interest test. It was simply not possible ethically to publish all the files.

Instead, ICIJ endeavoured to publish as many primary documents as possible. This decision was driven by ICIJ's mission to bring more transparency to society. But of equal importance is the credibility that it adds to reporting by allowing readers to scrutinise the process and the data directly.

## Lessons learned

The truism that change is the only constant certainly pertains to data journalism, where the pace is rapid and relentless. Although cutting edge at the time, much of the technology employed to produce the Panama Papers is already obsolete. However, the foundational theories and processes driving massive data investigations remain constant.

This idea that good journalism begets good sources begets more good journalism played out directly and specifically in the case of the Panama Papers. This continues to hold true. ICIJ's next investigation, the Paradise Papers, published 18 months later, was based on another massive trove of leaked data that revealed the questionable conduct and wrongdoing enabled by tax havens and financial secrecy.

This dataset was leaked to the same German reporters, who then brought the information to ICIJ – validation for the impact of the Panama Papers. It worked for the whistleblower and the news organisation that shared it (Allsop 2017).

Data momentum has continued at breakneck speed. In the years since the publication of the Panama Papers, ICIJ has published several cross-border investigations based on leaked material whose authors never envisaged it would be held up to public scrutiny. More material continues to arrive on a regular basis – some financial and some more general information, ranging from human rights abuses to kleptocracy.

Developing cutting-edge technology requires specialist knowledge and skills – skills that many journalists do not possess. In the lead-up to the Panama Papers, ICIJ had already learned the importance of taking the time to process data before wandering around blind in a mountain of unstructured data. ICIJ also understands the benefits of forging carefully vetted technology partnerships to better parse the data it has at its disposal.

Ultimately, ICIJ realises the stories it aims to tell cannot be told to maximum effect without the unparalleled local knowledge of its partners. Similarly, these partners appreciate an inability to achieve similar impact should they publish these stories on their own (even if they were capable of doing so). This symbiotic relationship underpins the ICIJ ethos and will continue to do so. In summary, the whole is immeasurably greater than the parts.

## References

Alfter, B. (2016). 'Cross-border collaborative journalism: Why journalists and scholars should talk about an emerging method'. In *Journal of Applied Journalism & Media Studies*, vol. 5, no. 2, pp. 297–311.

Alfter, B. (2018). 'New method, new skill, new position? Editorial coordinators in cross-border collaborative teams'. In Sambrook, R. (ed.), *Global teamwork: The rise of collaboration in investigative journalism*. Oxford: Reuters Institute for the Study of Journalism.

Allsop, J. (2017). The quiet impact of the Paradise Papers. [Online]. *Columbia Journalism Review*. Available from: www.cjr.org/watchdog/paradise-papers-icij-tax-havens.php [Accessed: 18 May 2020]

Bernstein, J. (2017). *Secrecy world: Inside the Panama Papers investigation of illicit money networks and the global elite*. New York: Henry Holt and Company.

Cabra, M. (2016). Wrangling 2.6TB of data: The people and the technology behind the Panama Papers. [Online]. *ICIJ.org*. Available from: www.icij.org/blog/2016/04/data-tech-team-icij/ [Accessed: 18 May 2020]

Greenberg, A. (2016). How reporters pulled off the Panama Papers, the biggest leak in whistleblower history. [Online]. *Wired.com*. Available from: www.wired.com/2016/04/reporters-pulled-off-panama-papers-biggest-leak-whistleblower-history/ [Accessed: 18 May 2020]

Hamilton, M. (2015). All together now: News partnerships increase in digital age. [Online]. *American Journalism Review*. Available from: https://ajr.org/2015/05/18/all-together-now-news-partnerships-increase-in-digital-age/ [Accessed: 18 May 2020]

Leigh, D. and Harding, L. (2011). *WikiLeaks: Inside Julian Assange's war on secrecy*. London: Guardian Books.

Listening Post. (2016). Behind the Panama Papers. [Online]. *Al Jazeera*. Available from: www.aljazeera.com/programmes/listeningpost/2016/04/panama-papers-media-160409024928741.html [Accessed: 18 May 2020]

Obermayer, B. and Obermaier, F. (2016). *The Panama Papers: Breaking the story of how the rich and powerful hide their money*. London: Oneworld Publications.

Reich, Z. and Barnoy, B. (2016). The anatomy of leaking in the age of megaleaks: New triggers, old news practices. In *Digital Journalism*, vol. 4, no. 7, pp. 886–898.

Ryle, G. (2016). In Raab, B. Behind the Panama Papers: A Q&A with international consortium of investigative journalists director Gerard Ryle. [Online]. *Ford Foundation*. Available from: www.fordfoundation.org/ideas/equals-change-blog/posts/behind-the-panama-papers-a-qa-with-international-consortium-of-investigative-journalists-director-gerard-ryle/ [Accessed: 18 May 2020]

Walker Guevara, M. (2016). Frequently asked questions about ICIJ and the Panama Papers. [Online]. *ICIJ.org*. Available from: www.icij.org/blog/2016/04/faqs/ [Accessed: 18 May 2020]

WikiLeaks. (2007). Website homepage. [Online]. Available from: http://web.archive.org/web/20070202025339/http://wikileaks.org/ [Accessed: 18 May 2020]

WikiLeaks. (2016). Post on Twitter. [Online]. Available from: https://twitter.com/wikileaks/status/717753531483168768 [Accessed: 18 May 2020]

Zetter, K. and Poulsen, K. (2010). 'I can't believe what I'm confessing to you': The WikiLeaks chats. [Online]. *Wired.com*. Available from: www.wired.com/2010/06/wikileaks-chat/ [Accessed: 18 May 2020]

# 2

# NATIONAL SECURITY

*Paul Lashmar*

## Introduction

"What's the cadet motto at West Point? You will not lie, cheat, or steal, or tolerate those who do. I was the CIA director. We lied, we cheated, we stole."

*Former CIA Director Mike Pompeo – Texas A&M University (April 15, 2019)*

Hidden behind a veil of secrecy, intelligence agencies can be a force for public good or bad. In authoritarian nations, they can protect or even install dictators. Consider, for instance, the assassination operations against critics of President Putin by the Russian secret service agency, the GRU.[1] This chapter, though, mainly focuses on the relationship between intelligence agencies and news media in Anglophone democratic countries, where the secret services should play a vital role in protecting the state from non-democratic change.

Since the emergence of Islamist terrorism in the 21st century, and the globe-wide counter-terrorism offensive, the attrition on civil liberties in many nations has been high. The threat to those countries posed by terrorism has been high also. For example, by November 2019, the British security services were conducting a staggering 800 'live' terrorism investigations (Casciani, 2019).[2] *The Guardian's* former national security reporter Richard Norton-Taylor sagely warns: "We may need the security and intelligence agencies more than ever. But more than ever we need to know that they are not abusing their ever-increasing power" (Norton-Taylor, 2020, p. xiii).

As Mike Pompeo's words previously make clear, the way intelligence agencies work, as we shall see, is not always ethical, and that is a reason journalists have a duty to monitor the national security apparatus. The news media monitor for betrayal, wrongdoing and incompetence, for which there is no shortage of historical evidence.[3] Thirty years before Pompeo's speech, academics Hulnick and Mattausch portrayed the CIA's *modus operandi* in similar terms:

> Professional standards require intelligence professionals to lie, hide information or use covert tactics to protect their 'cover,' access, sources, and responsibilities. The Central Intelligence Agency expects, teaches, encourages and controls these tactics so that the lies are consistent and supported ('backstopped'). The CIA expects intelligence officers to teach others to lie, deceive, steal, launder money, and perform a variety of other activities that would certainly be illegal if practiced in the United States. They call these tactics 'tradecraft.' And intelligence officers practice them in all the world's intelligence services.
>
> (Hulnick and Mattausch, 1989, pp. 520–521)

There is little reason not to think that British spies have demonstrated a similar operational ethos to Pompeo's CIA and other national secret services over the years. Since the advent of the modern intelligence services in the United Kingdom in 1909, they have from time to time ignored basic democratic principles, especially in the British colonies, where torture, rape and murder were part of their repertoire against nationalist uprisings (see Lashmar and Oliver, 1998; Cobain, 2012).

Intelligence agencies, cloaked in a culture of secrecy, are the most challenging organs of the state on which the news media can shine their Fourth Estate spotlight. Norton-Taylor observes:

> The role of the media in a struggle that goes to the heart of parliamentary democracy is crucial, given the reluctance of MPs to subject intelligence agencies to effective scrutiny. Well aware of the potential influence of the media, these agencies, MI6 in particular, seduce or smear journalists, give heavy spin to news events and even plant false stories in the media.
>
> (Norton-Taylor, 2020, p. 2)

With the exception of 'the eavesdroppers', the Government Communications Headquarters (GCHQ), UK agencies do not have press offices, and GCHQ's is mainly for community liaison. In the United States, media access is more accepted but varies across the 17 or so intelligence agencies. Journalists from Canada, Australia and New Zealand, experienced in covering national security, have told me that media access is restricted, difficult and sometimes tense in their countries, unless you play the agencies' game.

Former current affairs TV producer and now intelligence academic Kenneth Payne notes that covering national security for the mainstream media draws in what he defines as the 'access', the "clippings" and the "investigative" journalists (Lashmar, 2018b).[4] The access journalists are those for whom national security is their specialism, or 'beat'. In the United Kingdom, most major news organisations have one or two reporters who are 'accredited' and have mutually authorised contact with intelligence organisations. Norton-Taylor observes that this encourages only positive rather than objective coverage, "Too many journalists persuaded themselves that questioning what these sources tell them will end their 'special access'" (2020, p. 2).

In Payne's second category, when a major story involving national security breaks, an inflow of general reporters may cover the story, making the best contacts they can in the moment and using the 'cuttings' library for content. But it's the third category that is the most significant, as the revelatory public interest stories about national security are predominately produced by investigative journalists. The world of intelligence has been encapsulated as a 'wilderness of mirrors' needing considerable expertise to locate the truth of any story. Highly experienced investigative journalists' skill bases of nurturing inside sources, handling whistle-blowers, procuring leaks and grasp of law are a good fit for this demanding task. The current generation of these reporters tends to be comfortable with data journalism, knows how to handle high standards of data security and is wired into supportive international journalism networks.

## Historical context

The acceptance in the news media that questioning intelligence agencies is part of the Fourth Estate role is a relatively recent phenomenon. The first generation of post–World War Two journalists saw it as wise not to be critical of their own nation's spies (see Lashmar and Oliver, 1998; Knightley, 2006; Moran 2013). Many journalists had worked in intelligence during the Second World War and had close ties (see Lashmar, 2015, 2018a). Intelligence historian Richard Aldrich proposes that it was not until the early 1960s that the 'era of exposure' began after a series of scandals. He cites critical coverage of the U2 spy plane incident in 1960, the disastrous Bay of Pigs invasion in 1961, the Vassall spy case in 1962 and the Profumo Affair in 1963 (Aldrich, 2001, p. 607).

The UK media slowly began to take a more robust approach after intelligence agencies suffered reputational damage as a result of the gradual exposure of the Cambridge Spy Ring process that started in the 1950s but took many years. This handful of Cambridge University graduates, apparently paid up members of the British establishment but in reality Soviet agents, had inveigled their way into Britain's intelligence services (Boyle, 1979). The gullibility of the British establishment's 'old boys' network' was beyond embarrassing, and the spy ring had caused the death of many agents and the loss of many important national secrets before it was exposed.

Aldrich describes the subsequent, more aggressive reporting by the news media of the agencies as 'regulation by revelation'.

> Thereafter, during the last two decades of the Cold War, other journalists developed a counter-culture of revelation, focusing the spotlight of investigative journalism upon what they considered to be governmental miscreants. Yet even where the relationship was prickly, there remained an underlying appreciation that journalism and espionage were cognate activities and shared common professional ethics, including the diligent protection of sources.
>
> (2009, pp. 13–14)

The cultural breakthrough came with the California-based monthly publication *Ramparts*, one of the first of a new breed of radical 'underground' magazines that would spring up across the United States in the 1960s. Faced with the futility of the Vietnam War, they ignored the mainstream media's 'sacred cows', an unspoken consensus such as not criticising intelligence agencies when they failed. The *Ramparts* office was situated in Menlo Park near San Francisco, and with its editor, Warren Hinckle, increasingly drawn to the embryonic counterculture, the magazine engaged with radical politics and began taking an interest in the CIA as early as 1966. *Ramparts'* journalists had been alerted to a covert CIA operation by the scientist Stanley K. Sheinbaum. In the 1950s, he had coordinated a development project for South Vietnam called the Michigan State University Vietnam Advisory Group (MSUG). This project had been secretly financed and used as a cover by the CIA, including to train the Saigon police force and to write the South Vietnamese constitution. Published in April 1966, the investigation caused enough reaction for *Ramparts* to achieve a George Polk Award for Magazine Reporting (Richardson, 2009).

On 14 February 1967, the *New York Times* ran a front-page story headlined, 'A student group concedes it took funds from the CIA'. The story was by-lined Neil Sheehan, one of the paper's first investigative reporters, in a joint publication with *Ramparts* which exposed how, for many years, the CIA had sponsored the National Student Association (2009, pp. 74–81). It was becoming clear that the CIA was far exceeding its democratic mandate.

The ensuing period saw the mainstream media, led by the *Washington Post* and *New York Times*, spurred on by the radical press, challenging a corrupted government and the deep state. As revelations poured out about the deep state, it all built up to the Watergate scandal, which was to force the American president, Richard Nixon, to resign. It was a signal moment not only in American history but for the history of investigative journalism, best encapsulated in the movie *All the President's Men* (Pakula, 1976).

In the United Kingdom, extensive illegal and politically partisan operations by intelligence services were revealed more gradually. Perhaps the most important breakthrough was the detailed 1967 *Sunday Times* coverage of MI6's Kim Philby, a key figure in the Cambridge Spy ring. Historian Richard Aldrich noted that Whitehall's attempts to control the Philby story failed.

> The *Sunday Times* had ignored a D-Notice placed on the story. It also resisted efforts by Dennis Greenhill of the Foreign Office to persuade the editors to print unflattering material about the KGB alongside the Philby material. It is hard to recapture the sense of shock and outrage felt by some members of the establishment at the public parading of these secrets.[5]
>
> (Aldrich, 2004, p. 945)

In the new climate, the agencies were seen as fair game for exposure, and the controversial eavesdropping activities of the GCHQ were revealed, most notably by the investigative journalists Duncan Campbell and Mark Hosenball (1976). In addition British intelligence was shown to have been involved in many coups from Iraq to Indonesia, often with unintended and unfortunate consequences (Lashmar and Oliver, 1998, pp. 1–10).

I have argued that the introduction of accountability and oversight bodies post-Watergate looks good, but their record of efficacy has been poor, tending to be reactive rather than proactive (Lashmar, 2020, pp. 239–245). The intelligence academic Peter Gill observed that the growth of oversight was progress but not proactive:

> But we have learnt of highly controversial policies such as rendition and torture and mass communication surveillance not from these formal institutional mechanisms of oversight in the UK; rather they have come as a result of whistle-blowers, legal action and investigative journalists.
>
> (2013, p. 3)

Investigative journalists continued to monitor the agencies, sometimes assisted by whistle-blowers or inside sources. As Neal Ascherson has commented:

> The list of known names of government employees who for moral and patriotic reasons have broken their duty of silence – and often their pledge under the Official Secrets Act – is impressive. Some would call it a roll of honour. From recent years it would include Clive Ponting, Cathy Massiter, Sarah Tisdall and Katherine Gun.
>
> (Ascherson, 2020)

## Edward Snowden

Since the second edition of this book was published, by far the biggest national security story has been the leak of a huge tranche of National Security Agency (NSA) documents by Edward Snowden.[6] Snowden had been hired by an NSA contractor, Booz Allen Hamilton. By mid-2013, he was so disillusioned with the extent of global surveillance he had found at NSA that he established contact with Glen Greenwald, then of *The Guardian*, a journalist who had undertaken investigations. On 20 May that year, Snowden flew to Hong Kong after leaving the NSA base in Hawaii, and in early June, he made the documents available, initially to a small group of journalists including Greenwald, filmmaker Laura Poitras and investigative reporters Ewen MacAskill *(The Guardian)* and Barton Gellman (*Washington Post*).

Revelations from Snowden's leaked documents were splashed by media outlets worldwide, including *The Guardian* (Britain), *Der Spiegel* (Germany), the *Washington Post* and the *New York Times* (US), *O Globo* (Brazil), *Le Monde* (France) and news outlets, not least in Sweden, Canada, Italy, Netherlands, Norway, Spain and Australia. These articles revealed details of a global surveillance apparatus jointly run by the Five Eyes network in close cooperation with their commercial and international partners with scant regard for the applicable laws.[7]

Snowden stated: "My sole motive is to inform the public as to that which is done in their name and that which is done against them". He revealed that the agencies have secretly negotiated for 'backdoors' in the security of computer programmes, social networking sites, websites and smartphones. The largest GCHQ spying program – TEMPORA – and the NSA's PRISM showed "their extraordinary capability to hoover up and store personal emails, voice contact, social networking activity and even internet searches" (Hopkins and Harding, 2013).

An Australian journalist who had also worked in government, Phillip Dorling, told me, "Edward Snowden's revelations about the mass acquisition of telecommunications data and bulk interception of internet traffic by the US National Security Agency provide a salutary warning of how technological change has developed the architecture for a surveillance state" (Lashmar, 2017, p. 12).

According to the Snowden documents, GCHQ scooped up e-mails from journalists working for major media outlets. GCHQ had listed investigative journalists as a threat alongside terrorists and hackers (2017, p. 12). Journalists were targeted, and Germany's *Der Spiegel* reported that the NSA had intercepted, read and analysed internal communications at Al Jazeera which had been encrypted by the news organisation (Der Spiegel, 2013).

### The counter-attack

The reaction to publication of the Snowden documents was frequently hostile and particularly so in the United Kingdom. *The Guardian* was condemned not only by government, politicians and the agencies but also by some of the British media, notably the *Daily Mail*. Sir John Sawers, then head of MI6, appearing in front of a parliamentary committee in November 2013, addressed the impact of the Snowden revelations by questioning the qualifications of journalists and senior editorial staff in deciding what can be published.

> I'm not sure the journalists managing these publications are particularly well placed to make that judgement. . . . What I can tell you is that the leaks from Snowden have been very damaging, they have put our operations at risk. It is clear our adversaries are rubbing their hands with glee, al Qaeda is lapping it up.
>
> (Marszal, 2013)

The UK government and the prime minister, David Cameron, lambasted *The Guardian* while maintaining that the UK's intelligence agencies were fully accountable:

> So we have a choice, do we maintain properly funded, properly governed intelligence and security services, which will gather intelligence on these people, using all of the modern techniques to make sure that we can get ahead of them and stop them, or do we stop doing that? What Snowden is doing and to an extent what the newspapers are doing in helping him is frankly signalling to people who mean to do us harm, how to evade and avoid intelligence and surveillance and other techniques.
>
> (Hope and Waterfield, 2013)

My research into the leak suggests that journalists who wrote the Snowden articles acted responsibly and concentrated on material that demonstrated the extent of mass surveillance and other areas where the legitimacy was seriously in doubt (Lashmar, 2017). *The Guardian* editor Alan Rusbridger had told a UK parliamentary committee that the paper consulted with government officials and intelligence agencies, including GCHQ, the White House and the Cabinet Office, on more than 100 occasions before publication (Rusbridger, 2013). No documents from active anti-terrorist operations were published (Lashmar, 2020, p. 226).

## Impact on journalism

Snowden's revelations were to have significant impact on the practice of investigative journalism. Realising that the Five Eyes had the technology to snoop on journalists and their sources, a major revaluation of journalism tradecraft began. I published two papers on changes to tradecraft for which I interviewed investigative journalists and academics from the Five Eyes nations. One paper was researched six months after Snowden went public and the other four years later (Lashmar, 2017, 2018b).

When it came to protecting their sources, the interviewees' reactions to changing procedures were mixed. The Canadian investigative reporter David Seglins, for example, said that working with and reading the Snowden documents had fundamentally changed his understanding of operational security as a journalist.

> Everything from storage of documents to the use of encryption, encrypted communication, encrypted data storage, to how our mobile devices are potential listening devices and how that affects a journalist's ability to travel to places, meet sources, have discussions with absolute certainty we are not being recorded or monitored or tracked.
>
> (Lashmar, 2018b)

Encryption has become a regular tool. Scott Shane, then of the *New York Times*, said he now uses encrypted email. Some reporters had stepped up using PGP and TOR. Some also use encrypted phone apps:

> One of the things that has changed since we last talked is the proliferation of encryption communication apps. Many of us have run through the various ones, Silent Circle, What's App, Signal, so there is an increasing availability of encrypted communications. I'm certainly more aware of what I am putting into a storable electronic record.
>
> (Lashmar, 2018b)

Some interviewees now include a PGP key and other encryption contact information in their email or social media addresses. Australian *ABC* journalist Dylan Welch said he emphasised to potential sources that *ABC* is serious about source protection. Since Snowden, it has been hard for journalists to monitor the agencies to find out what is really going on in national security. In each of the Five Eyes nations (and many others), new and much more draconian laws have been passed to stop journalists, sources and whistle-blowers reporting on intelligence (ibid; Lashmar, 2020, pp. 239–249).

## Spy cops

There are still disturbing historical cases of unjustifiable and unethical intelligence operations coming to light. A British case study of the media acting as the Fourth Estate watchdog concerns the activities of an elite undercover police unit. The Metropolitan Police's Special Demonstration Squad (SDS) operated among civil rights, animal rights, anti-fascist left-wing groups, far-right activists and environmental activists from 1968 to 2008. Set up as a temporary operation at the height of student protests in 1968, male and female undercover police officers infiltrated these groups. However, they also undertook criminal acts to maintain deep cover, engaging in relationships with the people they were monitoring and in some cases having children with them.

A few of the groups infiltrated were engaged in violence, arson and other illegal activities. Some harm was prevented and some activists were convicted, but there was a major issue of proportionality. Only persistent digging by journalists and campaigners, mostly notably an award-winning seven-year investigation by Paul Lewis and Rob Evans of *The Guardian*, revealed this massive policing enterprise and its moral and accountability failure (Lewis and Evans, 2013). At the time of writing, a public inquiry was taking evidence to find out what did happen within SDS.

## The truth will out – eventually

For the 2008 edition of *Investigative Journalism*, I authored a chapter that analysed how well investigative journalism had dealt with the 'War on Terror' that had begun with 9/11 and the tragedy of the 3000 American deaths. My case study was British journalist Stephen Grey's investigation into rendition and torture by the CIA. His book *Ghost Plane*, published in 2006, had painstakingly identified over 1000 CIA 'ghost flights' criss-crossing the globe after 2001. Many of these flights were for 'extraordinary rendition' where, simply, terror suspects were secretly, without the suspect's agreement, taken by force from one country to another and in some cases kidnapped. As Bob Baer, a former CIA operative in the Middle East commented:

> If you want a serious interrogation you send a prisoner to Jordan. If you want them to be tortured you send them to Syria. If you want someone to disappear . . . you send them to Egypt.
>
> (Grey, 2004)

Rendition flights were not to move suspects from battle zones in Afghanistan or Iraq to the United States where these alleged terrorists could face the rule of law; the receiving nation was always a third country where the security services were cooperating with the CIA.

Grey described the cooperation by reporters:

> Beat reporters like me who have followed this story have worked cooperatively – not in concert but by picking up pieces of the jigsaw puzzle disclosed by others, and then adding new pieces to the picture of what we know so far. Much more remains to be discovered.
>
> (2006, p. vii)

Rendition is exactly the kind of practice that journalists are there to expose, as it involves nation states abusing fundamental human rights and seeking to avoid the rule of law. In December 2005, the then Labour Foreign Secretary Jack

Straw, the minister responsible for MI6 and GCHQ, categorically denied their involvement when he told the Commons foreign affairs committee:

> Unless we all start to believe in conspiracy theories and that the officials are lying, that I am lying, that behind this there is some kind of secret state, which is in league with some dark forces in the United States . . . there simply, is no truth in the claims that the United Kingdom has been involved in rendition.
>
> (Cobain, 2018)

Straw composed the party line for the government and the intelligence agencies to repeat *ad nauseam* for over a decade. Then, surprisingly, under the chairmanship of Dominic Grieve, the previously toothless Intelligence and Security Committee (ISC) revealed that Jack Straw had indeed misled the media and public. ISC's four-year inquiry, published in 2018, found that the United Kingdom had planned, agreed or financed some 31 rendition operations. Moreover, there were 15 occasions when British intelligence officers consented to or witnessed torture and 232 occasions on which the intelligence agencies supplied questions put to detainees during interrogation, whom they knew or suspected were being mistreated. MI5 helped finance a rendition operation in June 2003 (Cobain and MacAskill, 2018). In October 2004, Straw authorised the payment of a large share of the cost of rendering two people from one country to another (ibid).

Shortly before the ISC reported, an important independent tribunal judgment was delivered that had been triggered by the Snowden revelations about GCHQ operations, formally confirming that the British government had broken the law by allowing the eavesdropping agency to amass data on UK citizens without proper oversight from the Foreign Office. GCHQ had been given greatly increased powers to obtain and analyse citizens' data after the 9/11 terrorist attacks in 2001, on the condition that it agreed to strict oversight from the Foreign Secretary. The Investigatory Powers Tribunal (IPT) concluded that the Foreign Office had, on several occasions, given GCHQ 'carte blanche' to extract data from telecoms and internet companies. The tribunal reported:

> In cases in which . . . the Foreign Secretary made a general direction which applied to all communications through the networks operated by the [communications service provider], there had been an unlawful delegation of the power.[8]

*The Guardian* was vindicated, and the attacks by David Cameron and others on publication were demonstrably wrong headed. In both cases, these malfeasances would never have come to light if it had not been for dogged investigative journalism.

The 45-year veteran of national security reporting Richard Norton-Taylor ends his 2020 book on intelligence and the news media with a powerful warning:

> We have seen how Britain's top security, intelligence and military figures have failed to tell the truth to power for reasons of cowardice as well as convenience. As a result even their political bosses and those elected to monitor and question their activities are kept in the dark. That is all the more reason for the media to mount a sustained battle against an excess of official secrecy in the real interest, however perverse it may seem, of national security and of those agencies charged with protecting it.
>
> (Norton-Taylor, 2020, p. 312)

## Conclusions

Intelligence academics Gill and Phythian have commented on the importance of the media in bringing accountability to the intelligence agencies:

> The media in general remain significant, if inconsistent, contributors to oversight. Certainly, the heightened public concern with security in the wake of 9/11 has increased media attention to intelligence matters greatly, and the media have played an important role in alerting the public to concerns among intelligence professionals at the politicization of their product.
>
> (2012, p. 169)

As a result of the 1960s 'era of exposure', the news media in the Five Eyes countries have sought to bring accountability to the intelligence services with intermittent success but now face increasing resistance in fulfilling this role. The public mood has changed since 9/11, and reporting on national security has become more difficult and subject to greater attacks by government, its sympathetic media and the agencies. Over a decade ago, the US-based doyen of intelligence studies Loch K Johnson suggested the following proposition:

> In times of military crisis, a nation tends to rally behind its leader in favour of an efficient intelligence and military response to the threat, placing at a lower level of concern questions of civil liberties and intelligence accountability.
>
> (2009, pp. 50–51)

The proposition has proven accurate.

The Snowden affair has been the most fractious clash between the national security nexus and the media in Western countries in recent times. It highlights the variations within democracies as to what the right balance is between security and civil liberties. What that right balance is remains unresolved.

A profoundly serious issue for journalism is the use of surveillance techniques to prevent journalists acquiring and maintaining confidential sources, especially in the public sector. Surveillance is now so ubiquitous, it makes the development of intelligence sources in the sector very difficult, and consequently the news media's duty to provide critical accountability of power is much reduced. A UNESCO report expressed concern for the rule of law in the new environment:

> As a parallel to digital development, and occurs where it is un-checked by measures designed to preserve fundamental rights to freedom of expression and privacy, as well as accountability and transparency. In practice, this leads to what can be identified as a 'trumping effect', where national security and antiterrorism legislation effectively take precedence over legal and normative protections for confidential journalistic sources.
>
> (2017, p. 19).

It is important not to cry wolf. Nevertheless, over the last decade, national security apparatuses that make East Germany's Stasi internal security agency of the Cold War period, infamous for its ubiquitous intrusion to ordinary people's lives, look like a tiny cottage industry by comparison have secretly been installed in many democratic nations. With few exceptions, the oversight agencies have proved ineffective. What has proven more effective is investigative journalism, even if it is not a consistent monitor and itself subject to worrying levels of surveillance. Despite politicians and intelligence chiefs mouthing support for the freedom of the media as vital to democracy, they have no desire to provide legal protection to journalists and their sources, not least because they know they could be the target of investigations.

Despite all the increased difficulties in reporting national security, there is no doubt that investigative journalists will find a way. This crumpled specialism has been reported as dying for more than 40 years but has a particular way of surviving, a tribute to the stubbornness of practitioners. The rise of the security state has given it a new, and vital, importance; it must and will continue.

## Notes

1 These have been revealed, not least thanks to the work of the Bellingcat Investigative Collective
2 And had foiled 24 Islamist plots since March 2017
3 Mike Pompeo later became President Trump's Secretary of State
4 Academic Profile for Kenneth Payne: www.kcl.ac.uk/people/payne-dr-kenneth
5 Even to this day, we do not know the full scale of Philby's perfidy as a Soviet agent
6 The National Security Agency is the US equivalent of GCHQ but vastly larger

7 The Five Eyes is a partnership of the eavesdropping organisations of Australia (ASD), United Kingdom (GCHQ), United States (NSA), Canada (CSEC), and New Zealand (SIS)

8 The IPT judgment can be found at <www.ipt-uk.com/judgments. asp?id=45>

# References

Aldrich, R. J. (2001). *The Hidden Hand: Britain, America and Cold War Secret Intelligence*. London: John Murray.

Aldrich, R. J. (2004). 'Policing the past: Official history, secrecy and British intelligence since 1945', *English Historical Review*, 119: 483, 922–953.

Aldrich, R. J. (2009). 'Regulation by revelation? Intelligence, the media and transparency', in Dover, R. and Goodman, M. S. (eds.), *Spinning Intelligence: Why Intelligence Needs the Media, Why the Media Needs Intelligence*. London: C. Hurst, pp. 13–36.

Ascherson, N. (2020). 'Secrets are like sex', *London Review of Books,* 42: 7, 1 April.

Boyle, A. (1979). *A Climate of Treason*. London: Hutchinson & Co.

Campbell, D. and M. Hosenball (1976). 'The eavesdroppers', *Time Out*, 21 May.

Casciani, D. (2019). 'UK terrorism threat downgraded to "substantial"', *BBC News,* 4 November.

Cobain, I. (2012). *Cruel Britannia: A Secret History of Torture*. London: Portobello Books.

Cobain, I. (2018). 'What did Jack Straw know about the UK's role in torture and rendition?', *The Guardian*, 28 June.

Cobain, I. and E. MacAskill (2018). 'True scale of UK role in torture and rendition after 9/11 revealed', *The Guardian*, 28 June.

Der Spiegel (2013). 'Snowden document: NSA spied on Al Jazeera communications', *Der Spiegel,* 31 August, <www.spiegel.de/international/world/nsa-spiedon-al-jazeera-communications-snowden-document-a-919681.html>.

Gill, P. (2013). 'Obstacles to the oversight of the UK intelligence community', *E-International Relations*, 19 July, <www.e-ir.info/2013/07/19/obstacles-to-the-oversight-of-the-uk-intelligence-community/> (last accessed 4 February 2015).

Gill, P. and M. Phythian (2012). *Intelligence in an Insecure World*. 2nd ed. Cambridge: Polity.

Grey, S. (2004). 'US accused of "torture flights"', *Sunday Times,* 14 November.

Grey, S. (2006). *Ghost Plane: The Inside Story of the CIA's Secret Rendition Programme*. London: Hurst.

Hope, C. and B. Waterfield (2013). 'David Cameron: Newspapers which publish Snowden secrets help terrorists who want to "blow up" families', *Daily Telegraph*, 25 October.

Hopkins, N. and L. Harding (2013). 'GCHQ accused of selling its services after revelations of funding by NSA', *The Guardian*, 2 August.

Hulnick, A. and D. W. Mattausch (1989). 'Ethics and morality in United States secret intelligence', *Harvard Journal of Law & Public Policy*, 12: 2 (Spring), 509–522.

Johnson, L. K. (2009). 'A theory of strategic intelligence', in Gill, P., Marrin, S. and Phythian, M. (eds.), *Intelligence Theory: Key Questions and Debates*. Abingdon: Routledge.

Knightley, P. (2006). 'Journalists and spies: An unhealthy relationship', *Ethical Space*, 3: 2/3, 7–11.

Lashmar, P. (2015). 'Spies at the observer', *British Journalism Review*, 26: 3 (September), 60–65.

Lashmar, P. (2017). 'No more sources? The impact of Snowden's revelations on journalists and their confidential sources', *Journalism Practice,* 11: 6, 665–688.

Lashmar P. (2018a). 'Nest of spies', *British Journalism Review*, 29: 1 (March), 53–59.

Lashmar, P. (2018b). 'Journalistic freedom and surveillance of journalists post-Snowden', in Franklin. B. and Eldridge, S. A. (eds.), *The Routledge Handbook of Development in Digital Journalism Studies*. 5 September. Abingdon: Routledge.

Lashmar, P. (2020). *Spies, Spin and the Fourth Estate: British Intelligence and the Media*. Edinburgh: Edinburgh University Press.

Lashmar, P. and J. Oliver (1998). *Britain's Secret Propaganda War 1948–1977*. Stroud: Sutton Pub Ltd.

Lewis, P. and R. Evans (2013). *Undercover: The True Story of Britain's Secret Police*. London: Guardian Faber Publishing.

Marszal, A. (2013). 'Spy chiefs public hearing: As it happened', *Daily Telegraph*, 7 November.

Moran, C. (2013). *Classified: Secrecy and the State in Modern Britain*. Cambridge: Cambridge University Press.

Norton-Taylor, R. (2020). *The State of Secrecy*. London: I.B. Taurus.

Pakula, A. J. (1976). *All the Presdient's Men*. Warner Bros.

Richardson, P. (2009). *A Bomb in Every Issue*. New York: The New Press.

Rusbridger, A. (2013). 'Guardian will not be intimidated over NSA leaks, Alan Rusbridger tells MPs', *The Guardian*, 3 December.

UNESCO (2017). 'Protecting journalism sources in the digital age', *UNESCO Series on Internet Freedom*, <http://en.unesco.org/news/unesco-releases-new-publication-protecting-journalism-sources-digital-age> (last accessed 25 May 2017).

# 3

# NEW MODELS OF FUNDING AND EXECUTING

*Glenda Cooper*

On 30th July 2018, the *Guardian* newspaper led with an arresting front-page story: an influential thinktank, the Institute for Economic Affairs, had offered ministerial access to potential US donors which would help shape research in favour of free-trade deals during the Brexit process (Booth, 2018).

It was a great scoop, the result of six months worth of investigation, including some undercover reporting, but despite the by-line of *The Guardian's* social affairs reporter, the original investigative work had not been carried out by that media organisation. Instead it had been carried out by Unearthed, an investigative unit set up by the non-governmental organisation (NGO) Greenpeace. While the Guardian performed checks on the investigation, the genesis and the execution of this story belonged to the NGO (Mayhew, 2018).

Greenpeace is not the only NGO to have moved into the field of investigative journalism. In 2017, Global Witness was shortlisted for the prestigious Paul Foot award for investigative and campaigning journalism (Hazard Owen, 2017). The aid agency Christian Aid recruited former *Sunday Times* investigative journalist John Davison to head up its press office in the early 2000s, and Amnesty International set up its Digital Verification Corps.

Investigative reporting remains one of the most prestigious and well-regarded parts of journalism.

Yet many journalists find these aspirations to 'truth-tell', to pursue stories in the public interest, is increasingly difficult in a time of cuts and instability in the mainstream media. Lee-Wright (2011) talks of journalists' inability to go out and seek stories and, if confined to the office, finding themselves caught up in hot-desking as 'an unhappy version of adult Musical Chairs' and reduced to producing 'churnalism' (Davies, 2008), that is, rewriting press releases. Into this gap have stepped NGOs, and while the blurring of lines between investigative journalist and campaigning NGO may not be new, in these times of economic difficulty for media organisations, NGOs have become increasingly important for investigative journalism.

The presence of NGOs in the investigative journalism field, however, continues to stir up debate about *what* journalism is and *who* a journalist is. So this chapter will look at what current thinking is around what Gillmor (2008) once dubbed 'almost journalism' and how both sides are negotiating this boundary work.

## The stepping back of mainstream media from investigative journalism

While the advent of NGOs as players in the investigative journalism field is not new, their incursions into this field may have been speeded up because of the collapse in funding of media organisations. The Pew Research Center for the Project for Excellence in Journalism estimated that since the year 2000, US newspapers alone have lost US$1600 million annually (Requejo-Aleman and Lugo-Ocando, 2014). While subscription models have seen some revenue return, it remains a difficult time for legacy media organisations, and those areas of journalism which are expensive to carry out have been particularly hard hit. These include both foreign news (Harding, 2009; Sambrook, 2010) and investigative journalism (Lashmar, 2011). Speaking at a debate organised by the Frontline Club as far back as 2008, the award-winning photographer Marcus Bleasdale said:

> Over the last ten years I would say 80–85 per cent [of my work] has been financed by humanitarian agencies. To give one example, in 2003 I made calls to 20 magazines and newspapers saying I wanted to go to Darfur. Yet I made one call to Human Rights Watch, sorted a day rate, expenses and five days later I was in the field.
>
> (Frontline Club, 2008)

A decade ago, Hamilton (2009) estimated that it would cost a large metropolitan newspaper in the United States $500,000 a year to fund an investigative unit comprising an editor, three reporters and a researcher plus expenses that might result in two to three successful investigations a year – something that would be out of reach of many struggling media organisations. It is no wonder that in some parts of the world, journalists have looked to different models to fund investigative journalism.

In the United States, investigative non-profit outlets such as ProPublica, the Center for Public Integrity and the Center for Investigative Reporting received $184.5m over seven years (Birnbauer, 2018). Requejo-Aleman and Lugo-Ocando looked at non-profit investigative journalism in Latin America, where such initiatives talked about developing "investigative journalism more as a moral force" (2014: 523), but that relied hugely on foreign aid donations. "Therefore, we cannot really talk about a sustainable model of journalism and in many ways neither can we really talk of journalism independence," the authors concluded (2014: 528).

When the journalist Steve Crawshaw left the *Independent* newspaper in 2002 to join Human Rights Watch, where he worked as London director and then

UN advocacy director, he saw a considerable difference between investigative journalists and NGOs, a gap that he has seen to narrow since then because of the financial situation of mainstream media.

> The media in those days was very wary of NGOs bringing things along to them. They thought 'we need to do it [the investigation]' and that's shifted significantly. It's probably an economic thing I think. But if an NGO now brings a ready packaged story with video, not only will a little two-bit local television station take it, which might have happened in the old days, but you know, a big global television channel is also likely to go 'It's a good enough story and if we think you're doing it okay, then that's fine too'. That's an interesting change for me.
>
> (phone interview, January 2020)

Crawshaw went on to direct Amnesty International's International Advocacy Programme and the office of the Secretary General and at present is director of policy and advocacy at Freedom from Torture. He acknowledges that many NGOs are also financially squeezed but have the incentive to invest in investigative journalism. At the beginning of his career when he worked for the Granada investigative programme *World In Action*, he perceived that there was an attitude that money would be thrown at a story if media organisations thought a story was there. Such attitudes have changed since.

> NGOs of course don't have the money as such, but they have the impetus, the desire to feel that *this is what we do*. The NGO will say 'we need to nail this down because if we do, we can really make change'. So you have more of . . . an incentive. And that means that the NGOs have got more determined to do it . . . in parallel to the fact that editors, and managers in the media are kind of less keen to throw different lots of money at something often with no certainty of what's going to come back.
>
> (phone interview, February 2020)

The other practicality is the increasing speed of the news cycle, which can also make journalists more reliant on NGOs' work. As John Davison, a former investigative journalist with the *Sunday Times* who then went to head up Christian Aid's press operation in London, points out:

> You could take a bit more time over it and develop the story more . . . the reports we did were well researched, but they weren't just investigative, we had to get a top line out of them. You didn't have more resources but you did have more time. You know, you weren't trying to turn a story out every week.
>
> (phone interview, February 2020)

## Non-governmental organisations and investigative work

In the mid-1990s, Davison was working as part of the Insight team at the *Sunday Times* when the paper started looking into what became known as the Pergau Dam affair. In 1988, the Thatcher government had put in place a secret defence agreement linking the promise of civilian aid to Malaysia with a major arms export deal, despite objections from civil servants, who refused to sign off on the spending without written instruction from ministers. By the mid-1990s, details were beginning to emerge, and Davison was covering it for the paper. He was contacted by a small NGO called the World Development Movement (now Global Justice UK).

> Charities used to have a bit of a suspicious eye towards journalists especially . . . Murdoch journalists, but they (WDM) didn't seem to care. So I basically said, 'well, will you give us all your stuff?' And they said 'yeah'. I remember speaking to my then boss and he said, 'so, well you're going to nick all their research?'. When I said yes, he said 'brilliant'. It got us quite a long way.
>
> (phone interview, Feb 2020)

Davison recalls that as the first time he had worked so closely with an NGO in his career as an investigative journalist.[1] However, when he went to Christian Aid in the late 1990s, he incorporated his previous job's skills into his new role as head of press. At the time, aid agencies were increasingly hiring journalists for their press offices (Cooper, 2007), and Davison found that there was a market for such stories. In 2003, the Christian Aid press office, working with its researchers, found that billions in Iraqi oil revenue and other funds had disappeared into opaque bank accounts administered by the Coalition Provisional Authority (Christian Aid, 2003). The reaction was, as Davison recalls: 'it went global . . . absolutely bonkers'.

Christian Aid's press office and researchers were relatively small scale. Other NGOs such as Global Witness and Human Rights Watch (HRW) have grown massively. Amnesty in the early 1970s had 14 research staff; now it has 130 full-time researchers and 500 other staff in public relations, advocacy and fundraising, while Human Rights Watch has grown from 10 researchers in the 1980s to 400 full-time staff (Powers, 2015). Key investigations such as HRW's investigation into human rights abuses in the 2008 conflict in South Ossetia (HRW, 2009) or Global Witness's undercover investigation into lawyers in New York City (Global Witness, 2017). Two interesting approaches, however, have been Greenpeace's Unearthed and Amnesty's Digital Verification Corps.

Unearthed positioned itself as a journalistic unit set outside the NGO itself and works in a very similar way to traditional investigative journalism. The unit began life as Energydesk but changed its name in 2015 to reflect wider interest in any environmental issue of global importance. As editor Damian Kahya puts it:

> The name-change reflected a slight change towards longer-form investigative and in-depth reporting and away from relatively rapid-fire energy and climate commentary/fact-checks which had formed a large part of our output to begin with but which we now felt served more as the starting point for a longer piece of work rather than an output in itself.
>
> (personal communication)

Unearthed consists of eight journalists, three of whom started as interns after completing MAs in investigative journalism. Two came from trade magazines, one from *The Guardian*; one came from the *Guardian's* trainee scheme, and the final staff member was a former Greenpeace campaigner. The influence has been news led; Kahya sees strong news judgement, pursuit of a story and teamworking skills as key for those who work there and sees this hybrid of journalism and NGO work as fundamental:

> The difference between [Unearthed] and the work Greenpeace already did is important but also nuanced. It means we are more story-led and, by adopting our own editorially autonomous platform, we can ensure our reporting is put out in a clear and transparent way whilst allowing for key elements of journalistic work, such as the right to reply, to be effectively implemented. We have a different approach to legal risk and sometimes deploy different reporting techniques to those used previously e.g. we work a lot with sources. There's also a less-theoretical difference which is possibly more important to why Greenpeace has given space to this project. It sometimes allows you to be quicker and more impactful. Our staff journalists are directly accountable to fewer people than most investigators in NGOs. there are fewer meetings, there is less confusion of purpose, people have the freedom to chase a lead and see where it goes.
>
> (personal communication)

He is quick to say, however, that while the Unearthed model works for his organisation, there should be no 'one size fits all' approach and that different NGOs will have different models depending on the size of their organisation, funding and those people involved.

For example, the growth in open-source intelligence has allowed other NGOs to start using the kind of skills that were also seen as cutting edge in the journalistic world. Use of new technologies that could be used for verification was taken up with enthusiasm by those working in human rights, and some saw the possibility of collaboration with journalists. One of the most successful has been the aforementioned Amnesty International Digital Verification Corps, which now operates in six universities around the world. One of the founding partners was the Digital Verification Unit (DVU) at the University of Essex, now in its fourth year, where every year students compete for 16 places to work as volunteers at the unit. The students include human rights researchers, lawyers and journalists working together and must sign a contract to say they will dedicate 6–8 hours a week to the project.

The DVU has specialised in analysing user-generated content – the students are given a crash course in verification techniques in a weekend at the beginning of their contract, looking at geolocation, sundial calculations, search techniques and the discovery process. The result is, as the principal investigator at the DVU, Dr Daragh Murray, says, far more extensive than could have been managed in previous times, as was seen in the award-winning open-source investigation into airstrikes on Raqqa:

> What the open source work allowed us to do was to pretty much document every airstrike. We spent a lot of time on the verification, looking through videos of Raqqa before the fall of Raqqa, and immediately after, so that was everything from ISIS videos, propaganda videos, things that people had recorded, videos made by the Kurds as they drove around town. And then we essentially looked for destroyed buildings and geolocated them and we mapped all of those out in the different verification units. . . . So this allowed Amnesty to go to the coalition with much more specific dates, and then to go and investigate those specific sites with a lot more detail. So they were able to really effectively map out the whole, the whole attack.
>
> (Skype interview, Feb 2020)

The Amnesty report's findings was initially denied by US and UK forces, although the United States later conceded that civilians had been killed in the airstrikes (Cohen, 2018).

While journalists may taken part in these investigation processes, Murray says that they are often involved for their interest in the story – not because they are commissioned to do so – or that they may be involved at a strategic level rather than actually uncovering the detail needed:

> They're typically involved giving advice or at a strategic level as opposed to spending a lot of times themselves – like they can kind of outsource a lot of the hours. Either they don't have the skills or they don't have the time.
>
> (phone interview, February 2020)

## Non-governmental organisations: the 'almost journalists'?

The media are one means by which NGOs have traditionally tried to get their message across. They produce information, reports and press releases but also work closely with political players and communicate directly with the public, often through fundraising, to increase awareness of their particular causes (Cottle and Nolan, 2007; Waisbord, 2011).

In order to maximise their chance of media attention, scholars have argued that rather than challenging journalistic norms, NGOs have sought to mimic journalists (Fenton, 2009; Cottle and Nolan, 2009), using the idea of 'media logic', as described by Altheide and Snow (1979). Waisbord (2011) sees NGOs' actions as part of a widespread professionalisation of newsmaking in order to become 'news shapers' (Manheim, 1998). He puts forward the idea of 'journalistic' rather than 'media logic' as a better way of understanding the NGOs' approach, encompassing news values, media formats, labour conditions and editorial positions.

Powers (2015) talks about the NGO as 'journalistic entity', and this is a significant conceptualisation. He says that the content produced by NGOs expands the boundaries of journalism. This is happening in spite of the fact that NGOs themselves, he says, are not usually driven by journalistic instinct but aim for legitimacy by providing information to political elites via newsworthy coverage. Like others (Cottle and Nolan, 2007, 2009; Fenton, 2009), Powers also argues that NGOs are still subject to journalistic norms and practices rather than subverting them.

The question, however, that scholars return to time and again is whether NGOs can actually 'report' and 'investigate' in the same ways as journalists who subscribe to norms such as objectivity. Dan Gillmor (2008) famously dubbed activists who got involved in journalistic activities as 'almost journalists' doing 'almost journalism'. Gillmor criticised NGOs and human rights organisations who have entered the media field thus: "They're falling short today in several areas, notably the one that comes hardest to advocates: fairness" (2008).

This idea of lack of 'fairness' – a lack of commitment to straightforward reporting in favour of advocacy – is one that has dogged those NGOs that have engaged in journalistic activity. Yet NGOs have attempted to mimic classic journalism by attempting to provide deeply researched reporting on topics of public interest (Russell, 2013). Certainly, when teams such as Unearthed talked about the work they do, they are keen to stress their journalistic credentials (Damian Kahya, the editor of Unearthed, was a former BBC journalist) and the resources they used. In talking about the Guardian splash, Kahya said that they used three journalists at all times and that there was a distinction between Greenpeace and Unearthed:

> Greenpeace understands that and that's built into how we work and our decision-making structure, so we are completely outside of the rest of the Greenpeace decision-making structure. An article that goes on Unearthed doesn't have to be signed off the way a press release does.
>
> (Kahya, cited in Mayhew, 2018)

No money changed hands between Unearthed and *The Guardian* over the story, said Kahya, who added Greenpeace did not fundraise off the back of it "because when you're doing something that's quite high risk like this, you don't want to colour it with 'donate here'" (Mayhew, 2018).

Crawshaw takes issue with the idea that NGOs cannot report to the same high standards as investigative journalists. He thinks back to his own transition from journalist to NGO worker.

> The degree of extra checks [in NGO work], any set of facts was put through was very striking to me when I first moved. So if I was working for the *Independent* or the *Financial Times* or anyone else if I was covering a massacre in a village, broadly I would go there, I would get my notebook, I'd find as many people as I could and get a reasonable number of things. And that can just become to come the front page story of any foreign correspondent anywhere in the world. Whereas in a human rights organisation every single bit is check and double check and triple check.
>
> (phone interview, February 2020)

Sam Dubberley of Amnesty's Digital Verification Corps similarly talks about the need for caution on the part of NGOs when doing investigations and reports, compared with the mainstream media.

> The big difference is: how to decide what to publish. I think people working in the human rights sector are more careful, or reluctant, before they publish anything. Also, human rights people usually need far more information before they go out with anything than, for example, evidence from a video only. Overall, I think the human rights sector is generally more cautious before anything goes out, and there is a higher threshold than in journalism, partly because of the possible consequences.
>
> (Dubberley, quoted in Spangenberg, 2019)

Niall Couper, head of Media, PR and Supporter Communications at Amnesty International UK, sees the transition from investigative reporter for a media organisation to one in a NGO as being a difficult one to achieve. The overlap, he says, is smaller than people may realise.

> This is in part due to campaigning organisations not quite grasping the excellent skill sets investigative journalists do have. And also one of the key elements of a campaigning organisation's work is duty of care. Of course that is considered by the investigative journalist, but for researchers it is pretty much top of the list and comes with a large

amount of paperwork and training. I think there is a transition path, but it does need training to make it work.

(personal communication, January 2020)

## Boundary work, 'truth-telling' and the objectivity norm

Is the transition particularly difficult because of the fluctuating boundaries of journalism at present? Boundary (re)negotiation is a key struggle in the journalistic field at the moment (Carlson and Lewis, 2015), with journalists aiming to "defend [journalism] against incursions from non-journalists" (Carlson, 2015: 9).

This was seen clearly in the struggles around citizen journalism where journalists frequently denied that that those citizens were performing acts of journalism. Equally, journalists have been quick to deny that those working for NGOs can be seen as journalists. Phil Vine, a high-profile broadcast journalist who moved to work for Greenpeace New Zealand, wrote about the idea of the 'audacity' in still describing himself as a journalist while working at the NGO and that it was journalists who were the ones that principally objected to the idea that someone at an NGO could describe themselves as a journalist.

> New Zealand journalists took umbrage at my job description. Certain of them made it plain that by crossing this perceived Rubicon between 'recognised' media and a campaigning organisation 'with an agenda', meant that I would have to leave the tribe, hang up my pork pie hat with the reporter card in it. In footballing terms they seemed to see it as a clear case of divided loyalty. I'd taken on the manager's job at Liverpool while still insisting on wearing an Arsenal scarf at every game.
>
> (Vine, 2017: 45)

Added to this, journalists are frequently guided by a sense of professional norms such as truth-telling which Zelizer (2004) refers to as the 'God-term' of professional journalism. Codes for journalists foreground objectivity, with the journalist taking the stance of neutral observer (Schudson, 2001), autonomy and public interest as well, and other ethical stances include checking of facts, comprehensive reporting, truthfulness, fair representations of people's viewpoints.

Russell (2013) examined coverage of the 2011 United Nations Climate summit in Durban and found tension and overlap in the way that journalists and activists covered the summit. While journalists subscribed to conventional norms of objectivity and neutrality, Russell notes that this often resulted in amplifying the views of the elite or even creating false balance by giving space to the views of outlier climate change deniers. The activists, in contrast, had a more exhaustive coverage of the summit but also subscribed to a notion of

# NEW MODELS OF FUNDING AND EXECUTING

a 'public good' by going beyond their own specific agenda. Vine (2017) also questions the issue of bias in mainstream media and NGOs

> [Greenpeace's] bias in favour of the planet is intentional and transparent. I would argue that objectivity is an outdated and unachievable myth. As journalists we all come to stories with inherent biases – personal, financial or institutional. The manifest biases of the mainstream are far less easy to spot.
>
> (Vince, 2017, 48)

Crawshaw also thinks that bias needs to be understood in terms of the mainstream media as well as in NGOs; that the argument that only NGOs are approaching investigative work with an idea fixed in their mind is false – and the consequences for NGOs if the investigative work doesn't stand up if you do not scrutinise it properly.

> I mean an investigative journalist is kind of hoping for an outcome to the story that he or she is working on because otherwise there isn't a story . . . Usually you think there seems to be some funny business and you kind of smell where it might be coming from. And so in a sense everyone's starting with a possible idea. I think [with NGOs], if you all seem to have overstated your case, you may get better headlines in the short term, but you kind of lose respect if you could come to be seen as a cowboy, you lose respect in the medium and longer term.
>
> (phone interview, February 2020)

Davison agrees:

> I don't remember national newspapers being particularly objective about their targets. I'll put it another way around. If you were, as I was, an investigative journalist looking at anything, then you go and find the people who [cared]. Say you're doing something into political corruption, you go and find the people who cared about it, because they would also know about it and they would tell you things that you could then write about. I mean, you can't do journalism sitting in an objective bubble. Anybody you talk to has a point they want to make.
>
> (phone interview, February 2020)

## Conclusion

Investigative journalism is frequently time consuming and expensive, requiring the two commodities that mainstream media have in short supply at the moment. As such, there has been an increasing understanding that other actors may play a role in providing newsworthy investigations for public consumption. This is nothing new in one sense – NGOs such as Amnesty and Human Rights Watch have been investigating human rights abuses for decades. However, the ability to self-publish and the increased opportunities of open-source material mean that NGOs themselves have been examining different ways to bring their investigations to light.

The continued discussion over transparency and objectivity means that journalists are still liable to distinguish NGOs' work as separate from their own, and, as Vine makes clear, there is still hostility to the idea that someone can 'cross the line' and still be seen as a working journalist. Gillmor's 'almost journalism' description is still upheld by those working in the mainstream media, who still defend the boundaries of journalism.

Finally, Greenpeace's Unearthed and Amnesty International's Digital Verification Corps are both examples of how NGOs are seeking more innovative ways to carry out investigations with facilities and skills that mainstream media may not have. Yet as can be seen with Unearthed's collaboration with *The Guardian*, both sides still need each other in order to make maximum impact with both elite and public opinion.

## Note

1 WDM continued to research the Pergau Dam affair after the *Sunday Times* moved on and, after two parliamentary inquiries and a landmark judgment, the aid for Pergau was declared unlawful in 1994 in the case *R v Secretary of State for Foreign Affairs Ex p The World Development Movement*.

## References

Altheide, D. L., and Snow, R. P. (1979). *Media logic*. Beverly Hills, CA; London: Sage.

Birnbauer, B. (2018). *The rise of nonprofit investigative journalism in the United States*. London: Routledge.

Booth, R. (2018). Rightwing UK thinktank 'offered ministerial access' to potential US donors. *The Guardian*. Retrieved from www.theguardian.com/politics/2018/jul/29/rightwing-thinktank-ministerial-access-potential-us-donors-insitute-of-economic-affairs-brexit

Carlson, M. (2015). The many boundaries of journalism'. In M. Carlson and S. C. Lewis (eds.), *Boundaries of journalism: Professionalism, practices and participation*, 1–19. Oxford: Routledge.

Carlson, M., and Lewis, S. C. (2015). *Boundaries of journalism: Professionalism, practices and participation*. New York: Routledge.

Christian Aid. (2003). *Iraq, the missing billions*. Retrieved from https://reliefweb.int/report/iraq/iraq-missing-billions

Cohen, Z. (2018). *US-led coalition admits airstrikes killed 77 civilians in Raqqa, Syria*. Retrieved from https://edition.cnn.com/2018/08/06/politics/us-coalition-raqqa-civilians-killed/index.html?utm_content=2018-08-07T05%3A45%3A07&utm_medium=social&utm_source=twCNNi&utm_term=image

Cooper, G. (2007). *Anyone here survived a wave, speak English and got a mobile?: Aid agencies, the media and reporting disasters since the tsunami*. Oxford: Nuffield College.

Cottle, S., and Nolan, D. (2007). Everyone was dying for footage. *Journalism Studies, 8*(6), 862–878.

Cottle, S., and Nolan, D. (2009). *How the media's codes and rules influence the way NGOs work.* Retrieved from www.niemanlab.org/2009/11/simon-cottle-and-david-nolan-how-the-medias-codes-and-rules-influence-the-ways-ngos-work/

Davies, N. (2008). *Flat earth news: An award-winning reporter exposes falsehood, distortion and propaganda in the global media.* London: Chatto & Windus.

Fenton, N. (2009). Cloning the news: NGOs, new media and the news. *Annenberg and Nieman Journalism Lab, Harvard University Online Article Series.* Retrieved from http://www.Niemanlab.org/ngo/ (Accessed 27 August 2015).

Frontline Club. (2008). *The news carers: Are aid groups doing too much real newsgathering?* Retrieved from www.frontlineclub.com/the_news_carers_are_aid_groups_doing_too_much_real_newsgathering_-_new_york_-_fully_booked/

Gillmor, D. (2008). *Helping the almost journalists do journalism.* Retrieved from http://citmedia.org/blog/2008/07/23/helping-the-almost-journalists-do-journalism/

Global Witness. (2017). *Undercover in New York City.* Retrieved from www.globalwitness.org/shadyinc/

Hamilton, J. T. (2009). Subsidizing the watchdog: What would it cost to support investigative journalism at a large metropolitan daily newspaper. Paper presented at the *Duke Conference on Nonprofit Media,* 4–5.

Harding, P. (2009). *The great global switch-off: International coverage in UK public service broadcasting.* London: Oxfam, Polis, International Broadcasting Trust.

Hazard Owen, L. (2017). *How an environmental news initiative is bringing investigative stories to those most affected.* Retrieved from https://ijnet.org/en/story/how-environmental-news-initiative-bringing-investigative-stories-those-most-affected

Human Rights Watch. (2009). *Up in flames: Humanitarian law violations and civilian victims in the conflict over South Ossetia.* Retrieved from www.hrw.org/report/2009/01/23/flames/humanitarian-law-violations-and-civilian-victims-conflict-over-south

Lashmar, P. (2011). *The future of investigative journalism: Reasons to be cheerful.* Retrieved from www.opendemocracy.net/en/opendemocracyuk/future-of-investigative-journalism-reasons-to-be-cheerful/

Lee-Wright, P. (2011). The return of Hephaestus: Journalists' work recrafted. In P. Lee-Wright, A. Phillips, and T. Witscghe (eds.), *Changing journalism,* 35–54 London: Routledge.

Manheim, J. B. (1998). The news shapers: Strategic communication as a third force in news making. In D. A. Graber, D. McQuail, and P. Norris (eds.), *The politics of news. The news of politics,* 94–109. Washington, DC: CQ Press.

Mayhew, F. (2018). *Editor of Greenpeace-funded investigations unit behind IEA think tank sting says stories are not signed off by charity.* Retrieved from www.pressgazette.co.uk/editor-of-greenpeace-funded-investigations-unit-behind-iea-think-tank-sting-says-stories-are-not-signed-off-by-charity/

Powers, M. (2015). NGOs as journalistic entities: The possibilities, promises and limits of boundary crossing. In *Boundaries of journalism,* 186–200. Oxford: Routledge.

Requejo-Aleman, J. L., and Lugo-Ocando, J. (2014). Assessing the sustainability of Latin American investigative non-profit journalism. *Journalism Studies, 15*(5), 522–532.

Russell, A. (2013). Innovation in hybrid spaces: 2011 UN climate summit and the expanding journalism landscape. *Journalism, 14*(7), 904–920.

Sambrook, R. (2010). *Are foreign correspondents redundant? The changing face of international news*. Oxford: Reuters Institute for the Study of Journalism.

Schudson, M. (2001). The objectivity norm in American journalism. *Journalism, 2*(2), 149–170.

Spangenberg, J. (2019). *Interview with Amnesty's Sam Dubberley on verification challenges and approaches*. Retrieved from http://weverify.eu/blog/samdubberley-on-verification/

Vine, P. (2017). When is a journalist not a journalist? Negotiating a new form of advocacy journalism within the environmental movement. *Pacific Journalism Review, 23*(1), 43.

Waisbord, S. (2011). Can NGOs change the news? *International Journal of Communication, 5*, 142–165.

Zelizer, B. (2004). *Taking journalism seriously: News and the academy*. Thousand Oaks, CA: Sage.

# 4

# DIGITAL SLEUTHING[1]

*Félim McMahon*

A distinctive new form of investigative journalism has emerged in the age of the read/write web that has become famous for its leverage of material that is already in the public domain. The digital sleuths who practice it are singular in their ability to find, combine and extract probative value from the digital breadcrumbs strewn across the internet by every individual, organisation or device connected to it.

Thanks in part to the ready availability, pervasive nature and overwhelming volume of these data, this new form of journalism is more collaborative, transparent and iterative than its predecessors. It can lay claim to being just as effective. Following a series of substantive and painstaking investigations, its proponents have broken some of the most remarkable and consequential stories of recent years, finding innovative solutions to seemingly insurmountable problems of volume and verification to reveal facts that were hiding in plain sight.

## History and background

Technological and infrastructural advances in the latter half of the 20th century transformed the creation, storage, transmission and computation of data, giving rise to a digital and networked age where the virtual has become "an essential dimension of our reality" (Negroponte, 1996). In the era of "mass self-communication", power struggles are played out across the global multimedia systems of the "network society" (Castells, 2015, 2019; Howard, 2011) and traditional institutions are integrated and subordinated to the "networked public sphere" (Friedland et al., 2006). Journalists share this space – in real time – with those who have embraced, instrumentalised and weaponised it.

While technology has opened the door to new entrants and novel forms of knowledge production that are more "collective, distributed and participatory" (Bruns, 2018; Bruns and Highfield, 2016; Scott Wright et al., 2016), it has also given rise to doubts about the ability of journalists to maintain the "core normative practice" of verification (Hermida, 2015) and about the overall health of the system (Scott Wright et al., 2016; Rasmussen, 2016). For Kovach and Rosenstiel (2014), "a transparent method of verification [is] the most important tool for professional journalists trying to answer doubts . . . about their work" in this changed context.

One of the most advantageous and overlooked aspects of the new environment are its digital verification affordances. It is hard to imagine a news story today whose protagonists, observers and underlying events are not linked to an extensive corpus of online data. Over time, due to the nature of the World Wide Web, this body of information continues to be copied, linked and annotated by a wide variety of actors. It is also more searchable than ever. It can persist long after it is created and, because it is easy to transmit, may elude all efforts to secure it. Time permitting, this environment offers unprecedented opportunities for journalists to detect, cross-check and challenge information about real-world events and their contexts. Online and visual investigations focus on these opportunities, offering a powerful alternative to epistemic crisis.

## Development

The proliferation of mobile phones and the advent of simplified self-publishing on platforms such as Twitter, Facebook and YouTube has led to dramatic growth in the amount of content shared "with no professionals . . . in sight" (Shirky, 2009). Solicitation gave way to online searching, and journalists began to use the smart-phone-wielding, mass-communicating public as sensors and sources like never before.

Through a series of events that made global headlines – including the London bombings (2005), the Saffron Revolution in Myanmar (2006) and the Mumbai attacks (2008) – the unique value of user-generated content (UGC) for crisis reporting was firmly established. An early and much-documented pioneer in this regard was the BBC's UGC Hub, where verification procedures were initially based on direct contact and limited technical checks (Allan, 2013, 2007).

As a series of hoaxes and errors cast doubt on the reliability of reporting based on UGC, verification began to adapt to conditions of "virtuality" (Belair-Gagnon, 2015). One of the companies that was instrumental in this shift was Storyful, a social media news agency that provided discovery and verification as a service to newsrooms. Starting from 2010, the company's journalists and developers refined their methodologies and technologies across the events of the Arab Spring and Syria's civil war, working with clients such as *Channel 4 News*, the *New York Times* and the *Wall Street Journal*.

The newsroom culture at Storyful was shaped by five distinct factors:

1 A core of journalists with long experience in television and print news.
2 Strong representation of team members with a background in blogging, editing (fact checking) and technology.

3  A concept of operations closer to that of open-source intelligence or information management than storytelling (Little, 2012; Sheridan, 2012).
4  Explanation of its verification methodologies on a case-by-case basis (to build trust with clients).
5  Integration of the software development team into newsroom operations and *vice versa*, focused on the dynamic co-development of tools and the creation and automation of workflows.

Storyful popularised its verification methodologies through its public website, a blog, and through the "Open Newsroom" project on the now-defunct social networking site Google+, where members could engage in collaborative verification alongside its journalists (Bartlett, 2013).

## Methodology

Observing trends at the outset of the social reporting era, Hermida (2015) came to the conclusion that, "Far from being abandoned, verification is being rearticulated". In essence, the verification methods associated with user-generated content, which underpin online and visual investigation, seek to establish the 'who', 'when' and 'where' of that content; carefully approaching questions like 'what' and 'how', while being downright circumspect about the 'why'. The full range of methodologies is well described elsewhere (Dubberley et al., 2020; Lipinski, 2012; McPherson, 2015; Silverman, 2014; Trewinnard and Bell, 2018), but the evolving techniques include the following elements:

1  Monitoring and searching: Verification depends on the creation and maintenance of streams of data and operative filters across a broad range of social and non-social sources. Exhaustive searches using a broad range of strategies, tools and techniques are used to counter the repetition and distortion that are pervasive in the online environment. Essential skills include the use of advanced search operators, reverse image searching, knowledge of search resources including web archives, judicious use of machine translation and an understanding of how to work both with and without timestamps. The partiality of sources is assumed and assessed. Judgments about their credibility and reliability are made with reference to profile details, posting histories and network analysis.
2  Cross-verification: Due to the derivative nature of online information, any inferences must be supported by multiple strands of evidence and points of divergence heavily weighted. Whenever possible, external corroboration is sought to anchor "virtuality". Comparative and reconstructive visual techniques are used to establish, corroborate and understand the locations where imagery was acquired. This includes the geolocation of imagery with reference to mapping, satellite imagery and ground-level data, including street view imagery, photos and videos. Apparent weather

conditions can be checked against meteorological data, while shadows and other astronomical information can be used to query time, date and location. Verification techniques use metadata where available, though this is often stripped by social media platforms. Detecting synthetic and manipulated media via technical or manual means is emerging as an important skillset.

3 Content analysis: This includes the deeper interrogation of a range of items, including language, buildings and land uses, signage, weaponry, vehicles, accents, dialects, clothing, insignia and a plethora of other information. It also involves listening to the "conversation" around an event, entity or object. This leads to engagement with new communities, discovery of further sources and resources and the identification of new tactics and techniques.

4 Presentation: Due to the cumulative and/or visual nature of verification, presentation is a key skill set. This includes an emerging set of practices and conventions focused on both language and visual presentation

Online investigation is associated with seeking out and combining online information about individuals, organisations and objects, whereas visual investigation is a spatial-temporal approach focused on audio-visual information. The unifying assumption is that events and entities under investigation will leave a multimedia trail in their wake. Open source intelligence (OSINT) investigations combine both techniques, drawing on information that is already in the public domain.

The use of visual investigation techniques and remote sensing via satellite imagery, and the reimagining of the newsgathering as an intelligence discipline, closely mirrors and draws upon developments in the fields of human rights and non-proliferation (Aday and Livingston, 2009). In the past few years, this cross-pollination has developed into factual-analytical and storytelling collaborations across a range of human rights-related topics. Central to these partnerships have been two research agencies specialising in advanced spatial and media techniques: Forensic Architecture (FA), based at Goldsmiths, University of London, and New York-based SITU Research. Working with partners including Amnesty International and Human Rights Watch, Bellingcat, the *New York Times'* Visual Investigations unit and BBC Africa Eye, these two agencies have produced interactive reconstructions based on user-generated content, witness testimony and physical evidence, drawing on spatial analysis, photogrammetry, 3D modelling, animation and interactive visualisation. Their work has frequently been used in legal processes or official reports. In the spirit of the Internet, there have been notable individual contributions with a human rights focus, including the investigation –using satellite imagery and online documents – of alleged violations of human rights against China's Uighurs (Al Jazeera, 2019).

OSINT techniques in investigative journalism are heavily influenced by the field of cybersecurity, where publicly available information is used in investigations of individuals and organisations or to identify and mitigate security threats (Bazzell, 2020). Such information is often of a personal nature, in that it refers to the identities, biographical details and lives of people and the groups they belong to. The phrase OSINT is derived from military and intelligence doctrine, where it refers to the use of information from TV, books, radio, newspapers and other publicly available sources (CIA, 2010).

## Case study 1 – Bellingcat

Eliot Higgins first came to prominence by doing one simple thing: observing the weaponry being used by armed actors in the Syrian civil war (Chivers and Schmitt, 2013). Using crowdsourced funding, Higgins founded his own website in July 2014, focused on online investigation (Higgins, 2014a).

Between September 2018 and April 2020, Higgins and his colleagues named a slew of alleged assassins accused of hunting the Kremlin's enemies across Europe, compiling hefty dossiers on their links to the Russian state. In conducting their research, Bellingcat and its media partners brought online investigation into the mainstream.

So how did they do it?

One day after Bellingcat.com went live, Malaysia Airlines flight MH17 was shot down over war-torn eastern Ukraine, leading to the deaths of all 298 people onboard. Within the first few hours, Bellingcat and others began building a picture of the movements of an individual missile system, a Buk, through separatist-held territory close to where the passenger jet came down (Higgins, 2014b).

By early September, Bellingcat found and verified the location of videos and photographs that appeared to show the same individual system inside Russia just weeks before the tragedy. It was being transported as part of an eye-catching convoy that got locals posting videos and images to social media. Bellingcat identified the system as belonging to a Russian brigade based about three hours' drive from the border with Ukraine (Higgins, 2014c).

By November, Bellingcat (2014) had published a comprehensive report tracking the movement of the Buk system inside Russia in the weeks before and after the tragedy and charting its course through rebel-held areas of eastern Ukraine immediately before and after the aircraft was downed. They would go on to compile dossiers on the members of the Russian brigade most closely associated with the Buk system of interest and detailing their brigade's chain of command (Bellingcat Investigation Team, 2017).

In September 2016, the Dutch-led Joint Investigation Team (JIT) into the shootdown published a call for witnesses focused on two individuals, with callsigns 'Delfin' and 'Orion', publishing a series of intercepted conversations between them (Politie, 2016). Within 18 months, Bellingcat and its reporting partners had identified the men as Russian Colonel General Nikolai Tkachev and a "high-ranking GRU officer" named Oleg Vladimirovich Ivannikov, compiling extensive dossiers on their careers. They similarly exposed separatists allegedly linked to the downing of the aircraft and would go on to name another key individual highlighted by the JIT as a Russian Federal Security Service (FSB) general (Bellingcat Investigation Team, 2020a).

Starting with only the voices of 'Orion' and 'Delfin' and their first name/patronymic, the Bellingcat team used a wide range of sources in their investigations, including separatist digital media, Russian government websites, information published by the Security Service of Ukraine, Russian military-interest websites and archives, company records, court decisions and more. In the case of 'Delfin', Bellingcat sought confirmation of its findings by using scientific voice analysis. Obtaining the voice samples needed for the analysis necessitated their reporting partner, *The Insider* (Russia), using one of the more established practices of investigative journalism, adopting the cover of a reporter writing a story about a military school after it was established, via online sources, that Tkachev was chairman of its board of trustees.

Bellingcat identified 'Orion' nearly six months after 'Delfin', by which time there were further developments in its sourcing methods. Call data records were obtained for a Ukrainian phone number linked to 'Orion', and both this and related numbers were leveraged against contact-sharing apps, online telephone databases and leaked data from a defunct e-commerce site. The web store whose data had been compromised sent goods to a Moscow address that on-the-ground checks revealed to be the GRU's headquarters. Bellingcat also used residential registration records, obtained a 2003 passport application issued under Ivannikov's civilian identity and acquired border-crossing data between Russia and South Ossetia.

In terms of novel technical checks, the team outsourced graphological comparison of Ivannikov's signature across several documents. Finally, they used traditional door-stepping techniques, confirming his distinctive high-pitched voice with two human sources before making a phone call to an address they had linked to him, from where his voice was heard in the background.

In conducting these investigations, Bellingcat was establishing valuable new partnerships in two directions. Collaboration with Russian investigative magazine *The Insider* (Russia), extended the depth of their knowledge while a partnership with McClatchy DC Bureau extended their reach. At the same time, the team was offering training worldwide to journalists, police, human rights investigators and others.

In its ground-breaking investigations into the March 2018 poisoning in Salisbury of Russian double-agent Sergei Skripal and his daughter, Bellingcat combined open source research with the devastatingly effective use of a range of leaked databases and data supplied by insider sources with access to official records.

A week after the attack, the UK government had blamed Russia, leading to a tit-for-tat that saw nearly 350 diplomats expelled from 28 countries and NATO (Chughtai and Petkova, 2018). On September 5, 2018, UK police named and issued photographs of two Russian citizens they said were responsible for the attempted murders based on travel documents used by the pair (Barry, 2018; BBC News, 2018). Within a month of this announcement – in a series of extraordinary revelations – Bellingcat and its reporting partner *The Insider* (Russia) would first produce evidence that linked both men to the Russian security services, identified them as GRU operatives, disclosed details of their "prior European operations" and named them as GRU Colonel Antoliy Chepiga and Dr Alexander Mishkin, a military doctor employed by the same agency.

Bellingcat and *The Insider* (Russia) continued the trend of combining proprietary data – mostly leaked online and some from human sources – with open source information. The more proprietary records used in this instance included an Aeroflot passenger manifest, "extraordinary passport files", documents linking a phone number in the suspects' passport files to GRU HQ, border crossing data for a number of European and Asian countries, leaked Russian residential and telephone databases, the scan of a passport issued to Mishkin under his real name, car insurance databases and property records.

Bellingcat and its reporting partners have gone on to use similar methods in a string of high-profile exposés that including the following scoops: naming a second Russian intelligence officer suspected and later convicted *in absentia* of involvement in coup plot in Montenegro (2018b), naming a third Skripal suspect as Maj General Denis Sergeev – suspected of directing operations – and uncovering his alleged involvement in a string of GRU operations across several European countries (2019a, 2019b, 2019c, 2019d, 2019f; Urban, 2019), naming a Russian man arrested for killing Chechen-Georgian military commander Zelimkhan Khangoshvili in a Berlin park and compiling a dossier on his links to the FSB that pointed to their centrality to the operation (Bellingcat 2019e, 2019f) and exposing further GRU and FSB operations outside Russia (Bellingcat 2019g, 2020c).

The sources used in these stories have diversified to include census data, business records, criminal files, airline booking records, leaked passenger name record (PNR) data, Russian police passenger-monitoring data (accessed via whistle-blowers), driving licence data, call data records logging calls, data connections and cell-tower IDs (from a whistleblower working at a Russian mobile operator), tax records, criminal records and search warrant data. On the technical side, Bellingcat continued to leverage facial similarity testing to corroborate its findings and used call data record analysis. Its roster of partners grew to include Respekt (Czechia), BBC Newsnight, Swiss media group Tamedia, Der Spiegel and Russian exile Mikhail Khodorkovsky's Dossier Center.

## Case study 2 – the *New York Times* visual investigations

The *New York Times'* Visual Investigations series blends first-in-class production values, dramatic technique and explanatory journalism to deliver utterly compelling video presentations of its painstaking investigations. The series and team behind it have a strong thematic focus on human rights issues, especially pertaining to civilian harm in conflict and policing. In 2019, they produced three hard-hitting investigative pieces providing compelling evidence of the bombing – by the Russian Air Force – of hospitals, schools and residential buildings in insurgent-held northwestern Syria (Browne et al., 2019a).

The information collected by the team included flight data logged by a network of Syrian warplane trackers who provided an early warning system to areas facing bombardment and tens of thousands of intercepted radio communications between Russian Air Force pilots carrying out bombing missions and their controllers on the ground. This was cross-referenced against hundreds of reports, photos and videos of the air strikes that were posted to social media, unpublished videos and internal reports from sources on the ground, drone footage, satellite imagery and any available metadata.

Focusing on a 12-hour period in the midst of an offensive that saw dozens of healthcare facilities targeted in the northwest, the team documented four strikes on hospitals within 20 miles of each other using precision air strikes. The final video presentation blended plane spotter reports of the sorties with the intercepted communications. The ground controllers were heard delivering the coordinates of the targets and the pilots heard verifying that they had been hit using a phrase meaning "worked it" in Russian. This unprecedented picture of what was happening in the air was related to – and more importantly authenticated by – video, photographic, documentary and testimonial evidence of the attacks from the ground (Triebert et al., 2019).

Using the same techniques, the Visual Investigations team documented an attack on a housing complex for displaced Syrian families and a series of four strikes in 30 minutes the city of Maarat al Numan that left dozens of people dead. One appeared to be a double-tap strike, with the second explosion killing a medical worker who rushed to the scene. After firing his weapons, the Russian pilot who carried out the strikes was heard to confirm their release by using the phrase: "Sent Candy" (Browne et al., 2019b).

All four hospitals in the first investigation were reportedly on a "deconfliction list" compiled by the UN's Office for the Coordination of Humanitarian Affairs (OCHA) and provided to any warring parties in Syria with air power (Browne et al., 2019a; Triebert et al., 2019). In 2018, non-governmental organisations supplied OCHA with the coordinates of hundreds of such facilities in Syria, and the UN was urging them to register hundreds more in the rebel-held territory being contested in the northwest (Parker, 2018). By August 2019, however, UN Secretary-General António Guterres had ordered a board of inquiry to examine a series of incidents in northwest Syria involving attacks on facilities registered on the list. It found it "highly probable" that the "government of Syria or its allies" carried out attacks on three healthcare facilities, a school and a children's refuge (UNSG, 2020).

The Visual Investigations team stalked the official investigation, using the same methodologies and datasets to conduct a public inquiry and directly confront the issue of Russian responsibility, whereas the Security Council permanent member was not named in the official report (Hill, 2020). Although Russia denied involvement, the *New York Times'* investigations provided strong evidence that the hospitals were deliberately targeted by Russian pilots using precision weaponry. Their work also pointed to the systematic nature of the attacks. The Visual Investigations team's exposés were among the "winning work" as the newspaper scooped the 2020 award for foreign reporting (The Pulitzer Board, 2020).

Online and visual investigation uses the language of forensic science and criminal investigation, with differing standards of proof. While this was historically common within investigative journalism, the degree to which journalistic and criminal investigations now overlap in terms of their subject matter, methodology, information and evidence have set the scene for cooperation and confrontation.

## Case study 3 – BBC Africa Eye and "Anatomy of a Killing"

In January 2020, the trial of seven Cameroonian soldiers accused of killing two women and two children in the country's far north got underway (Kouagheu, 2020), a little over 18 months after a video of the killings began to circulate on social media. For several weeks after it emerged, members of the OSINT community on Twitter worked to ascertain the circumstances behind it. The ad-hoc investigative team included staff of Amnesty International journalists from BBC's newly launched documentary strand "Africa Eye", members of Bellingcat and their workshop participants, an Africa-focused investigative journalist and a group of online sleuths known mainly by their Twitter handles.

Within a couple of days, Amnesty International accused Cameroonian soldiers based on an analysis of the weapons, uniforms and geographical features seen in the video backed by information from sources on the ground (Amnesty International, 2018). Their press release – issued a day after a government spokesman dismissed the video as 'fake news' (@bendobrown, 2018) – pointed to the far north of the country where the military was fighting Islamist militant group Boko Haram. A few days later, Cameroon arrested four men suspected of involvement. Seven would eventually be put on trial (Kouagheu, 2018).

Working in public on Twitter and in private on business communications platform Slack, the ad-hoc team continued to work on the video with impressive results: pinpointing its location, using satellite imagery, astronomical information (shadows) and other data to narrow down the date it was taken, identifying some of the men in social media profiles. This was backed by a sophisticated video presentation that exposed the verification methodologies ("Anatomy of a Killing," 2010).

## Analysis – the new desk work

The investigative journalists who are the subject of this chapter have done the majority of their fact-finding behind a laptop lid. If that constitutes the power of their approach, then it is also its greatest limitation. This has been the cause of a sourcing debate within journalism that mirrors what McPherson et al. (2020) frame as a "knowledge controversy" within human rights. In journalism, the debate is best illustrated by differences of opinion around the remote investigation of chemical weapons attacks and other events in the Syrian civil war, which exhibit the signs a division along generational lines (CIJ, 2020).

Al Ghazzi (2014) says frames such as "citizen journalism" occlude "antagonistic, affective, and sometimes violent, aspects [embedded] in digital media", while Hauser (2018, 2019) notes that – compared to journalists – media activists in Syria had significant authority and power. For Harkin and Feeney (2019), remotely observed footage from partisan sources offers "a vanishingly narrow, excoriatingly subjective view of how conflicts unfold". Echoing lessons from the invasion of Iraq, they warn:

> The next world war might begin with a grainy, contested image launched online from some distant and inaccessible outpost right onto the pages of a newspaper that has recently sacked all its journalists.

On April 7, 2018, a chemical weapons attack that became central to debates about digitial investigative journalism and media reporting of the Syrian conflict took place on the insurgent-held suburb of Douma, Damascus. Digital investigative stories pointed towards government responsibility, suggesting that a chlorine cannister was dropped from a helicopter onto a residential building. The United States, the United Kingdom and France responded with missile strikes targeting the Syrian government's "ability to design, produce and stockpile" chemical weapons (Defense-Aerospace. com, 2018). Almost a year later, Harkin and Feeney's in-depth report (2019) revisited facts online and on the ground, exposing the climate of propaganda and conspiracy surrounding the incident and putting in context. They laid bare the willingness of actors on both sides to use imagery to bend the truth of what happened in ways that would make any digital investigator's hair stand on end. What is most remarkable, however, is the degree to which Harkin and Feeney's comprehensive research and on-the-ground fact-finding confirmed the conclusions reached by Bellingcat, the *New York*

*Times* Visual Investigations team and Forensic Architecture in the aftermath of that attack. In the midst of competing leads and in a heated atmosphere of propaganda, they focused on and accurately assessed information about an incident that saw a chemical weapon strike on one building cause the deaths of dozens of civilians (Bellingcat Investigation Team, 2018c; Browne et al., 2018; Forensic Architecture, 2018).

## Conclusion – rascals and rebels

Online and visual investigation is truly an effort to use "whatever media may be available" to dispel lies and establish the truth. In the finest traditions of investigative journalism, it has incorporated "sources and techniques that contemporaries thought reprehensible" (de Burgh, 2008) and its pioneers include "rascals and rebels" acting "deliberately outside the mainstream" (Deuze & Witschge, 2020; Higgins, 2021, Niezen, 2020).

If the years 2018/2019 are remembered as the moment online and visual investigation was established as distinct and indispensable part of mainstream journalism, then the stories mentioned previously – and the teams behind them – deserve much of the credit.

News executives appear to be taking notice. As the Black Lives Matter protests raged across the United States in May 2020, the *New York Times* Visual Investigations team faced fresh competition from newly established units at NBC News (@NBC_VC, 2020) and the *Washington Post* (Bennett et al., 2020a, 2020b), while the *Wall Street Journal* (2020) also produced a "video investigation". In the United Kingdom, BBC News Arabic and Newsnight are now producing regular investigative pieces using online and visual investigative techniques (BBC News Arabic, 2019a, 2019b, 2019c, 2020).

At a time of fears about surveillance, a networked system of *sousveillance* has emerged in a paradigm shifted from informed public to "monitorial citizenship" (Schudson, 2002). The power of this system, and its potential, lies in blending, linking and interpreting the aggregate actions of a range of actors, positioning journalists as investigators, analysis and intermediaries – not so much gatekeepers as pathfinders amidst a bewildering array of data. According to Bruns, this "thoroughly integrated complex" amounts to a "social news media network". If ever an academic phrase belonged in a Storyful investor pitch-deck. . .[2]

## Notes

1 This chapter was scrupulously and comprehensively referenced but, for reasons of space, secondary and following references have been omitted, as have detailed references to Bellingcat files.
2 The author directed the Human Rights Investigation Lab between 2018 and 2019; the author worked at Storyful between 2011 and 2014.

## References

Aday, S., Livingston, S., 2009. NGOs as intelligence agencies: The empowerment of transnational advocacy networks and the media by commercial remote sensing in the case of the Iranian nuclear program. *Geoforum* 40, 514–522.

Al Ghazzi, O., 2014. "Citizen journalism" in the Syrian uprising: Problematizing Western narratives in a local context. *Communication Theory* 24, 435–454. https://doi.org/10.1111/comt.12047

Al Jazeera, 2019. How virtual detectives exposed China's "re-education camps." In: The Listening Post, "Xinjiang: The story China wants the world to forget". *Al Jazeera.*

Allan, S., 2007. *Citizen journalism and the rise of "mass self-communication": Reporting the London bombings.* Global Media Journal (Australian Edition), Sydney.

Allan, S., 2013. *Citizen witnessing: Revisioning journalism in times of crisis, Key concepts in journalism.* Polity Press, Cambridge; Malden, MA.

Amnesty International, 2018. Cameroon: Credible evidence that Army personnel responsible for shocking extrajudicial executions caught on video. *Amnesty.org.* URL: www.amnesty.org/en/latest/news/2018/07/cameroon-credible-evidence-that-army-personnel-responsible-for-shocking-extrajudicial-executions-caught-on-video/ (accessed 6 August 2020).

Barry, E., 2018. From mountain of CCTV footage, pay dirt: 2 Russians are named in spy poisoning. *The New York Times.*

Bartlett, R., 2013. A look at Storyful's Open Newsroom verification project. *Media News.*

Bazzell, M., 2020. *Open source intelligence techniques: Resources for searching and analyzing online information.* IntelTechniques.com, Middletown.

BBC Africa Eye, 2010. Anatomy of a killing. *BBC News.* URL: https://www.bbc.co.uk/programmes/p0707w39 (accessed 23 November 2020).

BBC News, 2018. Novichok attack Russian "agents" named. *BBC News.*

BBC News Arabic, 2019a. Maids for sale: Silicon Valley's online slave market. *BBC News.*

BBC News Arabic, 2019b. Idlib 'double tap' air strikes: Who's to blame? *BBC News.*

BBC News Arabic, 2020. How an Iranian airline "helped spread coronavirus". *BBC News.*

BBC Newsnight, BBC News Arabic, 2019c. Libyan conflict: Suspected war crimes shared online. *BBC Newsnight.*

Belair-Gagnon, V., 2015. *Social media at BBC news: The re-making of crisis reporting, Routledge research in journalism.* Routledge, New York.

Bellingcat Investigation Team, 2014. Origin of the separatists' buk. *Bellingcat.*

Bellingcat Investigation Team, 2017. MH17 – drivers of the Russian June and July 2014 Buk convoy trucks. *Bellingcat.*

Bellingcat Investigation Team, 2018a. Open source survey of alleged chemical attacks in Douma on 7th April 2018. *Bellingcat.*

Bellingcat Investigation Team, 2018b. Second GRU officer indicted in Montenegro coup unmasked. *Bellingcat.*

Bellingcat Investigation Team, 2018c. Open source survey of alleged chemical attacks in Douma on 7th April 2018. *Bellingcat.*

Bellingcat Investigation Team, 2019a. The search for Denis Sergeev: Photographing a ghost. *Bellingcat.*

Bellingcat Investigation Team, 2019b. The GRU globetrotters: Mission London. *Bellingcat.*

Bellingcat Investigation Team, 2019c. GRU globetrotters 2: The spies who loved Switzerland. *Bellingcat.*

Bellingcat Investigation Team, 2019d. Third suspect in skripal poisoning identified as Denis Sergeev, high-ranking GRU officer. *Bellingcat.*

Bellingcat Investigative Team, 2019e. Identifying the Berlin bicycle assassin: From Moscow to Berlin (Part 1). *Bellingcat.*

Bellingcat Investigation Team, 2019f. Identifying the Berlin bicycle assassin: Russia's murder franchise (Part 2). *Bellingcat.*

Bellingcat Investigation Team, 2019g. The dreadful eight: GRU's Unit 29155 and the 2015 poisoning of Emilian Gebrev. *Bellingcat.*

Bellingcat Investigative Team, 2020a. An officer and a diplomat: The strange case of the GRU spy with a red notice. *Bellingcat.*

Bellingcat Investigation Team, 2020b. Key MH17 figure identified as senior FSB official: Colonel General Andrey Burlaka. *Bellingcat.*

Bellingcat Investigation Team, 2020c. "V" For "Vympel": FSB's secretive department "V" behind assassination of Georgian Asylum Seeker in Germany. *Bellingcat.*

@bendobrown, 2018. Benjamin Strick on Twitter: "#Cameroon government labels recent video of citizen executions as 'fake news'. #OSINT https://t.co/ls2BUPOLaS"/Twitter. Twitter/@bendobrown.

Bennett, D., Cahlan, S., Davis, A.C., Lee, J., 2020a. The crackdown before Trump's photo op: What video and other records show about the clearing of protesters outside the White House. *Washington Post.*

Bennett, D., Lee, J., Cahlan, S., 2020b. The death of George Floyd: What video and other records show about his final minutes. *Washington Post.*

Browne, M., Singhvi, A., Koettl, C., Reneau, N., Marcolini, B., Al-Hlou, Y., Jordan, D., 2018. One building, One bomb: How Assad gassed his own people. *The New York Times.*

Browne, M., Triebert, C., Hill, E., Hurst, W., Gianordoli, G., Khavin, D., 2019a. Hospitals and schools are being bombed in Syria. A U.N. inquiry is limited. We took a deeper look. *The New York Times.*

Browne, M., Triebert, C., Hill, E., Khavin, D., 2019b. A civilian camp in Syria was bombed. Here's how we traced the culprit. *The New York Times.*

Bruns, A., Highfield, T., 2016. Is Habermas on Twitter, in: Bruns, A., Enli, G., Skogerbø, E., Larsson, A.O., Christensen, C. (Eds.), *The Routledge companion to social media and politics.* Routledge, London.

Castells, M., 2015. *Networks of outrage and hope: Social movements in the internet Age.* Polity Press, Cambridge, UK; Malden, MA.

Castells, M., 2019. *Rupture: The crisis of liberal democracy,* 2nd ed. Polity Press, Cambridge, UK; Medford, MA.

Chivers, C.J., Schmitt, E., 2013. Saudis step up help for rebels in Syria with Croatian arms. *The New York Times.*

Chughtai, A., Petkova, M., 2018. Skripal case diplomatic expulsions in numbers. *Al Jazeera, English.*

CIA, 2010. The office of strategic services: Research and analysis branch. *Central Intelligence Agency.* URL: www.cia.gov/news-information/featured-story-archive/2010-featured-story-archive/oss-research-and-analysis.html (accessed 14 June 2020).

CIJ, 2020. CIJ Logan 2018: Investigation Khan Sheikhoun. *YouTube/The Centre for Investigative Journalism.*

de Burgh, H. (Ed.), 2008. Introduction, in: *Investigative journalism.* Routledge, Abingdon, Oxon; New York.

Defense-Aerospace.com, 2018. Successful strikes and targets hit in Syria. *Defense-Aerospace. com*. URL www.defense-aerospace.com/articles-view/release/3/192498/syria%3A-allied-air-strikes-hit-3-targets%2C-achieve-stated-goals.html (accessed 11 June 2020).

Deuze, M., Witschge, T., 2020. *Beyond journalism*. Polity, Cambridge, UK ; Medford, MA.

Dubberley, S., Koenig, A., Murray, D. (Eds.), 2020. *Digital witness: Using open source information for human rights investigation, documentation, and accountability*. Oxford University Press, Oxford, New York.

Forensic Architecture, 2018. Chemical attacks in Douma. URL: https://forensic-architecture.org/investigation/chemical-attacks-in-douma (accessed 23 November 2020)

Friedland, L., Hove, T., Rojas, H., 2006. The networked public sphere. *Javnost – The Public* 13. https://doi.org/10.1080/13183222.2006.11008922

Harkin, J., Feeney, L., 2019. What happened in Douma? Searching for facts in the fog of Syria's propaganda war. *The Intercept*.

Hauser, J., 2018. Citizen-activist as journalist: Network journalism and professional practices in the coverage of the Aleppo offensive. *Irish Communication Review*.

Hauser, J., 2019. Working the news: Preserving professional identity through networked journalism at elite news media. Doctoral. https://doi.org/https:/ /doi.org/10.21427/12h3-z337

Hermida, A., 2015. Nothing but the truth: Redrafting the journalistic boundary of verification, in: Carlson, M., Lewis, S.C. (Eds.), *Boundaries of journalism professionalism, practices and participation*. Routledge, New York, NY.

Hermida, A., Young, M., 2019. *Data journalism and the regeneration of news*. Routledge, London.

Higgins, E., 2014a. Brown Moses blog: What is Bellingcat. *Brown Moses Blog*. URL: http://brown-moses.blogspot.com/2014/07/what-is-bellingcat.html (accessed 1 June 2020).

Higgins, E., 2014b. Buk transporter filmed "heading to Russia" sighted in an earlier photograph. *Bellingcat*.

Higgins, E., 2014c. Video comparison confirms the Buk linked to the downing of MH17 came from Russia. *Bellingcat*.

Higgins, E., 2021. *We are Bellingcat: An intelligence agency for the people*. Bloomsbury Publishing, London.

Hill, E., 2020. U.N. inquiry into Syria bombings is silent on Russia's role. *The New York Times*.

Howard, P.N., 2011. *Castells and the media*. Polity Press, Cambridge.

Kouagheu, J., 2018. Cameroon arrests four soldiers suspected of executing women and children. *Reuters*.

Kouagheu, J., 2020. Cameroonian soldiers go on trial over shooting of women and children. *Reuters*.

Kovach, B., Rosenstiel, T., 2014. *The elements of journalism: what newspeople should know and the public should expect*, Revised and updated 3rd ed. Three Rivers Press, New York.

Lipinski, A.M., 2012. Truth in the age of social media. The Nieman Foundation for Journalism, Harvard University. URL: http://niemanreports.org/issues/summer-2012/ (accessed 23 November 2020).

Little, M., 2012. The human algorithm [archived]. *Storyful Blog*. URL: https://web.archive.org/web/20120902004946/http://blog.storyful.com/2011/05/20/the-human-algorithm-2/ (accessed 1 June 2020).

McPherson, E. (2015). Digital human rights reporting by civilian witnesses: Surmounting the verification barrier, in: Lind, R.A. (Ed.), *Produsing theory in a digital world 2.0: The intersection of audiences and production in contemporary theory,* Vol. 2, pp. 193–209. New York, NY: Peter Lang Publishing.

McPherson, E., Thornton, I.G., Mahmoudi, M., 2020. Open source investigations and the technology-driven knowledge controversy in human rights fact-finding, in: Dubberley, S., Koenig, A., Murray, D. (Eds.), *Digital witness: Using open source information for human rights investigation, documentation, and accountability.* Oxford University Press, Oxford; New York.

@NBC_VC, 2020. NBC VC – David McAtee. Twitter/@NBC_VC.

Negroponte, N., 1996. *Being digital, 1.* Vintage Books ed. Vintage Books, New York.

Niezen, R., 2020. *#HumanRights: The technologies and politics of justice claims in practice, Stanford studies in human rights.* Stanford University Press, Stanford, California.

Parker, B., 2018. What is humanitarian deconfliction? [WWW Document]. *The New Humanitarian.* URL: www.thenewhumanitarian.org/analysis/2018/11/13/what-humanitarian-deconfliction-syria-yemen (accessed 11 June 2020).

Politie, 2016. MH17 information Orion and Delfin. URL: www.politie.nl/en/themes/mh17-information-orion-and-delfin.html (accessed 15 June 2020).

Rasmussen, T., 2016. *The Internet Soapbox.* Oslo: Scandinavian University Press (Universitetsforlaget).

Schudson, M., 2002. *The good citizen: A history of American civic life, 1.* Harvard University Press paperback ed., 3rd print. ed. Harvard University Press, Cambridge, MA.

Sheridan, G., 2012. Newsrooms as intelligence agencies [archived]. *Storyful Blog.* URL: https://web.archive.org/web/20130728151954/http://blog.storyful.com/2012/07/30/newsrooms-as-intelligence-agencies/ (accessed 8 June 2020).

Shirky, C., 2009. *Here comes everybody: The power of organizing without organizations [with an updated epilogue].* Nachdr. ed. Penguin Books, New York, Toronto, London.

Silverman, C. (Ed.), 2014. *Verification handbook: An ultimate guideline on digital age sourcing for emergency coverage.* European Journalism Centre (EJC). URL: http://verificationhandbook.com/additionalmaterial/ (accessed 22 November 2020).

Trewinnard, T., Bell, F., 2018. Social media verification: Assessing sources and visual content, in: Ireton, C., Posetti, J. (Eds.), *Journalism, 'fake news' & disinformation: handbook for journalism education and training.* UNESCO, Paris. URL: https://unesdoc.unesco.org/ark:/48223/pf0000265552 (accessed 22 November 2020).

Triebert, C., Hill, E., Browne, M., Hurst, W., Khavin, D., Froliak, M., 2019. How times reporters proved Russia bombed Syrian hospitals. *The New York Times.* URL: https://www.nytimes.com/2019/10/13/reader-center/russia-syria-hospitals-investigation.html (accessed 23 November 2020).

The Pulitzer Board, 2020. The 2020 Pulitzer prize winner in international reporting [WWW Document]. URL: www.pulitzer.org/winners/staff-new-york-times (accessed 11 June 2020).

UNSG, 2020. Summary by the Secretary-General of the report of the United Nations Headquarters Board of Inquiry into certain incidents in northwest Syria since 17 September 2018 involving facilities on the United Nations deconfliction list and United Nations supported facilities. *UNSG.*

Urban, M., 2019. BBC two – Newsnight, Skripal poisoning: Did third Russian suspect command attack? *BBC.*

Wall Street Journal, 2020. Video investigation: How a Seattle protest ended in Chaos. URL: https://www.youtube.com/watch?v=MMjExztMbyA (accessed 23 November 2020).

Wright, S., Graham, T., Jackson, D., 2016. Third space, social media, and everyday political talk, in: Bruns, Axel, Enli, Gunn, Skogerbø, Eli, Larsson, Anders Olof, Christensen, Christian (Eds.), *The Routledge companion to social media and politics*. Routledge, New York.

# 5

# KILL ONE AND A DOZEN RETURN

*Stephen Grey*

There is a folk law that crooks say to themselves: don't kill a policeman or a journalist. That would only, as American reporters put it, "bring too much heat." But is that true anymore?

The death of two journalists in the European Union in winter of 2017/2018, plus the fiery popular rhetoric of President Donald Trump against media workers, raised widespread concerns about the danger.

The threat against reporters is not new. Over 1900 journalists have been killed between 1992 and 2020, according to the Centre to Protect Journalists, including both cases where the motive is confirmed or unconfirmed (CPJ, 2020).

Most have them died in wars in which they shared the danger with combatants and civilians of those conflicts. Most were not individually targeted. But the assassination of two journalists in the European Union who were both actively investigating corruption, Daphne Caruana Galizia in Malta on October 16, 2017, and Jan Kuciak in Slovakia in February 21, 2018, highlighted what appears to be a growing direct threat to freedom of expression in apparently peaceful places.

In the face of those concerns, something positive did happen: the revival of a strategy first pioneered in the United States in the late 1970s of bringing together a group of journalists from normally fierce competitors to continue their dead colleague's work. The previous project was called the Arizona Project (Lindsey, 1976). It followed the death of a reporter in that US state, Don Bolles, in 1976. Three decades later, the new version was christened the Daphne Project, taking up the work of Caruana Galizia. It involved up to 45 reporters from 15 countries and resulted in 86 articles (Forbidden Stories, 2020).

Laurent Richard, a French journalist who played a key role in founding the project, summed up why, as a collaboration, it was special.

It was not only about investigating a big leak, like WikiLeaks, and then doing a story, which is extremely important and difficult and tricky, but it was a bit more than that. Because it was about sending that strong signal at the end that you cannot kill the message (Richard, 2019).

This chapter explains how the project came together, organised itself, worked in practice and deployed techniques to make it successful.

## The Arizona Project

The car bomb on June 3, 1976, in downtown Phoenix that killed the 47-year-old state capital reporter Bolles of the *Arizona Republic* sparked outrage – but also a new way of working for journalists. The atrocity came not long before the inaugural conference of a new US organisation to promote journalistic sleuthing, the Investigative Reporters and Editors (IRE, 2020). At the time, investigative reporting was already in fashion – with the efforts of journalists at the *Washington Post* and other outlets credited for exposing the Watergate scandal that led to the resignation of Richard Nixon from the White House. But many of the rules of the investigative craft were still evolving.

Bolles was remembered in an IRE account of the project as a veteran sleuth: "the lone-wolf type, the kind who would attach a piece of Scotch tape to the hood of his blue Datsun to make sure that nobody had tampered with his engine" (Kovacs, n.d.). No one knew the motive for his death, but his colleagues believed it was revenge for articles he had written about land deals.

The death of Bolles inspired the fledging IRE to create what it called the Arizona Project. A team assembled in Phoenix at a temporary headquarters, the Adams Hotel, and together assembled a multi-part report with the help of 38 journalists from 24 newspapers and broadcasters. That report, which began publication on March 13, 1977, ran to about 80,000 words long, and at least some of its 23 parts were run in many papers, to support an objective as some described to "get revenge on deadline" (Wendland, 1977).

In an introduction to a book on the project, one of the reporters, Michael Wendland of the *Detroit News*, set out the objectives:

> First, the team attempted to pay tribute to a slain colleague by finishing what he had started, by getting to the heart of the political corruption and organized crime in Arizona that had made Bolles's killers believe that murder was a logical response to a reporter's work. Second, by clearly demonstrating the solidarity of the American press, the team effort would reemphasize the old underworld adage: "You don't kill a reporter because it brings too much heat."

One of the outline discussions is described between two reporters involved with the IRE:

> "The intent should not be to bring Don Bolles's killers to justice per se. The cops and the local papers are doing that right now. Instead, we should go into Arizona and describe the particular climate that caused his death."

"In other words, we should carry on Bolles's work, do the kind of stories that Don himself would have done if he had had the time and resources?"

"Precisely."

(Wendland, 1977)

This was a vital principle. The Arizona Project recognised from the start that reporters were not and could not be murder cops, but they could report on the wider context of the crime and continue the journalist's work. Established editors were not in favour, either of interfering in local media or of collaboration.

By the time of the Daphne Project in 2017, the value of collaboration had been well proven. After first running shy of it, even the *New York Times* joined collaborative projects such as the 2010 publication of State Department cables from WikiLeaks, NSA files leaked by Edward Snowden in 2013 and in 2016 the so-called Panama Papers (ICIJ, 2016).

In Arizona, law enforcement had been only partly successful in its work. A millionaire rancher, Kemper Marley, suspected at the time by reporters and prosecutors to have ordered Bolles' killing, was never prosecuted, and the convictions of two suspected middlemen in the arrangement also did not stand on appeal (Associated Press, 1990). Only the person who planted the bomb, John Adamson, who confessed, ever had a conviction sustained and served 20 years in jail. Both Marley and Adamson are now dead (Ruelas, 2016).

Yet many of the journalists' allegations of land fraud and corruption were sustained, and the series was widely praised by law enforcement. As the IRE account described: "The Arizona Project exposed widespread corruption pervasive in the state and was one of the first nation-wide efforts to bring together competitive investigative journalists to work as a team" (Kovacs, n.d.).

### How the Daphne Project unfolded

It was on October 21, five days after Daphne's death, that I first got a call from a friend working in Switzerland who had been in touch with her family. They were shattered and "feeling confused" about how to seek international support. He was in touch with Daphne's sister Corinne and her three sons. I already knew Matthew, Daphne's eldest son, as we were both members of the International Consortium of Investigative Journalists, the organisation that organised the publication of the Panama Papers. Once I had heard the extent of her allegations about corruption in Malta, it seemed obvious that we needed a big team to investigate.

Meanwhile, at a gathering of investigative reporters in South Africa, a similar idea took shape: that an "Arizona Project" Mark II could be created to look at Daphne's journalism. A new organisation based in Paris, Forbidden Stories, led by a French TV veteran, Laurent Richard, stepped up to provide leadership.

Just as I sent an email to fellow reporters asking who would like to join a collaboration, I got word from Laurent Richard that he was already trying to form such a group. *The Guardian* newspaper, which had a relationship with Daphne's family already, was also considering how it might cooperate with others, and they quickly agreed to join together. In a secretive meeting at a countryside hotel outside London, soon after the murder, *The Guardian* had taken the delivery from the family of one of the last collections of leaked material that Daphne had been working on.

## Forbidden stories

Laurent Richard, a French television producer of 20 years' experience, was one of the first at the scene of the massacre of journalists and cartoonists at the Charlie Hebdo magazine on January 7, 2015. This profoundly shocking experience convinced him of the need for a journalistic response to such crimes.

Richard had read of the Arizona Project and what was called the Khadija Project in 2015 (OCCRP, 2015). This was an attempt by the Organised Crime and Corruption Reporting Project (OCCRP) to continue the work of Azeri journalist Khadija Ismayilova while she was in jail.

Other examples inspired him, too, such as the work of reporters from the Brazilian Association of Investigative Journalism, ABRAJI, a non-profit, who kept alive the work of Tim Lopes, a reporter burned to death by drug traffickers in 2002 (ABRAJI, 2017).

During a sabbatical break at the University of Michigan, Richard developed the idea behind Forbidden Stories. It would be used as a platform systematically to continue the work of murdered and imprisoned journalists and to provide a technical system for reporters in dangerous situations to upload their secrets as a kind of insurance. In the event of their death or imprisonment, the secrets could be released.

The point was to focus on the journalism, not the outrage. "I was personally really looking for really what I can do as a journalist. I don't want to work for a NGO. I don't want to do advocacy. I don't want to do campaigning, because this is not what I am able to do and I really want to stay a journalist."

As he wrote later:

> Cooperation is without a doubt the best protection. What is the point of killing a journalist if 10, 20 or 30 others are waiting to carry on their work? Whether you're a dictator, the leader of a drug cartel or a corrupt businessman, exposure of your crimes is your biggest fear. Journalists are the enemy of the corrupt ecosystem that you have constructed. But what if this exposure becomes global, and the message amplified? Wherever you go, you will be questioned by the world's press. Whatever you are trying to hide will be magnified.
>
> (Richard, 2018)

## KILL ONE AND A DOZEN RETURN

To Richard, Daphne's case seemed like a perfect one to investigate. Before her death, she had alleged widespread corruption among the elite in her country and there was outrage across Europe about her death.

In some sense, Malta's stories might seem like quite small scale – local news, in effect, that might never reach the front pages of major international media. "But as a story I think this was universal," recalled Richard.

> You have one woman who was the last independent voice in the island, of this very tiny island which is part of European Union, but you have so many dirty businesses inside this island, so many corrupt people and some organized crime groups so active in this tiny island, that it makes the story extremely interesting for a journalist's point of view and extremely important that the public opinion should know.

The key thing was though that Daphne, he felt, had died isolated. "Daphne was fighting alone or almost alone."

Very soon after the killing, Richard spoke to Daphne's son, Matthew, and also got Bastian Obermayer, an investigative editor at the *Süddeutsche Zeitung* who was famed, with his team, of taking delivery of the so-called Panama Papers, involved. Also involved early was a Sarajevo-based organisation called the Organised Crime and Corruption Reporting Project. With a powerful technical infrastructure and experience of handling some of the most corrupt and dangerous people in the world, they would become the backend of the project. We also knew we would need a local partner, and Jacob Borg, a relentlessly dogged reporter who, unlike many local journalists, was shunned by the *Times of Malta*, was brought on board.

For Richard, a key moment was realising the quality of reporters coming forward. Although it was impractical for everyone to be invited, some of the best-known figures in investigative reporting in Europe were coming forward to help. Those early meetings showed, said Richard, "that I had some really very rock-solid reporters who could start working right away on continuing Daphne's work."

But a close look at that work also showed that an investigation presented some challenges. Daphne was a not a regular beat reporter or an investigative reporter who gathered only facts. She was an opinion writer who also took aggressive stances. The accusations she had made, such as that Prime Minister Joseph Muscat and his wife had received a one-million-dollar bribe from Azerbaijan, were subject to challenge, exemplified by the more than 40 libel suits she was fighting at the time of her murder (AFP, 2019).

The challenge for the Project was to continue her work as a reporter without endorsing her opinions or attempting to validate every accusation she had made. That string of libel suits, several key people argued, were a measure of the persecution she had faced before her death, an example of the global phenomenon of piling on pressure, particularly against freelance journalists, with intolerable legal threats that threatened freedom of expression. Nevertheless, until the team of journalists that became the Daphne Project re-investigated and verified her work, some involved felt there was need to be cautious. The act of being murdered was not proof that what Daphne wrote was correct. And what would be the impact on Daphne's family, for example, if the result of the project was to discover that Daphne had, in key respects, got it wrong? Said Richard: "We committed from the very beginning that if Daphne was wrong, we need to say that she was wrong. If she was not able to fact-check something that she was publishing, we need to say it" (Richard, 2019).

Still, as happens very often, key people involved trusted their gut instinct. After all, if Daphne had got everything wrong, why invest months following her leads? Juliette Garside of *The Guardian*, unlike many involved in the Project, had been to Malta and had met Daphne's family, if not Daphne herself, prior to the murder. She felt strongly that, even if Daphne had made some mistakes, she was 'onto something.'

Said Garside: "I was already convinced before she was killed that what she was investigating was of huge importance, a political corruption scandal that went to the top." After she was killed, she was certain: "Why was she murdered if she wasn't uncovering things that were true? She must have been killed for what she was about to expose or had exposed" (Garside, 2019).

Still, Garside, Richard and I all agreed early on that to protect the integrity of the investigation, Daphne's family should be treated as sources, not as an integral part of the Project. Since Matthew is a fellow journalist and known to me and others, it did make things awkward at times. But the arrangement was also good for the family, since it left them free to comment and campaign without being restrained by the need to stay neutral as the facts were investigated.

There was also an early emphasis on security. With the mastermind of the killing at large, no one knew what dangers awaited anyone else who looked at what Daphne had been investigating.

## Tools and techniques

In leading the organisation of the Daphne Project, the team at Forbidden Stories, advised by its experienced team, made use of evolving techniques and procedures that had been refined by leading media groups and the ICIJ in dealing with major projects like WikiLeaks, the Snowden files and the Panama Papers. For example, each journalist joined up with a formal, written participation agreement that bound not only the journalist but his or her editors to respect common rules, a stipulation that helped to neutralise the inbuilt tension when highly competitive reporters from rival organisations joined together for a common goal.

There was a need to make some sacrifices, recalled Richard.

> We are trained to be lone-wolf reporters [and] to never share information with the others. We are trained to scoop the others. We are trained [to work] in a very individualistic way, to be honest. But, but we know that for that kind of project, Daphne Project or for the Forbidden Stories entire project, that the paradigm is extremely different. That's the opposite we need to do. We need to let our egos somewhere far away from this kind of group.
>
> (Richard, 2019)

What made the Daphne Project different from other "typical" collaborations was its multi-dimensional aspect. This was not a look at one story or one set of documents that Daphne was working on. It was an attempt to pick up on multiple threads. She had written about and accused a large array of characters in the Maltese establishment. There was also an added dimension of danger inherent in looking at the case of a murdered journalist. This was not a matter of sharing access to and parcelling out a common set of documents, as was the case with the Panama Papers, but instead a story that involved developing and handling sources, many of them confidential. The handling of a secret source was not something that fitted naturally to a team approach.

Unlike the Panama Papers but like the Arizona Project, this was a locally focused project, turning global attention to a very small island. As in the Arizona Project, the question could be asked: why should readers of other foreign publications be interested in the ins and outs of Maltese characters and corruption? It was not clear that readers would be, but most felt readers would agree that this work was the right thing to do. The idea of the Project appealed to many editors, and substantial resources were invested.

There were five key principles by which the Daphne Project functioned:

First, there was a *solid technical infrastructure*. Unlike the original Arizona Project, the members of the Daphne Project did not all get dispatched to the scene of the crime and install themselves in a dedicated office. Instead they operated mostly virtually. At the core was a central hub for information run by the OCCRP. This included a Wiki (a user-updatable website), protected by various security measures, including encrypted connections and multi-factor authentication. In general, it is safer to store information in a central hub in the cloud rather than distributing information by email, even if those emails are secured by encryption as strong as PGP. Chats between reporters generally took place through chat groups within Signal, a peer-to-peer encrypted chat network. But reporters were advised not to use such chats to store information, as, while the communications might be secure, the local copy of that chat on a phone or laptop is highly vulnerable to being compromised.

Second, a *division of labour* in seeking out sources and materials and analysing it, combined with a pooling of the product. There were many complicated strands of Daphne's work, each requiring considerable effort to investigate, so it made sense to divide the reporters into teams. Seven teams were set up to probe the assassination, Malta's energy deals, political corruption, Malta's scheme to sell its passports to rich people, fuel smuggling, gambling and finally Pilatus Bank, an Iranian-controlled bank in Malta with close links to Azerbaijan and Maltese politicians. Every team went away and did reporting and then shared the results with the whole project. At the beginning, it was not clear which avenue would take us furthest.

Third was *mutual trust*. To enable teamwork, reporters needed to trust both the quality and integrity of other people's work and know they would not use their stewardship of one inquiry line to gain advantage. This requirement was underpinned by a selecting, as far as possible, the best and most trusted investigative journalists to join the project.

Fourth was *individual responsibility* for publication. The idea here, replicated from successful ICIJ and WikiLeaks collaborations, was to pool raw material but to make every partner responsible for his or her writing, editing and publication of finished material. For the ICIJ, refining this step had been critical for it in coordinating research into large and controversially obtained sets of data without risking legal liability for publication. For the media partners, it was also far more efficient to concentrate on their own editorial copy rather than wasting energy by attempting, as was done in the Arizona Project and early ICIJ collaborations, to edit and publish a commonly agreed-upon output, little of which might end up actually being published. A drawback of this approach, however, was that it limited the involvement of freelancers.

Fifth was an *agreed deadline*. A principle that holds together collaborations is an agreed-upon publication date and time that can be shifted only by mutual agreement. With a mixture of publications, including TV, radio and print, weekly and daily publications, any chosen time is rarely good for everyone.

The points of principle were formulated by Laurent Richard at Forbidden Stories and endorsed at the Project's first and only joint meeting, held in Paris early in January 2018. The key point, he recalled, was "We are not a human rights organization. We are not campaigning, we aren't doing advocacy. We are not here for defending the rights of Daphne. We are not here to make a tribute for Daphne. We are just here to make journalism. We're here to use journalism to defend journalism."

From the first meeting, research continued intensively with multiple group chats via Signal, conference calls and trips to Malta and around Europe.

### Issues and problems

Some potential issues in such a collaboration needed to be carefully thought through. And some journalists, including myself, felt a joint approach to such a serious matter risked compromising ethical standards, just as some had criticised the original Arizona Project. Unlike some collaborative projects that involved parcelling out a single major "leak" or were tightly focused on a single story, the Daphne Project involved investigating several allegations made by Daphne, all of which were contested, and where proof often relied on sensitive confidential sources who needed protection.

Given that Daphne had so firmly accused the Maltese government of corruption, it also required a careful approach to maintain objectivity until her allegations were evaluated. That meant, for example, not including in the team some journalists who had already made up their minds and said so publicly, however correct they might have been.

Some key dilemmas were:

- How publications should approach sources. As they approached people for comment, disclosing the existence of a secret collaboration could scare off some sources from commenting or encourage them to actively try to undermine the project. On the other hand, many felt it could be unethical to approach someone to comment on behalf of, say, Reuters, and for those comments to then appear in, say, *Le Monde*. A compromise was to re-approach people closer to deadline and explain that comments might be shared with others.
- How do you reconcile different media cultures: for example, willingness to publish unproven allegations or to use undercover footage? An example was French TV footage that secretly captured the occupants of a village bar describing how one of the alleged killers of Daphne, Alfred Degiorgio, had shared a drink with Chris Cardona, minister for the economy, investment and small business. Cardona denied the encounter. Some Daphne Project members published the conversation, while other media like Reuters and the *New York Times*, who had concerns about using undercover footage, ignored it.
- How do you reconcile different commitments of time and money from different publications? While the principle was to share all the reported material freely, in practice, different publications made considerably different contributions, particularly at later stages. Should they share all their material with others who had done less? As in other matters, these could be shared by good will – with discretion and appropriate credit where credit was due. But it was an issue that needed careful management.

## The investigation

Publication began in April 2018 that confirmed the weakness of the inquiry into Daphne's murder, verified as true some of the accusations that Daphne had made and also advanced some of her work.

Among the stories published were:

- How evidence against three suspects charged with Daphne's murder had been pieced together from mobile phone records but how the police focus on the people who planted the bomb had, so far, left the masterminds who ordered the killing at large. None of the people that Daphne was writing about, and could have been considered potential suspects, had been questioned by police (Garside & Kirchgaessner, 2018; Grey, The Silencing of Daphne, 2018).
- How documents in the Panama Papers indicated two senior figures in the Maltese government, the prime minister's chief of staff and a former energy minister, had secret Panama companies which, correspondence suggested, intended to receive cash from two mystery Dubai offshore companies, one called 17 Black and the other, Macbridge. Both people denied any wrongdoing or any knowledge of these projected cash flows (Pegg, 2018).

  Further investigation by Reuters and the *Times of Malta* later identified the director of a major power station project that was promoted by the Maltese government, Yorgen Fenech, as the secret owner of 17 Black (Grey & Arnold, 2018).
- How the same power project (a joint venture with Azerbaijan and Germany's Siemens) may have resulted in higher energy costs for the country (Garside, 2018).
- How Malta's passports-for-sale scheme was being abused as a cheap way of acquiring access to the European Union (Obermayer et al., 2018).
- How Malta was a centre for the fuel smuggling business (Rubino et al., 2018).
- How the Iranian-owned Pilatus Bank had seduced Maltese government ministers, been subject to lax regulation and then been used to funnel cash from Azerbaijan to secretly purchase property and investments across Europe (Chastand & Michel, 2018).
- How Minister Cardona frequented a bar regularly used by the one of the three people accused of Daphne's murder (Borg, 2018).

Investigations by the Daphne Project were, however, not able to verify Daphne's claim about a Panama company called Egrant that Daphne had alleged belonged to the wife of the prime minister, Joseph Muscat. (An official inquiry completely rejected the allegation; Willan, 2018.) In fact, no direct evidence was found to prove personal corruption by Muscat or any of his team, even if revelations, for example, about the planned transactions around the company 17 Black, suggested a need for further investigation. Instead, the articles broadly indicated a broader climate of corruption and favouritism.

### *Follow-up*

For her family and friends, the publication of the Daphne Project was a huge step forward, leaving them feeling her work would not be left ignored. In the week of publication, Daphne's husband, Peter, travelled to England and attended the daily editorial conference at *The Guardian*. Speaking on CNN, one of her sons said it "felt like some kind of justice" (CNN, 2018). After her murder, the family had doubted if anyone outside Malta would take an interest in what she had been writing about. The Daphne Project proved that wrong.

But the family pointed out that many of the key people whom she accused of corruption remained in office at the helm of the Maltese government. The Project was not enough in itself to achieve justice. It certainly focused the minds of many in Europe on what Malta needed to do to improve its record in fighting corruption. But the task of getting justice was colossal.

After the first publications, and revelation of the project, others took it as an inspiration. For example, after the death of three Russian journalists in the Central African Republic in July 2018 (Russian journalists killed in Central African Republic ambush, Guardian, 2018) exiled Russian oligarch Mikhail Khodorkovsky, who had funded them, set up his own initiative to fund investigations into the journalists' deaths.

Forbidden Stories, meanwhile, moved to a more wide-ranging investigation, called the Green Blood Project, for journalists killed or silenced for environmental reporting, which was to investigate mining (Forbidden Stories, 2019).

Elsewhere, Daphne Project inquiries continued, albeit with a smaller core group. The ultimate mastermind of the killing has not been discovered. A key development came in November 2015 when it emerged that one of the three suspects, Vince Muscat, had secretly provided an account to the police of how Daphne was murdered. His evidence led the police to a middleman, Melvin Theuma, who, when arrested, told police he had passed on a contract to kill Daphne from businessman Fenech, the same man the Reuters/*Times of Malta* investigation had named as the owner of 17 Black. Theuma was granted immunity from prosecution in return for his testimony against Fenech and the other co-accused. Fenech was charged with complicity in Daphne's murder and denied the charges.

At the time of writing, all the accused are awaiting trial. Police are continuing to investigate if there are others involved. Like the Arizona Project, the Daphne Project had focused attention on key people later accused of involvement in a journalist's killing. The Maltese judiciary will decide if those accusations hold water.

### Conclusion

Whenever a colleague is slain, there is always a temptation to get "revenge on deadline," but that emotion should not cloud judgement. If retribution is required, it is best delivered by an effective police investigation and prosecution. As articulated well by Forbidden Stories, however tempting it is to play detective and try to unravel the murder plot, the best thing that reporters can do is to continue the work of the murdered colleague. Continuing the thread of their investigations may provide material that ultimately proves vital to the official murder investigation – but that generally should not be an end in itself.

Sometimes, however, a police investigation may be weak and a justice system compromised. In those cases, it is vital that journalists be ready to hold those investigations to account, for example, by highlighting leads that the police are not following or weaknesses in the case they may be advancing. As with any aspect of our work, we are detectives of last resort. The case for our work is most obvious when authorities that rightly have greater powers to gather evidence (for example, by arrest or seizure) are evidently not doing their work. That is true just as much for authorities that should be looking at corruption allegations as it is for holding the murder investigation itself to account. After Daphne was murdered, both the murder case and the wider examination of corruption allegations in the country were weak.

Some cases, as with Daphne's murder, simply cry out for a collaboration, in particular where, as with Daphne, the victim is a freelancer or works for a small publication that does not have the resources to continue the journalist's work or where the journalist's work is of major public importance, even if that importance is mostly local and, finally, where that murder threatens to create a sense of impunity that threatens the wider liberty of expression. In some places where the deaths of people through murder or war are rife, there may be fewer good reasons to focus disproportionately on the death of our colleagues.

Even so, there comes a time when good reporters need to band together and show that – when it comes to murder and intimidation – even the fiercest of media competitors are willing to take a collective stand and work as a team. I hope the Daphne Project can provide a model and inspiration.

## References

ABRAJI, 2017. Projeto Tim Lopes. [Online] Available at: www.abraji.org.br/projetos/projeto-tim-lopes [Accessed 23 June 2020].

AFP, 2019. Malta urged to drop libel lawsuits against Daphne Caruana Galizia. [Online] Available at: www.theguardian.com/world/2019/sep/19/malta-urged-to-drop-libel-lawsuits-against-daphne-caruana-galizia [Accessed 23 June 2020].

Associated Press, 1990. Kemper Marley Sr. is dead at 83; name arose in '76 slaying inquiry. [Online] Available at: www.nytimes.com/1990/06/28/obituaries/kemper-marley-sr-is-dead-at-83-name-arose-in-76-slaying-inquiry.html [Accessed 21 May 2020].

Borg, J., 2018. Chris Cardona's presence at bar 'frequented by murder suspect' flagged to magistrate. [Online] Available at: https://timesofmalta.com/articles/view/cardona-presence-at-bar-frequented-by-murder-suspect-flagged-to.676636 [Accessed 23 June 2020].

Chastand, J.-B. & Michel, A., 2018. "Projet Daphne": Pilatus, la banque maltaise qui recycle l'argent de l'Azerbaïdjan dans toute l'Europe. [Online] Available at: www.lemonde.fr/

projet-daphne/article/2018/04/18/pilatus-la-banque-maltaise-qui-recycle-l-argent-de-l-azerbaidjan-en-europe_5287282_5286994.html#QTdyJepaeFuHJOeg.99 [Accessed 23 June 2020].

CNN, 2018. [Online] Available at: https://edition.cnn.com/2018/04/23/world/daphne-caruana-galizia-amanpour-intl/index.html [Accessed 23 May 2020].

CPJ, 2020. [Online] Available at: https://cpj.org/data/killed/?status=Killed&motiveConfirmed%5B%5D=Confirmed&motiveUnconfirmed%5B%5D=Unconfirmed&type%5B%5D=Journalist&start_year=1992&end_year=2020&group_by=year [Accessed May 2020].

Forbidden Stories, 2019. Green Blood Project. [Online] Available at: https://forbiddenstories.org/case/green-blood/ [Accessed 23 June 2020].

Forbidden Stories, 2020. The Daphne Project: Every story published so far. [Online] Available at: https://forbiddenstories.org/the-daphne-project-every-story-published/ [Accessed 23 June 2020].

Garside, J., 2018. The Daphne Project: Malta losing money 'hand over fist' from Azerbaijan energy deal, claim experts. [Online] Available at: www.theguardian.com/world/2018/apr/25/malta-azerbaijan-energy-deal-losing-money-claim-experts [Accessed 23 June 2020].

Garside, J., 2019. [Interview] (December 2019).

Garside, J. & Kirchgaessner, S., 2018. Mastermind behind Maltese journalist's murder is being protected, says husband. [Online] Available at: www.theguardian.com/world/2018/apr/17/malta-protecting-mastermind-journalist-daphne-caruana-galizia-says-husband [Accessed 23 June 2020].

Grey, S. 2018. The silencing of Daphne. [Online] Available at: https://www.reuters.com/investigates/special-report/malta-daphne/ [Accessed 30 November 2020].

Grey, S. & Arnold, T., 2018. Exclusive: Mystery company named by murdered Maltese journalist is linked to power station developer. [Online] Available at: https://uk.reuters.com/article/uk-malta-daphne-offshore-exclusive/exclusive-mystery-company-named-by-murdered-maltese-journalist-is-linked-to-power-station-developer-idUKKCN1NE196 [Accessed 23 June 2020].

Guardian, 2018. Russian journalists killed in Central African Republic ambush. [Online] Available at: https://www.theguardian.com/world/2018/jul/31/russian-journalists-killed-in-central-african-republic-ambush [Accessed 30 November 2020].

ICIJ, 2016. ICIJ offshore leaks database. [Online] Available at: https://offshoreleaks.icij.org/ [Accessed 23 June 2020].

IRE, 2020. Investigative Reporters and Editors Inc. [Online] Available at: www.ire.org/ [Accessed 23 June 2020].

Kovacs, K., n.d. The history of IRE. [Online] Available at: www.ire.org/about/history [Accessed 21 May 2020].

Lindsey, R., 1976. 18 reporters begin joint inquiry into Arizona crime. New York Times. [Online] Available at: www.nytimes.com/1976/10/05/archives/18-reporters-begin-joint-inquiry-into-arizona-crime-team-motivated.html [Accessed 20 May 2020].

Obermayer et al., 2018. Das Milliarden-Geschäft mit Pässen aus Malta. [Online] Available at: www.sueddeutsche.de/wirtschaft/das-daphne-projekt-das-milliarden-geschaeft-mit-paessen-aus-malta-1.3949570 [Accessed 23 June 2020].

OCCRP, 2015. The Khadija Project. [Online] Available at: www.occrp.org/en/corruptistan/azerbaijan/khadijaismayilova/ [Accessed 23 June 2020].

Pegg, D., 2018. The Daphne Project: Maltese politicians face pressure over $1.6m paid to offshore firms. [Online] Available at: www.theguardian.com/world/2018/apr/19/maltese-politicians-face-pressure-over-16m-paid-to-offshore-firms [Accessed 23 June 2020].

Richard, L., 2018. A warning to the corrupt: If you kill a journalist, another will take their place. [Online] Available at: www.theguardian.com/commentisfree/2018/apr/16/reporter-murdered-daphne-caruana-galizia-malta [Accessed 23 June 2020].

Richard, L., 2019. [Interview] (December 2019).

Rubino, G., Anesi, C. & Bagnoli, L., 2018. Daphne Project: Malta, a modern smugglers' hideout. [Online] Available at: www.occrp.org/en/thedaphneproject/malta-a-modern-smugglers-hideout [Accessed 23 June 2020].

Ruelas, R., 2016. Arizona Republic: 40 years later, final words of murdered reporter Don Bolles still a mystery. [Online] Available at: https://eu.azcentral.com/story/2016/12/20/40-years-later-final-words-of-murdered-reporter-don-bolles-still-a-mystery/84793594/ [Accessed 23 June 2020].

Wendland, M. F., 1977. *The Arizona Project: How a Team of Investigative Reporters Got Revenge on Deadline.* Kansas City: Sheed Andrews and McMeel.

Willan, P., 2018. Maltese PM Muscat cleared by inquiry into murdered journalist's corruption claim. [Online] Available at: https://www.thetimes.co.uk/article/maltese-pm-joseph-muscat-cleared-by-inquiry-into-murdered-journalist-s-corruption-claim-michelle-daphne-caruana-galizia-36tv0vxtm [Accessed 23 November 2020].

# 6

# LEGAL THREATS IN THE UNITED KINGDOM

*Sarah Kavanagh*

If there is one overriding responsibility of a journalist, it is the protection of sources. Whistle-blowers and sources need to be able to come forward and share information whilst keeping their identity protected. As Chris Frost, the chair of the (United Kingdom and Ireland) National Union of Journalists (NUJ) ethics council, said:

> It is difficult to measure the extent of stories from whistle-blowers because they are anonymous but in my experience virtually every serious investigation is launched on the back of a source or whistle-blower who needs to be kept anonymous for their protection.
>
> (NUJ 2015)

In practice, NUJ members will often come to the union for support and assistance when the authorities try to access their sources of information. For example, when London's Metropolitan Police decided to question journalist Amelia Hill under caution and then announced its intention to take *The Guardian* to court, Hill told the union:

> Scotland Yard believed my source was a serving detective on Operation Weeting, the police's phone hacking investigation. They claimed that I could have incited my source to break the Official Secrets Act and, in doing so, had broken the Act myself. The application for the production order required *The Guardian* and me to hand over material which would disclose both my source for the Milly Dowler story and my source for the information which had enabled me to reveal almost immediately the identities of those arrested in the hacking scandal.
>
> (NUJ 2017)

The legal action was scheduled to take place at the Old Bailey (England's main criminal court), but the police abandoned the case following widespread public condemnation. The incident was just one prominent example of the way in which the law is currently being used to threaten investigative journalism in the UK. The threats include police attempts to access journalists' sources, government clampdowns on national security reporting and big data leaks and the introduction of draconian legislation.

The NUJ seeks to tackle these threats, so first I will introduce the Union.

### *The National Union of Journalists*

The National Union of Journalists in the United Kingdom and Ireland is the only independent, collective and representative voice for media workers in both countries. The union was founded in 1907 and has 30,000 members representing staff, freelance and student journalists working at home and abroad in broadcasting, newspapers, news agencies, magazines, books and online.

The Union is democratic and membership led. It helps individuals and groups tackle their problems at work, and it can also mobilise thousands of media professionals, trade unionists and friends to campaign to defend investigative journalism.

The NUJ is affiliated to the International Federation of Journalists (IFJ), representing more than 600,000 media workers in 187 organisations from 146 countries. This enables the NUJ to operate within a global network that fosters mutual support and solidarity.

## National Union of Journalists ethics

In the United Kingdom and Ireland, the union's ethical *Code of Conduct* is the only code written for journalists by journalists. It forms part of the union's rules, and NUJ members strive to adhere to its professional principles. The NUJ code states:

> A journalist at all times upholds and defends the principle of media freedom, the right of freedom of expression and the right of the public to be informed.
>
> (NUJ 2011)

The code also repeatedly highlights the importance of the public interest and calls on journalists to protect their sources. The first NUJ code was published in 1936 and said a journalist "should keep union and professional secrets and respect all necessary confidences regarding sources of information and private documents" (NUJ 1936). The code was last updated in 2011, and more than 80 years after the first draft, it still says a journalist "protects the identity of sources who supply information in confidence and material gathered in the course of her/his work" (NUJ 2011).

## *Journalists and the legislation concerning secrecy*

Under the *Official Secrets Act 1989*, it is an offence for current or former employees of the security and intelligence services, government contractors or crown servants to make unauthorised disclosures of information. Doing so is technically described as a 'Primary Disclosure'. This means that if whistle-blowers or sources are found, they can be prosecuted. The category of Secondary Disclosure includes journalists and media workers because they receive information from a (primary) source and they make an unauthorised publication of the information. Under the *Official Secrets Acts 1911 and 1989*, journalists can be prosecuted for Secondary Disclosure. There is no public interest defence.

Under the *Police and Criminal Evidence Act 1984* (PACE), journalistic material (including hard copy notes, contact books, un-broadcast or un-published footage) is given special protection from seizure by the police. If the police want to access this material, they must first apply to a judge using a production order.

When Essex police applied for production orders to get access to the un-broadcast footage of scenes from the Dale Farm traveller site eviction in 2011: the *BBC*, *Independent Television News* (ITN), *BSkyB*, *Channel 5*, *Hardcash Productions* and the freelance video journalist Jason Parkinson were all notified of the application and opposed the requests. Some of the broadcast footage featured on the investigative current affairs programme *Dispatches* and the legal case lasted for 18 months. The production orders were eventually quashed at the Court of Appeal because they did not relate to any specific incidents of serious criminality. Instead the police had decided to embark on a 'fishing expedition' and wanted to trawl through the unpublished material. The final legal judgement said the police must have specific and clear grounds for a production order application, and it highlighted the clear and distinctive roles of the police and news gatherers. Responding to the judgement, NUJ member Jason Parkinson said:

> We will not be forced into the role of unwilling agents of the state . . . we are journalists and we are there to report the news and keep the public informed.
>
> (NUJ 2012a)

When the authorities wanted to access journalistic material or sources, they applied for a production order using the PACE legislation or the *Terrorism Act 2000*. This process had been well established, and the union had supported many NUJ members through lengthy legal proceedings in which they had successfully stood by the NUJ's ethics code.

What we did not know until 2014 was that the authorities were also using the *Regulation of Investigatory Powers Act 2000* (RIPA) to gain access to journalists' information and sources in secret.

## The secret state surveillance of citizens and journalists

The first of the Edward Snowden stories were published in *The Guardian* in 2013, and they revealed that various governments were spying on citizens. The newspaper came under attack for reporting the leaks, and the editor, Alan Rusbridger, was summoned to Parliament. The NUJ and IFJ decided to step into the public fracas. The IFJ president, Jim Boumelha, said:

> The IFJ and all the journalists worldwide are fully behind *The Guardian* and its journalists. It is mind-boggling that the revelations by *The Guardian* about the programme of mass surveillance are considered in some circles to be similar to aiding and abetting terrorism. This is an outrageous suggestion.
>
> (NUJ 2013)

The union also made a statement on behalf of the NUJ members (collectively referred to in each workplace as a 'chapel') employed at the titles. It said:

> *The Guardian* and *Observer* NUJ chapel, representing the overwhelming majority of journalists at both titles, strongly supports the editor's decision [to publish].
>
> (NUJ 2013)

Around the same time, the Metropolitan Police launched a criminal investigation focusing on the journalists working on the stories, and six years later, with no arrests or prosecutions, the police confirmed that their investigation had been dropped (Gallagher 2019).

NUJ member Ewen MacAskill, who worked on the Snowden files, explains the impact on journalism:

> What we learned from the Snowden documents is the ease with which journalists can be targeted and the speed with which the intelligence agencies and police can locate sources. They can – and do – gain access to emails, phone records and any other electronic data used by journalists, and, through that, can track journalists and identify sources.
>
> (2014)

The reporting of the Snowden leaks alerted the NUJ to the prospect that journalists' electronic communications could be targeted by the state. As a consequence, the union started paying more attention to legislation relating to investigatory powers and communications data (see also Chapter 3).

## The legislative battles to protect journalism

At the end of 2012, the UK government published a *Draft Communications Data Bill*. The NUJ supported calls, made by the pre-legislative committee, to amend the bill so that the home secretary was not given what the committee described as "carte blanche to order retention of any type of data" (Parliamentary Joint Committee on the Draft Communications Data Bill 2012).

The bill proposed to allow the government to order internet companies to collect and store communications data relating to all internet traffic, including websites visited, internet searches and private social media messages. Michelle Stanistreet, NUJ general secretary, said:

> The draft bill is a major assault on civil liberties for all citizens and a threat to press freedom. For journalists, it would be a direct attack on the way they work and would severely undermine their ability to protect their sources, materials and whistle-blowers. It must be dropped.
>
> (NUJ 2012b)

The Conservative Party and the Liberal Democrats were in a coalition government at the time, and Nick Clegg, the deputy prime minister and leader of the Liberal Democratic Party, said:

> I believe the coalition government needs to have a fundamental rethink about this legislation. We cannot proceed with this bill and we have to go back to the drawing board.
>
> (BBC 2012)

So it transpired that with one part of the government blocking another part of the government, the measures contained within the bill were temporarily dropped.

In the summer of 2014, the government published more draft legislation in the form of the *Data Retention and Investigatory Powers Bill* (House of Commons Library 2014). The government hurriedly pushed it through parliament over the course of three days without time for proper scrutiny or debate. It was unclear how the new law would impact the media.

With mounting concerns, the NUJ decided to organise a global conference with the support of the IFJ. The event brought together journalists, politicians, lawyers, human rights and privacy campaigners. We wanted to explore what we could do collectively and examine the practical steps needed to safeguard journalists and their sources. The conference was planned for October 2014 and was hosted by *The Guardian*.

## Police secretly grab journalists' phone records

A few weeks before the NUJ's global conference on safeguarding journalists and their sources, the trade publication *Press Gazette* ran a story revealing *The Sun*'s Political Editor Tom Newton Dunn's mobile phone records and the news desk's call data had been seized by police (Ponsford 2014a). The authorities had used the RIPA legislation to secretly access the phone records. They did not tap the phones or access phone messages; they took the records of which numbers were called and received. For the police to access this data, all they needed was sign-off by a police superintendent.

The *Press Gazette* story went to the heart of the matter. It showed that journalists could try to keep their sources confidential, but the RIPA legislation could be used to access information without their knowledge or consent. With the help of the NUJ, *Press Gazette* launched a 'Save our Sources' petition calling on the interception of communications commissioner to conduct an urgent investigation. Dominic Ponsford, the editor of *Press Gazette*, said:

> If law enforcement are able to secretly grab the phone records of journalists and news organisations then no confidential source is safe and pretty much all investigative journalism is in peril.
>
> (Ponsford 2014b)

The second RIPA case, reported by *The Times*, revealed that Kent police had used the legislation to obtain the phone records of the *Mail on Sunday*'s news editor David Dillon and freelance journalist Andrew Alderson (Ponsford 2014c). More cases followed, and it was clear that none of the journalists involved were accused of breaking the law.

The increasing number of cases brought increasing attention. The interception of communications commissioner announced an investigation and promised a report. The Home Affairs Parliamentary Committee also launched an investigation at which the NUJ gave evidence. The committee concluded the legislation governing communications data needed a complete overhaul. Keith Vaz, MP, the chair of the committee, said:

> We are concerned that the level of secrecy surrounding the use of RIPA allows investigating authorities to engage in acts which would be unacceptable in a democracy, with inadequate oversight.
>
> (House of Commons Home Affairs Select Committee 2014)

The NUJ, Law Society, Bar Council and British Association of Social Workers decided to launch a public alliance called the "Professionals for Information Privacy Coalition" and jointly demanded new legislation to protect professional data.

In February 2015, the interception of communications commissioner's report was published and showed that 82 journalists had had their data seized by police in relation to 24 out of 34 investigations involving 19 police forces over a three-year period. In total, the 34 police investigations concerned relationships between 105 journalists and 242 sources. Whilst deciding that police were not "randomly trawling" for data, the report revealed that a total of 608 RIPA applications were made for communications data to find journalistic sources (Turvill 2015).

The *Conservative Party Manifesto* in 2015 pledged there would be explicit statutory protection for the role of journalists and a commitment that "we will ban the police from accessing journalists' phone records to identify whistle-blowers and other sources without prior judicial protection" (The Conservative Party 2015). The party won the election, and a new *Investigatory Powers Bill* was published.

## The *Investigatory Powers Bill*

Throughout the different stages of the investigatory powers campaign, the NUJ engaged with cross-party parliamentarians, and our concerns were raised during every parliamentary debate. We fostered an informal partnership with the Media Lawyers Association, News Media Association and the Society of Editors, and by working across the news industry, we were able to put forward a united position. The union also backed the public campaigning initiative called 'Don't Spy on Us' involving Amnesty International, English Pen, Article 19, Privacy International, Liberty, Open Rights Group and Big Brother Watch.

Essentially, we were all advocating for improved protections that would replace the existing powers. The NUJ worked with Gavin Millar QC to draft a legislative amendment to the *Investigatory Powers Bill* that offered a "shield law" to protect journalists, their sources and material.

The *Investigatory Powers Bill* contained no equivalent of the production order procedures set out in the PACE legislation: there was no prior notification or right to challenge or appeal decisions relating to the authorities having access to journalistic communications. In addition, the bill also included broad new powers allowing for 'equipment interference'. This enables the authorities to take control of targeted electronic devices and access information stored including log in details, passwords, documents, emails, contacts, messaging chats and location records. The microphone, webcam and GPS technology can also be turned on.

The NUJ concluded that the bill was totally inadequate; the government had continually disregarded our objections, as well as the key recommendation from the parliamentary committee:

> The committee recommends that the Home Office should reconsider the level of protection which the Bill affords to journalistic material

and sources. This should be at least equivalent to the protection presently applicable under PACE and the Terrorism Act 2000.

(Parliamentary Joint Committee on the Draft Investigatory Powers Bill 2016)

The only significant concession contained within the Investigatory Powers Act (2016) was the introduction of a 'judicial commissioner' to provide oversight when the authorities want to access journalists' communications. Journalists or media organisations would not get the opportunity to make their case to a judge in an open court to explain why the authorities should not be allowed to access the information. The legislation passed through parliament without much opposition, and it remains one of the most draconian laws of its kind in the world.

In September 2018, in a successful challenge to the *Investigatory Powers Act*, the European Court of Human Rights ruled that mass surveillance, without adequate media safeguards, was unlawful. The judgement came after a four-year case brought by the Bureau of Investigative Journalism supported by the NUJ and IFJ (NUJ 2018a). The ruling represents the most significant blow to the government's dogmatic pursuit of this repressive surveillance legislation.

## Targeted for telling the truth

Over the course of the last decade, the most serious individual case that threatened investigative journalism and involved the NUJ was the targeting of two journalists who sought the truth about human rights abuses in Northern Ireland.

At the start of the bank holiday weekend in August 2018, two investigative journalists and NUJ members were arrested in Belfast. Trevor Birney and Barry McCaffrey were under investigation in connection with the suspected theft of a confidential report, and they were accused of handling stolen goods, unlawful disclosure of information under the Official Secrets Act and the unlawful obtainment of personal data.

The confidential report was from the office of the Police Ombudsman for Northern Ireland, and the leak was sent to the journalists by an anonymous source. McCaffrey had received a plain envelope in the post with no return address. The document related to the first police investigation into the killing of six men by a loyalist paramilitary group in 1994 in a Northern Ireland village called Loughinisland.

The report features in the film *No Stone Unturned*, which tells the story of the victims and their families. It also examines the police investigation into the murders, names the murder suspects and highlights allegations of collusion between the police and killers. Following the arrests of Birney and McCaffrey, Patrick Corrigan, Amnesty International's Northern Ireland director, said:

> When the police are arresting journalists who have investigated police collusion in the killing of civilians, rather than the killers and their helpers, then we all should be deeply worried.
>
> (NUJ 2018b)

## The police investigation

When the journalists were arrested, they had to wash and dress in front of police officers, they were questioned for 14 hours and their homes and office were raided. The police took away phones, computers and the entire computer server from the office. Durham police were leading on the investigation and had been brought in by the Police Service of Northern Ireland (PSNI).

During the investigation, the police ombudsman denied that his office had made a complaint about a theft to the PSNI, the police declined to comment and the *Irish Times* quoted Birney's solicitor as saying that it "undermines the entire integrity" of the arrests (McKay 2018).

The allegation of a data protection breach was linked to the whereabouts of Detective Albert Carroll, who is mentioned in the film. It was claimed by police that the journalists must have accessed his personal data, but they had actually found his contact details in the French telephone book.

The police had already known in advance that the film was likely to name the suspects in the Loughinisland case. During the film's pre-publication and editing process, the journalists offered the named suspects a right of reply sent by registered mail, and the letters went unanswered. They also informed the police ombudsman of the likely suspects the film would name. The ombudsman passed on the information to the PSNI. The journalists had wanted to be sure the PSNI was informed just in case there were any concerns for the safety of the suspects or in case the police had any other compelling reason the film should not be released. The journalists received no response.

During the course of the police investigation, both journalists were required to hand themselves in to a police station in Belfast on a regular basis for further questioning. Each time this happened, the union organised a solidarity protest outside. The union also supported a challenge to the legality of search warrants, arguing that the police had retained material that was not within the scope of their investigation: they had seized large quantities of journalistic material that was not connected to the film.

## The court challenge

In February 2019, Belfast's High Court granted a judicial review, and the journalists' legal argument rested on a series of technical points – the warrants did not cover all of the seized material, the police had used the wrong procedures (they had used the PACE legislation but not the sections that applied to journalists) and the judges' reasoning in granting the search warrants had not been recorded at the time.

Throughout the duration of the campaign, the NUJ had sought to secure media coverage of the case and organised public screenings of the film. The union contacted various politicians, and the Member of Parliament (MP) for County Durham, Grahame Morris, Labour, and David Davis, MP for Haltemprice and Howden, Conservative, both agreed to help. When the judicial review started in May 2019, some of the organisations from the *Investigatory Powers Bill* campaign also agreed to offer their support. The Media Lawyers Association intervened in the case, and English PEN and Index on Censorship also submitted evidence to court. After three days in session, Lord Chief Justice Morgan decided he was "minded to quash" the search warrants and said the two journalists were acting in "nothing other than a perfectly appropriate way in doing what the NUJ required of them, which was to protect their sources" (NUJ 2019).

The union came out of court that day demanding the PSNI lift the threat of criminal prosecution and, at a further hearing in June, the court confirmed that all the material inappropriately seized should be returned to the journalists. That night, the journalists were informed that the police had dropped the case.

## Is investigative journalism (still) a crime?

Journalists should never be targeted for simply doing their jobs. This chapter has highlighted some of the key threats to investigative journalism in the United Kingdom and Ireland. It has not been possible to provide a comprehensive account, but it has been possible to offer a snapshot of the problems and show the union's efforts.

Some of the NUJ's battles bear a resemblance to the threats posed in other countries. For example, a journalist in Australia had her home raided by police after she reported on state surveillance. The police warrant said the investigation was linked to the "alleged publishing of information classified as an official secret" (Murphy 2019). The public broadcaster ABC was also raided by police in response to stories it published about alleged human rights abuses perpetrated by the Australian military (BBC 2020).

The NUJ will continue to stand up for journalism and fight to defend the rights of investigative journalists to operate in the public interest and do so without interference from government or any other vested interest.

The UK government has repeatedly shown its disregard for investigative journalism through its attempts to clamp down on national security reporting and big data leaks and by introducing draconian legislation. In 2019, the government launched a campaign to promote media freedoms globally. The paradox was very clear to those of us who had spent many years campaigning for media freedom at home.

## References

British Broadcasting Corporation (2012) 'Draft communications data bill cannot proceed – Nick Clegg', *British Broadcasting Corporation*. 11 December. Available at: www.bbc.co.uk/news/uk-politics-20668953 [Accessed 10 April 2020]

British Broadcasting Corporation (2020) 'ABC raid: Australian public broadcaster loses legal challenge', *British Broadcasting Corporation*. 17 February. Available at: www.bbc.co.uk/news/world-australia-51526607 [Accessed 25 April 2020]

Conservative Party (2015) *Strong leadership, a clear economic plan, a brighter more secure future.* The Conservative Party General Election Manifesto. London: The Conservative Party. Available at: http://ucrel.lancs.ac.uk/wmatrix/ukmanifestos2015/localpdf/Conservatives.pdf [Accessed April 2020]

Draft Communications Data Bill (2012) Available at: www.parliament.uk/documents/joint-committees/communications-data/CM208359DraftCDBill.pdf [Accessed April 2020]

Gallagher, R. J. (2019) 'UK police Snowden probe declared "inactive"', *Ryan Gallagher*. 20 December. Available at: https://notes.rjgallagher.co.uk/2019/12/uk-police-curable-snowden-probe-inactive.html [Accessed 17 April 2020]

House of Commons Home Affairs Select Committee (2014) *RIPA not fit for purpose say MPs. Press release and report on the Regulation of Investigatory Powers Act 2000.* London: The Stationary Office. Available at: www.parliament.uk/business/committees/committees-a-z/commons-select/home-affairs-committee/news/141206-ripa-rpt-pubn/ [Accessed April 2020]

House of Commons Library (2014) *The data retention and investigatory powers bill.* London: The Stationary Office. Available at: https://commonslibrary.parliament.uk/research-briefings/sn06934/ [Accessed April 2020]

Investigatory Powers Act (2016) Available at: www.legislation.gov.uk/ukpga/2016/25/contents/enacted [Accessed April 2020]

MacAskill, E. (2014) 'Journalists must be vigilant with security and communications', *National Union of Journalists*. 15 October. Available at: www.nuj.org.uk/news/journalists-must-be-vigilant-with-security-and-communications/ [Accessed 20 April 2020]

McKay, S. (2018) 'Arrests of journalists queried as ombudsman denies reporting theft of documents', *The Irish Times*. 8 November. Available at: www.irishtimes.com/news/crime-and-law/arrests-of-journalists-queried-as-ombudsman-denies-reporting-theft-of-documents-1.3690026 [Accessed 23 April 2020]

Murphy, K. (2019) 'AFP won't rule out charging News Corp journalist Annika Smethurst after raid', *The Guardian*. 14 August. Available at: www.theguardian.com/australia-news/2019/aug/14/afp-wont-rule-out-charging-news-corp-journalist-annika-smethurst-following-raid [Accessed 26 April 2020]

National Union of Journalists (1936) 'The first NUJ code of conduct', *National Union of Journalists*. Available at: https://www.nuj.org.uk/about/nuj-code/first-nuj-code--1936/ [Accessed April 2020]

National Union of Journalists (2011) 'NUJ code of conduct', *National Union of Journalists*. Available at: www.nuj.org.uk/about/nuj-code/ [Accessed April 2020]

National Union of Journalists (2012a) 'NUJ victory on Dale farm production order', *National Union of Journalists*. Available at: www.nuj.org.uk/news/nuj-victory-on-dale-farm-production-order/ [Accessed April 2020]

National Union of Journalists (2012b) 'Data bill threatens journalistic sources and material', *National Union of Journalists*. Available at: www.nuj.org.uk/news/data-bill-threatens-journalistic-sources-and-material/ [Accessed April 2020]

National Union of Journalists (2013) 'IFJ offers support to Guardian editor at parliamentary committee', *National Union of Journalists*. Available at: www.nuj.org.uk/news/offers-support-to-guardian/ [Accessed April 2020]

National Union of Journalists (2015) 'NUJ submission to the joint committee on the draft investigatory powers bill', *National Union of Journalists*. Available at: www.nuj.org.uk/documents/nuj-submission-to-the-parliamentary-joint-committee-on-the/ [Accessed April 2020]

National Union of Journalists (2017) 'NUJ submission to the Law Commission consultation on official secrets', *National Union of Journalists*. Available at: www.nuj.org.uk/documents/nuj-submission-to-the-law-commission/ [Accessed April 2020]

National Union of Journalists (2018a) 'NUJ welcomes ECHR judgement on UK surveillance of journalists', *National Union of Journalists*. Available at: www.nuj.org.uk/news/echr-judgement-surveillance-journalists/ [Accessed April 2020]

National Union of Journalists (2018b) 'Bail extension for No Stone Unturned journalists "a travesty of justice"', *National Union of Journalists*. Available at: www.nuj.org.uk/news/bail-extension-for-no-stone-unturned-journalists-a-travesty-of/ [Accessed April 2020]

National Union of Journalists (2019) 'No Stone Unturned ruling "a victory for NUJ members and for press freedom"', National Union of Journalists. Available at: www.nuj.org.uk/news/no-stone-unturned-ruling-victory/ [Accessed April 2020]

Official Secrets Act (1911) Available at: www.legislation.gov.uk/ukpga/Geo5/1-2/28/contents [Accessed April 2020]

Official Secrets Act (1989) Available at: www.legislation.gov.uk/ukpga/1989/6/contents [Accessed April 2020]

Parliamentary Joint Committee on the Draft Communications Data Bill (2012) *Press release and report on the draft communications data bill*. London: The Stationary Office. Available at: www.parliament.uk/business/committees/committees-a-z/joint-select/draft-communications-bill/news/full-publication-of-report/ [Accessed April 2020]

Parliamentary Joint Committee on the Draft Investigatory Powers Bill (2016) *Draft investigatory powers bill report*. London: The Stationary Office. Available at: https://publications.parliament.uk/pa/jt201516/jtselect/jtinvpowers/93/9302.htm [Accessed April 2020]

Police and Criminal Evidence Act (1984) Available at: www.legislation.gov.uk/ukpga/1984/60/contents [Accessed April 2020]

Ponsford, D. (2014a) 'Police seized journalists' phone records in order to out Plebgate whistleblowers', *Press Gazette*. 2 September. Available at: www.pressgazette.co.uk/police-seized-journalists-phone-records-order-out-plebgate-whistleblowers/ [Accessed 16 April 2020]

Ponsford, D. (2014b) 'Keep up the pressure to save our sources', *National Union of Journalists*. 14 October. Available at: www.nuj.org.uk/news/keep-up-the-pressure-to-save-our-sources/ [Accessed 16 April 2020]

Ponsford, D. (2014c) 'Second police force admits using RIPA to spy on journalists and sources by seizing phone records', *Press Gazette*. 1 October. Available at: www.pressgazette.co.uk/second-police-force-admits-using-ripa-spy-journalists-phone-records-and-out-confidential-sources/ [Accessed 16 April 2020]

Regulation of Investigatory Powers Act (2000) Available at: www.legislation.gov.uk/ukpga/2000/23/contents [Accessed April 2020]

Terrorism Act (2000) Available at: www.legislation.gov.uk/ukpga/2000/11/contents [Accessed April 2020]

Turvill, W. (2015) 'Interception commissioner: 82 journalists' phone records grabbed by police in three years, judicial oversight needed', *Press Gazette*. 4 February. Available at: www.pressgazette.co.uk/interception-commissioner-82-journalists-phone-records-targeted-police-three-years-forces-should/ [Accessed 16 April 2020]

# 7

# MISSION-DRIVEN JOURNALISM

*Rachel Oldroyd*

More people than ever are reading content created by journalists, yet, since the birth of the Internet, an industry once used to substantial profits and annual revenue hikes has been hit by declining print sales and disappearing advertising revenue.

The storm has caused such enormous disruption that many fear for the very existence of the news industry. The facts are startling. In the first two decades of the century, the United States lost half its newspaper journalists, and in the 15 years until 2019, one in five papers across the country closed (Abernathy, 2018). It is the same across much of the Western world. In the United Kingdom, for example, there was a net loss of nearly 250 newspapers between 2005 and 2018 (Mayhew, 2019). The coronavirus pandemic hit the print industry hard, with many more newspapers expected to close and cuts across the sector. Meanwhile, smaller news teams are having to feed the ever-rapacious web with more and more stories from across the globe. In this environment, it is not only people that have been cut, it is also the time dedicated to digging and to the slow burn of an investigation. This loss is a major blow to transparency, accountability and democracy.

The problem is well understood in the news sector: an independent, well-resourced press informs, educates, scrutinises and questions. It provides the facts that help citizens better understand their world, and it holds to account those that wield the power. A country without a strong and free press is a much poorer society. Done well and in the public interest, journalism provides a crucial cornerstone of a functioning democracy. The question is: Who pays now that the commercial model that once sustained it is on the point of collapse and new models for sustainability such as paywalls and membership are still not assured?

In early January 2016, one of the United States' oldest newspapers, a once hugely profitable and highly regarded enterprise, was turned into the American equivalent of a charity. The *Philadelphia Inquirer* had become so stretched by tumbling revenues that its then-85-year-old billionaire owner Gerry Lenfest decided its best chance of survival, along with that of its sister paper, the

*Daily News*, was to transfer his ownership into a newly created non-profit organisation.

'Of all the things I've done,' said Lenfest, 'this is the most important. Because of the journalism' (Dobrin, 2018).

If the commercial model is no longer working – or if alternative commercial models have still to be proved in the long term – non-profit status perhaps provides a much-needed stepping stone that will save good-quality, important reporting. The *Inquirer*'s Lenfest is not the first to think so.

In the ten years before Lenfest's altruistic act, a number of journalists who had either left commercial newsrooms in frustration at reduced budgets and changed focuses, or found themselves at the sharp edge of the necessary cuts, founded dozens of alternative news organisations across the United States and in parts of the wider world. These newsrooms were set up as not-for-profit mission-driven enterprises, focused on public interest journalism, on delivering investigations or specialist stories that traditional newsrooms were finding increasingly hard to sustain. It is these newsrooms that are helping to keep the Fourth Estate alive.

The purpose of this chapter is to establish that this is a sector anybody coming into this profession should take seriously. It is one of the few growth areas in journalism, and with the rest of the news media shrinking, it could rapidly become the only place that ambitious, hard-hitting investigative journalism happens. The organisations in this space are not "transactional newsrooms" requiring their journalism to ultimately make profits. Instead they are driven by the need for change – "transformational journalism" – and this requires a different approach, a different value system, a different focus.

This chapter is dedicated to this not-for-profit, mission-driven sector. It looks at the structure of the newsrooms operating in the space, the attitude to reporting in these organisations, the value systems and how journalists are rediscovering that they really can pursue careers in the profession of journalism thanks to these new initiatives.

## From Philadelphia to the Philippines

The growth of not-for-profit journalism has been impressive. Especially in the United States, it has become a thriving, competing, hard-hitting sector in its own right, and over the past decade, not-for-profit newsrooms have been short-listed for dozens of Pulitzer prizes, the US's most prestigious journalism award, and several have been won by reporters operating in the sector.

The concept has spread beyond the United States and is rapidly catching on in countries across the world. The Global Investigative Journalism Network is an international grouping of organisations operating in this space and had 182 members at the end of 2019 across 77 countries.[1]

David Kaplan, who runs the organisation, explains:

> Non-profit groups have been pivotal drivers of the global spread of investigative journalism over the past 30 years. These include reporting centres, training institutes, professional associations, grant-making groups, and online networks.
>
> There were less than a dozen of these "investigative nonprofits" in the 1990s. In a 2007 survey we identified 39 groups in 26 countries. We updated that in 2013 and found 106 groups in 47 countries. Today there are more than 200 groups worldwide and the number keeps growing.
>
> GIJN limits its membership to nonprofit organizations committed to investigative journalism not because we don't think commercial media plays an important role, but because the nonprofits have been essential to the field's rapid global expansion. They provide the trainers, educators, and long-term commitment to building networks that are behind investigative journalism going global over the past 30 years.
>
> The demise of the advertising-based commercial model to support serious journalism has also given impetus to the nonprofit model. Particularly in this age of disinformation, the need for an independent structure to support public-interest investigations has never been greater.
>
> (2020)

In countries that still have a relatively strong press such as the United States, the United Kingdom and Germany, the not-for-profit sector provides a bolster to public interest journalism. In these countries, organisations like Propublica in the United States, the Bureau of Investigative Journalism in the United Kingdom (which I run) or Correctiv in Germany sit alongside the traditional media, often working with reporters from within larger newsrooms. Reporters in these groups have the privilege of time, the resources and the single focus to produce ambitious, often collaborative journalism that many larger cash-strapped and time-poor newsrooms lack. This is not to suggest that traditional newspapers are devoid of investigative journalism. Many in recent years have stepped up the level of public interest journalism for the very reason that this has proved another string to the bow in attracting reader attention and donations or subscriptions. But the days of traditional news desks putting a team of reporters on a subject for an unspecified period of time are rarer than unicorns, and it is this type of reporting that has become the domain of the not-for-profits.

Although it makes up the largest share of the not-for-profit journalism sector, investigative reporting is not the only discipline to turn to philanthropy. In recent years, there has also been a rush of local newsrooms setting up as charities or social enterprises. This again has come out of a reaction to the failure of the commercial sector to find a way to sustain vital local account-ability reporting. These might be large enterprises like the *Inquirer* or smaller new enterprises such as the *Bristol Cable*, a paper and online news outlet covering important public interest matters in the city of Bristol in southwest England.

In countries where the news is predominately provided by government-backed outlets, mission-driven organisations relying on reader donations have set up as independent challenges to the status quo. In the Philippines, for exam-ple, an extremely brave group of journalists launched *Rappler*, an online news-room where the reporters' main role is to hold the human rights abuses of President Duterte to account. In South Africa, the *Daily Maverick* produced a string of stories highly critical of the established Zuma regime and continues to dig up stories that the established media simply does not get near.

Fortunately, at the same time as reporters started to worry about the sus-tainability of an industry they loved but also a profession they believed in, so many philanthropic institutions started to worry about the impact a retrenching media would have upon democracy.

As the cracks started to appear in the news industry, large foundations stepped up to help. Grant makers such as the MacArthur Foundation, the Reva and David Logan Foundation and Luminate Group all poured millions of dol-lars into the sector. In the wider world, Open Society Foundations opened up applications for the funding of journalism, not just educating and bolstering – an area it had operated in for years. Other more localised foundations tradition-ally focused on civic society, such as Adessium Foundation in the Netherlands or the David and Elaine Potter Foundation in the United Kingdom, went in search of institutions that could fill the gap being left by traditional news. This flow of money, which has increased substantially through the first two decades of the twentieth century, provided the fuel that spurred on the growth of the sector.

The philanthropic support has meant that some of the largest not-for-profits have news teams that are starting to equal those of many papers both in scale and numbers. The Center for Investigative Reporting (CIR) in California, for example, has a budget of more than $10m and employs nearly 80 people. On the east coast, *Propublica*, which was set up in 2007 by Paul Steiger, for-mer managing editor of the *Wall Street Journal*, operates with a budget of over $25m.[2]

Both *Propublica* and CIR cover a wide range of subjects – all through inves-tigative reporting. Other non-profits operate in more niche areas, such as the well-respected Marshall Project, which focuses on injustices, and *Inside Climate News*, which reports on climate change issues. Others such as the *Texas Tribune* and *Voice of San Diego* have taken over local patches left by now-extinct print products. All are powerful, well-resourced newsrooms which pride themselves on providing the accountability and investigative journalism that keeps power in check.

## Holding the line between independence and funding

In some cases, campaign groups have become the journalists. Greenpeace, for example, supports a group of investigative reporters working on stories about climate change and environmental impact. The team is run as an independent unit, leaving the reporters largely free to pursue their own stories as long as the core of the substance is aligned to the mission of the NGO.[3] Other groups have embedded investigative journalism methods into their reports: Human Rights Watch and Global Witness regularly use traditional investigative journalism methods and techniques to produce their powerful evidence-based reports.[4]

Even in many of the independent not-for-profit newsrooms, funding can often come from foundations or individuals with particular interests that they want to see pursued, including climate change, the environment, human rights issues, financial corruption or development reporting. In local areas, the philanthropy has often come from interested local businesspeople. This 'project funding approach' has led to questions about influence and independence: a question of he who pays the piper plays the tune. It is a debate that causes as much hand wringing amongst those running and working in the newsrooms as many of those dishing out the dollars. Not-for-profits put in place strong governance; they publish heart-felt promises that they will not be led by their funders, and funders are often careful to stress that grantees must keep their independence. In NGOs in which journalism is practised, the reporters vociferously protect their independence from the campaigning side of the organisation. The debate – and sometimes criticism – has led many in the sector to seek to diversify their funding beyond philanthropy. Some are doing well. *Propublica*, for example, now gains more than 10 percent of its revenues from the public.[5] *Bristol Cable* eschewed foundation funding at the outset, instead seeking to sustain itself from local people's goodwill. It did a great job, attracting more than 2000 paying members.[6]

The sector has certainly put in the work to ensure the money does not drive the content, but it would be naïve to think that it has not had any impact on the sector. Those signing the cheques may not be looking for a commercial return, but they are looking for something: they want to see change, transformation. This is well discussed in *Investigative Journalism, A Mechanism of Impact*, by Christopher Hird.[7]

This search for 'impact' has become embedded in many not-for-profit newsrooms, and it has changed the type and the tone of the output. Success is not measured by clicks and by readers, but it is measured – by law changes, convictions and lives improved.

## Making a difference: a new value system

The mantra is 'public interest'. Only reporting that can be thoroughly tested against this purest of journalistic tests is taken on. This is not to say it is necessarily

## MISSION-DRIVEN JOURNALISM

worthy reporting. Many of the projects that come out of these newsrooms are gritty, hard-hitting stories. The characteristic thread that links them all is the desire, or even the drive, to deliver impact – to get their stories dominating the news agenda and to make a difference. The currency is change. But this does demand a different approach to reporting. It is not a return to the type of campaign journalism that for decades kept many newspapers, particularly those operating in the local space, in business. Many of the not-for-profit newsrooms do not have the weekly or daily platforms that a newspaper provided. Traffic to their websites can actually be quite limited. This new mission-driven reporting has embraced other techniques and methods aimed at making a difference. The stories, for example, can often be produced with a clear message or with a distinct level of engagement that drives readers to make a change.

Infographics and interactives can be used to let people discover for themselves the revelations discovered by the reporters. *Propublica*'s first story to properly engage – and one that for many years defined the organisation – was a database that revealed how much money every doctor across the entire country received from prescribing particular drugs. By building a vast database that allowed readers to find out about their own doctors, the organisation's *Dollars for Docs* series put a marker in the ground that virtually every not-for-profit that has come after has been trying to match – the perfect method of storytelling.[8] The Center for Investigative Reporting in California took a similar approach in their reporting on strawberry farms. Through a series of stories, the team revealed how heavy insecticides were being used on strawberry fields across California. The reporting told powerful stories, but the team wanted to let those most affected see the results of their work for themselves. They started from the position of: who does their reporting most affect? The answer was easy – the workers picking the fruit and the people living near the strawberry fields. The team built an interactive that let people enter their zip code to see the level of pesticides in their area.[9]

At the Bureau of Investigative Journalism in the United Kingdom, a team of reporters built a database listing all the public-owned assets that had been sold off by local authorities who had become desperate to raise funds. Again, the team wanted to let local people see how the policy was affecting facilities in their area so they could better do something about it. Their *SoldFromUnderYou* investigation included an interactive map that let the public see what properties had been sold in their area. The map was used more than 200,000 times.[10] Reporters in these newsrooms use other methods, even further removed from journalism, to make the impact they want. These include sending out press releases, sending briefing documents to members of Parliament or taking their stories to people affected through live events. Driven by the desire to make impact, new roles have also cropped up in the sector, armed with ensuring the journalism lives and breathes after it has been published.

At the Bureau of Investigative Journalism, we introduced the role of impact editor in 2019 in order to embed some of the processes that help the work be influential. Not all journalists would see this as part of their role, but in the not-for-profit sector, it is an approach that those working in these teams have little choice but to embrace.

## A co-publishing model

Job functions for reporters can also be different. Many of the newsrooms operating in the space do not produce a string of daily stories, and traffic to their websites or newsletters can be relatively small. Many partner with traditional newspapers or broadcasters, providing their stories for free in exchange for good placement and promotion. Partnerships of any kind are difficult. Reporters may, for example, see their work splashed across the front of a newspaper with no credit. For teams, pushing their work into different places can mean several packages and treatments. And with niche websites with often low profiles at a public level, it can be difficult to get people to tell their stories or attract whistleblowers, the lifeblood of investigative reporting.

Editors in these newsrooms find themselves having to hawk and market their stories around the bigger newsrooms. This task can sometimes fall on reporters. It is often the case, too, that reporters will have to be agile storytellers, capable of switching between making TV packages, writing long print pieces or even producing podcasts. The more inventive newsrooms have even turned to theatrical productions, comic books and speaking events as they find alternative ways to get their findings out into the world.

## A space for digging

For all the issues and concerns about the influence of funding and the focus on impact, the ability to spend proper time focused on the journalism, rather than clickbait (the latest obsession in news rooms desperately chasing allusive digital advertisers), has proved a huge draw. This has led some of the media's brightest young and some of the most senior journalists to this new model. Go into their newsrooms and there is a buzz, an enthusiasm that has long evaporated from many of the traditional print establishments. And this is leading not only to gap plugging but to unexpected stories and powerful journalism, as highly regarded *New Yorker* writer Nicholas Lemann noted in an article: "Their work is always good, and sometimes spectacular". *Propublica*, it is worth noting, has already received three Pulitzer prizes – the highest honour in American journalism – in its 12 years of existence.[11]

Time, focus, collaboration, innovation are words used often by editors or journalists working in these newsrooms, and it is these luxuries that are leading to the award-winning, high-impact stories. Investigative journalists have always operated away from the daily news desk. The investigative team buried in the basement, digging up important revelations over months in secret and only answerable to the editor, has long been the news industry's star turn to be cherished, rewarded and protected. Sir Harry Evans's Insight team at the UK's *Sunday Times* was his beloved creation. A similar example is Spotlight at the *Boston Globe*. It became the centrepiece of a cinema film.

The difference between these teams of the past and the new ones cropping up is that in the not-for-profit sector, these investigative teams are not isolated, rare, glorified beasts, they are the only journalists in town. The daily gossip, the daily agenda that comes with a busy, functioning newsroom is lost. Journalists operating in these spaces do not do the 'investigative' work on the side, slotted in between the demands of the daily news, but are instead focused solely on pursuing a hard, difficult story.

These not-for-profit newsrooms rarely have regular publishing cycles. They do not have newspapers or websites that require a constant flow of stories. Their focus is not getting something as ready as they can by a set date but instead gathering all the evidence they can to properly stand up the story. This evidence-based approach makes the reporting ambitious. But it also makes it time consuming and painstaking. Reporters can literally spend months building and analysing datasets, developing whistleblowers, collecting realms of testimony in order to hold the feet of the powerful to the fire or filing freedom of information requests by the hundreds. Stories tend to develop slowly and, without the divergence of a breaking news story, require immense fortitude, persistence and patience. This is not a sector that ego-focused, byline-driven reporters find comfortable.

## A chance to do journalism out of the reach of any lone wolf

Journalists in these newsrooms often work in teams, realising that to report on many of the complex stories of the world requires multiple skillsets rarely possessed by a single reporter. Again, this ability to put a team of reporters on a subject is largely a privilege of a newsroom whose function it is to provide evidence-based reporting rather than pinning down a top line of a story that might drive up social shares and clicks. The multi-disciplined teams often bring data specialists together with deep internet research and follow-the-money specialists as well as traditional shoe leather-type investigative reporters.

The team approach to reporting has brought a new need to develop communication techniques and software. Many of these newsrooms do not have physical space – this is a cost they chose not to take on, at least in the early days of launch. It means reporters have to develop communications methods that are safe and secure, even when they may be operating hundreds of miles apart. Encrypted email systems, communication channels and shared document folders have all become the norm. These systems become embedded in the culture of the organisation and are supported by the top team – again, this is something not found in traditional newsrooms where investigative reporters may find it hard to persuade their IT department that they need to install and support the latest encrypted messaging system.

Collaboration usually extends well beyond employed staff. Perhaps out of the necessity of small resources, but more likely out of a desire to get the big story, not-for-profit newsrooms are open collaborative spaces that reach out to reporters working in other outlets in order to build their teams and resources. Investigations in a global world often stretch across borders, but with stretched budgets and little money to pay freelancers, the solution has been to co-operate and share. This is anathema to those in commercial newsrooms, where the desire to be the first to the news still governs culture. But collaboration has proved an enormous string to the bow of the not-for-profit sector. The biggest global investigation of all time, the *Panama Papers*, for example, was co-ordinated by a small Washington-based not-for-profit organisation, the International Consortium of Investigative Journalists. The *Panama Papers* collaboration gathered journalists together from around the world to dig into millions of leaked financial documents. The result was the revelation of the inner workings of the off-shore system and those who used it to launder money. The work had enormous impact not only on the world's financial systems but also on the world of journalism. The *Panama Papers* showed the sector the value of collaboration on scale. Yet it remains the not-for-profit sector that has really embraced the power of collaborative reporting.

In 2017, the Bureau of Investigative Journalism applied the ambition of the *Panama Papers* collaboration to local journalism. In the second half of the twentieth century, local papers across the United Kingdom were decimated. Many were closed, staff were cut and reporters that were left were expected to cover ever larger beats, with very little time to dig into the stories in their local communities that took time. In answer to this problem, TBIJ launched the Bureau Local – a collaborative effort to bring dozens of local reporters together to work on a particular investigation. The premise was simple: reporters across the country would collaborate to build databases that reveal systemic problems about the country they live in and provide specific local stories that allow people to relate to the problem. The promise of the project was simple, too: by using the collaborative ambitions of the *Panama Papers*, local reporters could have more impact than even national papers if they worked together on projects. It took a not-for-profit organisation to bring reporters from different groups into the same investigation.

These collaborative environments mean there is no room for the lone wolf investigative reporter of old. Egos and territorial attitudes to by-lines have been suppressed. These newsrooms are places of sharing, of co-operation, of team effort and an alien environment still to many journalists coming from traditional environments. Working on such collaborative projects does also mean that journalists in these environments have had to become exceptionally good at organisation and project management. Figuring out how to run a right-to-reply process on an investigation involving dozens of journalists reporting

## Experiment and innovate

The experimental, ambitious approach of these newsrooms has also produced environments open to innovation. Over the past decade, many of the noteworthy innovations of the industry have come out of tiny not-for-profits. Perhaps the most extraordinary of these innovations has been Bellingcat, the citizen journalism community that uses the power of the Internet to search images and video to get at stories that even the best investigative journalists felt were out of reach. Bellingcat was the organisation that provided evidence proving Malaysian Airline Flight 17 (MH17) had been brought down by Russian missiles. It was also the organisation that coordinated the identification of the Russian spies that had attempted an assassination of a Russian double agent in Salisbury in England. The organisation uses methods that its founder Eliot Higgins developed. Calling it Open Source Intelligence, Higgins has built a community of journalists all trained in the techniques, many of whom use their spare time to track down information online and reveal stories that seem impossible to other reporters. It is the pursuit of the truth, not the commercial value of the findings, that drives the hundreds of volunteers that operate in the community.

This can be a risky business. Eliot Higgins is not a stranger to threat. But risk is something that the not-for-profit space has embraced. The organisations working in the space may be small, but it is through revealing wrongdoing and big-scale wrongdoing that attracts the funds. Traditional newspapers which have to balance the financial return (will it bring in readers?) with the financial risk (will it upset advertisers? can the potential cost of a lawsuit be balanced out by reader interest?) often find the calculations do not stack up in favour of investigative reporting. But in the not-for-profit newsrooms, these are not questions that need to be asked. This is not to suggest that they take unnecessary risks, or that they are not ultra-careful to ensure their work is thoroughly sourced, fact-checked and legalled. The level of fact checking and legal scrutiny undertaken in some of the better not-for-profits is second to none. It is the basis upon which the decision is made that differs, and this can affect the decision process right from the beginning. Not-for-profits are often much more open to trying what might seem an impossible investigation, because the reveal really would be important, global and impactful. It also means they are often more prepared to focus on potential litigious targets. The Organised Crime and Corruption Reporting Project in Bosnia, for example, has built a successful, well-funded organisation on the back of the mission to bring the corrupt to justice. Story after story take on some of the richest, most powerful individuals in the world. And they are proud of the level of risk they take. It is this sense of bravery, of taking on the world from often a small team, that makes these fun places to work.[12]

These approaches do not necessarily make the not-for-profit sector an easy place to work. These newsrooms are demanding. Burn-out is very real. Long hours a norm. Juggling usual. And few are known for their high salary cheques. There is also the question of sustainability. Even with the millions of philanthropic dollars pouring into the sector, it is still one searching for sustainability. But with these smaller newsrooms increasingly producing the great investigative scoops and taking the lead on proper accountability reporting – it is a sector that is finding its feet, getting recognised and attracting talent. Its successes also mean that the models, the methods and the value systems employed are starting to stick and seep into traditional newsrooms. As a result, many of the changes in investigative reporting are being inspired outside the traditional places known for their commitment to the practice, and are instead coming out of not-for-profit, small, new start-ups.

## Notes

1 https://gijn.org
2 www.revealnews.org/financialdocuments and www.propublica.org/about/documents
3 https://unearthed.greenpeace.org/
4 www.hrw.org/ and www.globalwitness.org/en/
5 https://assets-c3.propublica.org/pdf/reports/propublica-2019-annual-report.pdf, p26
6 https://thebristolcable.org/about/
7 www.documentcloud.org/documents/4638466-Impactreport-AUG-18.html
8 https://projects.propublica.org/docdollars/
9 http://apps.cironline.org/pesticides/
10 https://council-sell-off.thebureauinvestigates.com/
11 www.propublica.org/awards/
12 www.occrp.org/en

## References

Abernathy, P. M. (2018). *The Expanding News Desert*. www.usnewsdeserts.com/reports/expanding-news-desert/loss-of-local-news/
Dobrin, P. (2018). Obituaries, HF 'Gerry' Lenfest. *The Philadelphia Inquirer*. 5 August 2018.
Kaplan, D. (2020). Communication with author. 7 February 2020.
Mayhew, F. (2019). UK local newspaper closures: Net loss of 245 titles since 2005. *Press Gazette*. 11 February 2019.

# 8

# GRASSROOTS OPERATIONS

*Rachel Hamada*

2020 was a crossroads for local news journalism, as a pandemic swept the globe, threatening lives and also livelihoods. Media outlets large and small have been affected, and things look grim financially despite soaring traffic and engagement (Mayhew, 2020). With advertising revenue already nosediving this decade, Covid has helped to hammer home another nail in the coffin.

The future is uncertain: while the traditional media struggle and furlough staff, freelance journalists are struggling to find work, and many hyperlocal and niche publications, often run on the energy, passion and sometimes the personal finances of founders, are floundering.

The bright side of this picture is that, in the face of this stress, local newspapers, radio stations and hyperlocal sites are playing a vital role in the provision of reliable news and information. While conspiracy theories abound on WhatsApp and Facebook, local news providers share often real-time information on everything from food availability to support services. They are also asking hard questions about how crises are handled on a local level. They are illustrating exactly why knowledge is power and why news is a public good.

Many of us are currently more "local" than we have ever been before, stuck in a circuit of our flats, houses and immediate neighbourhoods, and we are more dependent on our geographic communities than ever before. The concept of "community" now seems more tangible and not just a buzzword.

There is much talk of reimagining the news so that it really serves the public and represents the issues that are at play in their daily lives – not just those of a still relatively middle-class, privileged core of newspaper, television and radio journalists. This is particularly true as the coronavirus crisis has exposed differences that were already present in society, for example, who can stay at home safely and who is forced to go out to work, or the disproportionate number of deaths of people from black and ethnic minority backgrounds.

The National Union of Journalists published its News Recovery Plan in 2020 with a view to mobilising its members and the wider public to demand short-term measures to protect the news industry – such as a windfall 6% tax on tech giants like Google and Facebook – as well as broader medium-term measures to create a foundation for a generation of media to serve the public good.

These include recommendations such as the establishment of a government-funded but independent journalism foundation to invest in local news and innovative journalistic projects; the establishment of an "asset of community value" status on local newspapers so that titles are preserved for potential community ownership and tax breaks, rate relief and other financial support for local social enterprises and journalistic cooperatives taking over titles from major regional operators, running them as not-for-profit enterprises.

NUJ head Michelle Stanistreet told an online gathering of NUJ member journalists at Edinburgh's freelance branch on 20 April 2020 that this is a time for "spearheading collective solutions . . . we need to use this crisis to see how we can collectively improve things", emphasising the need for a plurality of media. She added that journalism bodies around the world were having these conversations with their respective governments, too.

Time will tell if local journalists and outlets in the United Kingdom and in other countries can seize this opportunity and whether they will be supported by public sector and philanthropic funding and ultimately by the public directly. It could go either way.

In the meantime, it's important to recognise the recent historical context in order to understand where the local media sector finds itself.

Over the last decade, many local newspapers have been asset-stripped by their owners, and large numbers of journalists have been lost from the landscape. The number of full-time journalists in the UK newspaper industry dropped from around 23,000 in 2007 to 17,000 in 2017, and in the same period, over 300 local and regional newspaper titles were lost (Meditique, 2018, 57).

Industry shrinkage, the move to online and likely also a decrease in the volume of quality content saw weekly circulation of local and regional titles plummet from 63 million to 31 million over the same decade (2018, 6).

Senior journalists, seeing the writing on the wall, often accepted voluntary redundancy, and where there have been new posts, these have often been filled on a default basis by inexperienced journalists to save costs. This, coupled with an increase in casualisation, has led to a decline in the number of dedicated and knowledgeable council reporters, court reporters and other key beat reporters. Their ability to build up a network of sources and experts in their field, and a resulting understanding of key context and policy, has been lost.

Sometimes newspaper offices in smaller towns and rural areas have been closed by newspaper groups and events in those places covered by writers sat at desks tens of miles away or more, often unaware of local dynamics. Fewer journalists means more column inches to fill per head, more stories via press release and phone and fewer than ever through shoe leather and face-to-face conversation.

Local reporting and the health of local democracy are inextricably interlinked, and decisions that affect people's daily lives are now often going unscrutinised. The Cairncross Review, an independent review commissioned by the Department of Culture, Media and Sport, designed to investigate the long-term future of public interest journalism in the United Kingdom, was published in 2019 and makes the issues clear. The chair, Dame Frances Cairncross, underlined that as the number of local reporters has diminished, so has their news organisations' coverage of all aspects of local democracy (Hall, 2019).

Newspapers have been squeezed hard by the rise of Google and its peers, losing much of their key advertising revenue (almost a 70% decline between 2007 and 2017). In a declining market, traffic became king – and Kardashians tended to get a lot more clicks than councils.

The irony is that today there is actually more information available than ever before about our public services and how things are run, from a national level down to a hyper-local level. Freedom of Information (FOI) legislation heralded a new dawn for access to information. There are still many transparency battles to be won, but there is at least a consensus that government should be transparent and share statistics and other data online wherever possible.

All of this has led to an ocean of information but one which for the average citizen is incredibly difficult to navigate. Extracting the key data from that sea and understanding what it means is a critical skill that experts need to exercise on behalf of society.

This is where the journalist should come in. They should bring the ability to source and sift information, understand what is important and what is just noise and to help tell the human story that the data represents. This can help us all understand where society is succeeding, where it could be improved and where people experience harm as a result of government policy and implementation or neglect. However, if a journalist is inexperienced, unsupported and has eight stories to file a day, this process will not happen, these stories will go untold and these harms will continue to be done.

Not only this, it is clear that there is a relationship between quality local news and engagement with civic life. For example, where there are newspaper black holes, it has been shown that people vote less and that local institutions are less accountable (Howells, R, 2015). This is called the "democratic deficit", and it should worry us all.

There have been some attempts to address this issue on a structural level within the traditional media industry. For example, the BBC launched its Local Democracy Reporters programme with a view to strengthening reporting across the United Kingdom on local government. The scheme has had a mixed response and is far from perfect. Reporters often say that they only have the capacity to cover council and other local stories on a surface level and not go into any depth. Nonetheless, the scheme has helped fill some local news gaps, which is not to be sniffed at.

The Cairncross Review identified the likes of council reporting as somewhat of a conundrum – a public good with no obvious way of generating commercial revenue but also unsuitable for direct funding by the state (Cairncross, 2019).

The report states:

> As a result of falling revenues, publishers have cut costs dramatically. This has hurt the provision of all types of public-interest news, but local level democracy reporting the most. Some start-ups have begun to provide local coverage and there are promising examples of innovations to bolster the provision of public-interest news, but these are unlikely to be sufficient. While all types of public-interest journalism are in difficulty, the scale of the revenue gap of local publishers, combined with the public's limited appetite for local democracy reporting, creates a unique challenge.
>
> (2019, 9)

While the report has shed a valuable light on the challenges facing media for the public good, its recommendations were critiqued for not going far enough, and the implementation of the recommendations by the government were weaker still.

Sustainability is undoubtedly the holy grail for local news providers, old and new. There are a good number of new(ish) projects alluded to in the Cairncross report that are experimenting with ways of creating local accountability, investigating wrongdoing, rebuilding trust with members of the public and making enough cash to support that work.

What these projects have in common are the prioritising of public interest over profit; collective, democratic ownership structures; an ethos of collaboration over competition and the aim to report *with* communities rather than *on* them.

Traditional media models have been for profit and often held to formidable moneymaking standards. The profit margin sought by newspaper group owners has often been much higher than that generated even by the likes of UK supermarket giant Tesco (Mayhew, 2020). Meanwhile, news is undoubtedly a harder sell than groceries.

New models, in contrast, tend to be not for profit and often adopt collective ownership structures. *The Ferret* in Scotland, the *Bristol Cable* and the *Manchester Meteor*, for example, have all chosen to operate as cooperatives – allowing them to be community owned and rooted in the places they serve.

This means that journalists are now answerable to local communities rather than owners with a profit motive. Those who share in ownership of those models are acting in the role of citizen rather than the role of consumer, and this paradigm shift in journalism can be sited within a broader framework of societal change from consumerism to citizenship.

Strategy, decision-making and ideas about priorities and editorial themes to cover are all influenced by this wider community of member-owners in a way that is democratic, as opposed to the autocracy of the classic proprietor owner. The *Bristol Cable*, for example, often asks members at its Annual General Meeting (AGM) to give their thoughts on upcoming decisions. A recent *Ferret* AGM saw supporters vote against campaigning and advocacy on issues such as the environment (despite being very supportive of its reporting on the topic), as it was thought this would threaten the neutrality of the journalists – however, supporters felt it was appropriate for *The Ferret* to lobby on issues directly affecting journalism such as Freedom of Information, transparency and defamation.

Almost all of these new projects retain control over editorial on a story-by-story basis, free from interference by either member owners or funders. However, journalists often ask members and readers to offer a steer on the topics they think are the most important. When *The Ferret* crowdfunded for its launch in 2015, it also asked funders to vote on the topic they most wanted to see investigated. This turned out to be fracking, and thus this made up the first-ever investigation package published on the platform, which in turn contributed to a Scottish moratorium on fracking. Now, five years later, *The Ferret* continues to operate a model that allows readers to vote on the stories they want to see – and to suggest their own.

Transparency is also a keystone of many of these new projects, with *The Ferret*, for example, producing quarterly reports, including information on how money is raised and spent as well as stories covered. Interestingly, the publication of transparency reports often seems to stimulate a number of new member sign-ups, indicating that the public value not just stories that resonate with them but also being included and informed about a project, rather than being treated as merely consumers of its content.

As financial and editorial transparency and collaboration come to the fore as key principles, there also comes the question of spaces – are physical and digital community hubs that include journalists but also engaged citizens the direction that we are travelling in? The curation of spaces where resources and skills can be shared and ideas brainstormed mean that smaller local projects can punch above their weight.

These are the kind of innovations that the Bureau of Investigative Journalism is looking at with its ambitious Bureau Local project, where I am community organiser. This involves a network of over 1000 people across the United Kingdom – journalists, bloggers, coders, academics, lawyers, community leaders and activists – who all come together to work on investigations and commit "acts of journalism" beyond straight reporting.

Whoever is interested comes together to work on each specific story, and a dataset is usually compiled – sometimes from the top down through Freedom of Information requests, or sometimes from the bottom up through networked grassroots data gathering. This data is used for storytelling at a national, regional and local level, and partners work together to publish on the same date.

Part of the beauty of the project is that issues can be reported from a macro, systemic level down to a micro, granular level, creating multiple points of engagement and potential impact. For example, a domestic violence story could be reported on BBC News and picked up by a parliamentary committee, applying political pressure at a government level. Meanwhile, it could be reported on by the local newspaper and hyperlocal – reaching the communities directly affected and equipping them with evidence on what is happening but also applying pressure to MPs and local politicians who want to be seen as responsive to their voters.

Topics addressed must have relevance at a local level across the United Kingdom, but collaboration also helps to reveal national, systemic patterns, which can be reported on by national partners with the aim of securing positive change.

This model has proved effective and has inspired others – for example, *Correctiv* in Germany, who took on the same model to set up *Correctiv Lokal*, and *The Correspondent*, the global news features platform headquartered in Amsterdam, which has used the Bureau Local's collaboration model for its latest investigation into surveillance during the corona crisis. The Bureau Local operates on an open source basis wherever possible and shares open resources online – including a blueprint for its own model, *Building the Bureau Local: A User Guide*, as well as a *Manifesto for a People's Newsroom* and *Roadmap for Local News Collaboration*.

Perhaps the easiest way to understand how a model like this can work is to walk through an investigation from start to finish. A strong example of a Bureau Local investigation is Dying Homeless.

The seed was sown for this investigation in 2018 when a 35-year-old homeless man was found dead on the "doorstep" of the Houses of Parliament (Topping, 2018). MPs condemned the circumstances leading to the incident, saying it illustrated the rising problem of homelessness in the country as a whole. The Bureau Local team decided to take a look at numbers of deaths across the United Kingdom – but then came to the realisation that nobody was collating this data centrally. People were dying unacknowledged, without lessons being learnt and without commemoration.

So we put together a plan – we asked members of our network to look out in their areas for details of people who had died while homeless – whether they were rough sleeping, stuck in temporary B&Bs or sofa surfing. These could be submitted by online form; we would verify the case and build up a database to form a picture of what was happening around the country.

As part of this process, we gathered the stories of those who died – from Hamad Farahi, a quantum physicist from Iraq who nearly ended up working with Stephen Hawking but finally had to resort to sleeping in his car in a Tesco car park before dying in emergency accommodation, to Valerie Collins, a grandmother who was forced to sleep in shop doorways but still created a makeshift garden of potted plants.

It was important that we compile reliable data but also that we collect stories to show the real people behind the numbers and the things that might have led to their often-premature deaths. These causes varied.

One man who died was not yet 40 – he had been a successful sailor and had also regularly volunteered, including building schools and helping in a homeless kitchen. However, he lost two children in succession, and this sent him to rock bottom. One woman, in her early 30s, was found dead in the tent she shared with her partner in Cardiff, just a few days before Christmas. She had been suffering from chronic obstructive pulmonary disease.

Building up a database of deaths and stories was key to showing how, where and why these deaths were happening. We worked with our network of members all over the country and used social media to encourage as many submissions as possible to the database – using the hashtag #MakeThemCount.

We also wrote a reporting recipe, which was sent out to members. This is a standard part of our process and is a document that walks reporters through the data and how they can use it in their stories and also offers other content that reporters can use such as key quotes.

Members will also regularly support each other by brainstorming on reporting ideas, and the more experienced members often mentor others when it comes to the technicalities of Freedom of Information requests or data analysis and interpretation. We hold story clinics and regular check-ins so that people working on the story can touch base.

Participants also sign up to an embargo date, and then everyone publishes from that day onwards. This has the effect that many stories – local, national, newspaper, broadcast and specialist press – go out on the same day, creating momentum for the story.

In the end, when we published our Dying Homeless investigation, we showed that 800 people had died over the 18-month period. Almost 100 local stories were put out across the country, and Channel 4 News led its programme with a 20-minute segment on this story. We created a social media campaign around the findings on the same day, and this was taken up by many others, such as national homeless charities and public figures.

Next came the first wave of impact: we shared our methodology with the Office of National Statistics, and it decided to start gathering data on homeless deaths. National Records of Scotland also confirmed it would record this information.

This was a concrete victory, as this data will allow patterns to be identified and help government, national and local, to understand where services are failing people. This was reinforced by a piece we published in 2019, which showed that:

> Nearly a third of homeless people die from treatable conditions, meaning hundreds of deaths could potentially have been prevented. . . . The research by University College London also shows that homeless

people are much more likely to die from certain conditions than even the poorest people who have a place to live.

(McClenaghan, 2019)

At the end of this investigation, we needed to move on to new work. Although as an organisation, the Bureau of Investigative Journalism is able to focus on more long-term investigations than many news organisations, we can't stay on the same story forever. However, we had built up a community around this topic and didn't want to waste this.

Fortunately, we were able to find two solutions. First, we agreed with homelessness charity the Museum of Homelessness that it would take on the collecting of stories. From January to June 2019, its work showed that someone affected by homelessness died every 19 hours in the United Kingdom. *The Guardian* newspaper also launched a project aimed at recording the deaths and stories of people experiencing homelessness.

Second, we used this work to form the question that would shape our next investigation: "Why can't people get out of homelessness?" The exploration of this issue formed the basis of our subsequent Locked Out investigation, which used data to highlight the inadequacies of Local Housing Allowance, collected evidence to show the ineffectiveness of recent homelessness reduction legislation in England and used story circles in badly affected parts of the country, from Edinburgh to Bedford, to listen to experiences on the ground and then to feed back our findings to policy makers and politicians (Hamada 2020).

A totally different kind of local investigation that we ran was Sold from Under You, and this looked at public assets and spaces being sold off by councils in order to make ends meet. A data-driven story initially, this investigation was based on an exhaustive batch of FOIs to councils that were collated into a database.

Again, we collaborated with our network of members so that they could investigate what was going on in their area – and translate addresses into real places that meant something to people. From boxing clubs in Birmingham that had been real community hubs to libraries in Bristol and swimming pools in Leeds, places for congregating and talking, exercising or reading had disappeared off the map.

We worked, too, with a national media partner – HuffPost UK (we work with a range of publishing partners depending on the nature of each story) – and a sectoral partner – Locality – to show the big picture and to allow the public to tell their own stories. We created an interactive map that people could enter their own postcode into to find out which of their local spaces had been sold off. This also flagged up the councils that had failed to respond to Freedom of Information requests and meant that they could be held to account by their own citizens.

These are just a few of the projects that we have worked on as a collaborative network – we have also looked at domestic violence, police stop-and-search and risky council investments.

The Bureau Local's approach has won plaudits but most importantly has regularly led to change on the ground at the national level but also at the local level. This is because we work in collaboration with so many members who are local journalists and experts and know the specific landscape of their area. They in turn will ideally engage with under- or misrepresented communities in their postcodes to make sure that we capture the issues that most negatively affect people's lives and wellbeing.

Editorial judgement is still required to say what is a strong story, what has universality or some kind of systemic relevance, how data can be reliably collected and validated and how a story should be told for maximum impact and potential for positive change. But the story ideas should come from the ground up, not the top down, if journalism is to be relevant and useful to the public – and to survive.

Meanwhile, there are more and more news organisations springing up in the United Kingdom that are strongly rooted in place and have the public interest as their *raison d'etre*. These include the *Bristol Cable*, which is a democratically run cooperative running investigative journalism on topics from modern slavery to air pollution, and *The Ferret*, which has produced award-winning journalism on everything from surveillance and the far right to domestic abuse. Other notable publications include *Nation.Cymru*, the *West Highland Free Press*, Portsmouth's *Star & Crescent*, the *Manchester Meteor* and the *Clydesider*, as well as hyperlocals.

All of these have different aims, styles and content – but all have public interest at their heart over profit, and a desire to provide truthful, useful information and news for the areas they serve. ICNN, the Independent Community News Network in Cardiff, organises and lobbies on behalf of this sector and will have up-to-date information on which news outlets are currently active.

The legacy media sector – including big newspaper groups and broadcasters – remains a key pillar of local news despite the challenges it faces. Local newspapers can also drive big national stories. For example, the *Manchester Evening News* published a deep-dive news feature looking at Salman Abedi, the Manchester Arena bomber, and understanding the context of his life and radicalisation (Osuh, 2017), as well as an investigation into sexual offences in the Armed Forces (Gouk, 2020).

The BBC also continues to do essential work in this area through its Shared Data Unit, a partnership between the broadcaster and the News Media Association. One example is a vitally important story published by the BBC in 2019 on the number of disability benefit appeals winning at tribunal, which was also covered by 40 regional partners (Homer, 2019). The unit also published work looking at credit card advertisements targeting people looking for benefits advice on local government websites (Ferguson, 2020).

BBC East's Impact Hub spent four years investigating £10m missing from Northampton Town Football Club – and in the process uncovered secret payments to a local MP. As a result of the investigation, which comprised over

50 stories, the town's MP and chief executive were brought down, and a police investigation resulted. Files on 30 suspects are currently with the Crown Prosecution Service on charges of bribery and misconduct in public office.[1]

While traditional media continues to produce some good content, it's clear that serious innovation will be required to engineer the next generation of local public-interest news – not just technological innovation, but also editorial, creative and social innovation.

Across Europe and globally, brilliant projects are emerging all over – from *Pro Publica's* Local Reporting Network to brilliant one-off start-ups from Greece to India. There are too many to list, but local news is seeing a host of imaginative models emerging, and the collaborative spirit of this new ecosystem means that people are willing to share resources, technology and success stories, superpowering this movement. Forums such as Gather and databases such as the Engaged Journalism Database are great places to find examples, as are media news and collaboration hubs such as Nieman Lab in the United States and Splice Media in Asia.

There is also a great deal of experimentation with engagement techniques and storytelling going on. These range from the (on the surface) simple, such as *Médor* in Belgium's yellow posters, which they put up over town to let people know about the latest stories affecting their neighbourhoods, to *Journal Media* in Ireland, which funds investigations by letting users "pitch and pay" for stories they want published.

Pay, you say? There is no doubt that there are stories to cover and information to provide, journalists passionate about doing this and people who want this knowledge. The billion-dollar question, though, is where does the money come from to make this happen? Right now, there is no solid model for local news journalism, let alone local investigative journalism, which is even more expensive.

There have been inroads – some publications have been steadily building paid memberships to ensure a baseline income and cashflow. Others have been successful in repeatedly raising philanthropic funding for their work, or in crowdfunding. Some money still comes in from advertising and sponsorship. Some syndicate their work or operate side businesses. Most of the projects already mentioned work on a shoestring and operate a mixed revenue model, as no one financial stream is enough to guarantee their futures.

This looks unsustainable. There has, therefore, been a recent groundswell to show that journalism and information is a public good. Knowledge, like the air we breathe, the water we drink and the parks we walk and play in, should belong to all of us – and is a necessity for being an active citizen. Without accurate and timely local information, how can a person participate meaningfully in their local civic life? We all need to know which of our services are failing, which of our communities are ailing.

Campaigns such as the NUJ's Local News Matters, the Bureau's #LoveLocalNews and others are designed to show the public the benefit of good local news. The coronavirus breakout, forcing us all much closer to home, has also acted as an illustration of why we all need the right facts and the best scrutiny in a crisis.

So what next? There is widespread support for a tax on the tech giants that disrupted the advertising market that previously enabled the local news industry. They have sometimes pre-empted this – for example, Google has been a key and enthusiastic funder of local news and has recently pledged more to help struggling newsrooms.

However, media correspondent Jane Martinson argues: "Given the scale of the crisis, which comes after years in which Google itself has been the cause of so much disruption, this is like throwing a few planks of wood to those in the middle of a tsunami".

The Cairncross Review, the NUJ and others have called for a government-funded journalism foundation "to invest in local news and innovative national public interest journalistic projects, with particular encouragement for new models and startups across all platforms". This would certainly help establish an economic foundation for local and community news organisations.

There are some precedents – in New Jersey, the Civic Information Bill was drafted by free press and then passed.[2] Based on the foundation of solid months of work talking to communities and evaluating their news needs, as well as looking at which areas lacked local media coverage, the bill was proposed and included money to fund public-interest news, training and media literacy.

In Wales, the Welsh government recently created a small pot of money for hyperlocals, based on the findings of the National Assembly's Inquiry into news journalism. The sum itself was a drop in the ocean, but the implication – that this kind of journalism is deserving of public funding – is a breakthrough.

Projects such as info districts in the United States are working to understand how media, technology and events/public conversation can intersect to make something new. It's all a brave new world for investigative journalism, even for local journalism, with more to think about than ever. The rewards, though, are phenomenal – the building of deep connection and trust with communities could allow for journalists to build stories with those communities that are more powerful than ever.

### Notes

1 BBC East, 24/07/18, Northampton Town and the missing millions: A timeline of events
2 Gabbatt, A, 06/07/18, New Jersey pledges $5m for local journalism to boost state's 'civic health'

## References

Cairncross, F. (2019). The Cairncross Review: A sustainable future for journalism. *DCMS*. 12 February. www.gov.uk/government/publications/the-cairncross-review-a-sustainable-future-for-journalism

Ferguson, S. (2020). UK councils' benefits pages push credit card adverts. *BBC*. 5 February.

Gouk, A. (2020). Sexual offences in the armed forces. *Manchester Evening News*. 8 April.

Hall, T. (2019). Non-profit local news body could bring about 'sea change' in public interest journalism. *Press Gazette*. 4 November.

Hamada, R. (2020). Taking a story full circle: Reporting with people, not on them. *Journalism.co.uk*. 10 March.

Homer, A. (2019). Half of disability benefits appeals won in tribunal court. *BBC*. 14 November.

Howells, R. (2015). Journey to the centre of a news black hole: examining the democratic deficit in a town with no newspaper. PhD Thesis, Cardiff University.

Mayhew, F. (2020). News publishers hit new online records with coronavirus coverage. *Press Gazette*. 7 April.

McClenaghan, M. (2019). Homelessness kills: Study finds third of homeless people die from treatable conditions. *Thebureauinvestigates.com*. 11 March.

Mediatique. (2018) Overview of recent dynamics in the UK press market. *DCMS*. April 2018. https://secure.toolkitfiles.co.uk/clients/19826/sitedata/Reports/Press-report-for-DCMS.pdf

Osuh, C. (2017). The making of a monster: How Manchester boy Salman Abedi became a mass murderer. *Manchester Evening News*. 19 September.

Topping, A. (2018). Homeless man dies on 'doorstep' of Houses of Parliament. *The Guardian*. 14 February.

# Part II

# PLACES

# 9

# CHINA AND THE DIGITAL ERA

*Wang Haiyan and Fan Jichen*

Many people may think that there is no investigative journalism in the People's Republic of China. In fact, as a journalistic genre partly drawing on the Chinese tradition of critical reporting and partly modelled on the Anglo-American techniques, investigative journalism has been practiced in the Chinese media for several decades. The general belief is that investigative journalism in China burgeoned in the 1980s in the wake of economic reforms. Among the earlier examples, between July and August 1980, were the reports on the sinking of the Bohai No. 2 oil-drilling ship by the state media such as *Workers' Daily*, *People's Daily* and *Xinhua* news agency, which not only exposed the actual death toll but also criticised the government bureaucracy responsible for the disaster. As a result of the reporting, two ministers and several other officials were sacked, which was rare in China at that time. Since then, critical reporting and the exposure of social problems, disasters, policy failures, and even official corruption has gradually become a routine part of Chinese journalism. In the 1990s, with China further opening up to the world and gathering pace in economic reform, investigative journalism developed at phenomenal speed. The establishment of a wide range of commercially oriented newspapers, magazines and TV programmes, such as *Southern Weekend*, *Southern Metropolitan Daily*, *Caijing Magazine*, *China Youth Daily's Frozen Point Weekly*, CCTV's *News Probe* and so on, has greatly inspired nationwide media houses and journalists to pursue critical reporting. In particular, the late 1990s and early 2000s marked the heyday of Chinese investigative journalism. The widely remembered cases such as the reporting of Sun Zhigang's death in 2003 孙志刚之死[1], the Sanlu Milk Scandal in 2008 三鹿奶粉污染事件[2] and Chenzhou officials' corruption in 2006 郴州官场窝案[3] were all products of this period of time, creating a "golden age" of Chinese journalism when the Chinese audiences saw a swelling number of investigative reports that covered a wide range of social problems; some forced changes to the law, some brought down government officials and some saved citizens' lives.

Nevertheless, as we get to the second decade of the new millennium, investigative journalism in China has experienced profound changes. The rise of new media, especially the wide adoption of social media technologies, has moved news readership and advertisements from offline to online, and changed the ecosystem of Chinese media. Together with the collapse of the advertisement-based business model of traditional media and changing face of politics and administration, Chinese investigative journalism has reconfigured its grounds, practices and forms.

The editor of this book and author of this chapter are among the many who have written (i.e. de Burgh, 2003a, 2003b; Wang, 2016a, 2016b) about the development of Chinese investigative journalism and its practices in the 1980s, 1990s and 2000s. But very few wrote about how it has been practiced similarly or differently in the 2010s. In this chapter, our focus is the "new era", namely the second decade of the new millennium, or the "digital era". We will first analyze the changes in the technological, political and economic environment and contextualise the practice of Chinese investigative journalism in the 2010s. We will then analyze the key features of the practice of Chinese investigative journalism as it shifted away from the "golden age" to the new era. Following that, we will particularly focus on the changing mode of production of investigative journalism, by case studying former TV host Cui Yongyuan's 崔永元 endeavour to expose the tax scandal of entertainment celebrities and the genetically modified food (GMF) controversy based on personalised social media. We will conclude by discussing the industrial and sociopolitical implications of Chinese investigative journalism moving from legacy media to online media and from professional production to amateur production.

## The changing media environment in China in the "new era"

The 2010s are called a "new era" of Chinese investigative journalism because they involve new dynamics in all three big areas impacting Chinese society and media: technology, economy and politics (Wang & Sparks, 2019). Although the three aspects are often intertwined, it is worth examining each independently so that we can understand better why and how investigative journalism might be influenced.

New media technologies based on the Internet have gained rapid development in China in recent years, entering every corner of society and significantly reshaping people's daily lives. According to the latest report of the China Internet Network Information Center (CNNIC),[4] the number of Chinese netizens has reached 829 million in 2018, rising by 265 million since 2012. The Internet penetration rate has grown from 42.1% to 59.6% in this period, and among the overall Chinese netizens, 98.6% (or 817 million people) use mobile phones to get access to the Internet. At the same time, particularly noticeable is that 81.4% of Chinese netizens (or 675 million) consume news from the Internet, and mobile news users have reached 653 million, accounting for 79.9% of Chinese mobile netizens. These are not just dry figures. Behind the figures is a massive movement of news consumers migrating from offline to online, and particularly mobile phones, in this, the most populated country in the world.

On facing these changes, many legacy news organisations gradually realised that the Internet is a significant site to compete for the attention of audience and in response have established news websites and applications. Some media organisations have even given up offline offerings and turned to online-news-only operation. For instance, *Oriental Morning Post* 东方早报, a subsidiary of Shanghai Media Group, was closed on January 1, 2017, and its news reporting business and other functions all turned to *The Paper* 澎湃新闻 (thepaper.cn). Also, social media and platform media, such as *Weibo* 微博, *WeChat* 微信, *Today's Headlines* 今日头条, and *TikTok* 抖音, have flourished in this period and attracted several hundreds of millions of daily active users. Many organisations and individuals make use of these platforms to establish their own media. They label themselves "we media" or "self media" 自媒体 and release different kinds of information products on a regular basis and with immeasurable quantity, whether through text, images or videos, whether as personalised journals, promotions or news. These new kinds of information providers and platforms have become a powerful challenge to the legacy news organisations. They compete with legacy media not only for audience attention but also for advertising revenue, which used to be the major organisational and financial ground for the practice of investigative journalism in the pre-digital era.

On the economic side, the flourishing of new media outlets, especially those based on social media, has threatened traditional media's ability to generate revenue. Although revenue fall has been a long-standing phenomenon in Western media, it is a phenomenon relatively new to Chinese media. The so-called "golden age"[5] of Chinese journalism was made possible largely because of the success of the media economy, which lasted for about 20 years, from the end of last century to the beginning of this century. The Chinese media economy boomed without any serious interruption during this period of time, and many media organisations grew to be powerhouses of the national or local economy. It is only recently that media organisations started to experience revenue fall. To many people inside the Chinese media industry, it is a sudden, unexpected, unprepared-for yet drastic fall. According to official statistics, the turning point of advertising revenues of Chinese media appeared in 2012, while that of circulation appeared in 2013. A report on the development of China's media industry (2018–2019), which was published by a research group at Tsinghua University, argued that Chinese newspapers have entered a period of "cliff-like drop" 断崖式下跌 in advertising revenues since 2012. Advertising revenues of the newspapers in 2018 only accounted for 15.7% of that in 2011.[6] At the same time, newspaper readership has fallen drastically, too. According to reports from the General Administration of Press and Publications (GAPP), the highest number of printed copies of Chinese newspapers was 48.24 billion in total in 2013. Since then, the drop began and has been persistently deep. The rate of fall is by 9–10% each year, and in 2018, total printed copies recorded a low of 33.73 billion copies, less than 70% that of 2013.[7]

At the same time, it is necessary to bear in mind that most Chinese media organisations are state run. They are often affiliated with a larger media group at national, provincial or municipal levels, which contain a politically oriented "party" outlet and at least one other, commercially oriented, or "metro", title. The former plays a central political and propagandistic role and is mainly supported by subsidies, while the latter is most often supported entirely by advertising and circulation revenues. With the overall fall of the media economy, commercially oriented titles have experienced many more difficulties than politically oriented ones. And it is the former which had been the major engine of carrying out investigative reporting in the "golden age".

In order to survive through the financial difficulties, many news organisations attempted to reform their traditional business model and organisation structure. On the one hand, new investments are made into infrastructure and manpower, supporting the establishment of convergent newsrooms and online offerings. On the other hand, expenses in the production of traditional journalism genres, especially those involving long time and high costs, such as international reporting and investigative reporting, are cut and minimised. Some media organisations have tried to generate readership revenue through online paywalls to compensate for the loss offline. *Caixin* magazine 财新周刊, the major provider of investigative reporting in business and finance in China, is one of the pioneers. But so far it has shown no sign that this is going to be a workable solution, as people are adept at consuming news free from the internet. Other media organisations have tried to diversify revenue sources by turning to non-journalism business, such as cultural industries, property development, e-commerce and so on. More aggressively, there are also those who seek to remove the firewall between newsrooms and advertising departments and try to involve journalists in activities unrelated to journalism to pursue commercial interests. Amidst these changes, many media organisations dismissed their investigative reporting teams and closed investigation programmes, titles or pages, and a large number of journalists were laid off or resigned. According to a report[8] in Shanghai Journalism Review, at least 52 investigative journalists left their traditional media jobs from 2009–2015. Among them were CCTV's 中央电视台 Wang Lifen 王利芬, *Southern Weekend's* Fu Jianfeng 傅剑锋, *Oriental Morning Post's* 东方早报 Jian Guangzhou 简光洲, *Beijing News'* 新京报 Liu Binglu 刘炳路 and *Huashang Daily's* 华商报 Jiang Xue江雪, all famous names in Chinese investigative journalism of the "golden age". All these tend to suggest that, as the bottom line is threatened, it seems unrealistic to expect continuous and robust production of investigative journalism in the legacy media.

Politically, the coming into power of President Xi Jinping 习近平 since 2012 has meant that greater importance is attached to journalism in assisting the administration of the government and ruling party. From the end of

2015 to the beginning of 2016, Xi inspected major media houses, including *PLA Daily* 解放军报, *People's Daily* 人民日报, *Xinhua News Agency* 新华社 and *China Central Television (CCTV)*. In early 2019, he led the members of the Standing Committee of the Political Bureau of the Communist Party of China (CPC) central committee to inspect the new media building of *People's Daily* 人民日报 once again. By October 2018, Xi had published 14 speeches and 5 congratulatory letters on news, propaganda, public opinion, the Internet and other topics related to journalistic work.[9] Among these, the more important and influential conferences include *National Propaganda and Ideological Work Conference* 全国宣传思想工作会议, held on 19 August 2013, and *The Party's News and Public Opinion Work Symposium* 党的新闻舆论工作座谈会 held on 19 February 2016. Xi's thoughts on news and public opinion are mainly about how media and journalism should adhere to the correct political direction and public opinion orientation in the changing technological environment. As Xi stressed, all media in China should carry "Party as its surname". Facing the new demands from the top leadership, investigative journalism, which is traditionally critical and challenging in terms of reporting style, is made more difficult.

## The main features of investigative journalism in China today

The changing technological, economic and political dynamics have reshaped the media ecology and consequently influenced how investigative journalism is practiced. We contend that compared to the second "golden age", investigative journalism in the 2010s has new features at least in four aspects, namely new platforms, new actors, new routines and new reporting topics.

First of all, the publishing platforms for investigative reports have gradually shifted from traditional TV programmes and printed newspapers or magazines to social media. The publishers on social media include the investigative journalism departments of legacy news organisations and the so-called "we media" operated by individual users. The latter can sometimes be more powerful, in the sense that they are often able to attract greater attention of netizens, arouse more heated discussion and stronger public opinion and put more pressure on the relevant agencies. For example, on 22 July 2018, WeChat account "*ishoulc*" (*shouye*) 兽爷 published a feature entitled *Yimiao zhi Wang* 疫苗之王 (literally, the King of Vaccines),[10] exposing the fake vaccine business of one of the biggest vaccine manufacturers in China, the Changchun Changsheng Biotechnology Co. Ltd 长春长生生物科技有限责任公司. It went viral soon after the release. In the first hour of its publication, more than 2 million WeChat users read the report online. This is a number comparable to the readership size of a national-scale comprehensive newspaper which would be deemed successful in the "golden age". The coverage led the company to recall all problematic vaccines, pay a 9.1-billion-RMN fine and sack its chairwoman and 14 top management personnel.[11] The Association of Applied Journalism and Communication of China awarded the report "Top Ten Innovative Cases of Applied Journalism and Communication in 2018". Similarly, a number of other "we media" platforms, such as *Dingxiang Doctor* 丁香医生, *Low Voice* 小声比比, *Optical Valley Guest* 光谷客 and others achieved success in the same fashion. Their investigative stories online covered diverse topics, arousing nationwide concerns from the public, and forced the mainstream media to follow and the government to respond.

Second, as to the actors in investigative journalism, professional journalists from institutional news organisations wane, while amateurs wax. In recent years, for technological, economic and political reasons mentioned previously, the number of investigative journalists has been greatly reduced. Research by a team in Guangzhou-based Sun Yat-sen University shows that in 2011, there were 259 journalists nationwide working on investigative journalism, while by 2017, 57.5% of them had moved elsewhere, and only 130 still remain in the area.[12] Not only has the number of investigative journalists shrunk drastically, but so has the number of media organisations housing them. The 130-some investigative journalists are highly concentrated in about nine news outlets, such as *The Paper* 澎湃新闻, based in Shanghai, and *Caixin Media* 财新传媒, based in Beijing, which means that the geographical scale of investigative journalism coverage is limited.

However, at the same time, investigative journalism on social media platforms has flourished, and new actors have emerged. Some of the new actors are former investigative journalists of institutional news organisations, such as the founders of *Home of the Beast* 兽楼处 and Optical Valley Guest. After their leaving the job in legacy media, they continue to conduct investigative journalism based on social media, regarding it as a means of experimental entrepreneurship or a channel to express their own opinions. For example, Wang Keqin 王克勤, the former journalist of *China Economic Times* 中国经济时报, established a charity organisation called Love Cleans Up 大爱清尘基金 (literally, great love helps to clean the dust) to provide pneumoconiosis patients with medical advice and legal suggestions. Social media have become a very important channel for him and for volunteers on the team to disseminate information about their activities and raise funds. Also based on it, Wang Keqin himself continues to expose problems in society in the form of reporting, especially on topics related to migrant workers, environment, pollution and poverty. He regards his career as a special kind of investigative journalism. Many "we media" hosts similarly choose areas of their concern and conduct investigative journalism. Another prominent example is *Dingxiangyisheng* 丁香医生, which aims at promoting public health to metropolitan audiences. Publishing investigative reports has become its routinised practice and an effective mechanism to disseminate health-related information.

Third, production routines of investigative journalism have changed. This is mainly reflected in the changes in the sources of news and the way readers, or users, are involved. With the rapid development of social media, user-generated content (UGC) and civic journalism, 'supervision of public opinion'[13] by netizens has become common practice in China. Much influential investigative coverage originates from users' exposure on the Internet and then is picked up by the mainstream media, which continue to facilitate and conduct further investigation. In some cases, users of social media not only play the role of whistleblower but are active investigators who actually involve themselves directly in the production of investigative journalism. This is totally different from the traditional routine of investigative journalism in which it is a professional process mainly taking place within news organisations. For example, on 14 November 2018, a netizen named *Huazong Diule Jingubang* 花总丢了金箍棒 published a short documentary called *The Secret of Cups* 杯子的秘密 on Weibo, disclosing the cleaning irregularities of several five-star hotels in mainland China. Once published, this short film spread rapidly and widely on the Internet. Later, it received high attention from the mainstream media, such as *People's Daily* 人民日报, *Guangzhou Daily* 广州日报, *Beijing News* 新京报 and so on, and caused intervention by relevant departments of government, achieving an even better effect than some reports produced by professional news organisations.

Last but not least, the reporting topics of investigative journalism are significantly different. In the "golden age", investigative journalism in China heavily targeted "hard" topics such as abuses of power and wrongdoings of government departments and officials. But today, it tends to deal with "softer" topics such as health, environment, ordinary people's livelihoods and so on. Partly, this is due to the change in the political environment. Governments at all levels have strengthened control over mainstream media to limit the coverage of sensitive issues so that social stability may be maintained. At the same time, law and regulations prohibit alternative media (based on social media) from conducting 'formal' journalistic activities in the domain of 'hard' topics. As a result, 'soft' topics seem to be a good fit for all media.

## A case study: Cui Yongyuan's practice of investigative journalism

Cui Yongyuan 崔永元 is well known in China. He used to be one of the most popular TV hosts; now he is rather controversial. He was born in Tianjin in 1963. After his graduation from the Communication University of China (CUC) in 1985, he started a journalism career in China National Radio (CNR). In 1998, he transferred to China Central Television and gradually became a popular figure onscreen. In his early days at CCTV, he hosted different kinds of programmes, both news and entertainment, and he even played roles in comedy shows and films. Later he focused on two news programmes; one was *Oriental Horizon* 东方时空, a TV magazine, and the other *Tell It Like It Is* 实话实说, a current affairs commentary show. Both programmes bear some features of investigative journalism, as he often targeted sensitive social issues or current affairs topics, and the style of reporting or commenting was critical. In 2013, Cui resigned from CCTV and became a TV documentary lecturer at CUC. At the same time, he served as a member of the national committee of the Chinese People's Political Consultative Conference (CPPCC). Since then, he has no longer been a full-time career journalist working for any formal media organisation, but, based on social media, he has been able to utilise the social, political and cultural capital he has accumulated as a TV celebrity and public figure over the years to engage in the production and dissemination of investigative content as an individual and an independent journalist.

Two typical cases of Cui's investigative journalism based on social media are investigations on the safety of genetically modified food in 2013 and exposure of the tax scandal involving entertainment celebrities in 2018. These cases reflect not only the new features of investigative journalism in China today but also illustrate the possibilities and limits of such journalism in bringing about social changes in the new media environment. We examine each in turn in the following.

### Case 1: Investigation on the safety of genetically modified food

When Cui began his personal investigations on GMF, he had already resigned from CCTV. His name became associated with GMF first because of an online debate he had with Fang Zhouzi 方舟子, a net-based public intellectual. While Fang called upon netizens to support GMF production in China as a measure of solving food shortages and rallied a group of volunteers from online to join a GM corn harvesting and tasting tour, Cui questioned his motives and pointed out that the safety of GMF had not been proved and that GMF could contain huge health risks. The two sides challenged each other as to "whether or not GMF is eatable" on their respective Weibo accounts, on which both had millions of followers. In order to further understand the issue, in December of the same year, Cui conducted a reporting trip to the United States with the aim of shooting a documentary and enhancing public awareness of the issue. He visited six cities, including Los Angeles, Davis, San Diego, Chicago and Seattle, and interviewed more than 50 people, including academics, public intellectuals, food dealers, consumers from local communities, members of social organisations and so on. On 1 March 2014, the report, *Cui's Investigation of GMF in the United States* 崔永元美国转基因调查纪录片, was released.[14] The 68-minute documentary immediately attracted huge attention from the public. In the film, Cui showed the Chinese public how the scientific community, policy makers and society debated the safety of GMF in the United States and how a restrictive policy has been imposed on mass production of GMF due to the lack of scientific evidence supporting its safety. Cui ended the show with a personalised line: "This is my investigation. If you don't believe me, you can come to see it for yourself".

It's worth mentioning that in order to avoid any conflict of interest in the reporting and to be "objective" and "fair" as a detached journalist, Cui refused any sponsorship before the trip and paid all the expenses out of his own pocket, which was later estimated at nearly one million RMB.[15] Besides, Cui carried no CCTV title when he began this investigation. According to Cui, were he still a CCTV host, it would have been impossible to be involved in this project, because the organisational rules of CCTV do not allow staff to participate in personalised internet-based journalism.[16] In this sense, removing the formal title from a legacy media organisation actually released Cui's power as an individual journalist.

Since then, Cui has turned himself into a "warrior" against GMF. He paid close attention to its development in China and constantly involved himself in discussions with netizens online or with the general public offline. He even used his role in national politics and took the issue to the "two sessions" 两会, the annual assembly of the National People's Congress (NPC) and the National Committee of People's Political Consultative Conference, demanding that the Agricultural Ministry thoroughly investigate the issue and be accountable for relevant polices regarding the adoption of GMF in Chinese fields and introduction of GMF in the Chinese market.[17] Although government officials did not respond to his demand directly, the dynamics of policy-making in front of the public did show signs of greater care in the subsequent years. At the same time, the public awareness of GMF safety is greatly improved. Many ordinary Chinese people choose to trust Cui and regard him a custodian of conscience no less than a former CCTV journalist. As for Cui himself, GMF safety continues to be one of his major concerns and causes today.

### Case II: Exposure of tax scandal involving entertainment celebrities

Apart from the safety of GMF, Cui also exposed several social events, among which the tax scandal involving entertainment celebrities in 2018 was probably the most influential. On 25 May 2018, Cui posted copies of several contracts between a film star and an investor on Weibo. He stated that some entertainment celebrities had secretly evaded taxes by signing "yin-yang contracts" 阴阳合同, meaning dual contracts, with a small, taxable one in front of the public eyes (the yang contract) and a big, untaxable one under the table (the yin contract). One of these contracts clearly showed that Fan Bingbing 范冰冰, a 36-year-old superstar, was involved. She signed a taxable yang contract worth ten million RMB, while there was also a non-taxable yin contract worth five times more for one of her many film performances. The post attracted huge attention immediately, given the wealth involved and the fame of both Fan and Cui. Fan Bingbing's studio started public relations efforts swiftly, first denying the charge and vowing to sue Cui but later admitting the charges and apologising to Cui.

At the same time, Cui's online exposure raised the concern of the authorities. On 3 June, the State Taxation Administration (STA) claimed through its official website that it would thoroughly investigate the tax problems of the entertainment businesses. Later, local tax authorities and police stepped in to investigate Fan and her brokerage firm. All these were accompanied by intense reporting of legacy media and online media, which tried to get more information from Cui or investigate the long-standing black holes of taxation in the entertainment industry. In the process, Cui told the journalists that Fan's contract was only a small example from the problematic contracts he had collected, and he had a drawer of such materials, involving many "big names" people could imagine.

Cui did not post more contracts dealing with any particular individual film celebrities. But the impact on Fan Bingbing has been severe. On 3 October, Xinhua reported that the STA's investigation has proved that Fan Bingbing committed tax fraud. The total amount of overdue tax and fines she needed to pay back was 883 million RMB. Fan didn't revolt. She responded that she fully accepted the decision of tax authorities and sincerely apologised to the public for her behaviour. This was a deadly blow to the film career of Fan, once the most popular film star in China. Her studio was closed down, many commercial contracts involving her were suspended, the films in which she acted were pulled and she no longer appeared at public events. Meanwhile, the whole film industry experienced a tax earthquake. STA and its local authorities started to look into the tax records of all companies in the sector. The decade-old tax regulation of the industry was reformed. The general rate of tax was increased from 3–7% to about 20%.[18] Many individuals, including famous film directors and performers, were subject to huge sums of overdue tax payment and fines. Xinhua reported that by the end of the year, the total sum of overdue tax STA recovered from the film industry amounted to 11.747 billion RMB.[19]

Needless to say, Cui Yongyuan played a hugely important role in the case, which is telling of the practice and dynamics of contemporary investigative journalism in China. Individual users of social media first expose clues online, attracting traffic and drawing attention from the general public as widely as possible. Then, the mainstream media follow up and relevant government authorities intervene, leading eventually to the correction of wrongs and changes in people's lives. Although not every individual on social media has the influence of Cui, the case did show that in the digital era, investigative journalism conducted in the non-institutional domain is not only possible but also maybe even more powerful.

## Conclusion

Investigative journalism is an important component of journalism. By monitoring power, exposing corruption and wrongdoing, responding to social concerns and fighting against social injustice, investigative journalism worldwide is depicted as "custodian of conscience" and regarded as embodiment of the "watchdog" function of journalism. From the early 1980s, this journalism genre reappeared in China's media. Alongside economic reform and social liberalisation, it has experienced decades of rapid development. By promoting the public's right to know, correcting wrongs in society and holding power responsible and accountable, investigative journalism (IJ) has earned for its practitioners an elite status and contributed to the making of a new "golden age" of Chinese journalism. In recent years, however, influenced by technological, economic and political changes, investigative journalism has experienced difficulties. Although many hold a rather gloomy view of its future or think that digitalisation threatens traditional forms of IJ, there have also been opportunities for new IJ practices to grow.

Among the diverse forms being experimented with, especially noticeable is IJ practice based on social media and conducted by non-professionals. In the era of social media, Chinese citizens have more opportunities to express themselves and participate in public affairs than ever before; they can turn themselves into investigators. Cui Yongyuan's work is an illustration of the potential.

There are concerns. The new IJ is conducted by amateurs who do not necessarily have long-term commitment; this raises the matter of sustainability and continuity. It depends upon the individual's ability and will to mobilise public opinion, but they vary, and so will their influence. There is no established code of ethics governing their behaviour. Finally, there is the possibility of manipulation by special interests and lack of transparency. Nevertheless, as an experiment, investigative journalism based on social media is valuable, and its future development worthy of our attention and observation.

## Notes

1 Sun Zhigang 孙志刚 was a college graduate detained for being unable to produce his identity card when stopped by police. Soon he was found dead in detention. Two journalists from the local *Southern City Daily* 南方都市报 investigated. Their report of 25 April 2003 revealed that Sun had been beaten to death. The report caught public attention and eventually led to the repeal of the Detention Law 收容遣送制度.

2 Reported first by *Oriental Morning Post* 东方早报 on 11 September 2008 by its journalist Jian Guangzhou 简光洲, awarded a national journalism prize for it.

3 This case led to the downfall of 158 local officials, including the three leading executives. Investigations by Southern City Daily 南方都市报 journalist Long Zhi 龙志 were most influential.

4 CNNIC (Feb, 2019). Statistical report on China's internet development 中国互联网发展状况统计报告, available at: www.cac.gov.cn/2019-02/28/c_1124175677.htm

5 Wang uses this expression for the 1980s and 90s, but it was originally used by other authors to describe the 1920s–30s –ed.

6 The statistics are according to Cui Baoguo 崔保国 et. al. (2019) (ed.) *Report on Development of China's Media Industry* 中国传媒产业发展报告, Beijing: Tsinghua University Press.

7 These figures are calculated and summarized by the authors. Original statistics are based on GAPP's annually released *Analysis and Report on the Press Industry* 新闻出版产业

分析报告 from 2013 to 2019. The newest report was released on 28 August 2019, available at: www.chinaxwcb.com/info/555985

8 This is according to Chen Min 陈敏 (2016). Goodbye to the "Golden Age": A Discourse Analysis of 52 Journalists' Resignation from Traditional Media 告别"黄金时代" – 对52位传统媒体人离职告白的内容分析. *Shanghai Journalism Review* 新闻记者, No.2:16–28.

9 This is according to Chen Lian (2019). *Xi Jinping's 14 Speeches and 5 Congratulatory Letters about Journalism and Public Opinion* 习近平关于新闻舆论工作的14个讲话和5个贺信. *Journalism Lover* 新闻爱好者, 1:47–49.

10 The original article has been deleted, but many reprints remain visible on the Internet. One of the reprints is available at: www.freebuf.com/column/178589.html

11 This is according to Xinhua News Agency's reporting on 16 Oct. 2018. Available at: www.xinhuanet.com/politics/2018-10/16/c_129972780.htm

12 The report was conducted by Zhang Zhian 张志安 and Cao Yanhui 曹艳辉 (2017). *Report on the Changes of Ecosystem in Chinese Investigative Journalists in the Era of New Media* 新媒体环境下中国调查记者行业生态变化报告. *Modern Communication* 现代传播, 11:27–33.

13 Supervision by public opinion 舆论监督 is a Chinese expression in use since at least before the 1990s –ed.

14 The documentary is available at: www.youtube.com/watch?v=I3bzTRSK18c

15 This is according to an interview with Cui Yongyuan 崔永元 by a *Southern Weekend* 南方周末 journalist on 23 Jan. 2014. Available at: www.infzm.com/content/97730

16 This is according to another interview with Cui Yongyuan 崔永元 by a *Beijing News* 新京报 journalist on 22 Dec. 2013. Available at: www.bjnews.com.cn/inside/2013/12/22/298566.html

17 Cui also, rather wittily, exposed the fact that although the ministry advocated GMF for the nation, it prohibited it in its own ministerial staff canteen –ed.

18 This is according to reporting by Sina.com on 1 Dec. 2018. Available at: https://finance.sina.com.cn/china/2018-12-01/doc-ihmutuec5399873.shtml

19 This is according to reporting by Xinhua News Agency on 22 Jan. 2019. Available at: www.xinhuanet.com/ent/2019-01/22/c_1124026529.htm

## References

de Burgh, H. (2003a). Kings Without Crowns? The Re-Emergence of Investigative Journalism in China. *Media Culture & Society,* Vol. 25(6):801–820.

de Burgh, H. (2003b). *The Chinese Journalist: Mediating Information in the World's Most Populous Country.* London and New York: Routledge.

Wang, H. (2016a). *The Transformation of Investigative Journalism in China: From Journalists to Activists.* Lanham, MD: Lexington Books.

Wang, H. (2016b). Intellectual-Run-Newspapers Versus Statesman-Run-Newspapers: Wrestling Between Two Journalistic Paradigms in Pre-Reform China, 1949–1978. *Journalism Practice,* Vol. 10(5):663–679.

Wang, H. & Sparks, C. (2019). Chinese Newspaper Groups in the Digital Era: The Resurgence of the Party Press. *Journal of Communication,* Vol. 69(1):94–119.

# 10

# SYRIA

## The war and before

*Saba Bebawi*

Three young Syrian journalists, recently trained in investigative reporting, are 'drinking Arabic coffee and talking animatedly' in a café in Damascus. What are they talking about? What Arab people are worried about. '[N]ot only are these journalists talking, they are investigating and, more importantly, publishing'.

Such was the scene depicted by Rana Sabbagh, director of Arab Reporters for Investigative Journalism (ARIJ), in a famous article (Sabbagh, 21 June 2010), which I cite at the start of my *Investigative Journalism in the Arab World: Issues and Challenges* (Bebawi, 2016).

Alas, as I go on to note, Sabbagh wrote another article in December 2014 wherein he described that very place in which those three Syrian investigative journalists had not long before been exploring the possibilities of their new-found power as 'a graveyard for journalists' (Sabbagh, *Syria: Inside the World's Deadliest Place for Journalists*, 3 December 2014).

Before the 2011 civil war in Syria, there was a slow yet notable emergence of an investigative reporting movement which witnessed the publication of some investigations that dealt with grassroots issues. It was within that environment that those three Syrian journalists described previously were feeling a sense of power and momentum. Yet since the start of the conflict, such possibilities have been somewhat muted, thus reflecting the volatile politics of the region – a region Sabbagh describes as 'moving sands' (16 June 2013).

Not much has changed since 2011 in terms of the political, economic and social environment that journalists are operating under in Syria, and the conflict drags on. Yet there have been some individual attempts, notwithstanding the challenges the conflict offers, where we see a rise of an investigative reporting practice that is Syrian in nature. This chapter will cover this journey from the rise of investigative journalism in the Arab world more generally to the start of investigative reporting in Syria specifically before and during the conflict. This is based on the observation of training sessions; ARIJ Forum discussions from 2015–2019 and interviews with trainers, reporters, editors and board members of various organisations involved.

## Investigative journalism in Syria before the conflict

Investigative reporting in the Arab world is not new. In the past, there have been individual investigations that were carried out in the 1950s and 1960s by a few reporters such as Mohammad Hassanain Heikal, an Egyptian journalist who took the position of editor-in-chief of the Cairo-based newspaper *Al-Ahram* and who was focused on developing investigative reporting by training journalism graduates. Such initiatives were scattered across the Arab region and can be best described as individual and isolated and hence not sustainable.

However, now that some media organisations in Arab countries understand the importance investigative journalism can have in the region, they are making it a priority. This has been occurring across both big media organisations and small. Al Jazeera (AJ), for example, announced the establishment of its investigative unit in June 2010. The director general at the time, Wadah Khanfar, saw it as a major move for the network when other media institutions were stepping away from investigative reporting. He states that it was important to AJ because the established investigative unit was seen to 'not only to expand the breadth of . . . reporting, but also to drive further into stories for deeper narratives' (Press release, 29 June 2010). The unit dealt with both regional and international issues with a pan-Arab and global reach. However AJ's investigative unit ran a different operation to that of smaller local investigative units and programmes that operate within national boundaries. Many of these smaller units were established through the Arab Reporters for Investigative Journalism, launched in Amman, Jordan, as the first institutionalised investigative journalism training operation across the Arab world.

ARIJ was set up in 2015 through a Danish-Arab partnership, whereby a committee of Foreign Ministry officials from Denmark and members of the Danish Investigative Journalism Association came to Jordan to interview over a hundred journalists from Jordan, Syria and Lebanon. The Danish Ministry officials and the interviewed journalists came back with the suggestion to create a network through the establishment of ARIJ. The allocation of funds came through the Danish Parliament for ARIJ (Sabbagh, 16 June 2013). ARIJ was established as a pilot in Jordan, Syria and Lebanon and, as a result, a few Arab investigative units were set up with the assistance of ARIJ.

The emergence of investigative journalism was not a result of the Arab Spring. ARIJ was established before the protests of 2011. In fact, the development of investigative reporting in some Arab countries was more prominent prior to the Arab Spring. Elsewhere, on the other hand, investigative reporting was easier to pursue as a result of the political changes that came about due to the Arab spring. In Jordan, to illustrate, where protests did not lead to a leadership change but led to political reform, investigative journalism which only focused on social and environmental issues went on to address political matters such as corruption and election fraud. In Tunisia, investigative reporting was basic prior to the revolution in 2011 but flourished after the Arab Spring

(Bebawi, 2016). As for Syria, investigative reporting was slowly rising before the civil war but continued with difficulty during the conflict, as will be discussed in the following sections.

ARIJ began its operation in the Arab region in Jordan and then went on to expand to Syria, yet the possibility of training and doing investigative stories in Syria at the time was limited due to its strong political leadership. However, ARIJ was allowed to train investigative reporters in Syria as long as they avoided political investigations on corruption issues (Sabbagh, 16 June 2013). As a result, ARIJ began work in Syria and, according to Sabbagh, 'Syria was our success story' (16 June 2013). Sabbagh explains:

> We were very transparent, every time I go to Syria I would visit the Minister of Information and every month I would send him a report on what we were working on, and who was taking money. So all went well in Syria
>
> (16 June 2013).

Prior to the Syrian conflict, therefore, there were a number of investigations that were conducted as a result of a few Syrian journalists getting training by ARIJ in investigative journalism. One example of a successful investigation was conducted by a young journalist in Syria on local hospitals that were being negligent. At the time, trainers from ARIJ who were working with him were aware that this was a sensitive topic, yet they were curious to know whether the story could be published (Bebawi, 2016). The investigation was published and resulted in an intervention from the government, and a local commission was set up to deal with the matter. Anders Jerichow, who was an ARIJ board member, believes that this Syrian journalist 'paved the way for Syrian colleagues' (6 December 2014). In Syrian journalism, this story created a small 'media revolution', as suddenly Syrian reporters realised that they could hold official authorities accountable on local issues that affected the people (Jerichow, 6 December 2014). More examples such as this one came to light; however, the recent Syrian war which began with the Arab Spring protests in 2011 interrupted this briefly, but it slowly began to rise again during the conflict.

## Investigative journalism in Syria during the conflict

At the opening of a national workshop on investigative journalism, held on 25 May 2015, co-organised with the Syrian National Committee for the United Nations Educational, Scientific and Cultural Organization (UNESCO) promoting investigative journalism in Syria, Information Minister Omran al-Zoubi said: 'The extraordinary circumstances in Syria stress that investigative journalism is a need now more than any time before' in light of the various forms of misinformation and falsification that have targeted the Syrians since day one of the crisis (Said, 2015). He was especially focused on calling on

Syrian journalists to dive deep into social issues and touch on the daily needs and suffering of the Syrian people to better contribute to the efforts to protect citizens against the 'crisis opportunists' (Said, 2015). He had in February that year called for establishing an investigative journalism unit at every information and media institution to increase focus on social and daily life issues of concern to citizens (Said, 2015).

A few institutions have been established in Syria focused on investigative journalism which have set the basis for this. Notably, the Syrian Investigative Reporting for Accountability Journalism (SIRAJ) was launched in 2016. It was established by three journalists, Mohamed Bassiki, Ali Alibrahim and Ahmed Haj Hamdo, making it the first organisation in Syria for investigative journalism. Without funding, and working in exile, these journalists trained more than 30 local reporters on investigative journalism on a voluntary basis. Since then, SIRAJ has become a collective of 25 Syrian investigative reporters working from within and outside Syria, in cooperation with media partners from the Arab region who supported them with funding and publishing outlets. Its mission was to 'produce investigative reports about Syria by Syrian journalists, as well as to provide training to Syrian journalists, media activists and journalists on investigative methodologies and its development in the region and the world' (GIJN, 2019). They stress that investigations need to be carried out by Syrians themselves; Syrian reporters must have a local investigative voice.

As a training and publishing organisation, SIRAJ saw the need for stories and facts to be uncovered with the aim of enhancing accountability, revealing 'secrets in a professional and unbiased manner that are not linked to political or governmental bodies, especially after the country descended into anarchy and political, economic and social corruption increased' (GIJN, 2019). In a conversation with Majdoleen Hassan from the Global Investigative Journalism Network (GIJN), Mohamed Bassiki notes that:

> There was also a need for accurate and authoritative information about the situation in Syria for people living in the country as well as for a global audience. There wasn't a Syrian media organization that could accommodate Syrian investigative journalists able to write for publications inside Syria and publications outside of the country that could benefit from local expertise. It helps motivate local journalists to continue reporting. Death threats and the fear of arrest and imprisonment prompted a large number of Syrian journalists to flee to neighbouring countries and various places in the world, while others stayed inside the country. We worked on re-networking with those who are inside the country and those who are abroad.
>
> (GIJN, 2019)

Another notable player in the rise of investigative journalism in Syria is an organisation called Syria Direct, which is an organisation that focuses on independent and in-depth reporting. It was established in 2013 and aims to cover 'key military developments and track the country's shifting politics, province by province, to explain news as it unfolds, placing a particular focus on the individuals driving events on the ground' (Syria Direct, accessed 8 December 2019).

The establishment of such organisations that train and publish investigative journalism in Syria reflects a need to focus on establishing a tradition of this form of reporting, especially in times of conflict where issues such as chemical attacks and refugees are at the forefront of the conflict. Reports coming out of international news organisations often reflect global or national policies, whereas investigative reports coming out of local and independent Syrian journalists are more focused on covering issues that deal with grassroots issues of interest to the Syrian people. Such topics include smuggling, crimes conducted in Syrian refugee camps, corruption and bad conditions in hospitals, marriage of young girls and contamination within the environment (SIRAJ, 2019).

One example of an investigation during the Syrian civil war is one published by Daraj Media entitled '"Money" and "Propaganda Activities" Attract Children to "Al-Nusra" and Its Affiliates in Idlib', published 17 October 2018 (Daraj Media, 2018). As the title states, the investigation explores the different ways in which certain hardline Islamist factions recruit children in the Idlib area. By interviewing 'child' soldiers, the investigation found that '15 to 30 percent of all the children recruited [as soldiers] in Syria' were under the age of 15, tempting them with salaries and aid to their families (Daraj Media, 2018).

Another example of investigations carried out during the conflict is 'Homes of Syrian War Refugees Expropriated', by Mokhtar Al-Ibrahim and Ahmad Haj Hamdo, on Al Iqtisadi, 9 November 2014. An analysis of this investigation (Bebawi, 2016) looked into the impact this story had, which found that war profiteers were selling the properties of refugees who had fled the conflict using fraudulent documents. The reporters conducted the investigation by following and documenting the process the profiteers went through to sell the refugees' properties, tracking down the steps they would follow to forge a power of attorney (POA) which allowed them to sell the properties. The investigative process involved daily tours to Syrian districts, searching through records of civil and housing directorates, the Ministry of Justice and courts in the provinces of Damascus and its countryside and Aleppo (Al-Ibrahim and Hamdo, 23 December 2014). During this process, they identified the gaps in the legal system which facilitated the process of fraud and aided the war merchants in selling the refugees' properties. What they also uncovered was that there was a large number of judges and lawyers who had also been directly involved in this network of fraud.

Such topics are hard to investigate as a result of strict areas of control and mobility, barriers to access to information and lack of skills in investigative reporting in the first place. They require local reporters from the inside who know the system, the language and the issues that occur during conflict. Yet these local investigative reporters are not protected, and their investigations hit many roadblocks along the way. The following sections will discuss these challenges in relation to the processes of training and practice of investigative reporting in Syria through interviews conducted with Syrian investigative reporters and editors from SIRAJ and Syria Direct in November 2019.

## Training investigative journalism in Syria

Training in investigative reporting is still relatively new in Syria, and a lot of the skills that are used are either improvised on the spot or self taught. One example of this is one Syrian journalist who was not able to attend a training session in Jordan due to the conflict and instead read published investigative stories on the ARIJ website that included the reporter's and coach's notes and the ARIJ training manual. This provided the Syrian journalist with enough information to conduct an investigation on the homes of Syrian war refugees that were expropriated, discussed previously. This Syrian journalist also learnt from one of his colleagues who had attended an ARIJ training session (Bebawi, 2016). Manar Rachwani, editor-in-chief of Syria Direct, notes that investigative reporting is new and that a model of investigative journalism that suits and works in the region is therefore necessary:

> When we are talking about investigative reporting we are still talking about something new in the Arab world except when it comes maybe to having the necessary skills and acquiring the knowledge that is needed to produce high quality reports, and at the same time we talk about addressing some difficulties and overcoming problems that could face the journalist.
>
> (Rachwani, 22 November 2019)

However, when training is provided, there are also some issues in the delivery of training because a traditional way of teaching is more common in the region. This has been noted in previous observations (Bebawi, 2016), where trainers and university lecturers have not necessarily worked as investigative reporters themselves and hence find it hard to provide practical-based training. Yet even after training is provided, there are not many opportunities for trained reporters to practice investigative reporting, so the skills are never truly developed. Rachwani comments on this:

> What I noticed in the Arab World [is] that we don't understand the difference between training and lecturing. Many trainers till now go to the class . . . and they start giving us a talk or a lecture. It's not like about practice, it's not like about exercises and without practice people not only won't acquire the necessary skills from the beginning but

also, they might forget. Even if they managed to follow every step, and comprehend and to remember. But also after a while, without practicing, they usually forget. So this is one of the issues.

(22 November 2019)

Another issue that was noted during training sessions that were attended by the author is that trainers are usually from a non-Arab background or even a non-Syrian background, which makes it hard for the trainers to understand the intricacies, challenges and nature of doing investigative reporting specific to Syria, especially under conflict. Walid Al Noufal, from Syria Direct, notes that trainers are not Syrian, so they do not know enough about Syrian issues, and they also do not know enough about the nature of the situation within conflict areas in Syria (23 November 2019). This makes it very hard for Syrian journalists to indeed know how to deal with challenges and obstacles along the way, especially when conducting training from a Western perspective and narrative. Al Noufal notes that there needs to be more focus when training in Syria particularly, and in the Arab world in general, on developing skills that are a mix of a Western and Arab model. He also stresses the need for trainers to be from the same region the trainees are working in (Al Noufal, 23 November 2019).

However, even in non-conflict zones, Arab journalism has slowly been detaching from traditional methods of reporting, yet such traditional forms of doing journalism still remain very strongly in place when training for investigative reporting that requires a more detailed methodological and systematic approach. Ahmed Haj Hamdo, an investigative reporter for SIRAJ, talks in Arabic about what needs to be developed when adopting a systematic approach that works in an Arab environment of reporting:

> We have to adopt systematic work to conduct investigations. The best we can do is to train Arab journalists that investigative reporting is not an ad hoc approach – we need to have a clear plan on how to approach the investigation like who will our sources be, what angle are we investigating from, what information is available to us, what are our minimum or maximum expectations. A systematic approach to investigative reporting will ensure the development of Arab investigative reporting that can be described as more professional using evidence that is documented. To add, we also need to develop training on how to use open sources such as social media – we need to learn how to utilise them. We also need to learn more about media ethics, how to deal with war survivors from trauma which are sensitive issues in our area.
>
> (23 November 2019).

One other aspect that was noted in training sessions attended by the author is that it was difficult for reporters to understand the difference between fact and emotion. Investigative stories were built on a particular issue that journalists were passionate about, and whilst this makes for a strong and compelling driver towards uncovering facts, it could also be an obstacle to focusing on new findings or changing the angles available that come up during the investigation process. Trainers found themselves constantly having to remind trainees that they need to put their emotions aside and instead focus on dealing with facts and data that are provided to them as a basis for their investigations. Hamdo says in relation to this:

> The skills we need to develop as Arab investigative journalists are learning how to plan and develop a story, and not just go out and report based on emotion since it is a systematic form of journalism. Also journalists need to develop technical skills for storytelling such multimedia and podcasts. We also need skills to create infographics so if data becomes available then Arab reporters can ensure that their investigations are evidenced with infographics, statistics and tables.
>
> (23 November 2019)

One notable problem facing training investigative journalists is that there are very few training sources and learning materials in Arabic. Trainees not only find it hard to access these sources but also find it difficult to understand other international exemplars of investigative reports. Rachwani says in relation to this:

> It's so important in the case of the Arab world maybe being familiar with the international sources and this requires English language in some cases. It is not a secret that the quality of education is deteriorating all over the world, so also we have sometimes to be aware and know about the basic math related to the data we are dealing with.
>
> (22 November 2019)

A few training organisations, such as ARIJ, set out to provide English [language] training courses specific to investigative reporters and also online English-language material for those who could not attend these courses in person, which is a clear indication that there is an awareness of the need to address access to English courses. Having said that, there have been a few attempts to provide translations to Arabic of sources and material that could be of use to Arab investigative journalists.

## Practicing investigative journalism in Syria

The practice of investigative journalism has its separate set of challenges to that of training, although there are commonalities. One specific challenge Syrian reporters face when working on investigations is adapting to obstacles they face as a result of the conflict. This presents Syrian investigative reporters with an added layer of difficulty to what they are already enduring as Arab journalists. Al Noufal, from Syria Direct, notes that in the Arab world, there are differences between conflict zones and regions that have more stability, so the nature of investigative work would differ between the two areas. In countries with stability, it would be easier for the investigative journalist to go to the field and gather information and double-check the data and even gain access to government documents. Working in conflict zones is harder, he says, because reporters are a target and because they are working from afar. He states that '[m]ost investigative reporters are working outside conflict zones – even the reporters working from the inside, their mobility is limited as they are facing more obstacles to their work' (Al Noufal, 23 November 2019). According to Hamdo, co-founder of SIRAJ, the right to access information is one of those obstacles. He states in Arabic:

> In conflict areas we cannot reach every part and there is a lot of information that is restricted from us. When we work on money tracking, company contracts or agreements, as a result of my training in data analysis, I can now access some information. At this stage in the Arab world we still do not have access to information. . . . We need a law or method that allows us to get data or documents we can actually obtain. FOI laws exist but on paper only, and when we need to apply it, it is futile.
>
> (23 November 2019)

Another issue is the need for the protection of journalists. There have been a few funded initiatives for increasing awareness of Arab journalists of how to protect themselves in conflict zones, yet war zones in the region do not necessarily provide 'the full scope of protection granted to civilians under international humanitarian law' since 'Article 79 formally states that journalists engaged in dangerous professional missions in zones of armed conflict are civilians' (ICRC, 2019). Hamdo stresses the need to protect journalists in Syria:

> In Syria, journalists are killed, journalists are jailed, journalists are kidnapped in exchange of monetary ransoms, journalists are shamed, attacked with hate speech against them and their families, journalists are subject to untrue accusations when people don't like what they journalist says or does. How can we ask an Arab journalist to operate at a professional standard if we cannot guarantee some level of protection?
>
> (23 November 2019)

There is also the global issue of fake news that is affecting media around the world, and it becomes even a bigger issue in conflict zones such as Syria. The number of fabricated stories on Syria circulating the internet make it very hard for Syrian investigative reporters to operate within an environment of truth-telling. Rachwani states in regard to this:

> The most important part also, because of the internet, there is widespread belief in conspiracy theory in the Arab world – we need to be careful about this information, about tracking the sources of the information, and how we can verify, triangulate, not to be the victim of rumours, lies, etc. Especially now we are talking about well-produced lies.
>
> (22 November 2019)

The stories behind the stories laying out the journey that journalists go through to get accurate data and facts is reflective of the reality of the conflict, so not only is publishing stories a major impediment to initiating an investigation in the first place, but the dangers along the way could also act as a deterrent. This is a known fact – so nothing new there. However, one surprise is learning about the degree to which society itself is a major obstacle. Rachwani comments on this:

> In addition to the political and security issues, we have the social concerns. Not every issue can be addressed sometimes for religious obstacles, social problems, so we have to be – I would say – smarter. We have to be more creative in addressing these issues: how to show we are submitting a problem that needs to be solved and needs to be addressed instead of challenging the society as we challenge their values or their beliefs. Especially these are deeply rooted beliefs and religious beliefs in general.
>
> (22 November 2019)

Society has therefore been a hindrance to investigative reporters in many countries surrounding Syria, such as Jordan, where people see what the conflict has done to the Syrian people and therefore do not support any form of uncovering the truth, as investigative reporters are seen to be rocking the boat.

Generally, Arab investigative reporters aim to facilitate change and achieve impact, and in some cases in conflict areas, such as Syria and Iraq, investigative journalism can address war-related issues and set a base for building possibilities for political reform post-conflict. Al Noufal, from Syria Direct, suitably concludes in his interview that in conflict zones, there are many violations to human rights, and there is also a lot of corruption. Daily news reporting is often not sufficient to uncover these violations, so investigative reporting has the ability to uncover these violations and corruption. He states:

'[T]here is limited investigative journalism practice in Syria so this is what made me become an investigative reporter: in order to document the violations and corruption cases taking place' (Al Noufal, 23 November 2019). This explains why, despite the challenges facing Syrian journalists in general and investigative reporters specifically, there remains a determination to uncover as many stories as possible in conflict zones.

## References

Al-Ibrahim, Mokhtar and Hamdo, Ahmad Haj (2014) *Homes of Syrian War Refugees Expropriated*, ARIJ Website, 9 November [Online] http://arij.net/en/homes-syrian-war-refugees-expropriated, accessed 23 December 2014

Al Noufal, Walid (2019) *Reporter at Syria Direct*, Interview with Author, Amman, Jordan, 23 November 2019

Bebawi, Saba (2016) *Investigative Journalism in the Arab World: Issues and Challenges.* London: Palgrave Macmillan.

Daraj Media (2018) ' "Money" and "Propaganda Activities" Attract Children to "Al-Nusra" and Its Affiliates in Idlib', 17 October [Online] https://sirajsy.net/money-propaganda-activities-attract-children-al-nusra-affiliates-idlib/, accessed 15 February 2020

GIJN (2019) 'Starting up in Syria: Investigative Journalism in One of the World's Most Dangerous Countries', in *SIRAJ* [Online] https://sirajsy.net/starting-up-in-syria-investigative-journalism-in-one-of-the-worlds-most-dangerous-countries/, accessed 2 December 2019

Hamdo, Ahmad Haj (2019) *SIRAJ Co-Founder and Editor*, Interview with Author, Amman, Jordan, 23 November 2019

ICRC (2019) 'Protection of Journalists', in *International Committee for the Red Cross (ICRC) Handbook* [Online] https://casebook.icrc.org/case-study/protection-journalists, accessed 12 December 2019

Jerichow, Anders (2014) *ARIJ Board Member*, Interview with Author, Amman, Jordan, 6 December 2014

Press Release (2010) *Al Jazeera Network Launches a New Unit for Investigative Journalism*, 29 June [Online] www.facebook.com/notes/al-jazeera-english/al-jazeera-network-launches-a-new-unit-for-investigativejournalism/402479163262, accessed 9 January 2015

Rachwani, Manar (2019) *Editor in Chief of Syria Direct*, Interview with Author, Amman, Jordan, 22 November 2019

Sabbagh, Rana (2010) 'With the Help of the NGO ARIJ, Syrian Investigative Journalists Are Revealing Underreported Social Issues That Concern the Man in the Street', in *ARIJ News*, 21 June 2010 [Online] http://en.arij.net/news/with-the-help-of-the-ngo-arij-syrian investigative-journalists-are-revealing-underreported-social-issues-that-concern-the-man-in-the-street/, accessed 11 May 2015

Sabbagh, Rana (2013) *Executive Director of Arab Reporters for Investigative Journalism*, Interview with Author, Amman, Jordan, 16 June 2013

Sabbagh, Rana (2014) 'Syria: Inside the World's Deadliest Place for Journalists', in *Global Investigative Journalism Network*, 3 December [Online] http:// gijn.org/2014/12/03/syria-inside-the-worlds-deadliest-place-for-journalists/, accessed 12 May 2015

Said, Haifa (2015) 'Information Ministry Vows Support to Investigative Journalists to Fight Crisis Opportunists', in *Syrian Arab News Agency (SANA)* [Online] www.sana.sy/en/?p=42241, accessed 1 December 2019

SIRAJ (2019) *Investigations* [Online] https://sirajsy.net/category/investigations/, accessed 5 December 2019

Syria Direct (2019) *About Us* [Online] https://syriadirect.org/pages/about-us/, accessed 8 December 2019

# 11

# SURVIVAL IN TURKEY

*Selin Bucak*

Turkey's history is rife with examples of journalists being arrested, attacked, jailed or exiled. This has not changed under the government of President Recep Tayyip Erdoğan, although his Justice and Development Party (AKP) came to power in 2002 promising democracy and freedom for all, including journalists.

The initial years of the AKP government aside, Turkey has become the biggest jailer of journalists in the world since 2010. As of June 2019, there were 98 journalists convicted, 90 arrested and 167 wanted, according to the Stockholm Centre for Freedom (2019).

"This is the most oppressive period in the history of the Turkish Republic," said Prof. Dr. Emre Kongar, academic, author and journalist at *Cumhuriyet* newspaper. "There is a pressure on the media that has not been seen in any other period, including following the military coups".

> First of all, [the media is controlled] through outlets that they [the government] bought themselves or made their allies purchase. Those journalists outside of these groups are under immense pressure. They are constantly being judged because of the work they do and the articles they write, and they are being punished. Following most events, the government is also instituting a reporting ban, which is enforced by the courts. The government has direct control over how events are presented to the public.
>
> (Kongar, 2019)

Fear of litigation, violence and financial pressure have all been used by the government to silence journalism. In this climate, investigative journalism has been stifled, at a time when it is needed most. However, as it has always happened in Turkish history, a number of investigative journalists are continuing to defy the authorities.

Undeterred, but under constant pressure and with a diminishing number of free and independent news outlets, some have turned to book publishers to disseminate their work.

For Kongar, books have become the saviours of investigative journalists in Turkey.

> During this period, investigative journalism becomes even more important, because news is being hidden from the public. Because they are hidden, what's happening in the background is not very clear. That's why books are becoming increasingly important. When there is this much pressure on the media, books where journalists can expose wrongdoing become important. They can only do this by publishing books.
>
> (2019)

Journalist and academic Haluk Şahin has also highlighted this phenomenon, and in his view, "a book can become a lifeboat for an investigative journalist. That's why the investigator also needs to be a good writer" (Ş2012, p. 59).

Although the current desire to control the media has shone a spotlight on press freedoms, it is far from the first time Turkish investigative journalists have had to work under oppression. The periods following the three military coups that punctuated the last century also saw freedom of expression limited by the state.

In the 1990s, there was a clear rise in violence against journalists, with Turkey ranking as the second most dangerous place to report from. The first was the Bosnian civil war (Deutsche Welle, 2019).

Therefore, to understand how investigative journalism evolved in Turkey and why there is still an opportunity for it to survive and thrive under the current government, we need to consider its origins.

## The development of investigative journalism

Since the founding of the republic in 1923, Turkey has been ruled by numerous authoritarian regimes. Even outside of the military coups – there were three by 1985 – life has always been difficult for journalists. Successive governments adopted policies to limit the power and reach of the press. The closure of papers and magazines has always been commonplace.

Following the introduction of a multi-party system in Turkey in 1946, the media started evolving, giving a platform to different voices. New publications that held contrary views to the establishment began springing up. This freedom proved short lived, however, with the government starting to interfere following the elections in 1950 that brought the Democrat Party to power.

Between 1946 and the military coup of 1960, one of the most important publications was a weekly magazine called *Akis* – set up in 1954 by Metin Toker. Taking *Time* magazine in the West as its inspiration, *Akis* was the first political weekly in Turkey. It became a platform for investigative journalists, and over time, it increasingly took a critical stance against the ruling Democrat Party (Kurt Öncel, 2013, p. 94).

In 1960, the government, which was becoming increasingly oppressive, shut down *Akis*. Many of its journalists were sent to prison. But the magazine had already made an impact. Under Toker's leadership, journalists at the magazine had become both researchers and writers (Şahin, 2012). University graduates, who had doctorates and knew different methods of research, became journalists.

The military intervention on 27 May 1960 was the first coup in Turkey. It overthrew the government of Adnan Menderes, who was seen as becoming increasingly authoritarian. A National Unity Committee was established, composed of military officers, and members of the Democrat Party were put in prison.

In 1961, a new constitution was prepared, which was adopted following a referendum held on 9 July (Kaya, 2011). Some consider this the most democratic constitution Turkey has ever had.

> The constitution of 1961 introduced significant innovations. It strengthened the supremacy of the constitution by establishing a constitutional court, effectively restricting the powers of the elected branches of government, and strengthening the safeguards of fundamental rights and liberties through the rule of law.
>
> (Kaya, 2011, p. 1)

As a consequence, the 1960s saw the rise of critical thinking in Turkish society. With the freedoms granted by the new constitution, the public was exposed to new ideas. Journalists became investigators. Abdi Ipekçi, a prominent journalist who was later murdered in 1979, published his book called *İhtilalin İçyüzü* (The Inside Story of the Revolution) in 1965, looking into what led to the military coup, its execution and the National Unity Committee that was formed in its aftermath.[1]

## The case of the fictitious furniture

Although the relatively liberal atmosphere created in the 1960s under the new constitution was interrupted by another military intervention in 1971, with negative repercussions on press freedom, a new coalition government came to power in 1974, and in time, all this culminated in what is considered the first genuine work of investigative journalism in Turkey (Ertem, 2018, p. 658). In 1975, a series of articles was published exposing fraud by the nephew of the prime minister at the time. These articles were later turned into a book.

The term "investigative journalism" came into wider use following the publication of this book by journalists Uğur Mumcu and Altan Öymen. Entitled *Mobilya Dosyası* (The Furniture File), it exposed a fictitious furniture export operation conducted by the nephew of Prime Minister Süleyman Demirel.

At the time, the government was trying to incentivise foreign trade, offering a 75% tax refund on certain products in a bid to attract hard currency. While working at Anka Ajans – a news agency – Öymen and Mumcu received a tip-off phone call alerting them to a fraud involving furniture that was being exported by Yahya Demirel – the nephew. Demirel had set up an export business that was supposedly selling high-end furniture to countries such as Italy, Libya and Cyprus. However, the sales were really being made to fictitious companies in Geneva and Liechtenstein. Öymen, after travelling to Switzerland and tracking down the addresses at which they were registered, discovered that these companies did not exist. Öymen and Mumcu found out that Demirel's company was in fact buying up low-quality furniture and wood in Ankara on the cheap. The company then booked the fake sales and raked in hefty tax refunds from the bogus operation.

"We wrote all these articles about it and they kept saying they were lies. They filed lawsuits against us so we turned all our articles into a book to give to the courts," said Öymen (2019).

Both Öymen and Mumcu were acquitted.

Mumcu's name has now become synonymous with investigative journalism in Turkey. Following the publication of the *Furniture Files*, he went on to pen numerous investigative pieces. Sadly, like many other journalists in Turkey, he became the target of a violent attack. He was assassinated by a bomb placed in his car outside his home in Ankara in 1993 (*Milliyet*, 1993). His work established investigative journalism as a respected profession in Turkey. Following his death, his family set up the Uğur Mumcu Investigative Journalism Foundation.

His daughter, Özge Mumcu, said:

> After my father was murdered, our family founded the Uğur Mumcu Investigative Journalism Foundation . . . to encourage young people who are concerned about social problems and have ideals of hard work and humanity to enter the field of journalism.
>
> (2011)

## The changing media landscape in the 1980s

On the morning of 12 September, 1980, there was an announcement on the radio, heard everywhere in Turkey. The military once again had taken control of the government and declared a state of emergency. The liberal constitution of 1961 was suspended, to be replaced by a new one in 1982. Although the new constitution was voted for by 92% of the population, the electorate gave it their backing under threat of imprisonment for abstention (T24, 2017).

In the aftermath of the coup, 517 people received death sentences, 50 of which were carried out. Six hundred fifty thousand people were apprehended, 210,000 cases were opened and 30,000 people were fired from their jobs for being "unfavourable". One hundred seventy-one were killed during torture, and 300 in total died under suspicious circumstances. Journalists received prison sentences totalling 3,315 years and 6 months (T24, 2015).

The new regime had journalists firmly in its sights, with 3 shot dead and 31 imprisoned, and 927 publications were banned. Underlining the scale of the clampdown, around 40 tonnes of newspapers, magazines and books were burned by the government.

The military regime ended with the elections of 1983, which brought to power Turgut Özal, who would remain prime minister until 1989 and then become president, a position he held until his death in 1993.

The government of Özal oversaw a period of considerable change in the media landscape. While it sought to limit the freedom of the press as much as possible, the regime's economic policies gave rise to a burgeoning new class of tycoons who would go on to monopolise the ownership of news outlets. This was a development that would determine the shape of the Turkish media for years to come.

In his book on investigative journalism, Haluk Şahin recounts a conversation with prominent journalist Emin Çölaşan in 1990, when he talked about his work in the 80s.

> Both Uğur Mumcu and I came to journalism from other fields, bring-ing in new concepts. Between 1977 and 1980, when the government slacked off, there was a move from bureaucracy to journalism. Most of these were politically driven. A journalist had to be very careful not to be manipulated. And then the 12th of September happened and investigative journalism stopped. Everything was secret, nothing was leaking. And we couldn't use whatever did leak. But after 1984 there was a real explosion.
>
> (2012, p. 58)

Prior to 1980, newspapers had been owned by families who had been in jour-nalism for generations. After 1980, they started coming under the ownership of businessmen who were new to the media. Aydın Doğan, who bought *Milliyet* newspaper from Ercüment Karacan in 1979, was one high-profile example. Prior to this acquisition, Doğan had mainly been involved in the energy sector and had import and export businesses (Adaklı, 2003).

After the purchase of *Milliyet*, Doğan went on to set up DTV – later Kanal D – in partnership with another conglomerate, Doğuş Group. By 2003, the Doğan Group owned eight newspapers, numerous magazines, four TV chan-nels, four radio channels, a distribution business, internet sites, a music pro-ducer and a chain of bookstores (Adaklı, 2003).

Doğan's influence on the media landscape has been significant, but his has been just one empire. The Çukurova Group, owned by the Karamehmet family; the Uzan family's eponymous Uzan Group; the Bilgin family's Sabah

Group and Doğuş Group, founded by Ayhan Şahenk, have also been influential businesses in media.

The rise of the conglomerates led to the monopolisation of the industry as a whole. This was especially true when it came to distribution channels. By 2003, there were three main distribution channels, owned by the Doğan, Uzan and Bilgin families. Any independent organisations were at the mercy of the three giants who controlled distribution (Adaklı, 2003).

In an interview with *Hürriyet*, Professor Bilge Yeşil, author of "Media in New Turkey: The Origins of an Authoritarian Neoliberal State", said: "The 1980s were really important because they set the stage for the new commercialized media environment and the political-economic relationships between the government, state institutions, and the military" (Armstrong, 2016).

From the mid-1980s, media assets were turned into empires. The heads of these empires had the means to invest in and import the latest technology, and the technological developments at the time paved the way for investigative journalism to find a new outlet: television.

## The violence of the 1990s

The early 90s were peppered with violence. In 1992, 12 journalists were assassinated in Turkey, the highest number in any country that year (Committee to Protect Journalists, n.d.). The *Helsinki Watch Report* on this the following year wrote:

> During 1992, scores of journalists, editors and writers were beaten, interrogated, tortured, charged, tried and sometimes convicted for what they had written, edited or published in Turkey. Most were charged under the very broad Anti-Terror Law for such offenses as "criticizing" or "insulting" the president, public officers, Mustafa Kemal Atatürk or the military; printing "anti-military propaganda"; "praising an action proscribed as a crime"; "praising a terrorist organization"; or spreading "separatist propaganda".
>
> (United Nations High Commissioner for Refugees, 1993)

In 1993, Mumcu was killed. The following year, the office and printing house of the pro-Kurdish newspaper *Özgür Ülke* were bombed, killing one and injuring dozens.

In another incident, a bomb was placed in the car of Ahmet Taner Kışlalı, former culture minister who was also a professor and a writer, resulting in his death in 1999 (Hürriyet, 1999). Many others were killed, and investigations to find those responsible are still said to be continuing.

Those years were considered one of the darkest decades for journalism in Turkey. However, even in the face of constant threats of violence, investigative journalism was able to thrive. The rise of private TV channels looking for sensational content to drive ratings at the time also aided investigative journalists who needed a new channel of distribution.

Şahin wrote that the 90s were also a period marked by rampant corruption, which provided plenty of material to write about (2012, pp. 68–69). He was working as editor of a TV program called *Arena* at the time, alongside Uğur Dündar. *Arena* was famous for its investigations, and Şahin says that the show used to be inundated with calls from whistleblowers. This was a time when private TV channels could broadcast hard-hitting journalistic pieces.

> It was discovered that news and debate increased ratings. Journalism was freer than it had ever been or would ever be. . . . Turkey believed in the importance of seeming democratic to the European Union. This was an exciting and fruitful period for an investigative journalist. And it was a sad and shocking period for citizens.
>
> (*Hürriyet*, 1999)

*Arena* carried out investigations into a number of high-profile scandals that rocked society. The team unmasked an international organ mafia, revealed that Alzheimer patients at a care home in Istanbul were being beaten up and found out that numerous historical artefacts stored in Dolmabahçe Palace in Istanbul were being left to rot.

## Justice and Development Party and Erdoğan

There are many reasons for the rise of Erdoğan and the AKP. One reason for such strong support for a new and unknown party at the time of the 2002 elections was the hope of a bright new era.

In the aftermath of the election, *The Economist* wrote:

> In Turkey's general election on November 3rd, for the first time in 15 years one party seized an absolute majority: the conservative Justice and Development Party (AKP) led by Recep Tayyip Erdoğan. And it is a party which, though non-Islamist, has clear Islamic roots. But above all it was seen as a clean party (its Turkish initials, A and K, spell *ak*, white or clean). A wave of hope has swept a nation long hostage to economic mismanagement, repressive laws and corrupt politicians.
>
> (2002)

That wave of hope is now long gone.

In the decade and a half since Erdoğan came to power as prime minister, he has been systematically undermining the independence of the press. In recent years, his efforts to curtail free speech have become increasingly blatant, with Turkey becoming the world's biggest prison for journalists.

On numerous occasions, Erdoğan has targeted individual journalists, creating a climate of fear for reporters (Ahval, 2019). They have been subject to censorship, arrests, lawsuits, financial pressures and violence.

In 2018, at a press conference with French President Emmanuel Macron, Erdoğan described journalists as "gardeners" of terrorism (Deutsche Welle, 2018).

Investigative journalists who revealed corruption in Erdoğan's government, ties to shady organisations and dubious practices by the so-called "deep state" have all been accused of supporting terrorism and imprisoned.

In 2011, seven journalists were arrested, accused of being part of a plot to overthrow the government. They were said to be members of a clandestine group called Ergenekon which was allegedly trying to organise a coup against Erdoğan's government.

Investigative journalists Nedim Şener and Ahmet Şık were among those detained. The allegations were made by prosecutors who had links to the Gülen movement – a religious group led by cleric Fethullah Gülen, a former ally of Erdoğan who was later blamed for being behind the failed coup of 2016 (AP News, 2018).[2] The irony that the Ergenekon investigation was opened because of Şık's investigation into the organisation which had been published in 2007 in *Nokta* magazine was not lost on observers (PEN International, 2011).[3]

At the time, Şık also wrote a book called *The İmam's Army* which investigated the infiltration of the police and the judiciary by Gülen's followers. In a Q&A with the Committee to Protect Journalists while in prison in Istanbul, Şık said he was arrested because of this book, which had not even been published yet (*Hürriyet*, 2011). Erdoğan, who was prime minister at the time, compared the book to a bomb (Bianet, 2011).

Şık and Şener were eventually freed in March, 2012. Şık was later arrested again in 2016, this time for propaganda for the outlawed Kurdistan Workers' Party (PKK) as well as the Gülen group, which is now called the Fethullah Terrorist Organisation (FETO).

Just like Şık, Şener also investigated the Gülen organisation, among other issues. In 2010, he was tried over a book he wrote implicating Turkish security forces in the 2007 murder of Turkish-Armenian journalist Hrant Dink. He later wrote another book on Dink's murder called *Red Friday – Who Broke Dink's Pen?* and *Fetullah Gülen and the Gülen Community in Ergenekon Documents*. Şener said that he believed his arrest was linked to his books on Dink (Mahoney, 2011).

Pelin Ünker is another investigative journalist who has been prosecuted for her work. Ünker worked on the *Paradise Papers* investigation and wrote about the two companies in Malta that Binali Yıldırım, prime minister from 2016 to 2018, owned with his sons. Ünker was sentenced to more than a year in prison in January 2019 for defamation and insult (Borger, 2019). In May, the appeals court dismissed the prison sentence; however, it upheld the more than $1,000 fine that *Cumhuriyet* had to pay (Fitzgibbon, 2019).

Alongside this suppression of free speech through more traditional methods, such as imprisonment, Erdoğan and his supporters have adopted what in many ways is the blunter tactic of seizing ownership of the media over the last few years. Following the sale of Doğan Group's media assets to Erdoğan ally Demirören Group in 2018, approximately 97% of Turkish media has come under direct or indirect control of the government (Bucak, 2018).

Through such control, red lines were drawn. Bilge Yeşil describes it perfectly:

> If you look at 2007–08, that was a key turning point. The media back then learned that certain corruption or bribery scandals must not be covered, particularly after huge tax fines levelled against Doğan Media Group for reporting on the issue. Then again, during the Ergenekon and Balyoz coup plot trials, the media learned that there was another red line regarding the military and the Gülen movement. In 2013 with the Gezi Park protests new red lines emerged, and after the corruption scandal of December 2013 more red lines emerged. Now with the coup attempt there are even more red lines.
>
> (Armstrong, 2016)

Doğan Group's media empire had previously been a platform for journalists who were critical of Erdoğan's regime for years. Now there are only a handful of independent papers left who will publish the work of investigative journalists.

However, they have been struggling. *Cumhuriyet*, the independently owned newspaper famous for publishing investigative pieces exposing government corruption, was one of the few publications left that featured opposition voices. In 2018, 13 of its staff members received prison sentences for supporting PKK and FETO. The paper was already in a difficult financial position, struggling to keep its doors open since 2011, when it was denied public advertising (BBC News, 2018).

In September 2018, a controversial court ruling resulted in a new board of directors being appointed. Alev Coşkun, who was a prosecution witness in the trial against the *Cumhuriyet* journalists, was appointed as chairman of the Cumhuriyet Foundation. The changes led to many of the title's journalists, including Editor-in-Chief Murat Sabuncu, being fired (Ahval, 2018).

## Conclusion

There is no denying that investigative journalism under the current regime in Turkey is incredibly difficult. Even if journalists are able to find sources, unearth documents and discover wrongdoing, there are not that many places that will publish their articles. If they do find an outlet, they are faced with immediate persecution. They work under the threat of violence and prosecution from the government.

However, it is not impossible. Book publishers have thrown a lifeline to investigative journalists. There are numerous examples of this.

In early 2019, a book was published called *Metastaz*. It was written by two journalists, Barış Pehlivan and Barış Terkoğlu. The book is an investigation into the infiltration of the Turkish government by FETO and other religious organisations. It looks into events both before and after the coup attempt in 2016 and how other organisations are filling the gaps left by FETO (Haberler, 2019).

The same publishing house, Kırmızı Kedi (Red Cat), recently published the English translation of another book written by Haluk Şahin. The Turkish version was published in 2016. In the book, called *Hate Trap – The Anatomy of a Forgotten Assassination*, Şahin looks into the assassination of two Turkish diplomats by an Armenian-American in the United States in 1973 following recently declassified FBI documents (AVIM, 2019). He then goes on to discuss the connection between the killing of the Turkish diplomats and the assassination of Armenian-Turkish journalist Hrant Dink in 2007.

In addition to such journalists who are defying the government's suppression and finding ways around its censorship, there are organisations that are actively training a new generation of investigative journalists in Turkey. One we already mentioned is the Uğur Mumcu Investigative Journalism Foundation (Umag).

Another is the Objective program that was launched by international consultancy Niras and BBC Media Action in 2013 across several countries, including Turkey. In its first year, 48 journalists responded to a call for submissions, with more than 50 projects (Platform 24, n.d.).

The works selected to receive grants in 2018 were:

- Desislava Şenay Martinova Öztürk, "Bonsai's Journey in Turkey"
- Dicle Baştürk, "KanalIstanbul: An International Crisis in the Making"
- Merve Diltemiz Mol, "The LGBTI Movement in State of Emergency"
- Uygar Gültekin, "Can the Assyrians Return to Their Homeland?"
- Bekir Avcı, "From Satellite Dishes to Wireless"
- Tamer Arda Erşin, "The Impact of Asbestos Release from Demolition of Buildings on the Environment and Public Health"

Repression of journalists and especially of investigative journalists in Turkey has been going on since the foundation of the Turkish Republic, save for short periods of relative freedom, and has become almost ingrained in the political culture of the country. Consequently, it is not likely to end any time soon.

As T24 columnist Metin Münir said:

> The better a journalist is in Turkey, the more likely he or she will be fired. Ahmet Şık is the proof of this. If he was in the US, he would have received a Pulitzer. In Turkey, he was fired from his job and sent to prison.
>
> (2017)

## Notes

1 After the adoption of the multi-party state in Turkey, there were intermittent bursts of investigative journalism. These all impacted the way the media was viewed by the public and bolstered the confidence of journalists overall. However, it wasn't until the 1970s when the practice and the terminology came into wide use.

2 Fethullah Gülen is a cleric who has been living in self-imposed exile in the United States since 1999. His organisation operates schools and charities in multiple countries. However, they have also been known to have control over the judiciary and police in Turkey. Gülen has had a friendly relationship with several Turkish leaders in the past. He and Erdoğan were also previously allies. However, during the Gezi protests that took place in Turkey in 2013, cracks in that relationship began to appear. On May 2016, Erdoğan officially listed the Gülen organisation as a terrorist group known as FETO. On 15 July 2016, there was an attempted coup in Turkey. The efforts of the military men who were involved in the attempt were quashed overnight, and Erdoğan was quick to blame Gülen for it. Following the coup attempt, the government declared a state of emergency, which led to mass arrests.

3 The draft book was seized by the government in 2011, which claimed it was a document of the Ergenekon terror organisation. A version of the book was, however, eventually published in November 2011 under the title "oooKitap" ("oooBook"). It was put together by 125 journalists, activists and academics.

## References

Adaklı, G. (2003). Hakim Medya Gruplarının Kısa Tarihi. [online] *Bianet – Bağımsız İletişim Ağı*. Available at: http://bianet.org/bianet/medya/27919-hakim-medya- [Accessed 29 May 2019].

Ahval (2018). Cumhuriyet's New Board Sacks Editor-in-Chief, Reverses Editorial Policy | Ahval. [online] *Ahval*. Available at: https://ahvalnews.com/turkish-media/cumhuriyets-new-board-sacks-editor-chief-reverses-editorial-policy [Accessed 2 Jun. 2019].

Ahval (2019). 'Climate of Fear' for Journalists in Turkey – Atlantic | Ahval. [online] *Ahval*. Available at: https://ahvalnews.com/media-freedom/climate-fear-journalists-turkey-atlantic?amp. [Accessed 3 Jun. 2019].

AP News (2018). A Look at Turkey's Post-Coup Crackdown. [online] *AP News*. Available at: www.apnews.com/dbb5fa7d8f8c4d0d99f297601c83a164 [Accessed 29 Mar. 2019].

Armstrong, W. (2016). Interview: Bilge Yeşil on the Turkish Media, Past and Present. [online] *Hürriyet Daily News*. Available at: www.hurriyetdailynews.com/interview-bilge-yesil-on-the-turkish-media-past-and-present-103020 [Accessed 29 May 2019].

Avim (2019). Kitap: The Anatomy of a Forgotten Assassination – The Hate Trap – Haluk Şahin HATE TRAP – HALUK ŞAHİN. [online] *Avim.org.tr*. Available at: https://avim.org.tr/tr/Duyuru/KITAP-THE-ANATOMY-OF-A-FORGOTTEN-ASSASSINATION-THE-HATE-TRAP-HALUK-SAHIN [Accessed 1 Jun. 2019].

BBC News (2018). Turkey Cumhuriyet Trial: 13 Newspaper Staff Convicted Over Coup. [online] *BBC News*, 25 Apr. Available at: www.bbc.co.uk/news/world-europe-43899489 [Accessed 29 Jun. 2019].

Bianet (2011). Speech at Pace: PM Erdoğan Compared Journalist Şık's Book to a Bomb. [online] *Bianet – Bağımsız İletişim Ağı*. Available at: http://bianet.org/bianet/english/129243-pm-Erdoğan-compared-journalist-sik-s-book-to-a-bomb [Accessed 29 Mar. 2019].

Borger, J. (2019). Journalist Pelin Ünker Sentenced to Jail in Turkey Over Paradise Papers Investigation. [online] *The Guardian*. Available at: www.theguardian.com/news/2019/jan/09/journalist-pelin-unker-sentenced-to-jail-in-turkey-over-paradise-papers-investigation [Accessed 29 May 2019].

Bucak, S. (2018). Doğan Media Sale to Erdoğan Ally Is Blow to Press Freedom. [online] *Financial Times*. Available at: www.ft.com/content/3273aafc-4317-11e8-97ce-ea0c2b-f34a0b [Accessed 29 Apr. 2019].

Committee to Protect Journalists (n.d.). Explore CPJ's Database of Attacks on the Press. [online] *Cpj.org*. Available at: http://cpj.org/killed/1992/ [Accessed 29 Apr. 2019].

Deutsche Welle (2018). Erdogan in Paris: Journalists Are "Gardeners" of Terrorism | DW |. [online] *DW.COM*, 5 Jan. Available at: www.dw.com/en/Erdoğan-in-paris-journalists-are-gardeners-of-terrorism/a-42037145 [Accessed 1 Jun. 2019].

Deutsche Welle (2019). A Return to Dark Days for Journalists in Turkey. [online] Available at: www.dw.com/en/a-return-to-dark-days-for-journalists-in-turkey/a-46684187 [Accessed 24 May 2019].

The Economist (2002). Erdoğan Triumphs – With Plenty of Help From His Enemies. [online] *The Economist*. Available at: www.economist.com/europe/2002/11/07/Erdoğan-triumphs-with-plenty-of-help-from-his-enemies [Accessed 1 Jun. 2019].

Ertem, B. (2018). 12 Mart 1971 Askerî Müdahalesi Sonrası Ara Rejim ve Türkiye Siyasetine Etkileri (1971–1974). *OPUS Uluslararası Toplum Araştırmaları Dergisi*, 8(14).

Fitzgibbon, W. (2019). Turkish Journalist Spared Jail for Paradise Papers. . . [online] *ICIJ*. Available at: www.icij.org/investigations/paradise-papers/turkish-journalist-spared-jail-for-paradise-papers-investigation/ [Accessed 29 May 2019].

Haberler (2019). Metastaz' Kitabı Piyasada. [online] *Haberler.com*. Available at: www.haberler.com/metastaz-kitabi-piyasada-11707901-haberi/ [Accessed 1 Apr. 2019].

Hürriyet (1999). Yine o meçhul fail. [online] *Hurriyet.com.tr*. Available at: www.hurriyet.com.tr/gundem/yine-o-mechul-fail-39108944 [Accessed 3 Jun. 2019].

Hürriyet Daily News (2011). Banned Book Goes on Sale in Istanbul Book Fair. [online] *Hürriyet Daily News*. Available at: www.hurriyetdailynews.com/banned-book-goes-on-sale-in-istanbul-book-fair-6901 [Accessed 29 Mar. 2019].

Kaya, Ö. (2011). *On the Way to a New Constitution in Turkey Constitutional History, Political Parties and Civil Platforms*. Bonn: Frederich Ebert Stiftung.

Kongar, P. (2019). Interview with Journalist & Author Emre Kongar.

Kurt Öncel, G. (2013). *Türkiye'de soruşturmacı gazetecilik*. İstanbul: Evrensel.

Mahoney, R. (2011). Q&A: Two of Turkey's Leading Journalists Speak From Jail. [online] *Cpj.org*. Available at: https://cpj.org/blog/2011/08/qa-two-of-turkeys-leading-journalists-speak-from-j.php [Accessed 29 Jun. 2019].

*Milliyet* (1993). Mumcu'ya Bombalı Suikast.

Munir, M. (2017). Beş soruda araştırmacı gazetecilik. [online] *T24*. Available at: https://t24.com.tr/yazarlar/metin-munir/bes-soruda-arastirmaci-gazetecilik,16527 [Accessed 30 May 2019].

Mumcu, Ö. (2011). Out of Tragedy in Turkey Emerges a Journalistic Mission | Nieman Reports. [online] *Nieman Reports*. Available at: https://niemanreports.org/articles/out-of-tragedy-in-turkey-emerges-a-journalistic-mission/ [Accessed 29 Apr. 2019].

Öymen, A. (2019). Interview with Journalist and Former Politician Altan Oymen.

PEN International (2011). Turkey: PEN Free Expression Award Winner, Nedim Sener, and Writer Ahmet Şık Arrested. [online] *PEN International*, 11 Mar. Available at: https://pen-international.org/news/turkey-pen-free-expression-award-winner-nedim-sener-and-writer-ahmet-sik-arrested [Accessed 2 Jun. 2019].

Platform 24 (n.d.). Investigative Journalism Program. [online] *Platform24.org*. Available at: http://platform24.org/en/objective/10/investigative-journalism-program [Accessed 1 Apr. 2019].

Stockholm Center for Freedom. (2019). Jailed and Wanted Journalists in Turkey – Updated List – Stockholm Center for Freedom. [online] Available at: https://stockholmcf.org/updated-list/ [Accessed 1 Jun. 2019].

Şahin, H. (2012). *Kim korkar soruşturmacı gazeteciden?* Istanbul: Say Yayinlari, p. 59.

T24. (2015). İşte 12 Eylül darbesinin kanlı bilançosu. [online] Available at: https://t24.com.tr/haber/iste-12-eylul-darbesinin-kanli-bilancosu,296166 [Accessed 29 May 2019].

T24. (2017). 1982 referandumu: Hangi koşullar altında yapıldı, "Hayır" diyenler neyle suçlandı? [online] Available at: https://t24.com.tr/haber/1982-referandumu-hangi-kosullar-altinda-yapildi-hayir-diyenler-neyle-suclandi,397263 [Accessed 1 Jun. 2019].

United Nations High Commissioner for Refugees (1993). Refworld | Human Rights Watch World Report 1993 – Turkey. [online] *Refworld*. Available at: www.unhcr.org/refworld/docid/467fca705f.html [Accessed 1 Jun. 2019].

# 12

# POLAND SINCE 1989

*Marek Palczewski*

What follows is a brief history of investigative journalism in Poland since1989, with particular emphasis on the recent years. I analyse, with case studies, notorious investigations from 2017–2019; assess the condition of modern investigative journalism in Poland and discuss its future. In defining investigative journalism, I locate myself with de Burgh, Kovach and Rosenstiel's analyses, which hold that several conditions must be met in order to define journalism as investigative: investigative journalism 1) must reflect original research, 2) should uncover the truth, 3) permits the use of undercover reporting techniques and 4) can include the analysis of documents to reveal something hidden (de Burgh 2000; Kovach and Rosenstiel 2001). Investigative journalism should always be in the public interest.

## 1. The history of investigative journalism after 1989

Investigative journalism began to develop in Poland after the change of regime from a communist to a democratic state in 1989. Previously, the media were more or less subordinated to the ruling Communist Party (PZPR). The acceleration of political transformation and the increase of media independence from political power, dating back to the first free elections in 1991, highly influenced the work of journalists (Bereś 2000).

In the 1990s, there appeared the first articles that could be described as investigative journalism. They were written by journalists of *Gazeta Wyborcza*, Poland's liberal daily newspaper. Jerzy Jachowicz (an article about former secret service officials were still present in the democratic structures of the new state) and Piotr Najsztub and Maciej Gorzeliński (an article about corruption in the police headquarters in Poznań), as well as Rafał Kasprów and Jacek Łęski (from the daily *Życie* newspaper, articles on banking scandals and connections between Polish politicians and Russian agents).

During this early period in Poland, undercover reporting was first employed as a method of gathering information and evidence of wrongdoings in politics, health care, banking, businesses and so on. Among the most famous cases were: purchase of explosives from a terrorist group at Okęcie Airport by an unnamed journalist of *Super Express*; sale at auction of a painting claimed to be the work of Polish painter Starowieyski (arranged by *TVN* and *Rzeczpospolita* journalists Jarosław Jabrzyk and Wojciech Cieśla); purchase of a fake ID card by Grzegorz Kuczek (a *TVN* journalist) and its use at a bank to rent a car, sports and construction equipment or even a flat. These are just a few examples of successful undercover reporting. Other popular methods were masquerades, sting and stunt journalism, including changing the reporter's identity and impersonating employees, customers or clients of various firms or institutions, that is, a report by Alicja Kos and Wojciech Cieśla titled *Wędliny drugiej świeżości (About the Meat Plant Constar in Starachowice)*. There were also reports by Mirosław Majer, *Mordercy Dzieci (TV Polsat)*; Jarosław Jabrzyk, *Prokurator* and Daniel Zieliński, *Kardiochirurg (TVN)*, in which journalists changed their identities and prepared entrapments (sting operations) which revealed corruption and exposed a paedophile web and conspiracy against a colleague physician. In the following, I would like to recall two investigations among many.

### 1.1. TNT at Super Express

In early 1995, (an) anonymous *Super Express* (*SE*) reporter(s) bought six sticks of TNT (weighing 4.5 kg) from an anti-terrorist police unit at Okęcie Airport. It happened during the time of wars between the mafias from Wołomin and Pruszków, when the gangs wanted to take control of the Warsaw underworld. The atmosphere of danger was increasing. There were frequent explosions; cars were being blown up and bombs were going off in bars and homes. The reporters decided to investigate from where they could buy explosives (*Super Express* 1995). There were 84 attacks using explosives in Poland in 1994, some being in Warsaw. Surprisingly, they purchased them from people who claimed to be anti-terrorist police officers working at the airport. The TNT (trinitrotoluene), bought for 50m old zlotys (c.a. 1k Euros), was then locked in the editorial safe at the *SE* office.

This undercover operation was carried out to make people realise how easy it was to purchase such materials. *SE* wanted to call a press conference, but the police first entered the building and confiscated the explosives. The chief editor, Urszula Surmach-Imienińska, and the newspaper's publisher, Grzegorz Lindenberg, were questioned by the police and later charged with possession of explosives. The journalists explained that they acted for the public good and they simply wished to disclose the source of leaking such dangerous explosives within the police. In 2004, the District Court in Warsaw and the Appellate Court shared their opinion and dismissed the case (*Wprost* 2004).

### 1.2. Anti-paedophile provocation

In 2002, *TV POLSAT* broadcast Mirosław Majeran's report *Mordercy Dzieci (Murderers of Children)*. Together with Jacek Błaszczyk from the weekly *Wprost*,

Majeran organised a sting operation which led to exposing and breaking up a paedophile gang. Its members had contacts in the West and were involved in the production of child pornography. The journalists decided to disclose these activities. Jacek Błaszczyk went undercover to infiltrate the group and deceive their members into thinking that he had a client in France who was interested in the film. When the final negotiations considering the film's production took place, the journalists provided the information to the Central Investigative Office (CBŚ), which joined the investigation. During an arranged meeting at a castle in Książ with the boss of the gang nicknamed "Waga", Błaszczyk was equipped with a hidden microphone. The conversation was recorded, and the police decided that they had enough evidence to prosecute. In several cities around Poland, at the same time, CBŚ officers proceeded to stop the gang's other members. The paedophiles were arrested in their homes and at the castle during negotiations on the details of the criminal transaction (Palczewski 2008).

## 2. The changing picture of investigative reporting in the 21st century

Between 2002 and 2008 there were great developments. At that time, many articles and investigative reports were written, the most famous of which were: *Skin Hunters* in 2002 by Tomasz Patora, Marcin Stelmasiak (*Gazeta Wyborcza*) and Przemysław Wojciechowski (*Radio Łódź*) about paramedics and physicians from the Polish city of Łódź. These workers were convicted of murdering at least five elderly patients and later selling the information about their deaths to competing funeral homes. The perpetrators were arrested in 2002. The next ones were the report *Mafia Fuel* in 2004 by Witold Gadowski and Przemysław Wojciechowski *(Superwizjer TVN)* describing the Polish mafia and illegal trade in oil, gas and petrol, and *Work for Sex* in 2006 by Marcin Kącki (*Gazeta Wyborcza*) about sexual services provided to the leading politicians of the Self-Defense Party by the female employees of this party. A huge controversy was sparked when secret tapes were disclosed by two journalists from *TVN* – a commercial TV station. On 26 September in 2006, in a *TVN* programme conducted by Tomasz Sekielski and Andrzej Morozowski, *TERAZ MY*, fragments of conversations between Renata Beger (a member of the Self-Defense Party, Polish Samoobrona) and Adam Lipiński (the Law & Justice Party; Polish PiS), recorded by Beger using a hidden camera in her flat in the Sejm hotel, were broadcast. The talks took place after Andrzej Lepper's dismissal (he was earlier a vice-minister of the Polish government), when the future of the coalition was being decided. PiS wanted to get some S–DP deputies' support and have them switch parties so that they could form the government without S–DP. The taped conversations showed – just as *TVN* journalists had planned – proof of political corruption (*TERAZ MY* 2006).

The tape scandal had an essential influence on what happened on the Polish political scene. As a result, Jarosław Kaczyński's government resigned a year later. The disclosure of the tapes' content sparked a heated discussion in the media and social debate regarding ethical standards in politics and journalism. It should be noted, though, that the recorded politicians (Lipiński and Mojzesowicz) did not sue the journalists. But ethical dilemmas still remain. Journalists need to be independent of external influences (politicians, authorities, media companies, sources of information, etc.) and internal ones (journalists' subjective opinions and prejudices). Did the journalists act independently in this case? There is no certainty.

In the first decade of the 21st century, investigative journalists often worked in teams (e.g., *Gazeta Wyborcza*, *Dziennik*, *Rzeczpospolita* or *Superwizjer TVN*); they dealt with corrupt politicians, businessmen, judges, prosecutors and health care. Journalistic teams organised entrapments and sting operations and practiced investigative reporting to reveal abuses of power, financial misappropriation or fraud (for instance, those of Andrzej Stankiewicz and Małgorzata Solecka, Anna Marszałek, Bertold Kittel and Wojciech Cieśla from *Rzeczpospolita* and Ada Wons and Jarosław Jabrzyk from *TVN*). Their activities led to the arrest of the bribed prosecutors, disclosure of a case in a meat factory where old meat was being "refreshed" and uncovering of the existence of incompetent 'experts' in the art market.

## 3. Revival of investigative journalism? The last decade (2010–2019)

Stagnation in Polish investigative journalism after 2008 had various causes. Among others were media involvement in relations with politicians, the economic crisis, restrictions on the financing of "investigatory" projects, problems of a legal nature (judicial processes against investigative journalists), self-censorship, tabloidisation of media messages and declining interest in this type of journalism. The renaissance of investigative journalism in Poland, however incomplete, took place about 2016. Earlier, especially during the second period of governance (2011–2015) by the coalition of the Civic Platform (PO) and the Polish People's Party (PSL), investigative journalism was in crisis. Anti-government scandals revealed at that time (conversations between politicians on civic platforms recorded by hidden microphones in The Sowa & Przyjaciele Restaurant) had nothing to do with investigative journalism but were primarily the result of games of the secret service related to the opposition, using journalists for their purposes. The leaked scandals (Gambling Scandal, Tape Scandal) were used by the opposition in the political fray. At that time, high-quality journalism, independent of political powers, was sustained among journalists like Tomasz Patora from *TVN*, who revealed the so-called Salt Scandal (contaminated salt was being sold as edible), Cezary Łazarewicz (*Newsweek Polska*), Piotr Pytlakowski (*Polityka*), Ewa Ornacka, Krzysztof M. Kaźmierczak and Piotr Talaga (*Głos Wielkopolski*), whose journalistic books addressed matters related to the communist past of the country; the fights inside the Mafia or the death of one of the first Polish investigative journalists Jarosław Ziętara, who was murdered (in 1991), probably by the Mafia. In turn, Justyna Kopińska (*Gazeta Wyborcza*) described the problem of sexual harassment, mobbing and rape of women in the Polish Army (see Popielec 2018).

The most outstanding examples of investigative journalism were recognised in the Grand Press Competition organised by *PRESS* magazine and the Polish Journalists Association (SDP). In 2016, the Grand Press Award went to Iwona Szpala and Małgorzata Zubik for the article titled *To Whom the Plot* (*Gazeta Wyborcza*), in which they described the abuses and "scams" during the pathological re-privatisation of buildings and plots in Warsaw. In 2017, the award for the report *Death at the Police Station* was given to Wojciech Bojanowski (*Superwizjer TVN*), who discovered the truth about the death of 25-year-old Igor Stachowicz, killed by policemen at the police station in Wrocław. In 2018, the prize in the category of investigative journalism was awarded to Bertold Kittel, together with Anna Sobolewska and Piotr Wacowski (*Superwizjer TVN*), for the TV report *Polish Neo-Nazis* (see the following).

The newest period of investigative journalism seems to announce the return of a better climate for this type of journalism in Poland, although financial resources are still lacking. In this context, it is worth noting that the Sekielski brothers (Tomasz and Marek) made a film about paedophilia in the Catholic Church in Poland, *Tell No One*, using resources raised on a crowdfunding platform only. The reception of this documentary by public opinion and further interest in its sequel can herald mental as well as organisational and technological transformations (the film was first made available on YouTube) in how investigative journalism pieces will emerge and be disseminated in Poland. The last three aforementioned reports will be analysed in this article as case studies in terms of their history, political and media contexts and social implications.

### 3.1. Death at the Police Station

Wojciech Bojanowski, a reporter at the *TVN* station since 2007, was awarded the title of Journalist of the Year 2017 in Poland in the Grand Press Competition for his investigative report *Death at the Police Station*. Bojanowski is a young reporter with long work experience. He specialises in reporting on criminal and wartime topics. For a few years now, he has been working for *Superwizjer*, a weekly investigative program broadcast on *TVN* since 2001, and which, so far, has been awarded 12 Grand Press awards. In 2014, Bojanowski reported on the civil war in Donbas and another about drug gangs; in 2016, about the dramatic efforts of immigrants who wanted to get to Great Britain through La Manche channel in Calais.

His report, *Death at the Police Station*, for *Superwizjer TVN* describes tragic events at the Stare Miasto police station in Wrocław (Bojanowski 2017).

On 15 May 2016, after 6 a.m., at the Market Square in Wrocław, 25-year-old Igor Stachowiak is arrested. He has just left a pub. He looks like 22-year-old Mariusz Frontczak, wanted for drug dealing, who escaped the police 2 days before. Now, when the police officers see Stachowiak at the Market Square, they take him for Frontczak. The report shows these places and the whole event from the recordings of city monitoring and three random witnesses' mobile footage. We can see two police cars arrive. Four policemen wrestle with Stachowiak; they handcuff him, and one of the policemen tases Igor on his back with Taser X2. Two of the witnesses recording the incident are later detained by the police and taken to the police station where Stachowiak is held. This is where the drama will take place.

The further course of action was made public due to the journalistic investigation carried out in 2017 by Wojciech Bojanowski. He reached the witnesses, got documents hidden from the public and used anonymous sources of information. Thanks to his work, everyone found out about the circumstances of Stachowiak's death. Before it happened, the policemen beat one of the witnesses in the washroom. Next, they escorted Stachowiak to the washroom. There – as recorded on the taser – they tasered him three times with 5-second impulses of 1200 volts. He breathed heavily and died of cardiopulmonary insufficiency. The photos taken by Maciej Stachowiak, the father of the victim, showed facial and neck injuries. Although the police station was equipped with a monitoring system, none of the cameras recorded the described events. According to forensic experts, the death resulted from three factors: the victim's substantial drug and legal high intake, being paralysed by taser a few times and hard neck pressure (Bojanowski 2017).

The investigation in this case was run by the district prosecutor's office in Poznań. Prior to the broadcast of the report, no charges had been pressed. The prosecution's investigation did not manage to explain why Stachowiak had been searched in the washroom. It was Bojanowski's report that stopped this case from being swept under the rug; the journalist showed that the police officers overstepped their powers and wanted to cover their tracks, and the use of taser against a handcuffed person was unlawful. The law enforcement representatives, obligated to act lawfully, violated it themselves.

The case didn't move on until after the broadcast of the report. If it hadn't been for the media, no one would probably have been sentenced for the death of an innocent man. In the resulting trial, the police officers who contributed to Stachowiak's death were sentenced to 2 and 2.5 years in prison. The sentence was set on 21 June 2019, over 2 years after Igor Stachowiak's death. His father, Maciej Stachowiak, said that "it was the first step to punish the guilty". He was not satisfied with it, however; he said, "the police hadn't even apologized" (*TVN24.pl* 2019).

### 3.2. Polish Neo-Nazis

*Gazeta Wyborcza* has been tracking neo-Fascist and neo-Nazi groups in Poland for many years; Jacek Harłukowicz writes about the world of fascist bands and calls Lower Silesia a hub of neo-Nazism. This is where they organise concerts of groups whose participants greet one another with the Nazi 'Sieg Heil'. This is also where Polish neo-Nazis meet with those from German lands, from Saxony and Brandenburg.

*Superwizjer* reporters who learned about those concerts decided to investigate the activity of such groups. They managed to infiltrate the circle of Polish neo-Nazis. Seventy years after World War II, in which Poland suffered so terribly, there are people who worship Adolf Hitler and build altars to celebrate his birthday. In Poland, organisations, associations and behaviours glorifying Fascism, Nazism and Communism are prohibited in law. The report took months to prepare, and its publication was delayed to boost its reception with new facts. Bertold Kittel, Anna Sobolewska and Piotr Wacowski, acting undercover, showed the alternative world of the Polish neo-Nazis who publicly organise political happenings, music festivals and ceremonies dedicated to the memory of Hitler (Kittel, Sobolewska and Wacowski 2018).

The report *Polish Neo-Nazis*, was broadcast on *TVN* on 20 January 2018. In the foreground, in one of the scenes, the report showed swastika flags and a shrine in memory of Hitler. Some of the participants of the event wore WW2 German uniforms. The reporters were criticised for provoking the neo-Nazis and for encouraging the participants to utter pro-Hitler declarations. As a result, the prosecution charged Piotr Wacowski, a *TVN* cameraman, with propagating Nazism. The case never came to court (*Newsweek* 2019).

In November 2018, the portal *wpolityce.pl* and a weekly associated with it, *wSieci*, wrote that the *Superwizjer's* report could have been a 'set-up' for which the organiser of 'Hitler's birthday' was paid 20k PLN (Biedroń 2018).

The editorial office of *Superwizjer* categorically denied these suggestions and called them innuendos (*TVN24.pl* 2018/3). Mateusz S., the organiser of the event, talked about the alleged set-up. He testified that he had received 20k PLN in a carrier bag when he was collecting his son from kindergarten. The prosecutor's inquiry in this case is still on. There has also been a thread interpreting the TV camera operator's Nazi salute during the party as unlawful.

In this case, the prosecutor initiated and discontinued the proceedings. The division in the journalistic environment, however, became clear: the journalists opposing the ruling party supported their colleagues from *TVN*, and the pro-government ones discredited and disregarded their achievements. They tried to show that all this 'masquerade' involved just a tiny minority of people and that Nazism in Poland is marginal.

After the broadcast of the report, there has been some backlash from the secret services and the judiciary. The activity of "Pride and Modernity" and other fascist groups has been branded by the prime minister and the minister of justice. Steps have been taken to outlaw it. The chief prosecutor and the minister of justice, Zbigniew Ziobro, initiated an investigation into "Pride and Modernity". Upon the broadcast of the report, the governor of Wodziław Śląski submitted a claim to dissolve "Pride and Modernity". The claim was supported by the prosecutor's office in Gliwice. The association was outlawed by court in August 2019 (*TVN24.pl* 2018/1).

There were also punishments for the participants of the 'birthday' party. Adam B. was fined 13k PLN (about 3k euro). He was found guilty of public propagation of fascism and illegal gun possession. The other suspects were charged with propagation of a Nazi system. The police found in their homes, among other things, uniforms, badges and publications glorifying Nazism (*TVN24.pl* 2018/2)

The reporters' work was appreciated by the main Polish journalistic competitions. For their report about the neo-Nazis, Bertold Kittel, Anna Sobolewska and Piotr Wacowski were awarded Radio ZET's Andrzej Wojciechowski Award and the Grand Press Award for investigative journalism, and Bertold Kittel won the Journalist of the Year 2018 Award.

### 3.3. Tell No One

On 11 May 2019, Marek and Tomasz Sekielski broadcast on YouTube their film about cases of paedophilia in the Polish Catholic Church. It was an independent production financed through crowdfunding. Tomasz Sekielski, one of the document's authors, has been an investigative journalist working for years for *TVP* and *TVN*. The program which he realised together with Andrzej Morozowski in 2006, *TERAZ MY* on *TVN*, in which they revealed secret talks between the politicians of the Law and Justice Party and those from the Self-Defense Party, led to the outbreak of the so-called Tape Scandal of Renata Beger, which resulted in the resignation of Jarosław Kaczyński's government in 2007.

The documentary *Tell No One* places emphasis on hiding paedophilia among the clergy by Church hierarchs. Murky scenes from the victims' stories contrast with the complacency of their oppressors and the reaction of Polish Episcopacy representatives, who didn't want to speak before the camera or claimed that the problem was being effectively fought within Church structure itself. The film presents both old and new cases. The victims' accounts abound with various instances of sexual harassment of boys and girls and their families' lack of interest in their children's stories about the priests' misdeeds. Already adult, the women and men, with tears in their eyes or simply crying, describe drastic scenes of rape and sexual harassment (Sekielski 2019).

The film, which was originally broadcast only on YouTube, had over one million views within the first 5 hours, which was an audience record in Poland (at the end of November 2019, it had over 23 million views on

YouTube). The film was later published by the *Wirtualna Polska* portal and its associated TV channel and by a private station, *TVN*. *TVP*, a public television station, decided not to show the film, and in its flagship information program, *Wiadomości (The News)*, criticised both the content of the film and its authors, accusing them of lack of objectivity and launching an attack on the Catholic Church. Some Law and Justice politicians claimed that the issue was fabricated and its main purpose was to provoke (*Rzeczpospolita* 2019).

After the broadcast, moved by what they had seen, Polish prelates published a statement, and Cardinal Kazimierz Nycz apologised for not having appeared in it (*Onet.pl* 2019/2). However, there were different reactions within the church hierarchy; some of them talked about an attack on the Church or even "a paedophilia industry"; others treated it as an expression of concern. One of the violators, priest Dariusz Olejniczak, after the broadcast of the film, asked Pope Francis that he be relegated to the secular state.

According to some commentators, the film didn't show what is hidden in Church, that is, 'homo-lobby' activity, the molesting of clerical students and young priests by their supervisors. Priest Tadeusz Isakowicz-Zaleski, known for his controversial public appearances, pointed at some scandals connected with this issue, among other things the case of Archbishop Juliusz Paetz, who was accused of molesting clerical students from Poznań. There are also cases of priests cooperating with the communist secret services (SB), which have not been completed (*PCh24.pl* 2019).

In March 2019, the Episcopacy presented data concerning child sexual abuse in the Church. In the period of 1990–2018, the total number of victims of paedophilic priests was 625. Eighty-five priests out of the accused 168 have been charged in trials. Only 68 priests have been expelled from the priesthood (Kalisz 2019). In October 2019, the Court of Appeal in Gdańsk sentenced priest Andrzej S. – one of the infamous characters in the film – to apologise to his victim and pay him 400k PLN in compensation (*archive.today* 2019). The National Public Prosecutor's Office announced that it had set up a special team to investigate the cases covered in the film, and the politicians from the main parties promised more severe punishments for paedophilia (*Onet.pl* 2019/1).

On 15 May 2019, Press Club Polska awarded the Sekielski Brothers a Special Award for "making a documentary about one of the most appalling phenomena, which is paedophilia of the clergymen. It is the expression of gratitude towards the authors, who reminded us that the role of a journalist is to stand on the side of truth" (*Wprost* 2019). The film by the Sekielski brothers was also awarded a Radio ZET award and GRAND PRIX from the City of Łódź, as well as the White Cobra Statue at the festival Człowiek w Zagrożeniu 2019 for their "courage to stand against evil". In December 2019, they received the 1st Grand Press prize in the category TV/Video Reportage, and Tomasz Sekielski won the title of Journalist of the Year 2019. The Sekielski Brothers are planning to make another film about paedophilia in the Church.

## Discussion

The aforementioned cases point to the diversity of the investigative methods used (reporting techniques). *Death at the Police Station* is an attempt to reconstruct the events and a journalistic investigation held after the proper one had failed. The reporter plays the part of a detective and investigator trying to explain the causes of death of Igor Stachowiak. Bojanowski's report illustrates archetypes of investigative journalism: a socially significant topic of the abuse of power, a figure of an innocent and helpless victim and a violent authority who is callous and unfeeling towards their fate, covering up the case and stalling the investigation. It also draws attention to the so-called whistleblowers (anonymous informers and witnesses), whose testimony contributes to publicising the story and informing the public opinion about the true course of action. Bojanowski uses their recordings and testimony in his report, thus revealing what was supposed to stay hidden from the public. The results of the report should not be evaluated just by the court sentences (relatively low according to public opinion), but the wider, prospective consequences should be considered: the police in Poland may not act with impunity, for their actions are monitored by the Fourth Estate, and what was supposed to stay hidden was revealed thanks to the work of investigative journalists.

Another of the discussed reports is a typical example of undercover reporting. The use of methods from the area of investigative journalism makes it similar to American 'masquerades', in which journalists play different roles – change their identities – in order to find out about wrongdoings, shortcomings or infringement of law. That was the case of the Mirage Tavern – a famous action of *Chicago Sun Times* reporters comprehensively described in the subject literature. However, whereas Pamela Zekman and other reporters from the Chicago newspaper thoroughly planned, prepared and carried out their sting operation, the *TVN* reporters were, in this case, participants and not the organisers of the masquerade. Despite that, some reporters decided to carry out a 'journalistic investigation' directed against the *TVN* reporters. The *TVN* reporters did their best to obtain the most extensive material illustrating the existence of neo-Nazi groups and associations in Poland, so their use of undercover techniques (masquerade, hidden camera, hidden microphone) was a last resort; otherwise, they would not have found such evidence. Reproaching them for that does not show the journalists' exceptional ethical sensitivity but rather some journalists' lack of understanding of the essence of investigative journalism.

The last case – the documentary by Marek and Tomasz Sekielski – is an example of reliable investigative journalism. It was the result of original work by the reporters, who managed to get to the source of information on their own, found open and anonymous informers and tackled an important social and moral problem which was supposed to stay hidden, and many people did not want it to see the light of day. Perhaps the results of the reporters' investigation were not sensational, for they revealed only a few cases of paedophilia in Catholic Church in Poland; however, the film triggered an extensive debate on the topic which, before then, had been taboo. They also forced an official acknowledgement from church authorities stating that paedophilia is a problem for this institution. Thereby, *Tell No One* not only fitted into the discourse concerning paedophilia among Polish priests, but also, in some aspects (concerning Poland), it was a continuation of the investigation carried out in the USA by an investigative team of the American *Boston Globe* in the years 2001–2003. In 2003, as part of a court settlement, the Boston Archdiocese paid a total of 85 million dollars compensation to 522 victims of sexual harassment (Gostkiewicz 2017).

All three cases of investigative journalism revealed a discursive 'grey area' – an area of silence which was supposed to stay that way: violence in a place which should symbolise opposition to violence, a return to historical narration with which the Polish State is fighting, sexual abuse in an institution which should set a moral example. The truth about these phenomena revealed by the reporters sparked a debate, whose effects remain open.

## Conclusion

Investigative journalism was relatively stagnant between 2008 and 2014. The reasons were, *inter alia*, legal restrictions, financial shortcomings, tabloidisation, decline in newspaper readers and limitations in access to information. Despite the restraints, since 2014 there has been an increase in valuable publications. Recently, there has been a return to crime and economics, although more and more involve political scandals and moral issues. The three case studies analysed previously show the versatility of Polish investigative journalists. There were 57 investigative reports entered for the 2019 Grand Press Competition. The entries covered the corruption of authority, a paedophile scandal with a famous musician in the main part and murky political business. Investigative journalism in Poland, after years of relative stagnation, has reminded us of its existence once more.

## References

### 1. Literature

Bereś Witold (2000), *Czwarta Władza: Najważniejsze Wydarzenia Medialne III RP*, Prószyński i S-ka, Warszawa.

de Burgh Hugo, ed. (2000), *Investigative Journalism. Context and Practice* (2000), Routledge. Taylor & Francis Group, London and New York.

Kovach Bill, Rosenstiel Tom (2001), *The Elements of Journalism: What Newspeople Should Know and the Public Should Expect*, Three Rivers Press, New York.

POLAND SINCE 1989

Palczewski Marek (2008), *Prowokacja dziennikarska. Definicja – aspekty prawne i etyczne – typologia*, "Studia Medioznawcze", 2(33), 71–91. https://studiamedioznawcze.pl/Num ery/2008_2_33/pelny.pdf

Popielec Dominika (2018), *Dziennikarstwo śledcze. Istota, funkcjonowanie, perspektywy*, Wydawnictwo Uniwersytetu Kazimierza Wielkiego, Bydgoszczy.

Super Express (1995), Kupić trotyl – żaden problem!, from 27.02.1995. 12 Poland since 1989.

## 2. Broadcast TV and online sources

archive.today (2019) – http://archive.is/jpCWA [access 30.11.2019]

Biedroń Wojciech (2018), *Znamy kulisy śledztwa w sprawie "urodzin Hitlera". W tle tajemniczy zleceniodawcy, duże pieniądze i dziennikarka TVN*, wpolityce.pl, 8.11 – https://wpoli tyce.pl/media/420145-tylko-u-nasurodziny-hitlera-byly-maskarada-znamy-kulisy [access 30.11.2019].

Bojanowski Wojciech (2017), *Śmierć na komisariacie*, "Superwizjer" TVN24, 20 maja – www.tvn24.pl/superwizjer-w-tvn24,149,m/smierc-igora-stachowiaka-w-komisariacie-zobacz-reportaz-superwizjera,741647.html [access 30.11.2019].

Gostkiewicz Michał (2017), *Przez lata tuszował pedofilski skandal w kościele. Kardynał Law nie żyje*, (without date of the Issue) – http://weekend.gazeta.pl/weekend/1,152121,19 697030,prawdziwa-historia-spotlight-jak-sledztwo-upartych-reporterow.html [access 30.11.2019].

Kalisz Paweł (2019), *Ponury obraz polskiego duchowieństwa. Oto najważniejsze dane z raportu KEP o pedofilii*, 14.03. – https://natemat.pl/266853,raport-kep-kto-najczesciej-zostaje-ofiara-ksiezy-pedofilow [access 30.11.2019].

Kittel Bertold, Sobolewska Anna, Wacowski Piotr (2018), *Polsce Neonaziści, "Superwizjer" TVN* – https://tvn24.pl/superwizjer-w-tvn24,149,m/superwizjer-tvn-z-kamera-w-srodowisku-polskich-neonazistow,807953.html [access 30.11.2019].

"Newsweek" (2019), 27.02 – www.newsweek.pl/polska/reportaz-o-polskich-nazistach-sledztwo-przeciwko-operatorowi-superwizjera-zostalo/3fbbesc [access 31.11.2019].

Onet.pl (2019/1), 13.05 – www.onet.pl/?utm_source=pl.wikipedia.org_viasg_wiadomosci& utm_medium=referal&utm_campaign=leo_automatic&srcc=ucs&pid=7d46bff5-6744-4a76-b9e4-da8e5a830281&sid=b177a2c9-166f-4113–9b28–185bbe554807&utm_ v=2[access 30.11.2019].

Onet.pl (2019/2), 22.05. – https://wiadomosci.onet.pl/kraj/kep-prowadzi-prace-nad-systemowa-odpowiedzia-na-pedofilie-w-kosciele/gmzbs13 [access 30.11.2019].

PCh24.pl (2019), 19.12 – www.pch24.pl/o-czym-nie-mowi-film-tomasza-sekielsk iego–zobacz-komentarze-zatroskanych-o-kosciol-i-furie-lewicy,68193,i.html[access 30.10.2019].

"Rzeczpospolita" (2019), 13.05. – www.rp.pl/Prawo-i-Sprawiedliwosc/190519805-Saryusz-Wolski-Pedofilia-w-Kosciele-Problem-wydumany-zeby-jatrzyc.html [access 30.11.2019].

Sekielski Tomasz, *Tylko nie mów nikomu* (2019) – www.youtube.com/watch?v=Br UvQ3W3nV4 [access 30.11.2019].

"TERAZ MY" (2006), 26.09.

TVN24.pl (2018/1), 21.01. – https://tvn24.pl/wiadomosci-z-kraju,3/sledztwo-po-repor tazu-superwizjera-ziobro-podjal-decyzje-po-emisji,808217.html [access 30.11.2019].

TVN24.pl (2018/2), 9.10 – https://tvn24.pl/wiadomosci-z-kraju,3/pierwszy-wyrok-ws-urodzin-hitlera-po-reportazu-superwizjera,874690.html [access 30.11.2019].

TVN24.pl (2018/3), 8.11 – https://tvn24.pl/wiadomosci-z-kraju,3/oswiadczenie-redakcji-superwizjera-w-sprawie-reportazu-polscy-neonazisci,882104.html [access 30.11.2019].

TVN24.pl (2019), 21.06. – https://tvn24.pl/wiadomosci-z-kraju,3/maciej-stachowiak-o-wyroku-w-sprawie-smierci-igora-stachowiaka,946640.html [access 30.11.2019].

*Wprost* (2004), 22.03. – www.wprost.pl/kraj/58015/Sad-po-stronie-dziennikarzy.html [acces 30.10.2019].

*Wprost* (2019), 14.05 – https://www.wprost.pl/kraj/10216516/tylko-nie-mow-nikomu-bracia-sekielscy-laureat ami-nagrody-specjalnej-press-club-polska.html [access 30.11.2019].

# 13

# INDIA'S PARADOX

*Prasun Sonwalkar*

'The frustrating thing about India is that whatever you can rightly say about India, the opposite is also true'[1]. It is a conundrum most researchers face while navigating contemporary India's sub-continental size, deep diversities, stark inequalities, 1.3-billion-plus population with over 65 per cent below the age of 35 and a large middle class. The growing numbers of the super-rich co-exist with abysmal poverty as a globalised India continues to face major challenges in issues such as health, education, food security, environment, energy and rural development. At the time of independence from Britain in 1947, the unlikely nation-state was not expected to survive long due to many fissiparous tendencies, yet democracy has flourished for over 70 years, consolidating India's position as a modern nation-state, unlike others that gained independence around the same time. Underpinning the turbulent decades since independence is a diverse, raucous and largely free news media, aiding the state's development initiatives in the early decades and increasingly holding power to account with effective examples of investigative journalism since the mid-1970s, particularly after the Indira Gandhi government-imposed Emergency (1975–1977) that included press censorship, curtailing civil liberties and suspending elections.

The general election of 2019 presents a convenient backdrop to explore the contemporary context of Indian journalism and recall the paradoxical story of its investigative genre: highly effective at its peak but tamed in recent years as part of news discourse to the point that it has become increasingly anodyne by a combination of extreme examples of political economy of news and governments intolerant of criticism imposing overt and covert curbs. India presents a rich menu for investigative journalism: ideological conflicts, gaps between policy and implementation, corruption, imperfect application of the rule of law and serious deficiencies in practices at various levels, among others. Ministers have been forced to resign, top politicians shamed, new laws enacted and corporate illegalities exposed by telling examples of investigative reporting that rocked India, particularly during the 1970s and 1980s and some in the 1990s and later. Indian investigative journalists and newspapers are increasingly part of global networks such as the International Consortium of Investigative

Journalists and WikiLeaks and access information abroad to bring to light anomalies in the country.

However, such examples have dwindled in recent years, particularly after the phenomenon of 'Murdochization' entrenched itself in Indian journalism and posed a serious challenge to the news media performing its role of holding power to account, particularly since the early 1990s (Sonwalkar, 2002, 2013, 2016). 'Murdochization' is based on the corporate culture devised by Rupert Murdoch to drive profits and involves privileging the 'marketing' or 'business' side of journalism over the 'editorial' and thus catering to the lowest common denominator, tabloidisation, pricing wars, non-unionised workforce, journalists employed on short-term contracts and censorship to suppress negative news about business partners, advertisers or political parties. The trope of 'manufacturing consent', set out in academic literature, may have reached its extreme in India since 2014, when overt and covert curbs ensured the dominance of one political party and its government and the marginalisation of the rest in news discourse, with newsrooms openly pushing propaganda or journalists self-censoring material to avoid offence to those in power.

Blurring the lines between advertising and news in the form of advertorials and stating it as such is a common practice, but one of the manifestations of 'Murdochization' in India is 'paid news', which refers to paid political advertising passing off as news without stating that it is sponsored. 'Paid news' itself became the subject of a series of investigative reports in the 2010s by P. Sainath, one of India's leading journalists. Identical 'news' reports, plugging a candidate or party, appear in various newspapers on the same day during elections; television news channels have their versions. In the context of feverish competition for revenue, 'paid news' has become a normal, if officially undeclared, source of income for news organisations, even though it is seen by many as a threat to the democratic process, since readers and viewers are misled into believing that editorial content has been produced by independent journalists. By the 2014 general election, 'paid news' had ceased to be a surprise, as parties, candidates and news organisations devised ingenuous ways to push claims to electoral success and power. Given the vast news media infrastructure in the country, 'paid news' became one of the key ways to influence voters.

In India's increasingly corporate-driven news mosaic, in recent years, journalists and media groups critical of the party in power have faced raids by official agencies, threats to life and employment or lack of access to sources of news. As news content increasingly turned anodyne, investigative journalism was almost non-existent. The role of the editor has been downgraded since the early 1990s as media owners place a premium on their own proximity to the party in power. In 2017, Arun Shourie, one of the icon of investigative journalism, compared democratic India's news media to that in North Korea (Bose, 2017).

This chapter explores the story of India's investigative journalism by situating it in historical and contemporary contexts, with major examples that had impact, and dwells on reasons for its recent neutering to the extent that reporters' instincts to probe an issue deeply have been virtually annihilated. 'Newspapers no longer invest in investigative journalism, not because they have no money but because they are afraid to antagonize the rulers', says Arun Sinha, one of India's most-known investigative journalists, who broke the infamous 'Bhagalpur blindings' story in 1980.[2] After a brief overview of Indian journalism, three examples of investigative reporting are recalled before focusing on some reasons for the decline in recent years of what Protess *et al.* called 'journalism of outrage' (1993).

## Indian journalism: an overview

India's ancient oral tradition of argument and debate (Sen, 2006) was reinvigorated when the British introduced their energetic style of public debate through print journalism in the late eighteenth century. The printing press arrived in Goa with Portuguese missionaries in the mid-sixteenth century, but it was not until 1780 that the first English-language journals were launched in Calcutta (the first was *Hicky's Gazette or Calcutta General Advertiser*, by James Augustus Hicky), followed by journals in Bengali, Persian and Hindi in Calcutta and in other Indian languages in colonial Madras and Bombay. By the early nineteenth century, a 'multifarious culture of the print medium' had come into existence, which quickly became the first fully formed print culture outside Europe and North America, distinguished by its size and a large number of languages (Dharwadker, 1997: 112). Print journalism soon emerged as a key site of public discourse, as leading Indians of the time such as Rammohun Roy presented arguments from Indian perspectives and countered colonial measures (Sonwalkar, 2015). It went on to play a crucial role in the long freedom struggle before independence in 1947, as nationalist newspapers took on a distinct anti-establishment posture against the British and British-owned newspapers. One of them, *Indian Express* (founded 1932), continued the posture after independence, establishing itself as the foremost forum of investigative journalism in contemporary India.

Press laws enacted during British rule continue in amended form today. After independence, the press was left largely free, with the first prime minister, Jawaharlal Nehru, insisting that he would 'rather have a completely free press with all the dangers involved in the wrong use of that freedom than a suppressed or regulated press'. The first governments of free India tolerated criticism in editorial pages; there were rare attempts to muzzle the press or the expression of dissent, which aided the creation of a professional culture in which Indian journalists aspired to reach the (then) standards of British journalism.

However, subsequent governments sought to curb press freedom, particularly the Indira Gandhi government that imposed the Emergency. The press fought back, often exposing leading politicians and corrupt practices that also influenced elections. As Sen has famously argued, the principal reason 2 to

3 million people perished in famines in China in the 1950s and 1960s while only thousands died in India, in spite of there being no major differences in agricultural growth rates and food-grain supply, was the existence of a relatively free unofficial media in India and its absence in China. The press played the role of an effective advance warning system. It became a major agency of communication, information dissemination and public debate; newspapers contributed to raising public and governmental awareness on a range of issues, from changing social values, to poverty and starvation, to policy and programme failures.

Figures reflect the scale and diversity of the Indian press: as of 2018, the number of registered publications was 118,239 (17,573 newspapers, 100,666 periodicals). The largest number of publications are in Hindi (47,989), followed by those in English (14,626). The circulation of publications was 43,00,66,629 (Hindi: 19,56,21,990, English: 5,34,53,564). English is one India's 22 'official languages', and given its aspirational and historically privileged status in the country, English-language newspapers published from New Delhi are considered the national press, often setting the agenda in parliament and exerting influence in the public sphere. Technology has transformed India's media universe, providing new tools for investigative journalism. Since the mid-1980s, television has opened new avenues of information, entertainment and connectivity for individuals, institutions and regions. There are over 400 twenty-four-hour news channels in all major languages. But, as in other countries and aided by rising literacy, television did not obliterate the position of the press as a mature, reasonable and sober forum of public debate. The news discourse includes exponential growth in the use of the Internet and growing numbers of citizen journalists with smart-phones providing audio and visual footage to mainstream news organisations during times of crisis.

## Investigative reports that rocked India

The most-known examples of investigative journalism are from *Indian Express*, which describes itself as practicing 'journalism of courage'. Its focus on anti-establishment reporting peaked from the late 1970s until the mid-1980s, when its publisher, Ramnath Goenka (1904–1991), allowed significant freedom to his editors: Arun Shourie, B. G. Verghese and S. Nihal Singh, who went on to acquire legendary status in Indian journalism. The newspaper led with several exposés after the Emergency, when the news media increasingly asserted itself against the government. Three examples published in *Indian Express* from the period are: a series on the purchase of a young woman, Kamla, by Ashwini Sarin (1981); the gory blinding of suspects awaiting trial by the police in police custody in Bhagalpur, by Arun Sinha (1980) and the plight of juvenile suspects in Delhi's Tihar Jail, by Sanjay Suri (1985). The first two became the subject of Bollywood films: 'Kamla' (1985) and 'Gangajal' (2003). A summary of the three

# INDIA'S PARADOX

in the following sets out how they held up a mirror to Indian society beyond its feel-good narratives of democracy, culture and diversity.

### *Buying Kamla*

Ashwini Sarin, an unassuming man of 29 in 1981, was known for his investigative reports in the aftermath of the Emergency. He learnt of trafficking in women in the Agra-Morena-Mainpuri-Etah area near New Delhi, where they were sold as servants or prostitutes under the patronage of the local police and politicians. He, along with his editor, Arun Shourie, decided to probe further but realised that a straight story would not have the necessary impact. They decided to actually buy a woman. After months visiting the area known for its gun culture, Sarin, posing as a doctor, bought a young woman named Kamla for a little over 300 dollars and brought her to his home in New Delhi.

Sarin's series on the purchase on the front page of *Indian Express* began thus:

> Yesterday I bought a short-statured skinny woman belonging to a village near Shivpuri in Madhya Pradesh for 2,300 rupees. Even I find it hard to believe that I have returned to the capital this morning after buying the middle-aged woman for half the price one pays for a buffalo in the Punjab. . . . There were not many customers for Kamla, so I decided to emancipate her.
>
> (April 27, 1981)

Sarin recalled the effort behind the series in 2018:

> It took me almost a year to penetrate the racket. It was an area where country-made pistols were bought like packs of cigarettes. Arun Shourie, my editor, knew the project we were embarking upon could land us in trouble with the law. We worked out a strategy. He wrote letters to three prominent persons, including the then chief justice of India, setting out our intentions in participating in that crime of purchasing a woman. In sealed envelopes, along with covering notes requesting them not to open the letters until they were requested to do so.
>
> (Sarin, 2018)

As the story unfolded, officials were shown in a bad light, and the police promptly filed a case against Sarin, who had committed the crime under the Indian Penal Code of buying the woman. Shourie approached the Supreme Court and got a stay on Sarin's arrest, while the government ordered an inquiry by three states adjoining New Delhi, which confirmed the existence of large-scale trafficking of women.

Shourie, who oversaw several such exposés as editor, said at the time:

> We will ask the court if the law can be broken for a legitimate investigation and afterwards approach the court with a request to initiate steps to mitigate the evil laid bare by the investigation and thereby enlarge the scope of the citizen's rights. . . . I can't change the society. It will change when people will want it. I am just holding a mirror to society. I am using the Gandhian technique: pick up small issues, remove fear, try and educate people about the evils in society, and coax his contribution out of every individual.
>
> (Gupta, 1981)

S. Nihal Singh, who was editor-in-chief, added:

> Nothing was done by the authorities to check this organized crime spread over three states. Kamla is the symbol of slavery still prevalent in that area. Our action was the only effective way to tell our readers what was happening around them and that something must be done to get rid of the evil.

The story raised questions of ethics and law, but Sarin insisted it was appropriate for a journalist to participate in a crime to show it exists. He wrote in 2018:

> It boggles the mind that it's almost 40 years now. But why is it not surprising to realize that the issues have not changed one bit? Should an aberration, an abnormality, a wrong, be allowed to exist unreported? Is it more intolerable that a crime is committed, every minute, silently, or that it is reported? Which is worse? That a grievous flaw exists? Or that it is demonstrated to exist, so that something can be done about it? Should a journalist push the envelope by participating in a crime to show it exists? My answer, after all these years, is still yes.

Kamla has since become the foremost example of investigative reporting in India.

### *The Bhagalpur blindings*

The town of Bhagalpur in the economically backward eastern state of Bihar rarely makes news in the national press. The state has long grappled with issues of caste, crime, gun culture, left-wing extremism and extra-judicial killings. Arun Sinha had acquired a reputation for investigations into Bihar's social and political problems when he dug into an innocuous single-column report in the inside pages of the newspaper of October 11, 1980, by the newspaper's legal correspondent. The report said a lawyer had moved a *habeas corpus* petition in the Supreme Court on behalf of 10 individuals in the Bhagalpur jail awaiting trial for suspected crimes, adding that they 'alleged that the police deprived them of their eyesight by using acid'. Two Calcutta-based publications followed it up with detailed features for their early November issues, but printing problems delayed publication by two weeks. Sinha's account was the first to appear, narrating gory details of over 30 jail inmates blinded by the police, who inserted metal spokes in their eyes and poured sulphuric acid on them as extra-judicial punishment for their alleged crimes. His report was splashed on the front page with a photograph of one of the victims and the headline: 'Eyes punctured twice to ensure blindness' (*Indian Express*, November 22, 1980).

The story and Sinha's follow-ups soon had impact. The policemen were suspended from their jobs, while human rights groups and others approached the Supreme Court, which ordered compensation for the victims, including monthly pension, in the first such case in which the court ordered compensation for the violation of human rights in India. But that was not the end of the story. The police's illegal act was widely welcomed by the local population that was weary of growing crime in the town. Journalists who followed Sinha's exposé were harassed and hounded by the local people, who saw the blindings as an act of instant justice, instead of the long, drawn-out proceedings in courts. Sinha recalls:

> I heard of it in early November 1980. I made initial inquiries in Patna and went to Bhagalpur to find out more. Fortunately, the superintendent of the Bhagalpur jail, where the blinded under-trials were lodged, was a conscientious officer and he showed me documents that clearly suggested the police were directly or indirectly irresponsible for the barbarous acts. I returned to Patna (the state capital) and wrote a report which was carried on the front page. It was after the report was published that my editors asked me to do a detailed investigation. I went back to Bhagalpur and conducted detailed interviews with the jail officials, the families of the victims, some victims who were on bail, police and administration officials and common people. The documents and facts did not come to me in one basket. I had to get pieces of information from various sources – jail officials, police officers, officers of civil administration, lawyers, human rights activists and in the villages and small towns of the district where the incidents took place, as well as sources in the departments of police and prison in state headquarters. There was risk to my life as many policemen were suspended and the public had come out on the streets to support them, saying they had done the right thing. I had to go around Bhagalpur with a disguised identity. I found it puzzling to hear lawyers, teachers, doctors and other middle-class professionals residing in Bhagalpur town and other parts of the district justify the blindings as 'an

excellent method' of crime control. Most of the district police officers echoed their feelings, some even acquitting their juniors manning police stations who were involved in the blindings as 'innocent' as they had only done what the people wanted – in short, they had acted in 'public interest. I met very few people from the middle class who still remained committed to the rule of law dealing with people accused of violating the law. The height of barbarity of the perpetrators of blindings and the height of irrationality of the middle-class champions of the horrendous campaign was evident from the fact that most of the victims were not even hardcore outlaws but suspects. Some were picked up only because they were members of the lower social classes who defied local elite power and stood up to their excesses.

The story raised awareness about human rights and exposed the reality of extra-judicial killings in police custody. It was followed up widely, but instead of stooping such acts, it also inspired copycat acts against suspects elsewhere. Sinha's exposé was published in 1980, but recent developments suggest such illegal acts continue. Filmmaker Amitabh Parashar produced a documentary in 2017 titled *The Eyes of Darkness*, presenting contemporary evidence, decades after the Bhagalpur blindings (Ramnath, 2017).

### Children in Delhi's Tihar Jail

Sanjay Suri was a reporter on the crime beat in *Indian Express* in the 1980s. He was known for his reporting of the separatist 'Khalistan' movement in Punjab and of the killing of a large number of Sikhs in Delhi following the assassination of Indira Gandhi in October 1984. One of his exposés, published in 1985 under the headline, 'The Shame of It', highlighted the plight of children and juveniles detained for alleged crimes in Delhi's Tihar Jail, the largest prison complex in south Asia. They were lodged in cells with hardened criminals. Using opportunities provided by lax supervision during visiting hours, Suri met and interviewed several children. His reports led to an inquiry and eventual transformation of the jail's infrastructure that now includes separate cells to house children and juveniles accused of crime.

Suri recalls:

A single thought runs through my recollection of the stories: how little we reporters were managed. It is the memory of an enabling freedom. That freedom gave me room to visit Tihar Jail several times over the course of about six weeks to interview children that I had learnt from a source in jail were being sexually abused and enslaved into hard labour by senior convicts. Most of the children I met one by one as a visitor were visibly sick, many of them seemed to have skin infections. Something extraordinary happened the morning my first report appeared. The chief justice of the Supreme Court, P.N. Bhagwati, admitted it as a petition in his own court and ordered an inquiry by the chief judicial magistrate of Delhi, who confirmed what I had reported and amplified it. That led to a court order to restructure the jail to build in an entirely separate section for juveniles. This brought institutional protection for children who had been abused for years.

Journalists such as Suri and Sinha who made an impact recall the support they enjoyed from their editors, without which, they admit, their catalogue of exposés would not have been possible. As Sinha observes, 'I had full support of the editors'. In 1986, in a newsroom culture of what Suri calls 'enabling freedom', I did a three-part investigative series on the front page of the Patna edition of *The Times of India* on corruption and anomalies in the Bihar government's computerisation drive, titled 'Bihar's Computer Muddle', which led to an inquiry and action.

Suri reflects on the contemporary situation:

> Fighting off the usual urge of assuming that the self always does great things and all who follow are lesser, it does still seem that barring the occasional exception, the days of investigative reporting of the kind we did so much of and at such length, are mostly gone. The reporter's story needs a supportive editor to be what it is. The reason this culture of reporting has dwindled is pressure to be frequently if not constantly productive, and not be seen for long stretches as having, on the face of it, 'done nothing'. In some leading publications editors are now are undisguisedly managed by managers. They in turn do not commit enough resources over what they fail to see as immediately visible returns. Ad budgets have been swallowed substantially by television, and much of that finds flash and noise a cheaper way of offering allegedly lively content. Television can be a great medium for investigations but its logistics demand a great deal of time and money. We are into a culture of quick turnaround. Journalists work now with expectations of early career arrivals and not of launching into painstaking investigations. This is why we get so much by way of lazy offerings arising from relatively little work.

Besides the three examples, some investigative reporting in recent years had impact. N. Ram, editor of *The Hindu*, and Chitra Subramaniam, his former colleague, relentlessly investigated the Bofors arms purchase controversy that later contributed to the defeat of Prime Minister Rajiv Gandhi and his Congress party in the 1989 elections. Other journalists whose reporting made an impact include Sucheta Dalal, Aniruddha Bahal, Rana Ayyub, Murali Krishnan, Ritu Sarin, P Sainath, Paranjoy Guha Thakurta, Chitra Subramaniam, Neha Dixit, Tarun Tejpal, Amitav Ranjan, Manoj Mitta and Josy Joseph.

Besides newspapers such as *Indian Express* and *The Statesman*, until recently, news magazines *India Today* and *Outlook* also devoted resources for investigative journalism.

Journalism, particularly its investigative genre, does not exist in isolation but is part of a complex matrix of laws, core values and practices in a democracy. The default position in a democracy is for the idea, ideology and idealism of journalism to flourish, so that it can diligently perform its normative role, but to what extent it can do so when powerful political and corporate forces steer it to one partisan extreme is open to debate. As I have shown, investigative journalism in India has a glorious record, but that is increasingly in the past. The contemporary text and context are different. There has been a proliferation in the last 30 years of what I call the 'hardware' of journalism (enabling factors such as technology, capital, rising literacy, training centres), which offers new potential and opportunities for the 'software' of journalism to flourish: by 'software', I mean the quality of the editorial content that empowers citizens, holds those in power to account and strengthens democratic institutions. Online journalism is increasingly making its presence felt, providing new spaces to reclaim credibility, but, as the now-embedded idea of 'Murdochization' acquires ever more extreme forms in India, the genre of investigative journalism faces a serious challenge, when mainstream journalism itself is facing a crisis of trust.

## News media itself as focus of investigative journalism

The support from editors that enabled exposés declined progressively after the early 1990s, by when Indian journalism had been well and truly 'Murdochized'. Josy Joseph, whose catalogue of investigative reporting since 2001 in leading newspapers featuring high-profile individuals and corporate houses created ripples and won him awards and lawsuits, penned a lament in a piece titled 'The Byline Is Dead: How Indian Newsrooms Became Morgues for Investigative Journalism':

> More than a decade ago, I opened a folder in my email called 'Morgue'. I began saving in it stories I had written that met journalistic standards but still failed to see the light of the day. Stories have continued to pile up in that folder even as I have changed jobs. . . . In the mortuary of these dead stories, I have a collection of reporting on some of our biggest political leaders and corporate giants that, in a country with robust media, would have been celebrated, and in a law-abiding society, would have triggered major criminal investigations. But in India, these stories have found few takers. There have been times when I have seen individual editors stand up for journalism, but they have been rare exceptions. The culture of the newsroom has

degenerated slowly, and self-censorship has become second nature to young journalists.

(2018: 12)

Joseph's words marked a new low. In May 2018, in an ironic twist to the story of investigative journalism in India, top news organisations themselves became the focus of a series of sting operations, which exposed their willingness to consider 'news packages' to further a particular ideology, defame politicians and create a religious atmosphere to help a political party in the build-up to the 2019 general elections – for a big price (Rowlatt, 2018). The revelations disappointed many and spread more cynicism about the state of Indian journalism; one leading commentator saw the news media as a 'principal threat' to India's famed democracy (Mehta, 2018).

As mentioned previously, some governments in independent India sought to curb press freedom, but the contribution to journalism of the Narendra Modi government, which has been in office in New Delhi since 2014 (it was re-elected in 2019), has been significant in the history of media–government relations. Leading figures in the government fuelled public distrust in journalism by referring to journalists as 'presstitutes' and 'news traders' or restricting their access to news sources and forcing journalists and news organisations to censor news that may be critical of the government (the 2019 World Press Freedom Index ranked India at 140). Prime Minister Modi does not address press conferences, prefers scripted interviews and addresses the people through twitter and the state-owned media. The fear of reprisals from those in power among news media organisations and journalists has effectively prevented investigative reporting in recent years (Rao, 2019; Subrahmaniam, 2019).

Journalism, particularly its investigative genre, does not exist in isolation but is part of a complex matrix of laws, core values and practices in a democracy. The default position in a democracy is for the idea, ideology and idealism of journalism to flourish so that it can diligently perform its normative role, but to what extent it can do so when powerful political and corporate forces steer it to one partisan extreme is open to debate. As I have shown, investigative journalism in India has a glorious record, but that is increasingly in the past because of the present text and context: there has been a proliferation in the last 25 years of what I call the 'hardware' of journalism (enabling factors such as technology, capital, rising literacy, training centres), which offers new potential and opportunities for the 'software' of journalism to flourish. By software, I mean the editorial content that empowers citizens, holds those in power to account and strengthens democratic institutions. Online journalism is increasingly making its presence felt, providing new spaces to reclaim credibility, but, as the now-embedded idea of 'Murdochization' acquires more extreme forms, investigative journalism faces a serious challenge, when mainstream journalism itself faces a crisis of trust.

## Notes

1 Reportedly said to Professor Amartya Sen by his supervisor at Cambridge, Professor Joan Robinson.
2 Quotes from Arun Sinha and Sanjay Suri are from personal communication, 2019.

## References

Bose, M. (2017) 'Tale of two republics: Why Shourie compared our media to N. Korea's', *The Quint*; www.thequint.com/news/india/tale-of-two-republics-arun-shourie-indian-media-north-korea; accessed December 26, 2019.

Dharwadker, V. (1997) 'Print culture and literary markets in colonial India', in *Language machines: Technologies of literary and cultural production*, edited by Masten, J., Stallybrass, P., Vickers, N.J., 108–133. London: Routledge.

Gupta, O. (1981) '*Indian Express* pulls off a smart journalistic coup, exposes a sordid flesh trade', *India Today*, May 31.

Joseph, J. (2018) 'The byline is dead: How Indian newsrooms became morgues for investigative journalism', *Caravan*, December.

Mehta, P.B. (2018) 'Where anything goes', *Indian Express*, May 29.

Protess, D. et al (1993) *Journalism of outrage*. New York: Guilford Press.

Rao, S. (2019) 'India's TV journalists cannot speak truth to power – or even the truth', *Newsclick.in*; www.newsclick.in/India-TV-Journalists-Cannot-Speak-Truth-to-Power?fbclid=IwAR3XgP7HzRUZUTXc7poHA8XDJDzgBKSl98I1PuCy4ANYGx7CIop2U3EP690; accessed March 8, 2020.

Ramnath, N. (2017) 'Documentary *The Eyes of Darkness* reveals the horrific copycat effect of the Bhagalpur blindings', *news-views website: scroll.in*; https://scroll.in/reel/826748/documentary-the-eyes-of-darkness-reveals-the-horrific-copycat-effect-of-the-bhagalpur-blindings; accessed December 16, 2019.

Rowlatt, J. (2018) 'The story barely reported by the Indian media', *BBC News*, May 28; www.bbc.co.uk/news/world-asia-india-44280188; accessed July 15, 2019.

Sarin, A. (2018) 'Reporter's case diary', *Outlook*, January 12.

Sen, A. (2006) *The argumentative Indian*. London: Allen Lane.

Sonwalkar, P. (2002) 'Murdochization of the Indian press: from by-line to bottom-line', *Media, Culture & Society*, Volume 24, Number 6, pp. 821–834. ISSN: 0163–4437.

Sonwalkar, P. (2013) 'Where more is not better: Challenges before quality journalism in "shining" India', in *The future of quality news journalism: A cross continental analysis*, edited by Anderson, P. J., Ogola, G., Williams, M., 267–281. London: Routledge.

Sonwalkar, P. (2015) 'Indian journalism in the colonial crucible: A nineteenth century story of political protest', *Journalism Studies*, Volume 16, Number 5, pp. 624–636.

Sonwalkar, P (2016) 'A conundrum of contras: Murdochization of Indian journalism in a digital age', in *The Routledge companion to digital journalism studies*, edited by Eldridge, S., Franklin, B., 528–536. London: Routledge.

Subrahmaniam, V. (2019) 'Daring and drumbeat: An essay on the media in two parts', *The Hindu Centre*; www.thehinducentre.com/the-arena/current-issues/article26664258.ece/binary/Vidya%20Subrahmaniam-Essay_Part%201%20and%202%20-%20final.pdf; accessed December 16, 2019.

Trehan, M. (2009) *Tehelka as metaphor*. New Delhi: Roli Books.

# 14

# MALAYSIA

## A case study in global corruption

*Clare Rewcastle Brown*

This is a case study of how persistent and long-term investigative journalism, using new media, can expose the corrupt in political power and also how the very rich have harnessed the same tools to retaliate through online intimidation and disinformation.

I became involved in the Malaysian corruption issue back in late 2006 when I returned to Sarawak, East Malaysia (the place of my birth), to take part in a Media and Environment conference. Malaysia is a Southeast Asian nation of two halves, cobbled together in 1963 by the British when they relinquished control of previously separate colonies. To the west is the more developed mainland, which includes the capital, Kuala Lumpur; across the South China Sea, East Malaysia comprises the two states in the northern part of the island of Borneo, Sabah and Sarawak, made up of several polities previously in the British Empire. Once known for rubber plantations, pepper and spice trade but nonetheless retaining a largely intact forest landscape, this beautiful region was soon to fall prey to mass timber extraction, followed by the rolling out of an imported cash crop monoculture. The blight of palm oil is today well understood, and Malaysia has become the epicentre of the business that is now driving the mass obliteration of natural forests through Indonesia, Papua New Guinea, the Solomons, the Congo and beyond. The discovery of oil, coal and other valuable resources has consolidated the power of political office holders.

In Borneo, considered the richest area of biodiversity on the planet, the effects have been devastating. Meeting up with local journalists and scientists, I rapidly concluded that poor governance was responsible, driven by state-level, political corruption, abetted by the federal Malaysian government. The local ruling family of then-Chief Minister Abdul Taib Mahmud (now governor) had been in power since the 70s and had taken the opportunity to appropriate all the profit for themselves and a handful of political cronies working hand in glove with the 'big six' timber conglomerates, an inter-related web of family concerns based in the Chinese seaboard communities in the towns of Sibu and Miri.

The local indigenous populations were being stripped of their native customary land rights and bullied and beaten out of the areas they depended on for their food and livelihoods. The landgrabs were carried out in the name of development that did not arrive. With thousands of square miles of prime timber extracted at virtually no profit to the state revenues (officially, the wood was exported for nominal prices), it was whispered that Taib Mahmud was a billionaire several times over.

Why was the federal government allowing such abuses? Why was none of this being reported locally or internationally? And why were the Mahmud family and their cronies apparently able to siphon out so much wealth from their country through the international banking system into what I swiftly identified as a series of massive property portfolios across the Americas [1], United Kingdom [2] and Australia [3]?

Having retained a grip on government since independence, the ruling Barisan Nasional Party utilised a raft of oppressive measures to silence critics, including sedition laws (left over from colonial times) and tight media licensing controls.

The federal government was allowing local potentates such as Taib Mahmud of Sarawak and his alter ego in the neighbouring state of Sabah, Musa Aman, a free hand to pillage their states in return for an illegal deal signed off on in 1974 (the Petroleum Development Act was never ratified by the state parliament as legally required), whereby the federal government obtained 95% of the fabulous oil wealth of both those states. Thus unchecked, Taib set about awarding his family and cronies vast concessions and contracts: his children soon emerged as the shareholders of the biggest companies in the state, enriched by assets privatised from public ownership. They worked together with a handful of increasingly powerful businesses, Sarawak's 'big six' timber companies, which diversified into plantations, oil and gas, construction and of course media ownership. All the major private news outlets, such as the *Borneo Post*, were owned by the logging interests connected to Taib, which have now spread their interests throughout Southeast Asia and beyond. In the speech made in 2016 by then Deputy Head of the FBI, Andrew McCabe he confirms the corruption I identified and that spurred the Department of Justice to the biggest ever seizure of assets in the United States [4].

To enforce such unscrupulous theft by the political classes in a nominal democracy where most people were seeing their ancient rights and livelihoods removed without compensation necessitated strongarm tactics [5]. I was banned from the state almost as soon as I started reporting on Sarawak's problems [6]. No local journalist dared to report on the true state of corruption in the state, let alone the brutal treatment of the indigenous people who were losing their lands or the disastrous environmental impacts of Taib's policies. As they explained to me, at best, they would lose their jobs and see their families penalised in various ways, and at worst, they could be hauled up for 'spreading false news' or 'activities detrimental to democracy' (both of which I, in the relative safety of the United Kingdom, would later be charged with from afar), punishable by up to 20 years in jail. The courts were subject to much political influence, leaving the Malaysian media to all intents a state propaganda machine operating one of the most controlled media environments in the world, languishing around the bottom quarter of the 180 countries in the Press Freedom Index compiled by the organisation Reporters Without Borders [7].

Researching the money flows, it was clear that what enabled the whole system of exploitation to work so smoothly for the dominant political and business families in East Malaysia was the manner in which western professionals and the global financial system were willing to assist these local kleptocrats in processing their corruptly gotten gains out of the locality where they were blatantly abusing their positions of trust, through the off-shore system and into tax free investments across the developed economies. Thanks to these rogue jurisdictions and the willing participation of sophisticated foreign helpers, including bankers, lawyers, tax advisors, business consultants, media and policy strategists, these political criminals had got away with thieving the wealth of their nation from under the feet of its people. Each time a journalist like myself attempted to trace disappearing assets, we would hit the world of 'Treasure Islands' secrecy, making it virtually impossible to untangle ownerships without the help of official investigations or whistleblowers to crack open the money trails [8].

The consequences in terms of environmental devastation and human misery are global, affecting the well-being of billions of lives. In Sarawak, great rivers that were once teeming with life are now stained red and clogged with mud and toxic chemicals. Nearly all the larger animals, including the orang-utan, clouded leopard, proboscis monkey, sun bears, dwarf rhinoceros and pygmy elephants, have become critically endangered, and thousands of plant and animal species have doubtless hit extinction even before being discovered by science.

Marine nurseries for billions of fish have been wiped out with the loss of mangroves and coral reefs. The loss of the natural habitat has been a catastrophe for the native peoples of the region – dozens of tribes and languages existed in the state of Sarawak alone. Bulldozed out of their native lands, many of these groups are being left on the edge of starvation on the fringes of massive plantations without compensation, basic services or any of the benefits of the vast wealth released from their lands. As I started to report on the situation in the interior for such communities, it became clear that none of the profit from logging or palm oil was being returned into health, education, infrastructure or even basic provisions for people who had been deprived of their jungle living. Most still do not have running water, electricity or roads, and very many have been deliberately kept undocumented, which has obstructed them from being able to make demands or vote for a better outcome. Later reporting trips have shown this pattern is repeated everywhere across the region, such as in the vast timber island of Papua New Guinea [9] and the Solomon Islands [10], which are being stripped bare by the very same Sarawak companies who exported their tactics of buying decision-makers and promising development that never came.

Annual choking fires set by the agri-businesses to clear the scrub from logged land to create oil palm plantations now regularly turn these key natural environments into pollution hotspots, affecting the health of the populations in the entire region who suffer the smog for weeks on end – and are a leading driver of climate change.

## How new media took on a totalitarian state

In 2009, the internet presented a staggering window of opportunity, offering small news portals the chance to compete with major news groups – free from censorship and potentially able to catch the attention of a population that was greedily plugging into new possibilities to learn about previously forbidden information. Deep-seated dissatisfaction with the very same corruption and environmental and human rights issues that troubled me was already starting to be expressed online. As an experienced western journalist used to challenging powerful interests as well as digging up information and confirming facts, I felt I could add to the effectiveness of what was being written so far. Facts that nailed the allegations, evidence that corroborated the arguments, clear exposés and a strong narrative were the tools of my trade as I set about providing what I hoped would offer at least a small sampling of public interest journalism to a community that had for decades been fed nothing but wall-to-wall pro-government propaganda through its media. Apart from a £1,000 grant to create the site, I launched it without backers and on my own without any commercial elements.

It was named Sarawak Report in deference to the subject matter and target audience, who were the general public of the East Malaysian state. Yet by calling out the unexplained wealth and blatant conflicts of interest of the ruling family, I started to see immediate impacts in terms of thousands of hits from further afield in Malaysia, too. Articles were being shared and made viral through the developing new media networks of Facebook and Twitter. They were reaching the local audiences in Malaysia without any assistance needed from the previous dominant cartels of mainstream news. And because I was remotely based in the far freer media environment of the United Kingdom, I presented my Malaysian targets with a novel challenge in that, although I was soon banned from the state, they could not silence me.

As I pointed to the international assets of the Taibs and their associates and questioned how a salaried government official together with his immediate family could have amassed such wealth [11], I soon began to receive anonymous insider leaks and tip-offs, another revolutionary by-product of the new media pathways.

These leaks led me to further story after story, as I started to chase the companies belonging to the leading family, which since the early 80s had spread its tentacles into wealth and properties across the globe. The journey of discovery continued as the world of online data started to open up, giving access to public records across the world. Moreover, data that had been suppressed could be sneaked out of back offices and emailed – for example, I received the land survey data detailing the secret handouts of native lands appropriated by the government. I learnt to which front companies they had been granted, whose shareholders I could then research online and who invariably turned out to be connected to Taib through family, political or business ties.

Questioning contacts and NGOs, I tracked down a whistleblower in California who had managed a multi-million-dollar property portfolio for Taib [12]. More leads in the United Kingdom revealed major London holdings [13]; likewise in Australia. By the time of the state election of 2011, Sarawak's chief minister–cum–finance minister–cum–planning resources minister, who had for so long seemed all powerful and untouchable, had an angry populace on his hands.

The result saw his party's share of the popular vote down to a mere 51% of the electorate, despite notorious election rigging practices and gerrymandering by the ruling parties [14]. He had been particularly hit in the urban areas, where young and old were now online.

## Moving up

Following on the heels of that debacle, the 2013 general election likewise presented the closest shave ever for the ruling party. It lost the popular vote for the first time, retaining power thanks only to gerrymandering [15] and vote buying [16].

To survive an unprecedented challenge by a newly invigorated opposition led by Anwar Ibrahim, running on an anti-corruption manifesto, Malaysia's prime minister, Najib Razak, pumped hundreds of millions into winning the election, taking Malaysia's infamous 'money politics' to a new level [17]. It was treated as common knowledge by insiders who spoke to me that the source of the cash appeared to be a new 'sovereign wealth fund' set up by Najib named One Malaysia Development (1MDB) that he was using as a personal slush fund rather than for its ostensible purpose of investing in development [18].

Notwithstanding the close election result and the discontent with corruption it expressed, the federal government did not confront Taib and his brutal regime. Najib's attitude to the East Malaysian states was a long-standing one in his party – they were Barisan Nasional's so-called 'safe deposit': a vital source of cooperative MPs and oil revenues [19]. A Malaysian Anti Corruption Commission investigation had been opened on Taib Mahmud in response to the public outcry over the Sarawak Report's exposés into his assets and sweetheart contracts and concessions. Now it was closed. Najib had merely taken the opportunity to leverage more control over the totalitarian state leader by using the investigation to bargain him out of his executive roles into the ceremonial governor's office. However, thanks to his vast wealth, the elderly politician still holds a commanding control over the economy and management of the state.

The disappointing shutting down of all investigations against Taib and his cronies, despite the overwhelming evidence of their blatant corruption, underlined the extent to which Taib and his ilk were being protected by their partners in crime at the federal level. I realised that without change at the very top of Malaysian politics, they would remain entrenched and their destruction of the last tracts of forest would continue unchecked. I therefore started to expand my investigations, insofar as I could, towards West Malaysia and central government.

My opening to look into Najib and his 1MDB fund came at the end of 2013. Christmas had seen the release of the hundred-million-dollar Hollywood film *The Wolf of Wall Street*. The producer bankrolling it was a newcomer to the movie business named Riza Aziz, Najib's stepson, born to his second wife Rosmah. Rosmah was by then a widely hated character in Malaysia, known for her gargantuan spending sprees, her greed and her interfering presence in her husband's government. Malaysians were widely speculating how the couple had acquired so much money (displayed, for example, at her daughter's lavish wedding [20]) from his career in politics, and now I wondered how her son had managed to fund a blockbuster film, given his previous career as a junior bank officer lasting just two years.

I browsed reports on the film online and noticed that present in all the photo shoots was a young Chinese Malaysian financier named Jho Low, who had already attracted headlines thanks to his big spending in global hotspots. Jho had been in his 20s when he started to gain notoriety in the nightclubs of New York [21], Las Vegas, London and St Tropez, whilst at the same time having coincidentally emerged as the key advisor to Prime Minister Najib over the 1MDB fund and a rumoured confidant of his wife Rosmah. Now it was clear Jho was also involved in Riza's film.

This all raised questions [22]. Jho Low had never provided a consistent explanation for his access to so much cash, at first claiming he was investing on behalf of parents of rich school friends (he went first to Harrow and then Wharton College in Pennsylvania), then later asserting that he was a third-generation billionaire, which came as a surprise to his former neighbours in Penang [23]. It was *The Wolf of Wall Street* leading actor Leonardo DiCaprio who publicly put the pair in the spotlight; when receiving a Golden Globe Award for the film in January, he thanked 'Jho and Riza for taking a risk on the movie' [24]. I had already arrived in Hollywood by that time, since the questions I had raised in articles on Sarawak Report had prompted tip-offs about a series of massive Beverly Hills properties Riza and Jho had secretly bought – again with unexplained millions of dollars through anonymous companies based in Delaware, the United States' secretive domestic tax haven [25]. I would later dig up plenty more on Riza's business activities, all covert and mysteriously funded [26].

Riza and his company, Red Granite Pictures, employed some of the most expensive lawyers in the United States, who immediately started bombarding me with aggressive threats about my reporting. This form of pushback is highly effective against most mainstream news organisations with businesses to protect and a wide range of issues to cover. However, with truth and public interest on

MALAYSIA: GLOBAL CORRUPTION

my side and with just one issue in my sights, I called their bluff, on the basis that the people I was investigating would be disinclined to appear in a witness box in a court of law. I also released their 'confidential' legal letters to the Hollywood media [27]. Predictably, the lawyers never pursued their threats.

## Pushback

Nonetheless, unscrupulous operators (in many cases former journalists who had identified a new form of PR known as 'reputation management') had started pitching to wealthy individuals and oppressive governments, claiming they could outsmart the social media challenge and take back control of the media landscape. Najib Razak had spent millions on online campaigns to vilify his opponent, Anwar Ibrahim [28]. Taib Mahmud purchased the assistance of firms such as the UK-based production company FBC Media [29], Bell Pottinger [30] and SCL [31] (the parent company of Cambridge Analytica) to attack and discredit me online and promote his election chances [32]. FBC Media was working with Rogue Strategic Communications, run by close associates of the (now-jailed) Trump campaign manager Paul Manafort [33].

FBC and Josh Trevino of Rogue Strategic Communications were originally hired to target Sarawak Report in 2011 by Taib Mahmud on a three-year contract worth $15 million [34]. It was an early manifestation of the very real industry of 'fake news'.

I found myself the target of a burgeoning crop of online sites dedicated to attacking and defaming me in a concerted effort to discredit my reporting. Fake Facebook and Twitter identities were created in order to spread their stories [35].

In 2014, soon after my exposés about the Beverly Hill properties, I established that Jho Low had lied over a statement issued through a top PR company that he had ceased involvement in 1MDB shortly after the fund's May 2009 launch. A UK High Court judgement recorded that he had been financially backed by 1MDB in an attempted billion-dollar buy-out in 2011 of London's most luxurious hotel chain [36]. Meanwhile, tracking Jho Low and the Najib family through social media, Sarawak Report had started to unveil details of an astonishing trail of debauchery and excess surrounding these characters and a circle of willing Hollywood hangers-on (including Paris Hilton and DiCaprio) as they partied and gambled in Las Vegas and the world's hotspots. Alongside his Hollywood homes, Jho had acquired a super-yacht for $250 million, a private jet and iconic New York properties, while Rosmah had become a notorious collector of hundred-thousand-dollar Birkin handbags (274 were discovered still boxed when her properties were eventually raided), as well as hundreds of millions of dollars' worth of diamonds and haute couture.

This was all eye-catching material and was laying bare the connection between a kleptocracy, which was destroying the world's third largest rainforest, leaving its people marginalised and destitute, and mammoth expenditure and investments in high-profile sectors of the world's advanced economies.

## Whistleblowers

Despite the current fixation with 'data journalism', nothing beats a good human source. I obtained my first key insider on 1MDB in Xavier Justo, a Swiss former director of the first company that engaged in a so-called 'joint venture' with 1MDB, PetroSaudi International [37]. His (initially anonymous) contact details were passed to me by an aide to an opposition politician whom Justo had approached through an intermediary, offering to sell information that would 'destroy Najib'.

That politician was Anwar Ibrahim, whom Najib was seeking to return to jail (on spurious charges of sodomy, for which he had been previously jailed under former Prime Minister Mahathir Mohamad) in order to cripple the growing opposition threat before the next election, due in 2018. However, Anwar's people were very sceptical about the approach; anyway, they didn't have the $2 million being asked for the promised information. I, of course, didn't have any funds to pay for it either, but I knew enough about the deal to suspect from the tantalising snippets Justo had relayed to the politicians that the documents he was offering were probably genuine. PetroSaudi, owned by a Saudi prince, Turki, and a Swiss-based friend named Tarek Obaid, was essentially a shell company looking to peddle access through Prince Turki's royal connections, but it had posed as a major player in the oil business.

I went to Bangkok to meet Justo (who now lived in Thailand) and try to find out more. I learnt that, having fallen out with his former colleagues, he had left, taking with him a copy of the company email server – the database contained hundreds of thousands of documents which revealed how the joint venture with 1MDB had fronted an immense and deliberate theft from the fund. We scrolled through some of the damning material that plainly showed how Jho Low, representing 1MDB on behalf of the 'Big Boss' (Najib) and his wife Rosmah, was acting behind the scenes as the real orchestrator of the development fund. The plan had been pulled together at a meeting of the key players –Turki, Obaid, Najib, Rosmah and Jho – on board a super-yacht off the coast of Monaco shortly after Najib had taken power in 2009. They had even emailed each other the pictures, providing handy visual evidence. As the plan unfurled, the official board and management of 1MDB were no more than window dressing; such was the power of the prime minister-cum-finance minister over Malaysia's highly centralised and corrupt regime.

Bank transfers showed that of $1.83 billion transferred by 1MDB into the joint venture, over $1.3 billion had been siphoned into an off-shore company based in the Seychelles that was owned by Jho Low, whilst the rest went into funding PetroSaudi's private ventures and kickbacks. Jho Low had used $260 million to buy out, at vast profit, one of his own investments in Sarawak, a conglomerate named UBG half owned by Taib Mahmud himself, who thus also profited handsomely from this theft of Malaysian public money.

## Big banks, accountancy giants, global law firms and the United Nations

Intermediaries on this first set of deals were RBS Coutts in Zurich, J P Morgan Suisse and BSI Bank. Dozens of international banks were eventually caught facilitating the transfers and thefts from 1MDB 'without due care and attention'. BSI Bank has been closed down over the fraud [38] and several others fined [39] and prosecuted [40]. The top London law firm White & Case managed PetroSaudi's side of the deal, whereby $700 million was transferred out of the joint venture company on the very first day of operations in the guise of a bogus loan repayment. Many other law firms, including Shearman & Sterling and Kobre & Kim, were later caught up in the scandal (millions were laundered through their client accounts to fund Riza's movies) [41], along with three of the world's top four accountancy firms who failed to do basic due diligence on 1MDB's audits [42] and waved through Jho Low's fraudulent transactions on behalf of prime minister Najib. Politicians and officials in Western countries and global institutions were likewise beneficiaries of the 1MDB conspirators' efforts to buy influence and cover up their criminality on the international stage. By the time I got the story, Jho had reinvented himself as a global philanthropist fêted by the UN Foundation for funding its Global News service, ironically dedicated to supporting investigative journalism [43]!

The Malaysian scandal has become a case study in how global financial institutions, law firms and other governments have flocked to do business with corrupt authoritarian regimes, providing kleptocrats with impunity not just in their own countries but across the world. Foremost amongst these was the banking giant Goldman Sachs, central to the next set of blatantly corrupt manoeuvres orchestrated by Jho Low on behalf of his 'Big Boss' through 1MDB [44]. This constituted the borrowing by 1MDB, ostensibly for investment in power plants and urban development, of $6.5 billion via three major bond issues managed by the bank. As I wrote at the time, the extortionate interest rates offered – which I discovered from a leaked document related to this secretive deal – and suspiciously high fees exacted by the bank ought to have triggered regulatory alarms but never did [45a]. The FBI later traced how half of the cash raised was again siphoned off within hours into off-shore companies connected to Jho Low and his co-conspirators [45b].

After several months trying to get Justo to part with the evidence, I finally persuaded a Malaysian media baron to pay his price and received a copy of the data as part of that agreement. Together with the *Sunday Times*, I published the exposé on PetroSaudi in February 2015, calling it 'The Heist of the Century' [46] (which indeed it was, as 1MDB is now recognised as the largest theft tackled by the US Department of Justice, totalling $5 billion and rising as investigations around the world continue). Thereafter I was contacted by several more insiders, including one with key information about those Goldman Sachs bond deals, which had been conducted in collaboration with a second 1MDB 'joint venture partner', a company called Aabar which was itself a subsidiary company of another sovereign wealth fund, Abu Dhabi's International Petroleum Investment Company (IPIC).

My source had been close to the sovereign wealth fund manager and chief executive of IPIC, Khadem Al Qubaisi, popularly known as KAQ, who was also chairman of Aabar. Jho Low and KAQ had already been revealed to me by a separate source to be party companions in Las Vegas, where the salaried fund manager had mysteriously funded a major nightclub chain named Hakkasan [47]. Working with Jho Low, KAQ had agreed, in a complex arrangement constructed by Goldman Sachs' South East Asia boss, Tim Leissner (who has now pleaded guilty to bribery and fraud [48]), that Aabar would act as the 'guarantor' for the bonds raised by 1MDB. In return for the guarantee on the loans, 1MDB secretly agreed to pay around half of the money raised to companies allegedly owned by Aabar.

What my new informant was able to demonstrate through documents obtained from KAQ's account at Edmond de Rothschild bank in Luxembourg was that the companies into which around $3 billion was paid (ostensibly for the nonsensical loan guarantee) were merely bogus off-shore entities based in the British Virgin Islands and Seychelles, owned not by Aabar but by KAQ. Half a billion dollars from those payments had gone straight into KAQ's private accounts to pay for his lavish lifestyle (he owned a fleet of more than 50 customised sports vehicles and over a dozen properties in Paris and the Côte D'Azure) [49] and also for the upkeep of one of the world's largest superyachts, *Topaz*, which belongs to KAQ's ultimate boss at IPIC, Sheikh Mansour, a member of the ruling family of Abu Dhabi. After I published the story in March 2015, KAQ was sacked and soon imprisoned, the first arrest related to 1MDB [50].

Compliance officers within Goldman Sachs had consistently raised concerns about these extraordinary arrangements but were over-ruled, and I wrote numerous reports demanding accountability, which for years the bank stonewalled while Najib remained in power. Following investigations in the United States and other jurisdictions, the bank has now paid more than $7 billion in fines and compensation for its role in the affair, and some of its star bankers have been struck off and arrested [51]. The new Malaysian government pressed charges against 17 senior executives at the bank (later settled in return for an alleged $3.9 billion), and a major shareholder class action has accused the former CEO and president and others of complicity and cover-up in the illegal transactions that made unprecedented profits for the bank. It is worth noting that until a tiny online blog, Sarawak Report, published these exposés, there had seemed little chance that any regulatory or investigative body would take

## MALAYSIA: GLOBAL CORRUPTION

action to investigate what had by 2015 emerged as billion-dollar losses from a government fund through the good offices of Goldman Sachs.

### Power vs publicity

My stories on the initial 1MDB joint venture with PetroSaudi were picked up by the wider media and prompted investigations by anti-corruption authorities in Malaysia. Initially these were permitted by Najib, who sought to distance himself as a mere advisor to the fund. Amendments to the articles of association later proved he had in fact established himself as the sole shareholder and decision-maker [52]. The FBI also began its own enquiries based on the dollar transactions involved and the huge assets caught up in the United States.

In late June 2015, my own sources within the Malaysian investigations passed me crucial confirmation that nearly a billion dollars from the money funnelled out of 1MDB through the fake Aabar accounts had been transferred to Najib's own personal bank account in KL just a week before he called that 2013 general election which had witnessed so much vote buying. I was passed documents showing the transfer of $681 million into his account from a company in Singapore owned by Jho Low. After weeks of denial, during which time Xavier Justo had been arrested and jailed in Bangkok on trumped-up charges of blackmail (and forced to make a false confession in which he accused me of doctoring the documents [53]), this was the game changer.

I passed on the documentation to the *Wall Street Journal*, and we jointly published the evidence on 2 July [54]. Najib was on the run, and many of the entities that had been hired to intimidate and impede my reporting, including a team of private investigators who had ostentatiously stalked me in London over several weeks and reported my movements back to their bosses in Malaysia, now noticeably fell away [55]. Instead, Najib moved to secure his position at home. He aggressively clamped down on dissent, bringing in new regulations against online media and one of the world's first 'fake news' laws to intimidate social media users. My site was banned entirely, the first such case in Malaysia (happily, many savvy internet users were able to get around the ban) [56]. Then he shut down the domestic investigations of 1MDB and sacked the attorney general and several senior politicians who had led calls for more accountability over 1MDB [57]. He replaced the top personnel in the anti-corruption agencies, and his new attorney general was wheeled out to make a press statement claiming the enquiries had shown there was 'no wrongdoing at 1MDB' and that Najib was 'cleared' [58]. The billion dollars in Najib's account was explained as a gift from an anonymous Middle Eastern royal who appreciated Najib's contributions to the promotion of moderate Islam.

I was leaked a charge sheet which showed that prosecutors had drawn up charges against Najib for criminal breach of trust and theft and had been on the verge of charging him. It was obvious that this had precipitated his sudden virtual coup against his own government. I published the document, which caused a huge stir.

Najib's regime responded by bringing charges against me for 'spreading false news' and 'activities detrimental to parliamentary democracy', for which the penalties amounted to 20 years imprisonment on each charge [59]. Malaysia requested INTERPOL issue a Red Notice seeking my arrest and extradition to face the charges (thankfully it was publicly rejected by that organisation) [60]. I remained in the United Kingdom and refrained from visiting the region where Xavier Justo remained imprisoned owing to Malaysian influence in Thailand for a full 18 months before Swiss pressure finally obtained his pardon and release.

There was worse to come. Soon after Najib executed his internal coup, a young prosecutor was reported to have been abducted from his car in moving traffic in KL (the incident was captured on CCTV), only to be found dead ten days later, submerged in a concrete-filled drum [61]. It became clear that it was he who had drawn up charges against Najib for criminal breach of trust and theft [62]. Following the murder, several frightened officials in Malaysia told me that they could do no more to counter the scandal.

Yet in mid-2016, Najib received a major setback. A joint team from the US Department of Justice and the FBI – which had contacted and interviewed me after I published my stories on 1MDB – held a stunning press conference headed by US Attorney General Lorretta Lynch to announce a billion-dollar asset seizure of mansions, jets, super-yachts, businesses and even *The Wolf of Wall Street*, all bought with money traced from 1MDB through the bogus joint ventures that Jho Low had framed with PetroSaudi and Aabar. Their court deposition [63] laid out in excruciating detail exactly how hundreds of millions had been transferred through off-shore companies and a string of private and major multi-national banks. Over the next months, the investigations expanded globally, exposing further billions in stolen assets from the fund [64].

Jho Low and several officials from the fund fled into hiding but Najib continued to dig in, declaring emergency powers and imprisoning critics without trial [65]. The fact that money from the fund had been found by the FBI to have supplied Najib's holidays and diamonds, luxuries and anti-ageing treatment for his wife was alternately denied or dismissed as a 'mistake'.

Najib had such control over the country that all the experts opined that, notwithstanding the scandal, he would breeze through the next general election [66]. Yet, despite the domestic media clamp-downs, news of the scandal and the international investigations now being undertaken by the Swiss, Singaporean, Luxembourgish and French authorities reached the public in Malaysia – thanks again to social media. My banned articles recording the unfolding investigations were circulated through Facebook, WhatsApp and emails.

When the election was finally called, in early 2018, the electorate, revolted by the blatant corruption and the authoritarian repression, deserted Najib and the decades-old Barisan Nasional regime in droves. The scandal had brought together old enemies from the opposition, who created a united front under the 93-year-old former prime minister, Mahathir Mohamad. The popular strongman and predecessor of Najib himself bore a good deal of culpability in the eyes of reformers for the systemic corruption and over-centralisation of power; nonetheless, he had signed up for the reform agenda of progressive parties and pledged to hand over power to the imprisoned Anwar Ibrahim as the next prime minister designate. Amazingly, despite more bribes and gerrymandering than ever before, that coalition swept the dishonoured and discredited Najib from power when the country finally went to the polls. It was a historic moment and a new dawn for Malaysia [67].

For me, the outcome of that election of the 9th of May 2018 represented a massive vindication of the role of independent investigative reporting, empowered by the reach and impact of social media platforms. Despite the hugely funded professional counter-attacks, the population in Malaysia learnt the truth about their prime minister and voted on the guidance of evidence-based reporting as opposed to propaganda based on blatant lies. The unravelling of the 1MDB scandal has demonstrated that effective investigative journalism can still make a difference.

## Notes

1 www.sarawakreport.org/2010/06/exclusive-taibs-foreign-property-portfolio/; www.sarawakreport.org/2010/07/saktisakto-another-taib-exclusive/
2 www.sarawakreport.org/2010/07/growing-scandal-the-london-connection/
3 www.sarawakreport.org/2011/03/cash-for-honours-at-adelaide-university/
4 https://aliran.com/web-specials/2016-web-specials/fbi-1mdb-malaysian-people-defrauded-enormous-scale/
5 www.sarawakreport.org/2013/10/spotlight-on-melikin-how-gangsterism-and-politics-mix-in-sarawak/; www.sarawakreport.org/2012/08/gangster-state/; www.sarawakreport.org/2012/07/what-justice-for-the-victims-of-timber-gangs-in-sarawak/; www.sarawakreport.org/2011/05/how-len-talif-salleh-objective-civil-serv antbn-politiciantimber-company-boss-swindled-long-terawan/
6 www.telegraph.co.uk/news/worldnews/asia/malaysia/10159557/Activist-sister-in-law-of-Gordon-Brown-deported-from-Malaysia.html
7 https://rsf.org/en/malaysia
8 www.sarawakreport.org/2011/11/sean-murrays-kuching-construction-connection-expose/; www.sarawakreport.org/2014/02/questions-for-taib-after-new-revelations-over-japanese-kickbacks-special-investigation/
9 www.sarawakreport.org/2020/01/new-malaysia-should-clean-up-its-present-day-colonial-shame/
10 www.sarawakreport.org/2020/01/predator-logging-company-thrown-out-of-solomon-islands-is-owned-by-sons-of-sarawak-mp-expose/
11 www.sarawakreport.org/2010/06/a-key-question-for-taib/
12 www.sarawakreport.org/2011/03/film-tribute-to-ross-boyert/
13 www.sarawakreport.org/2010/11/hide-park-taibs-london-bolt-hole/

14 www.sarawakreport.org/2011/04/thief-minister-stole-election/; www.sarawakreport.org/2010/04/give-us-our-vote/

15 www.economist.com/asia/2018/03/08/how-malaysias-next-election-will-be-rigged; www.sarawakreport.org/2013/05/bns-money-politics-leaves-malaysia-with-same-crime-minister/

16 www.sarawakreport.org/2013/04/what-tiong-gets-for-his-rm1000-per-vote/; www.sarawakreport.org/2013/05/down-at-the-airport/; www.sarawakreport.org/2013/05/caught-on-camera-bns-hatchet-faced-vote-buyers/

17 www.sarawakreport.org/2017/05/bustari-the-bag-man-how-najib-bought-the-sarawak-election-further-exclusive/

18 www.malaysiakini.com/news/145649

19 www.iseas.edu.sg/images/pdf/ISEAS_Perspective_2018_27@50.pdf

20 www.malaysiakini.com/news/330605

21 https://nypost.com/2009/11/08/big-spending-malaysian-is-the-mystery-man-of-city-club-scene/

22 www.sarawakreport.org/2013/12/wall-street-greed-malaysian-money-expose/

23 www.thestar.com.my/business/business-news/2010/07/30/low-dispels-talk-he-received-rm500mil-airbase-job

24 www.fraud-magazine.com/cover-article.aspx?id=4295001869

25 www.sarawakreport.org/2014/01/wow-we-enter-riza-azizs-secret-beverly-hills-mansion-hollywood-exclusive/

26 www.sarawakreport.org/2016/05/riza-linked-company-seeks-to-invest-millions-in-multiple-ventures-globally/

27 https://deadline.com/2014/01/wolf-of-wall-street-producers-cease-and-desist-sarawack-report-clare-brown-671868/;www.hollywoodreporter.com/news/wolf-wall-street-financiers-threaten-668550

28 www.sarawakreport.org/2011/07/dirty-tricks-campaign-targets-anwar-too/

29 www.sarawakreport.org/2011/08/taib-paid-out-5-million-to-attack-sarawak-report-international-expose/

30 www.newyorker.com/magazine/2018/06/25/the-reputation-laundering-firm-that-ruined-its-own-reputation; www.independent.co.uk/news/uk/politics/the-arms-company-the-oligarch-and-the-ex-pms-sister-in-law-lobby-firms-wikipedia-hit-list-6274541.html

31 www.sarawakreport.org/2018/05/najib-lied-about-umno-links-to-sclcambridge-analytica/; www.theguardian.com/politics/2019/aug/01/revealed-johnson-allys-firm-secretly-ran-facebook-propaganda-network

32 www.sarawakreport.org/2015/10/defamation-games-a-swiss-pr-anonymous-attacks-a-fake-twitter-army-and-information-they-all-share/

33 www.sarawakreport.org/2012/08/malaysias-poison-blogger-exposed-in-the-us/; www.politico.com/blogs/media/2013/03/joshua-trevinos-malay-payday-158247

34 www.sarawakreport.org/2011/08/bbc-suspends-all-fbc-programmes-pending-enquiry/

35 www.sarawakreport.org/2015/11/liars-forgers-and-paid-pr-people-posing-as-activists-black-pr-against-sarawak-report-exposed/

36 www.sarawakreport.org/2014/05/1mdb-backed-jho-low-with-uk1billion-exclusive-expose/

37 www.sarawakreport.org/2015/02/heist-of-the-century-how-jho-low-used-petrosaudi-as-a-front-to-siphon-billions-out-of-1mdb-world-exclusive/

# MALAYSIA: GLOBAL CORRUPTION

38  https://theconversation.com/how-a-swiss-bank-was-toppled-by-a-financial-scandal-in-malaysia-and-what-can-be-learned-from-it-100130
39  www.straitstimes.com/business/mas-imposes-penalties-on-standard-chartered-bank-and-coutts-for-1mdb-related-breaches
40  www.reuters.com/article/us-malaysia-scandal-swiss-falcon-private/falcon-bank-faces-swiss-criminal-probe-in-1mdb-case-idUSKCN12C134
41  www.justice.gov/archives/opa/page/file/877166/download
42  www.scmp.com/news/asia/southeast-asia/article/2184302/malaysia-fines-audit-firm-deloitte-serious-breaches-linked
43  www.sarawakreport.org/2016/03/jho-lows-latest-party-pals-are-from-the-un/
44  www.ft.com/content/3f161eda-3306-11ea-9703-eea0cae3f0de; www.sarawakreport.org/2019/11/goldman-sachs-lied-and-denied-over-1mdbs-billion-dollar-thefts/
45a www.sarawakreport.org/2013/07/goldman-sachs-us200million-charge-for-1mdb-bond-issue/
45b www.justice.gov/archives/opa/page/file/877166/download
46  www.sarawakreport.org/2015/02/heist-of-the-century-how-jho-low-used-petro saudi-as-a-front-to-siphon-billions-out-of-1mdb-world-exclusive/; www.thetimes.co.uk/article/harrow-playboy-linked-to-troubled-malaysian-fund-7fq32lf5vdr; www.nytimes.com/2016/07/21/world/asia/1mdb-malaysia-us-assets-seized.html; www.theguardian.com/world/2016/jul/28/1mdb-inside-story-worlds-biggest-financial-scandal-malaysia
47  www.sarawakreport.org/2015/12/more-on-the-massive-us-investment-portfolio-of-disgraced-ex-falcon-bank-boss-khadem-al-qubaisi/
48  www.nytimes.com/2019/12/16/business/goldman-sachs-1mdb-tim-leissner.html
49  www.sarawakreport.org/2016/03/khadems-kool-cars-cash-buyer-wanted/
50  www.sarawakreport.org/2016/08/90-federal-police-officers-raided-edmond-de-rothschild-bank-how-aabar-scandal-could-dward-1mdb/
51  https://dealbreaker.com/2020/02/andrea-vella-banned
52  www.euromoney.com/article/b12kmz59m12yj8/jho-low-says-it-aint-so-malaysian-tycoon-denies-role-in-1mdb-heist-of-the-century
53  www.theguardian.com/world/2016/jul/28/1mdb-inside-story-worlds-biggest-finan cial-scandal-malaysia; www.youtube.com/watch?v=CDYIzTME6zE
54  www.sarawakreport.org/2015/07/sensational-findings-prime-minister-najib-razaks-personal-accounts-linked-to-1mdb-money-trail-malaysia-exclusive/; www.wsj.com/articles/SB10130211234592774869404581083700187014570
55  https://time.com/5463070/malaysia-1mdb-clare-rewcastle-brown-sarawak-report-interview/; www.theguardian.com/media/greenslade/2015/jul/28/british-journalist-im-being-followed-in-london-by-teams-of-stalkers
56  www.theguardian.com/world/2015/jul/20/sarawak-report-whistleblowing-website-blocked-by-malaysia-over-pm-allegations
57  www.asiaone.com/malaysia/malaysias-najib-appoints-new-ministers-strengthen-coali tion; www.sarawakreport.org/2015/07/cameron-ought-cancel-his-malaysia-visit/
58  www.sarawakreport.org/2016/01/bungling-ag-gives-away-more-evidence-at-press-conference-meant-to-clear-najib-exclusive/0
59  www.nst.com.my/news/2015/09/police-have-arrest-warrant-sarawak-report-editor
60  www.thestar.com.my/news/nation/2015/09/14/cops-still-want-clare-interpol-red-notice/

61  www.nst.com.my/news/2016/04/138783/kevin-morais-was-smothered-death-being-stuffed-drum-pathology-expert
62  www.sarawakreport.org/2015/07/arrest-warrant-for-the-prime-minister-the-real-reason-the-attorney-general-was-fired-exclusive/
63  www.justice.gov/archives/opa/page/file/877166/download
64  www.thetimes.co.uk/article/jho-low-the-man-accused-of-stealing-5bn-to-buy-his-way-into-hollywood-xnvx6hlqz
65  www.reuters.com/article/us-malaysia-scandal-idUSKBN13I1XP
66  www.economist.com/leaders/2018/03/10/malaysias-pm-is-about-to-steal-an-election
67  www.bbc.co.uk/news/world-asia-44036178

# 15

# TEN YEARS IN NIGERIA

*Emeka Umejei and Suleiman A. Suleiman*

Between 1999 and 2019, there has been a marked decline of investigative journalism in Nigeria's traditional media and a corresponding shift towards the online media. This chapter holds that the rise of digital media has disrupted the business model of traditional media organisations in Nigeria, leading to plummeting advertising revenues and consequences for investigation.[1] The first section is a brief overview of investigative journalism as a liberal democratic norm both in the wider political communication literature and in Nigeria specifically. The second section discusses the decline of investigative reporting in traditional print media due to the death of magazines and depleting investigative units over time. This is followed by a detailed analysis of the marked shift to online media and the accompanying changes in journalistic processes and practices as investigative reporting goes online. The final section offers our concluding arguments.[2]

## Context

The role of the traditional media in the establishment of democracy in Nigeria is well documented (Ogbondah 1994). At the outset of democratic governance in 1999, it was evident that the traditional media were well prepared to take on the watchdog role to shepherd Nigeria's fragile democracy (Onabanjo 2004). The media reinforced this role barely one month after the return to democratic governance when Salisu Buhari, a former speaker of the Nigerian House of Representatives, was exposed for certificate forgery and age falsification. The tempo of watchdog journalism was sustained with exclusive investigative stories that helped shape democratic governance. The investigative reporting tradition was most evident in the magazines, which had prioritised investigative reporting since the era of military dictatorship, and newspaper publications that incorporated investigative reporting in their news work. For instance, the first author of this chapter started off his journalism career in the Cover and Investigation unit of one national newspaper in Nigeria that no longer maintains that desk. In addition, the arrival of *Next* newspaper in the Nigerian media landscape in 2008 added impetus to investigative reporting in the traditional

203

media space. *Next* was published by Pulitzer-prize-winning journalist Dele Olojede. However, it soon collapsed from the coordinated exclusionary tactics of advertisers, which detested its investigative reporting bias. After the collapse of *Next* in 2011, some journalists who had worked there founded *Premium Times*, Nigeria's leading online newspaper. Before *Premium Times*, *Sahara Reporters*, a diaspora online platform based in New York, had been the torch bearer of investigative journalism in the online media space in Nigeria. Though fashioned as a citizen journalism platform, it has provided in-depth investigative reporting that shook the political establishment in Nigeria. And from 2011, a noticeable shift emerged in investigative journalism in Nigeria; newly established online publications such as *Premium Times*, the *Cable* newspaper and International Centre for Investigative Reporting (ICIR), in collaboration *with Sahara Reporters*, began to focus exclusively on investigative reporting. Significantly, these online publications prioritised investigative reporting over other news genres. In this sense, while investigative reporting was conceived as having a roving role in the traditional media, in the online media space, it was prioritised; it became an institutional practice.

This digital turn in investigative reporting in Nigeria was further consolidated with a grant of $5 million offered by the MacArthur Foundation to strengthen investigative reporting capacity and data journalism in Nigeria.[3] Nine organisations were awarded various amount of money; among these, only one was from the traditional media space, *Daily Trust* newspaper, which got $350,000 through the foundation. The remaining included the usual online media organisations, including *Sahara Reporters*, *Premium Times*, *ICIR* and the *Cable*. Some others are the Wole Soyinka Centre for Investigative Journalism, Bayero University, Kano and Reboot, Abuja. This grant is believed to have strengthened investigative reporting and helped entrench it as an institutional practice in the online media space.

## Investigative journalism as liberal democratic norm in Nigeria and beyond

Classical liberal theory assumed that publicity and openness, which investigative journalism engenders, were the most effective guarantees against the corrupting influence of power. As such, investigative journalism is regarded as the most important function of the media (Coronel 2010, p. 111; Norris and Odugbemi 2010, p. 5; Jones 2009, pp. 5–6; Feldstein 2006, p. 105). Nord (2007, p. 518) points out that investigative journalism is "universally perceived as the cornerstone of journalistic practice and a more or less uncontroversial function of independent media organizations in a free and democratic society". Similarly, Ettema and Glasser (1998, p. 189) identify three 'core values' that inform the democratic potentials of investigative journalism, namely *publicity* (bringing abuse of power into public attention to instigate reforms); *accountability* (calling wrongdoers into account) and *solidarity*, or creating bonds of compassion between the public and victims of wrongdoing. Mellado (2015, p. 602) contends that investigative reporting is the most important aspect of all news reporting styles through which watchdog journalism is enacted in journalistic content, the others being questioning, critiques, denouncing, conflict, coverage of trials and external research. In short, investigative journalism is about investigating the operation of democracy to help actualise its normative claims (Hamilton 2016, p. 8). As such, investigative reporters are described as the "elite special forces of Fourth Estate's armies" (Walton 2010, p. 19). Therefore, definitions of investigative reporting emphasise features that differentiate it from other journalistic practices: reporter initiative, methodological rigour in collecting evidence and writing up the story and the impact of the story in instigating reforms (Lanosga et al. 2017; Lanosga 2015; Starkman 2014; Stetka and Örnebring 2013; Jones 2009; Ettema and Glasser 2007; Feldstein 2006).

However, neither the ideal nor the practice of investigative journalism is without critics. It is criticised for invoking conflicting values such as its claim to be 'detached' or 'objective' and 'watchdog' or 'custodian of conscience' at the same time (Cunningham 2003, pp. 1–5; Ettema and Glasser 1998, pp. 7–9). Some doubt its claim to 'truth-telling', since investigative reporters depend mostly on powerful sources who often manipulate the press for their own political agenda (Feldstein 2007, pp. 546–457; Waisbord 1997, pp. 121–124, 1996, p. 344). Starkman (2014) contends that investigative journalism sometimes goes to sleep when the public needs it the most, as in failing to expose the malfeasance that resulted in the Great Recession of 2008. Others are worried by increasing sensationalism and celebritisation of investigative reporting and hence transformation of 'Watergate' into 'Zippergate' (Street 2011, p. 192; Tumber and Waisbord 2004, p. 1145). More broadly, Altschull (1995) argues that by merely exposing corruption, investigative reporting, in fact, protects an inherently unequal capitalist system rather than exposing its systemic contradictions (in Lanosga 2015, p. 368). What promise, then, does the foregoing discussion hold for investigative journalism in Nigeria, particularly since the return to democracy in 1999?

### *Watchdog journalism and investigative reporting in Nigeria*

Nigeria has between 400 and 1000 news publications (EU 2015, p. 22; Kuenzi and Lambright, 2015, p. 14), most of them owned by proprietors who were themselves former journalists and editors, although an increasing number are owned by politicians or businessmen with political connections (Musa and Domatob 2007, p. 322). Broadband penetration remains generally low, but internet access is available to nine in ten Nigerians through mobile devices (PEW 2015). In addition, the Freedom of Information Law, designed to promote whistleblowing and investigative reporting of corruption, has been in effect since 2011, after years of bickering and buck-passing between government and civil society (Berliner 2014, p. 483; Ojebode 2011, p. 268).

Furthermore, the Nigerian press is described as the most politically vibrant in Africa and has espoused liberal ideas of free press and watchdog journalism since its inception in 1849 (Oso 2013, p. 17; Rønning 2009, p. 165; Olukotun 2000, p. 33, 2002, p. 319; Omu 1978). According to Omu (1968, p. 285), by the 1900s, Nigerian newspapers had a political clout and impact that matched the colonial government itself. Colonial governors in Nigeria in the 1930s and 1940s were known to complain "bitterly" about critical coverage by newspapers like *The Comet* and *West African Pilot* that was ultimately instrumental in rolling back colonialism altogether (Olukotun 2004, p. 74; Shaw 2009, p. 496). Following political independence in 1960, the press, it is claimed, exposed corruption and human rights abuses of Nigerian civilian and military governments, often forcing the resignation from office of top government officials (Olukotun 2004, p. 74; Jibo and Okoosi-Simbene 2003, p. 181). Moreover, since the return to democracy in 1999, newspapers found renewed vigour in exposing corruption in high places, often leading to resignations of several top office holders, including two speakers of the House of Representatives for certificate forgery and corruption, respectively (Iwokwagh and Batta 2011, pp. 327–328; Ojo 2003, pp. 831–833). Newspapers also preserved the constitutional order in 2006 by preventing former President Olusegun Obasanjo from perpetuating himself in power (Olaiya et al. 2013, p. 57). The overall argument, then, is that through watchdog journalism and investigative reporting, Nigerian newspapers have been at the forefront of democratic development in the country.

However, some observers argue that Nigerian newspapers are as elitist, corrupt and anti-democratic as the governments they claim to challenge (Hall 2009; Ette 2000; Obadare 1999; Agbaje 1993). In consequence, therefore, much of what is called investigative journalism in Nigeria and elsewhere in Africa are biased, poorly written stories by ill-motivated reporters, often published to settle political scores, maximise profits or impress foreign donors (Behrman et al. 2012, p. 87; Rønning 2009, p. 166; Camara 2008, p. 291; Berger 2002, p. 38; Kasoma 1995, p. 547). How, then, has investigative journalism in Nigeria changed from the return to democracy in 1999 to date?

## Decline of investigative reporting in the traditional media

### *'Death' of magazines*

The rise of digital media has disrupted the media landscape globally, and Nigeria is not an exception. The magazine segment of the Nigerian media has suffered the most from digital disruption. The magazine segment of the Nigerian media was reputed for establishing investigative journalism as an institutional practice. This was the case during the military era when magazines such as *Tell*, *The News* and *Newswatch* were thorns in the side of several military juntas. The founding of *Newswatch* magazine in 1984 by American-trained journalist Dele

Giwa and colleagues redefined investigative journalism in Nigeria. Incidentally, Dele Giwa also met his death in the course of investigating corrupt practices under a former military dictator, General Ibrahim Badamasi Babangida.[4] The *Newswatch* magazine pioneered a magazine segment that was reputed for hard-hitting investigative stories. The same tradition was sustained by *Tell* and *The News*. A few colleagues also left *Newswatch* to establish *Tell* magazine, while a group of journalists who had been 'unfairly' treated at *The Concord* newspaper started *The News* magazine. These magazines were responsible for most of the exclusive investigative reporting that rattled the top hierarchy of the military establishment during years of military dictatorship. Unfortunately, these magazines have either collapsed, gone online or are in skeletal production. For instance, *The Newswatch* collapsed after it was bought and became enmeshed in civil litigation; *The News* has stopped running a print edition and basically operates as an online magazine.[5] Bayo Onanuga, editor-in-chief, explained that its transition to the online media space "has been informed by the rising costs of production and declining advertising income, which make the continuous production in print form, very unprofitable". For its part, *Tell* is struggling to make an appearance on newsstands every week. In the same vein, some journalists from these magazines have shifted to the online media space, where they have prioritised investigative journalism. For instance, the publishers of ICIR and Premium Times are both products of some of these magazines.

### Declining advertising revenues

There is a consensus among journalists in print, electronic and online media that the decline of investigative journalism in the traditional media is a consequence of limited financial resources. Respondents agree that media viability has become challenging in the face of the disruptive influence of digital media. The situation is more complicated in Nigeria, where a section of the traditional media has not been able to pay salaries to journalists when due.[6] This means that traditional media organisations do not have additional financial resources to fund investigative reporting assignments. Hence, embarking on investigative reporting assignments is considered a luxury that many traditional media organisations cannot afford. In this sense, advertisers are considered precious objects that must be courted by traditional media organisations. For instance, respondents emphasised that advertisers wield influence over media content in the traditional media space. They contend that in the face of depleting advertising revenues, most traditional media organisations are cautious not to offend potential advertisers and are likely to defer investigative reporting if it is considered offensive to an advertiser. The experience of the first author at a national newspaper in Nigeria is quite relevant. The author had been recruited to the Cover and Investigation desk of a national newspaper and was assigned to investigate a car manufacturing company that was short-changing Nigerian owners. The outcome of the assignment was scheduled to be published in series. The publication of the first report in the series elicited widespread attention and attracted the subject of the investigation. The car company intervened, and the report was halted. This reflects the power of advertisers in the Nigerian media landscape. This was also highlighted by the publisher of *Next Edition*:

> Advertiser influence is a major issue why most of these conventional media organisations are not running investigative stories because they are afraid that when you run it you will hurt your advertiser and they will not come to you but that is a false notion.
>
> (personal communication with Ibanga, May 2019)

In addition, media owners wield enormous influence in the Nigerian media landscape (see Okwuchukwu 2014). In the traditional media space, media owners decide the genre of content to be published or not. For example, media content that adversely affects an owner's political or economic interests is often not allowed to fly; it is 'killed' during gatekeeping (Okwuchukwu 2014). Hence, one of the easiest routes to losing a job in the traditional media space is to provide a report that adversely affects corporate organisations or political allies of media owners.

### *Depleting investigative units*

Respondents agreed that investigative units are getting fewer in traditional media in Nigeria. In both electronic and print media, there are only a few media organisations with investigative units that have dedicated funding. For instance, in the print segment which accounts for more than 20 daily newspapers, there are only 4 newspapers with dedicated investigative reporting units. These include the *Nigerian Telegraph*, *The Daily Trust*, *The Nation* and most recently, *The Punch*. The investigative unit at *Punch* is manned by four reporters, with the head domiciled in Abuja; this is the same for *Daily Trust*, which also has a foundation that is dedicated to investigative journalism. For the *Nigerian Telegraph* and *The Nation*, both have very limited funding to pursue investigative reporting projects; while the *Nigerian Telegraph* has just the editor of investigation on the investigation desk, *The Nation* has two persons, including the editor of the desk.

The electronic media is less enthusiastic considering that its resources are tied to advertising from both commercial and political sources. Channels Television was considered Nigeria's version of the BBC, but it has been accused of compromising its investigative reporting in recent times. A broadcast media columnist at *Punch* recently described the downplay of investigative reporting at Channels Television as 'akin to The NTA-nisation of Channels TV'[7] in reference to the state broadcaster, the Nigerian Television Authority (NTA), which is considered a propaganda outlet for any government in power. In a rebuke, Channels Television countered that the allegation "was false, misleading and a figment of the imagination of the writer and her sponsors" and threatened to "use all within our means to seek legal redress against anyone who chooses to malign us or bring our media organisation to disrepute".[8]

### *'We do more than investigative reporting'*

Observers point out that the traditional media landscape in Nigeria largely operates in a 'roving' mode, in which an investigative reporter, who may or may not be assigned to a specific investigative desk, combines investigative reporting with regular news reporting. In this sense, every desk in the news-room is a potential unit for investigative reporting instead of having a unit that is wholly dedicated to it. The foregoing suggests that investigative reporting in the traditional media is operationally part of general news reporting rather than a distinct activity within the newspapers' overall editorial operations. It is not allocated separate resources or fully coordinated under a specific unit. Most investigative reporters combine regular news reporting along with doing investigative stories, earn just the same salaries and incentives as other reporters and are assessed by the same indicators of performance. Yet time, significant resources and different standards of performance evaluation are crucial elements of investigative reporting practice and a significant aspect of its institutionalisation in media organisations (Hamilton 2016, p. 10; Tong and Sparks 2009, pp. 340–343; Doig 1992, p. 46). In sum, then, one way to conceptualise investigative reporting in the traditional media is to say that while the norm is deeply entrenched among journalists through education and occupational socialisation, the practice is not institutionalised or professionalised as a distinct editorial activity. Journalists, who have practised journalism in both traditional and online media explained, however, that the outcome of an investigative reporting assignment may be compromised if it is not prioritised. For instance, they noted that in traditional media, when an investigative reporting assignment is initiated at the headquarters of a print or electronic medium in Lagos, the lead investigator will be directed by the management to contact a state correspondent of the organisation in another part of the country to provide a local perspective without considering that state correspondents are susceptible to compromising such reports. This is informed by the perception that state correspondents would want to maintain good relations with state government officials, political and economic elites in the state. Hence, when an investigative report is turned in from the state or region, what emerges is merely a press statement that mirrors official position. A senior journalist recounts his experience in the traditional media that:

> When you want to conduct an investigative story, the traditional media organisation will ask you not to travel to other parts of the country since that will increase expenditure. A correspondent in the state or region is assigned to cover the story. In many instances, state

correspondents are in bed with the political establishment in their various locations. In the long run, the investigation will be watered down, and it won't amount to anything different from a press release.

(personal communication with Fatade, May 2019)

## Investigative reporting goes online

Investigative reporting in the online media space was pioneered by diaspora-based media outlets, which operated largely out of the United States. Fashioned as citizen journalism platforms, these diaspora online platforms have shaped and influenced the course of democratic governance in Nigeria since 1999. One of the earliest of these platforms was Elendureports.com, owned by Jonathan Elendu in collaboration with Omoyele Sowore, who later founded Sahara Reporters.[9] Others, including huhuonline.com, pointblanknews.com and elombah.com, contributed in no small measure to the digital turn in investigative reporting in Nigeria and influenced the emergence of online media in Nigeria. A fraction of Nigerian journalists who exited traditional media to online media is believed to have been inspired by these diaspora online media platforms.

### *The shift to online media*

Respondents have identified several factors for the digital turn in investigative journalism in Nigeria. Some of these include the collapse of the magazine segment of the Nigerian media and lack of financial resources to fund investigative reporting assignments. In addition, respondents emphasised that the shift to online media is also influenced by the perception that online media is easier to run and largely does not require a fully fledged newsroom to run. One respondent noted that a journalist who wants to focus on investigative reporting could decide to move online and recruit five other staff to support himself. Hence, he contended that the gradual shift to online is "maybe because of its flexibility because it is easy to run and sustainable". In this sense, some of the journalists who were responsible for investigative journalism in the traditional media space have also moved to the online media segment. So, most of those responsible for investigative reporting in these magazines and newspapers have left to work for online media organisations or established their own media outlets online. Some traditional media leaders lament that they are losing competent professionals to the online media space. This means that journalists with the requisite skill and gravitas for investigative reporting are embracing online media:

Another fundamental issue which is very critical is that we are losing professionals to the online media because that is where the action is for now. People see the traditional media as a boring process because you have to identify the topic, you have to go through editorial judgment for them to even give you the approval and many other processes of gatekeeping. I think that is why you see a lot of investigative reporting in online media because people who are bold enough to do these stories are leaving to the online media.

(personal communication with Saá May 2019)

In addition, respondents claimed that they moved to online media because they could not function effectively in the traditional media. One senior journalist emphasised that many serious-minded journalists, who were trailblazers responsible for investigative reporting in traditional media, have moved to online publication because it is an area of specialisation. They argue that investigative journalism is an institutionalised practice in online media, while in traditional media, it is complementary. For instance, the editor of International Centre for Investigative Reporting in Abuja, Nigeria, explained that he had to move to online media after his suggestion for the establishment of an investigative desk at a traditional media organisation where he worked was rejected:

When I came back from the study of a masters in data journalism at Columbia University, I suggested to my former employer to establish an investigative reporting desk, where I would apply my expertise in data journalism but this was turned down. That is why I left my former employer for an online media organisation, where investigative reporting is prioritised.

(personal communication with Ajibola, May 2019)

### *Online media anonymous*

Respondents from traditional media organisations argue that the shift of investigative reporting to online media could be attributed to the fact that journalists who work for online media are anonymous and can operate from anywhere, unlike traditional media journalists, who have to report at their workplaces daily. In addition, they argue that online media organisations could be considered invisible because some of them don't have operational addresses, which they claim not to be the case with traditional organisations that can be traced and attacked if they investigate stories that adversely affect political or economic elites. This was highlighted by the managing director of Abubakar Rimi Television (ART) in Kano: that online media journalists can afford to be reckless because they can get away with it, unlike traditional media organisations that are traceable to their office addresses:

Some of them are anonymous, the writers are anonymous, they don't have faces. So, they have nothing at stake; they don't lose anything. But for us in the traditional system of broadcasting, we pay attention to credibility because we are liable to legal action. They know

Abubakar Rimi Television Station in Kano and they can come after me or any of my staff.

(personal communication with Sa'a, May 2019)

The publisher Next Edition countered that it is not entirely true that online media organisations are anonymous, because it is mandatory for promoters to be registered with the Corporate Affairs Commission (CAC) in Nigeria when they operate in the country. He emphasised that online media organisations do not practise some kind of 'ghost journalism', where reporters are anonymous and organisations have no official addresses. However, he added that what obtains in online media is that "when you publish a certain story that could cause trouble for the organisation, it is advisable to evacuate the office for some days and allow staff, who can handle any crisis to preside over the office". In addition, he claimed that a common practice in the online media space is the use of pseudonyms to evade pressure that may arise for the author of the article. However, he emphasised that this practice is not exclusive to online media because "some people could go the extra mile to harm the person that wrote such stories but this is used by both online and traditional media".

## Conclusion

This chapter examines the evolution of investigative journalism in Nigeria since the return to democracy in 1999. The findings identified there is a digital media turn in investigative journalism in Nigeria. This has resulted in the shift of investigative journalism to the online media space. The chapter identified several factors that account for this shift, such as prioritisation of investigative reporting, media viability, financial resources and the collapse of the magazine segment. The prioritisation of investigative reporting in the online media space has attracted many investigative journalism professionals, who have left traditional media to concentrate on their specialty. This means that well-trained and experienced journalists, who would have provided leadership for investigative reporting in the traditional media space, are moving to the online media space. In the face of rising digital disruption to the business model of traditional media organisations, cuddling up to advertisers and allowing them to influence media content has become fashionable. This suggests that limitation on advertising revenues is likely to have an adverse impact on investigative reporting in the traditional media space. In addition, owners' influence is pervasive in the Nigerian media landscape, and their power over media content is far reaching. Hence, investigative reporting that may adversely impact their friends and business partners is 'weeded out', and sometimes reporters may get punished. Last, the death of magazines, which had established investigative reporting as an institutional practice, has accelerated the digital turn in investigative reporting in Nigeria.

It is necessary to point out that investigative journalism in traditional media may never recover to the pre-1999 era, because some of the magazines that helped define that epoch have mutated into online media. In addition, more traditional media organisations are packing up and moving their productions online. Journalists are also embracing the online option because it affords them an opportunity to be their own boss and prioritise investigative reporting. It is expected that *Premium Times*, the *Cable*, ICIR and Sahara Reporters will continue to be leaders in the online media category. Even though many media organisations are mushrooming online, they have yet to make an appreciable impact to compete with these established brands.

## Notes

1 www.thepassivevoice.com/plummeting-newspaper-ad-revenue-sparks-new-wave-of-changes/
2 Data presented in this chapter is obtained from two sets of semi-structured interviews with 34 Nigerian journalists in 2015 and 2019. The first set of interviews was conducted with 24 respondents across four traditional newspapers (*Daily Trust*, *Punch*, *This Day* and *The Guardian*) in 2015. These include investigative reporters, political and business journalists, editors, officials of anti-corruption agencies and activist NGOs working in the areas of investigative reporting and corruption in Nigeria. These interviews were a part of the second author's doctoral research on investigative journalism and press coverage of corruption in Nigeria (1999–2012), awarded by the University of East Anglia, Norwich, UK, in 2018. The second set of interviews was conducted by the first author in May 2019 with ten journalists across online, print and electronic media, particularly those journalists who transited from traditional to online media during the period 1999–2019.
3 www.macfound.org/press/press-releases/macarthur-a
4 https://punchng.com/dele-giwa-30-years/
5 www.premiumtimesng.com/news/top-news/187247-%E2%80%8Bthenews-bids-farewell-to-print-moves-online.html
6 www.channelstv.com/2018/12/03/campaign-of-calumny-against-channels-tv/
7 https://punchng.com/thenta-nisation-of-channels-tv/
8 www.channelstv.com/2018/12/03/campaign-of-calumny-against-channels-tv/
9 http://saharareporters.com/2016/02/28/my-saharareporters-story-sowore

## References

Agbaje, A., (1993). Beyond the state: civil society and the Nigerian press under military rule. *Media, Culture & Society. 15*(3), 455–472.

Altschull, J. H., (1995). *Agents of Power: The Media and Public Policy.* London: Longman.

Behrman, M., Canonge, J., Purcell, M. and Schiffrin, A., (2012). Watchdog or lapdog? A look at press coverage of the extractive sector in Nigeria, Ghana and Uganda. *Ecquid Novi: African Journalism Studies. 33*(2), 87–99.

Berger, G., (2002). Theorizing the media–democracy relationship in Southern Africa. *Gazette (Leiden, Netherlands). 64*(1), 21–45.

Berliner, D., (2014). The political origins of transparency. *The Journal of Politics. 76*(2), 479–491.

Camara, S. M., (2008). Media, civil society, and political culture in West Africa. *Ecquid Novi, African Journalism Studies. 29*(2), 210–229.

Coronel, S., (2010). Corruption and the watchdog role of the news media. In: P. Norris. ed. *The Public Sentinel: News Media and Governance Reform.* Washington, DC: The World Bank. pp. 111–136.

Cunningham, B., (2003). Re-thinking objectivity. *Columbia Journalism Review. 42*(2), 24–32.

Doig, A., (1992). Retreat of the investigators. *British Journalism Review. 3*(4), 44–50.

Ette, M., (2000). Agent of change or stability? The Nigerian press undermines democracy. *Harvard International Journal of Press/Politics. 5*(3), 67–86.

Ettema, J. S. and Glasser, T. L., (1998). *Custodians of Conscience: Investigative Journalism and Public Virtue.* New York, NY: Columbia University Press.

Ettema, J. S. and Glasser, T. L., (2007). An international symposium on investigative journalism: introduction. *Journalism. 8*(5), 491–494.

European Union Election Observation Mission (2015). *Final Report: Nigeria General Election.*

Feldstein, M., (2006). A muckraking model: investigative reporting cycles in American history. *Harvard International Journal of Press/Politics. 11*(2), 105–120.

Feldstein, M., (2007). Dummies and ventriloquists: models of how sources set the investigative agenda. *Journalism. 8*(5), 499–509.

Hall, P., (2009). Think imperially: the private press mediation of state policy and the global economy within colonial and postcolonial Nigeria. *Journal of African Media Studies. 1*(2), 247–262.

Hamilton, J. T., (2016). *Democracy's Detectives.* Cambridge, MA: Harvard University Press.

Iwokwagh, N. S. and Batta, H. E., (2011). Newspaper coverage of corruption issues in Nigeria. *African Communication Research. 4*(2), 323–342.

Jibo, M. and Okoosi-Simbene, A., (2003). The Nigerian media: an assessment of its role in achieving transparent and accountable government in the fourth republic. *Nordic Journal of African Studies. 12*(2), 180–195.

Jones, A., (2009). *Losing the News: The Future of News That Feeds Democracy.* New York: Oxford University Press.

Kasoma, F. P., (1995). The role of the independent media in Africa's change to democracy. *Media, Culture & Society. 17*(4), 537–555.

Kuenzi, M. and Lambright, G., (2015). Campaign appeals in Nigeria's 2007 gubernatorial elections. *Democratization. 22*(1), 134–156.

Lanosga, G., (2015). Partners in power: alliances between investigative journalists and officials in the United States, 1917–1960. *Journalism Practice. 9*(3), 367–382.

Lanosga, G., Willnat, L., Weaver, D. H. and Houston, B., (2017). A breed apart? A comparative study of investigative journalists and US journalists. *Journalism Studies. 18*(3), 265–287.

Mellado, C., (2015). Professional roles in news content: six dimensions of journalistic role performance. *Journalism Studies. 16*(4), 596–614.

Musa, B. I. and Domatob, J. K., (2007). Who is a development journalist? Perspectives on media ethics and professionalism in post-colonial societies. *Journal of Mass Media Ethics. 22*(4), 315–331.

Nord, L. W., (2007). Investigative journalism in Sweden: A not so noticeable noble art. *Journalism. 8*(5), 517–521.

Norris, P. and Odugbemi, S., (2010). Evaluating media performance. In: P. Norris. ed. *The Public Sentinel: News Media and Governance Reform*. Washington, DC: The World Bank. pp. 3–30.

Obadare, E., (1999). The press and democratic transition in Nigeria: comparative notes on the Abacha and Abubakar transition programs. *African Issues*. 27(1), 38–40.

Ogbondah, C. W., (1994). *Military Regimes and the Press in Nigeria, 1966–1993: Human Rights and National Development*. Lanham, MD: University Press of America.

Ojebode, A., (2011). Nigeria's freedom of information act: provisions, strengths, challenges. *African Communication Research*. 4(2), 267–284.

Ojo, E. O., (2003). The mass media and the challenges of sustainable democratic values in Nigeria: possibilities and limitations. *Media, Culture & Society*. 25(6), 821–840.

Okwuchukwu, O. G., (2014). The influence of media ownership and control on media agenda setting in Nigeria. *International Journal of Humanities Social Sciences and Education*. 7(1), 36–45.

Olaiya, T. A., Apeloko, D. O. and Ayeni, O. O., (2013). Factors in mass media, third-term agenda and governance in Nigeria. *New Media and Mass Communication*. 10, 48–63.

Olukotun, A., (2000). The transition and the media. *African Journal of Political Science*. 5(2), 32–44.

Olukotun, A., (2002). Authoritarian state, crisis of democratization and the underground media in Nigeria. *African Affairs*. 101(404), 317–342.

Olukotun, A., (2004). Media accountability and democracy in Nigeria. *African Studies Review*. 4(3), 69–90.

Omu, F. I., (1968). The dilemma of press freedom in colonial Africa: the West African example. *The Journal of African History*. 9(2), 279–298.

Omu, F. I., (1978). *Press and Politics in Nigeria, 1880–1937*. London: Longman.

Onabanjo, O., (2004). The watchdog role of journalists in a nascent democracy: the Nigerian example. *International Journal of Communication. 1.*

Oso, L., (2013). Media and democracy in Nigeria: a critique of liberal perspective. *New Media and Mass Communication*. 10, 13–22.

PEW Research Centre (2015, April). *Cell Phones in Africa: Communication Lifeline*. Washington, DC: PEW Global.

Rønning, H., (2009). The politics of corruption and the media in Africa. *Journal of African Media Studies*. 1(1), 155–171.

Shaw, I. S., (2009). Towards an African journalism model: a critical historical perspective. *International communication gazette*. 71(6), 491–510.

Starkman, D., (2014). *The Watchdog That Didn't Bark: The Financial Crisis and the Disappearance of Investigative Journalism*. New York: Columbia University Press.

Stetka, V. and Örnebring, H., (2013). Investigative journalism in central and Eastern Europe: autonomy, business models, and democratic roles. *The International Journal of Press/Politics*. 18(4), 413–435.

Street, J., (2011). *Mass Media, Politics and Democracy* (2nd edition). Basingstoke: Palgrave Macmillan.

Tong, J. and Sparks, C., (2009). Investigative journalism in China today. *Journalism Studies*. 10(3), 337–352.

Tumber, H. and Waisbord, S. R., (2004). Introduction: political scandals and media across democracies, volume II. *American Behavioral Scientist*. 47(9), 1143–1152.

Waisbord, S. R., (1996). Investigative journalism and political accountability in South American democracies. *Critical Studies in Media Communication. 13*(4), 343–363.

Waisbord, S. R., (1997). Can investigative reporting tell the truth? The modernity of journalism in Latin America. *Ecquid Novi, African Journalism Studies. 18*(1), 115–131.

Walton, M., (2010). Investigative shortfall: many news outlets are doing far less accountability reporting than in the past, bad news indeed for the public. New non-profit investigative ventures have emerged, but they can't pick up the slack by themselves. *American Journalism Review. 32*(3), 18–34.

# 16

# THE EUROPEAN UNION AND THE RISE OF COLLABORATION

*Brigitte Alfter*

Leap in time to the autumn of 1998 and until mid-March 1999: For the Brussels press corps and the European Commission, those were dramatic months. Would the power struggle between European Commission and European Parliament lead the Commission to resign? Would the accusations of nepotism, unveiled by a network of Brussels correspondents, have political consequences? In March 1999, the European Commission under Luxembourgish Jacques Santer did indeed step down, forced by the European Parliament and the findings of a special committee.

This case from the late 20th century is worth understanding for several reasons. Jacques Santer considered himself and his cabinet "a victim of the international press" or rather of "a certain part of the press, that which plays investigative journalism American style rather than fulfilling its mission to inform" (Meyer 2002, p. 115). Initially, a team of correspondents from Britain, Germany, Luxembourg and France had met in cafés in the EU quarter of Brussels to exchange notes and documents on the allegation that a commissioner had given a lucrative position to a personal friend. "For a long time no other media would pick up on the case, 'it was the Brussels press corps against the rest' and it was 'the Nordics versus the French'", according to one early member of that group (Alfter 2019, p. 72).

At the time, Scandinavian and British journalists kept pushing for more transparency and Nordic-style access to documents, for example (Meyer 2002, p. 138), and even the perception of what constituted a breach of norms varied according to country. What British, German and Swedish interviewees considered a clear case of nepotism was seen as a private matter and "essentially about romance" by a Southern European interviewee, or it was framed as part of a political plot by Northern EU media against Southern EU countries (Meyer 2002, pp. 138–139).

Here I will address journalism as an expression of the underlying mindset and of the role of journalism in a given society. Then, I will describe journalism practice, including how to trace those responsible, which topics are investigated and which methods applied to do so, citing several investigations. Finally, I will introduce the recent trend of cross-border collaborative journalism.

## 'Investigative journalism' in a European context

So is there investigative journalism in and about the EU? Is there a *European* investigative journalism?

The first question can be answered with a clear "yes": There is thorough, elaborate investigative journalism in and about the EU. Professional journalists seek to get as close as possible to what *really* happened or what is *really* going on.

The second question, whether there is a *European* investigative journalism, is more tricky. Though English is widely used, the continent is divided not only by language but also by media, research and storytelling traditions; legal and ethical standards and practices and general freedom of expression conditions. Dutch editor Dick van Eijk in 2005 tried to compile an overview over the status of investigative journalism in Europe ahead of the 3rd Global Investigative Journalism Conference of 2005. "If anybody ever thought that there is something like 'European journalism', he or she should be cured from that after having read the 20 country reports. Journalism traditions vary widely in Europe, and so do traditions of investigative journalism," he wrote afterwards (van Eijk 2005, p. 227).

Nevertheless, cross-border collaborative journalism was developed predominantly in investigative journalism networks, and the will and capacity actually to work together indicate that journalists indeed *do agree* on what constitutes "a good story". "The criteria as to what constitutes a viable investigative project and what does not appear to be similar throughout Europe" (Tillack 2013).

## Journalists investigating in Europe

Mapping investigative journalism in Europe and even just attempting an overview of such a diverse mosaic of languages; practices and academic, literary and journalistic traditions appears to be an impossible task. The quest has been attempted twice, van Eijk (2005), as mentioned previously, and – more narrowly focusing on the investigation of fraud with EU funds – Smit et al. (2012).

In the following, several aspects of *investigative journalism practice* in Europe will be addressed, followed by selected examples.

## Investigating in Europe – where to find the villain

Any journalist – be that on the local, regional, national or international level – will have to understand power structures in order to follow money flows, paper trails or otherwise find information, in order to hold those in power to account, in order to understand who may be responsible and who may be capable of finding solutions.

Many will think of the European Union Institutions in Brussels, Luxembourg and Strasbourg when pondering investigative journalism in Europe.

Academics study the Brussels press corps covering the European institutions (typically in all three cities) and reporting via international, national, local or specialised media. Investigative journalists as well as the European Ombudsman and civil society groups repeatedly complain about opaque decision-making processes and administration. Yet, while investigations about the European institutions may be scarce, there is a steady flow of information from the institutional level to national and local levels. The information flow the other way round, from citizens' experience back to Brussels decision makers, looks more like an unsolved challenge.

When covering issues on a local or national level, very often journalists are not aware of the international dimensions of a given problem, nor would they know where to turn. An ambulance company declares bankruptcy and halts the service in an entire county. Public authorities rush to find a solution, adding significant amounts to the local budgets. Even if journalists make investigations into the background of the ambulance company and the contract, few if any of them consider addressing the underlying legislation. Many may not even be aware of the European legislation obliging public authorities to offer public services to competitive bidding along a certain set of rules and to ask the obvious question, whether these rules – in force for decades – are still adequate or are adequate for a given service such as ambulances for citizens in a potentially life-threatening emergencies. Further, international agreements in a wide range of fields such as trade, fisheries, labour, migration or defence between nation states or groups of nation states such as the EU, the EEA, NATO, WTO, WHO, IMO, Interpol and so forth significantly influence and overrule national or local regulations. Yet the political level of such agreements, and not least the role such agreements play on local and national levels, are sparsely covered outside specialised media. It is thus a challenge to navigate the levels of competence beyond the local and national in almost any subject – and a particular strength for those specialised journalists who know the territory.

## Investigating in Europe – what to investigate?

Journalists throughout Europe have different views on priorities and selection of topics. Even on obviously connected topics like the labour market, pan-European teams struggle to find a shared storyline (Alfter 2019, p. 111). But this is only part of the picture.

Tracing categories of subject matter, the mapping by Dick van Eijk (2005) shows widely shared interests as well as some differences in subject matter. Classic investigative 'follow-the-money' stories or – as van Eijk puts it – "chasing crooks" are prevalent. He categorises them as stories on breaches of law (van Eijk 2005, p. 233). Others investigate breaches of "commonly shared moral convictions" (van Eijk 2005, p. 234) or individual breaches of moral convictions – where "'catching a politician with his pants down' – literally – is often a big story in the United Kingdom . . . similar cases would not be reported at all in

Scandinavia, the Netherlands or Belgium", yet in Sweden a politician enjoying "an advantage of a few thousand euro . . . may run into serious trouble" (van Eijk 2005, p. 235).

Investigations into politics, party funding, broken promises and so forth appear to be widespread, investigations into arts or sports less so at the time and investigations into social matters such as poverty or the lives of drug addicts prevalent only in some countries (van Eijk 2005, pp. 235–237).

The 2012 (Smit et al.) mapping exercise covering fraud with EU funds had difficulties in tracing such cases: "When mapping stories on misappropriation, fraudulent use, lost revenue or waste of EU funds, the research team had to throw the net wider than first intended," Smit writes (2012, p. 34). Rather than only looking three years back in time, instead the researchers almost doubled the time span to search for investigations on fraud with EU funds in then 27 countries. Though the compilation of examples was "relatively small considering the timeframe (5 years in 27 countries)", the study allowed for some qualitative findings indicating journalism with focus on "individual people or companies" or "on 'silly' projects instead of structures enabling fraud", amongst others (Smit et al. 2012, p. 88).

Cross-border collaborations – as described in the following – indicate that, regardless of such apparent diverse views on subject matters, collaborations are increasingly attractive and bridging such differences.

## Investigating in Europe – professionalisation of journalism and differences in methods

There is general agreement that the last decades of the 20th and the first decades of the 21st centuries have brought a professionalisation of journalism, not least investigative journalism. The various methods are described, discussed and developed. Beyond journalism education – be that academic or vocational – journalists gather for professional exchange on national and international levels (Alfter 2019, pp. 5–9; Smit et al. 2012, p. 31). Early developments in that field began in the 1970s in the United States, when journalists and editors organised IRE, the Investigative Reporters and Editors, an association to work with the development of investigative journalism. Annual gatherings, peer-training (not least in the field of computer-assisted reporting, freedom of information requests etc.) were among the core activities. In the 1990s, the Nordic countries founded similar membership-based professional groups, and in 2001 and 2002, Germany and Netherlands/Flanders followed. When McFadyen (2008, pp. 138–156) listed a series of methodology considerations, his overview was embedded in an era of professional method development and sharing: entire books are published in various languages about topics such as freedom of information requests, computer-assisted and data journalism and working with whistleblowers or digital self-defence for journalists, as well as investigative journalism methods in general (see, for example, Hanson 2009; Ludwig 2014). This move towards professionalisation is also widespread geographically.

Yet which methods are preferred varies from country to country in Europe, obviously, since legal context and traditions of doing journalism vary from country to country. Though the use of methods surely has developed since 2005 (not least when it comes to data journalism), the overview by van Eijk (2005, pp. 237–244) is indicative. In Scandinavia, for example, journalists relied upon documents obtained from government bodies – likely because there was a strong freedom of information law and practice. In Italy, journalists used court documents a lot, whereas it appeared difficult for them to obtain government documents. In France, Belgium and Central and Eastern European countries, informal access or leaked documents were a usual way to obtain information (van Eijk 2005, p. 240).

Not only the use of methods of obtaining information varies, journalists' views also vary as to which methods are preferable or even acceptable. A survey study of journalists behind the Panama and Paradise Papers revelations of tax avoidance showed congruent as well as differing views on methods in a group of journalists that the authors considered rather homogenous, for example, whether an unauthorised piece of material – for example, from an interview – could be published or whether journalists could claim to be someone else when doing their research (Lück & Schultz 2019, p. 102). With methods explicitly named and described, similarities and differences in different parts of Europe can be better understood. On the optimistic side, practitioners can collaborate across borders and supplement each other's material.

## Investigating Europe – the example of freedom of information requests

Journalists using freedom of information legislation – the right to documents held by public authorities – is a very telling example. To a certain extent, history may provide insights. In Sweden, citizens' right to access documents held by the public administration was introduced in 1766; today it has constitutional status along with freedom of expression. Other Nordic countries and the Netherlands introduced similar rights from the 1950s to 70s, and the United States introduced its well-known FOI Act in 1966. A later wave of freedom of information laws was introduced after 2000, when Central and Eastern European countries eager to join the EU introduced such laws in the name of democracy. The United Kingdom, Germany and the EU introduced such laws following, not least, pressure from transparency advocacy groups.

Freedom of information laws are a sound – if in some cases and countries administratively cumbersome – way of obtaining information for journalism. Yet it may feel like a revolution within an administration. Imagine an administrative culture where – for decades and centuries – officials have considered it the highest virtue to *protect* the valuable documents and information from disturbance by the potentially less knowledgeable public. The overall purpose was, of course, to safeguard smooth and efficient working of the political machinery. Imagine, on the other hand, an official in an administration where public insight and, maybe even on a case-by-case level, involvement of the public was considered of the highest democratic value. Also in the latter, some information has to be protected such as business secrets, private personal information or matters concerning security. In the latter system, each document needs to be traceable in a well-functioning archive system, and officials on all levels need to be aware of and follow best administrative practice in case there comes a request for access.

The "weight of tradition" thus should not be underestimated: An in-depth comparative description of the Nordic countries' (Jørgensen 2014, pp. 33–34) documents how historical differences prevail and influence freedom of information legislation as well as practice even within this rather homogenous group of countries. Translating that to Europe, including the European institutions, tensions and conflicting approaches is inevitable. Anecdotal evidence shows that officials from some traditions consider a freedom of information request an aggressive way of seeking information, a notion that would be flabbergasting in the comparably low-key Nordic access traditions considering requests day-to-day business.

## Investigating in Europe – storytelling

Once research is carried out, journalists have to consider how to present their findings. And they differ from country to country. Particularly in cross-border teams, it becomes visible how journalists present findings about the same subject in different ways. "My Romanian version would read like a soap-opera if I translated it directly into English – it had much more context and background atmosphere", recalls one journalist from an international team. Another recalls "raised eyebrows and gaping jaws" at the "lighthearted approach" by team members from another tradition (Alfter 2019, p. 113).

"While the content of news changes every day, form and style assure the ritual function of news", writes Marcel Broersma (2007, p. ix) in the introduction to an anthology about form, style and strategies of the presentation of news. The anthology is among the first addressing news presentation, and Broersma calls for more research in the field, not least interdisciplinary between scholars from the social sciences, history and literature (Broersma 2007, p. xii). It could be added that for journalists, not least, the international comparison would be helpful to gain a deeper understanding of own and others' traditions. At the publication of this edition, academic literature comparing storytelling and presentation of journalism across borders still is scarce. The previously mentioned attempts by Meyer (2019) and Grzeszyk (2019), representing social sciences and culture studies, respectively, do give some indications as to the challenges in understanding the differences.

## Investigative cases

Given the vast number of investigative journalism published throughout Europe, any selection will be nothing but a glimpse of the vast material available. The examples thus are indicative only to illustrate fields of cases.

### *Investigating European funds*

Investigating the flow of EU funds – a classic 'follow the money' approach – is carried out all over Europe with varying intensity and frequency. One key case worth knowing is the Cresson case, analysed by Meyer (2002); this case is an early example of cross-border collaboration between Brussels correspondents. Another key case is the so-called Tillack case, referring to German Brussels correspondent Hans-Martin Tillack, who – based upon information from a source whose identity was never disclosed – was able to publish highly critical articles on "allegations of a European civil servant concerning irregularities in the European institutions" (ECHR 2007), more precisely concerning fraud in the Commission's Eurostat department (Kirk 2005) and on the institutions' reactions to these allegations. The journalist's home and newsroom were raided by Belgian police and material, computers and telephones seized. Tillack and his magazine took the case all the way to the European Court of Human Rights in Strasbourg, where Tillack won (ECHR 2007). Both cases must be considered landmark journalism, leaving a trace on the relationship between journalists and EU institutions. Two other cases are worth emphasising: older and more recent investigations into the EU's generous farm subsidies and recent years' investigations into EU funds spent in Hungary.

Since the founding of the EU, large funds have been handed out to individual farmers, agricultural projects and investments and indeed price guaranties in the form of export subsidies. By 2019, the sum of subsidies for the EU with 28 countries amounted to around 60 billion EUR or 51 billion GBP. Research into the actual spending of the EU's farm subsidies began on a national level in Denmark in 2002. In the early 2000s, two Danish journalists teamed up for an FOI request on national level to access information on which farmers actually got which amount. Such data would allow them to geo-tag and analyse distribution and the potential effect of the subsidies. Eventually, in 2004, they got access to the documents. They found that the EU subsidies were not supporting their intended targets in Denmark, the poorest farmers. A follow-up FOI with the European Commission in Brussels was turned down and led to the first large cross-border journalism collaboration in Europe, where a loose network of journalists filed requests to access the data on the national level and published as information was obtained over the years from 2005 onwards (Farmsubsidy. org 2017; Alfter 2019, pp. 64–66). The wider network of the Farmsubsidy team kept reporting about the topic for years, yet with a loose coordination and intensity waning after 2012. The actual effect of the Farmsubsidy reporting on the public debate is not documented, though its effect on 'Europeanisation' has been analysed (Heft et al. 2017).

In 2019, a *New York Times* investigative team set out to scrutinise European agricultural subsidies with findings mirroring previous articles (Apuzzo 2019).

One of the findings of the *New York Times* concerned how people and companies with close ties to the Hungarian government were receiving farm subsidies. This story of how lucrative EU funds were granted, via national tenders or grants, to the strongmen around, for example, the Hungarian government, is another 'follow-the-money' story. It was covered persistently by Hungarian media, not least investigative non-profit media, over years and years (for examples in English, see Atlatszo 2020 or Direkt36 2020).

## Investigating EU decision making and administration

Following EU funds is one classic subject. Scrutinising EU decision making and controlling how EU rules and agreements are carried out is another. There are numerous examples: the internal market's affect on consumer affairs and business, lobbying, opaque lawmaking and the administration of European legislation counter to agreed-upon rules. One representative example is cited here.

In its treaties, the EU emphasises the precautionary principle, aiming at insuring a high level of environmental protection and food, human, animal and plant health (European Commission 2000). Having heard of a particular pesticide well known in the scientific literature to cause brain damage to babies and young children, a group of journalists from Denmark, France, Norway, Belgium, Slovenia, Spain, Poland and the United States set out to investigate. The starting point was to investigate residues on food and question authorities about what was being done about it (Dahllöf 2019), a classic big chemicals versus consumers case. Using FOI requests, reports by scientists and administrative bodies, interviews and other classic research methods, the team was able to document that the producer had presented a report to the EU authorities at the time of authorisation which lacked data and included modified statistical protocols. Furthermore, it appeared that the authorities had not even looked at the report. They only did so years later (Horel, S. 2019c). The reporting was noted and quoted by industry lobbyists (Horel 2019a), and as of 2020, the use of the chemical will be forbidden all over the EU (Horel 2019b).

Further examples of scrutiny of lawmaking and administration can be found at Euobserver.com 2020.

## Investigating topics of general interest

Though not directly influenced by shared decisions, subject matter may be relevant in multiple EU countries or be partially linked to European politics: Tax avoidance has been scrutinised by journalists on a national level as well as internationally (see, for example, ICIJ's Lux Leaks 2014; Panama Papers 2016;

EIC's Football Leaks 2018). Taxes are a national competency, yet excessive tax advantages are considered distorting competition and thus EU regulated.

Investigating royal families is another strictly national subject, yet inspired by colleagues in other countries, journalists from different countries have started filing FOI requests and in other ways started looking into ownership and spending of their royal families (see, for example, Koningshuizen.be 2019). Another story within the national realm concerned investigations into the security weaknesses of the Internet of Things – where, for example, digital cameras installed in private houses to protect against burglars or security cameras in public spaces were used systematically to spy on family bedrooms or on public swimming pools (see, for example, Sandli 2013; Svensson 2015; Brühl & Wormer 2016).

The Daphne Project is worth mentioning. When Maltese blogger Daphne Caruana Galizia was killed in Malta in 2017, a team of journalists set out to finalise her reporting on alleged corruption in Malta (Daphne Project 2018), thus insisting on finalising the work of the killed colleague – a clear statement from the journalism community.

## Further reading

Any journalist wishing to follow investigative journalism in Europe will start by learning to read "Googletranslatish" to open the vast field of investigative journalism in Europe. English speakers have the advantage of their language being the working language in many journalism contexts. To gain familiarity with investigative journalism, collections of cases can be traced at the meeting places of investigative journalists in Europe.

One such meeting place is Dataharvest – the European Investigative Journalism Conference (Dataharvest 2020). Grown out of the Farmsubsidy.org project and open to all journalists since 2011, the conference has gathered a growing number of journalists from all over Europe; the programme thus gives an insight into what is going on in Europe. The programme includes, however, only cases of potential relevance in other European countries, be that for methodology or subject matter.

## Cross-border collaborative journalism

Since the late 1990s and onwards, investigative journalism communities have emerged in the United States, in Europe and beyond, and collaborations have become more commonplace. Surmounting the competitive mood journalists have been conditioned to work within is a challenge but worth the effort: "you have to haul through that. You have to change your mindset to say they are not your rivals, that you can actually collaborate with people. There are ways in which you have more in common than you have against each other. The psychological thing is a big change for a lot of journalists," says David Leigh, former investigations editor at *The Guardian* and one of the pioneers in cross-border collaboration in the United Kingdom (Alfter 2019, p. 55). Obvious advantages cited are sharing costs and information and ability to set the news agenda (Konow-Lund et al. 2019, p. 8).

By 2019, cross-border collaboration was well on the way to the mainstream in many countries; journalism schools have started teaching it (see Newsreel; Gothenburg), and academia is picking up on the method (Konow-Lund et al. 2019; Sambrook 2018; Alfter 2016, 2019).

## Conclusion

Investigative journalism can be found all over Europe – yet it will not always look the same. Parts of Europe are more influenced by Anglo–American-style reporting and story-telling, while other parts of Europe follow different traditions. Research methods vary according to journalism tradition and context, including legal practice, thus providing the potential for journalists to supplement each other in collaborative teams on topics of shared interest.

## References

Alfter, B. (2016). Cross-border collaborative journalism: Why journalists and scholars should talk about an emerging method. *Journal of Applied Journalism & Media Studies.* Vol. 5 (2): 297–311.

Alfter, B. (2019). *Cross-border collaborative journalism: A step-by-step guide.* New York/London: Routledge.

Apuzzo, M. et al. (2019) The money farmers. *New York Times.* [November- December series of articles, viewed on 4 January 2020]. Available from: www.nytimes.com/2019/11/03/world/europe/eu-farm-subsidy-hungary.html, www.nytimes.com/2019/11/03/reader-center/eu-farm-subsidy-reporting.html, www.nytimes.com/2019/11/06/opinion/eu-hungary-farm-subsidies.html, www.nytimes.com/2019/11/04/world/europe/EU-farm-subsidy.html, www.nytimes.com/2019/12/11/world/europe/eu-farm-subsidy-lobbying.html, www.nytimes.com/interactive/2019/12/25/world/europe/farms-environment.html

Atlatszo (2020). Atlatszo. [Selection of articles in English, viewed 4 January 2020]. Available from: https://english.atlatszo.hu/

Bettels-Schwabbauer, T., Leihs, N., Polyák, G., Torbó, A., Pinto Martinho, A., Crespo, M. & Radu, R. (2018). Newsreel – New skills for the next generation of journalists. University of Pecs, Hungary. [Viewed 3 January 2020]. Available from: newsreel.pte.hu/sites/newsreel.pte.hu/files/REPORT/new_skills_for_the_next_generation_of_journalists_-_research_report.pdf.

Broersma, M. (ed.) (2007). *Form and style in journalism: European newspapers and the presentation of news, 1880–2005.* Leuven/Paris/Dudley, MA: Peeters.

Brühl, J. & Wormer, V. (2016). Das Internet der Dinge ist kaputt. Süddeutsche Zeitung. [Viewed 1 December 2020]. Available from: https://gfx.sueddeutsche.de/apps/58343704f38f33fb247b637d/www/.

Burg, H. de (2008). *Investigative journalism*, 2nd Edition. New York/London: Routledge.

Chalaby, J.K. (1996). Journalism as an Anglo-American invention: A comparison of the development of Anglo-American and French journalism 1830s–1920s. *European Journal of Communication*. Vol. 11 (3): 303–326.

Dahllöf, S. (2019). The most dangerous pesticide you've never heard of. *Euobserver.com*. [Viewed 4 January 2020]. Available from https://euobserver.com/health/145146.

Daphne Project (2018). Daphne project. Coordinated by *Forbidden Stories*. [Viewed 28 March 2020]. Available from: https://forbiddenstories.org/case/the-daphne-project/

Dataharvest – the European Investigative Journalism Conference (2020): Dataharvest – Previous years' programmes. [Viewed 4 January 2020]. Available from: https://dataharvest.eu/previous-years-programmes/

Direkt36 (2020). Category: Blackholes of EU funds. [Series of articles, Viewed 4 January 2020]. Available from: www.direkt36.hu/en/category/elnyelt-eu-penzek/.

Eijk, D. V. (2005). *Investigative Journalism in Europe*. Amsterdam/Zellik: Vereniging van Onderzoeksjournalisten VVOJ.

ECHR, European Court of Human Rights (2007). Chamber judgement Tillack vs. Belgium. [Viewed 4 January 2020]. Available from: https://hudoc.echr.coe.int/eng-press#{%22itemid%22:[%22003-2189531-2328879%22]}

EUobserver.com (2020). Investigations. [Category of articles, Viewed 4 January 2020]. Available from: https://euobserver.com/investigations.

European Commission (2000). The precautionary principle. [Commission Communication, Viewed 4 January 2020]. Available from: https://eur-lex.europa.eu/legal-content/EN/TXT/?uri=LEGISSUM%3Al32042

European Investigative Collaborations, EIC (2018). Football leaks. [Viewed 4 January 2020]. Available from: https://eic.network/projects/football-leaks

Farmsubsidy.org (2017). Farmsubsidy.org at a glance/Farmsubsidy.org Extended history. [Viewed 4 January 2020]. Available from: https://farmsubsidy.org/about/

Grzeszyk, T. (2019). Diversity matters! How cross-border journalism calls out media bias. In: Alfter, B. & Candea, C. (eds.) Special Issue on Cross-Border Journalism, *Journal of Applied Journalism and Media Studies*. Vol. 8 (2): 169–189.

Hallin, D. C. & Mancini, P. (2004). *Comparing media systems: Three models of media and politics*. Cambridge: Cambridge University Press.

Hanitzsch, T. (2009). Comparative journalism studies. In: Wahl-Jorgensen, K. & Hanitzsch, T. (eds), *Handbook of journalism studies*. New York/London: Routledge.

Hanson, N. (2009). *Grävande journalistik*. Stockholm: Ordfront.

Hanusch, F. & Hanitzsch, T. (2017). Comparing journalistic cultures across nations. *Journalism Studies*. Vol. 18 (5): 525–535.

Heft, A., Alfter, B. & Pfetsch, B. (2017). Transnational journalism networks as drivers of Europeanisation. In: *Journalism* (online), pp. 1–20. Sage.

Horel, S. (2019a). Chlorpyrifos: les fabricants contre ‐ attaquent. *Le Monde*, 3 December, p. 15. (English translation available at www.ir-d.dk/2019/12/producers-fight-back-to-prevent-pesticides-ban-eu-bows-for-pressure-from-ngos-and-media/).

Horel, S. (2019b). Le chlorpyrifos va être interdit dans l'Union européenne. *Le Monde*. [Viewed 4 January 2020]. Available from: www.lemonde.fr/planete/article/2019/12/06/le-chlorpyrifos-va-etre-interdit-dans-l-union-europeenne_6021924_3244.html.

Horel, S. (2019c). Chlorpyrifos, une toxicité passée sous silence. *Le Monde*, 18 June 2019, pp. 10–11. [Viewed 6 January 2020]. Available from: www.lemonde.fr/planete/article/2019/06/17/chlorpyrifos-les-dangers-ignores-d-un-pesticide-toxique_5477084_3244.html

International Consortium of Investigative Journalists, ICIJ (2014). Lux leaks. [Viewed 4 January 2020]. Available from www.icij.org/investigations/luxembourg-leaks/.

International Consortium of Investigative Journalists, ICIJ (2016). Panama papers. [Viewed 4 January 2020]. Available from www.icij.org/investigations/panama-papers/.

Jørgensen, O. (2014). *Access to information in the Nordic countries – a comparison of the laws of Sweden, Finland, Denmark, Norway and Iceland and international rules.* Gothenburg: Nordicom. (This is an English language summary of the extensive study by the same author: *Offentlighed i Norden*).

Journalismfund.eu (2015). What is investigative journalism? [Viewed 2 January 2020]. Available from: https://web.archive.org/web/20150215024022/www.journalismfund.eu/ what-investigative-journalism

Kirk, L. (2005). Stern reporter drags Belgium to European court of human rights. *Euobserver. com.* [Viewed 5 January 2020]. Available from: https://euobserver.com/justice/18847

Koningshuizen (royal houses) (2019). Immo royal. [Viewed 4 January 2020]. Available from: www.koningshuizen.be/

Konow-Lund, M., Berglez, P. & Gearing, A. (2019). Transnational cooperation in journalism. In: *Oxford research encyclopedia, communication.* Oxford: Oxford University Press.

Löffelholz, M., Rothenberger, L. & Weaver, D. H. (2018). *Journalism across borders – The production and "produsage" of news in the era of transnationalization, destabilization and algorithmization.* Institute of Media and Communication Science, Technische Universität Ilmenau/Germany. [Viewed 1 January 2020]. Available from: www.tu-ilmenau.de/mw/ conference/program/

Lück, J. & Schultz, T. (2019). Investigative data journalism in a globalized world. A survey study on ICIJ journalists. In: *Journalism Research.* Vol. 2 (2), pp. 93–114. Cologne: Herbert-von-Halem-Verlag.

Ludwig, J. (2014). *Investigatives Recherchieren*, 3rd Edition. Konstanz: UVK.

McFadyen, G. (2008). The practices of investigative journalism. In: Burgh, H. de (ed.) *Investigative journalism*, 2nd Edition. London/New York: Routledge.

Meyer, C. O. (2002). *Europäische Öffentlichkeit als Kontrollsphäre: Die Europäische Kommission, die Medien und politische Verantwortung.* Berlin: Vistas Verlag.

Meyer, G. (2019). Varieties of cross-border journalism. In: Alfter, B. & Candea, C. (eds.) Special Issue on Cross-Border Journalism, *Journal of Applied Journalism and Media Studies.* Vol. 8 (2), pp. 151–168.

Meyer, G. & Lund, A. B. (2008). International language monism and homogenisation of journalism. In: *Javnost, the Public.* Vol. 15 (4), pp. 73–86.

Offerhaus, A. (2010). EU-Korrespondenten als Wegbereiter einer europäischen Öffentlichkeit? Vergemeinschaftung und journalistische Selbstkontrolle by Korrespondenten in Brüssel. In: Pöttker, H. & Schwarzenegger, C. (eds.) *Europäische Öffentlichkeit und journalistische Verantwortung.* Köln: Herbert von Halem Verlag.

Sambrook, R. (ed.) (2018). *Global teamwork: The rise of collaboration in investigative journalism.* Oxford: Reuters' Institute.

Sandli, E. et al. (2013): Null Ctrl (zero control). [Viewed 4 January 2020]. Available from: www.dagbladet.no/nullctrl/

Smit, M. et al. (2012). *Deterrence of fraud with EU funds through investigative journalism in EU-27.* Brussels: European Parliament, Directorate General for Internal Policies, Policy Department D, Budgetary Affairs.

Svensson, T. G. et al. (2015). Fri Adgang. [Viewed 4 January 2020]. Available from https:// ekstrabladet.dk/nyheder/friadgang/

Tillack, H.-M. (2013). Geld von der Stiftung. *Stern Blogs Hans-Martin Tillack*, 11 November 2013. [Viewed 1 January 2020]. Available from: www.stern.de/politik/deutschland/tillack/hans-martin-tillack-geld-von-der-stiftung-6823138.html

Worlds of Journalism (2015). Worlds of journalism network. [Viewed 1 January 2020]. Available from: https://worldsofjournalism.org/about/.

Wormer, V. & Brühl, J. (2016). Das Internet der Dinge ist kaputt. Süddeutsche Zeitung. [Viewed 4 January 2020]. Available from: https://gfx.sueddeutsche.de/apps/58343704f38f33fb247b637d/www/

# 17

# INVESTIGATIVE JOURNALISM IN LATIN AMERICA TODAY

*Magdalena Saldaña and Silvio Waisbord*

This chapter examines the state of investigative journalism in Latin America. The focus is on four major trends: the rise of collaborative forms of regional and global reporting, the consolidation of vibrant digital news sites that scrutinise political and economic power in relation to a range of social issues (e.g. human rights, women's rights, environmental issues), the use of data journalism techniques, and the rise of fact checkers to debunk misinformation in the region. All together, these novel forms open opportunities for critical news and complement the limited interest in investigative work among traditional news organisations. These trends are particularly significant in the context of old and new challenges for in-depth, hard-hitting journalism – from legal and physical attacks to digital harassment of reporters perpetrated by states, para-state actors, and citizens.

## Background

Understanding the current state of investigative journalism in Latin America demands a consideration of unprecedented changes in news ecologies in the past two decades. Just as in other regions of the world, news industries, journalistic practice, and information flows have been transformed. News industries and journalism are in a vulnerable situation. News companies have been losing advertising revenue to global digital platforms. Legacy news media struggle to compete for audience attention with Google and Facebook. Shifts in press economies and the painful transition to digital news have deepened labour precarity amid massive job losses (Waisbord, 2019).

Amid these conditions, investigative journalism is a vibrant, important yet limited aspect of the Latin American news landscape. Only a small number of national news organisations consistently offer investigative stories aimed at revealing power abuses and illegal actions. Investigative journalism remains, especially at the local level, a rarity, even though press exposés oftentimes gain wide attention, especially when they uncover wrongdoing at the highest level of political, economic, and cultural power. Out of hundreds of legacy and digital news companies and websites, a handful of news organisations in each country in the region consistently investigate corruption and produce explosive stories.

Immediately after the return of democratic rule in the 1980s and 1990s, investigative journalism emerged vigorous. As a journalistic practice primarily anchored in commercial news organisations in countries with a spotty record of democratic rights and the rule of law, it has been torn between contradictory forces. Investigative reporting reflected the commitment of journalists and news organisations to holding power accountable by exposing many forms of power abuses: corruption, wrongdoing, cover-ups, collusion. It sparked legislative and judicial investigations that yielded limited yet significant forms of accountability. It contributed to processes that culminated in the resignation of powerful politicians, military officers, and corporate executives.

Investigative journalism was, nevertheless, hamstrung by powerful political and economic forces, both at the level of the state and media corporations more interested in pursuing narrow industrial interests than in truth-telling. It was oftentimes too dependent on leaks from political and economic elites as well as intelligence services. It was also bound by editorial and partisan allegiances of individual reporters and news organisations. Exposés resulted from complex, multi-layered political dynamics, including the politics of sources, rather than only journalism's concern with serving the public good.

These tensions have continued in recent times. News organisations, particularly legacy media companies, have tried to balance economic, ideological, and partisan commitments with investigative journalism. News organisations have continued to play critical roles amid political battles, especially in contexts of polarised politics in much of the region. Whereas some have vigorously confronted administrations with hard-hitting exposés, others opted to champion official causes. Investigative journalism has often been aligned with the editorial positions and corporate calculations of news organisations. Oftentimes, the threat of economic punishment by governments and corporations discouraged news organisations from publishing critical investigations of political and economic powers.

In this context, legacy news organisations have produced numerous investigations that revealed wrongdoing and corruption in government, corporations, religious institutions, and other sectors of society. Leading news organisations and journalists participated in the regional and global networks that broke the biggest stories in the past decade, such as the Panama Papers and the Paradise Papers, Brazil's *Lava Jato*, Argentina's *Los cuadernos de la corrupción*, Mexico's *Peña Nieto's Casa Blanca*, and Colombia's *Las Chuzadas*. Without going into the specifics, all investigations revealed the collusion of political and corporate actors in various forms of wrongdoing for personal benefit. In some cases, corporations delivered paybacks to public officials in exchange for government contracts. In other cases, government officials and wealthy individuals collaborated in setting up offshore financial networks to avoid taxes. Other investigations revealed the action of rogue intelligence services spying on politicians, reporters, and activists with the knowledge and support of prominent politicians.

## Collaborations in investigative projects

Collaborative journalism is "a cooperative arrangement (formal or informal) between two or more news and information organisations, which aims to supplement each organisation's resources and maximize the impact of the content produced" (Stonbely, 2017; p. 14). The Panama Papers and the Paradise Papers are probably the best examples of recent collaborative, investigative projects conducted by journalists from all over the world. Through the analysis of millions of leaked files, both investigations revealed financial dealings of global prominent figures who sheltered their wealth in secretive tax havens.

Both the Panama and the Paradise Papers demonstrate a paradigm shift where exclusivity and immediacy are replaced by a culture of information sharing and "slow" journalism. Global investigations like these cases cannot be conducted by a single news organisation or small team of reporters. Instead, news outlets collaborated in these projects in unprecedented ways. During the Panama Papers investigation, 96 journalists from 15 countries in Latin America were part of the International Consortium of Investigative Journalists team that reviewed 11.5 million records from the Panamanian law firm Mossack Fonseca, one of the world's top creators of shell companies used to hide ownership of assets. Similarly, 60 journalists from 13 Latin American countries were involved in the management, reporting, and editing of the Paradise Papers, analyzing massive volumes of documents leaked from offshore law firm Appleby.

Besides the Panama and the Paradise Papers, other examples show that Latin American news organisations have embraced the potential of collaborative work. In 2016, the Salvadoran site *El Faro* worked in conjunction with the *New York Times* to expose violent gangs in El Salvador. In 2017, *El Faro* worked with *Univision* to produce a multimedia report about the migrant crisis in Central America. In both cases, the information was published simultaneously in English and Spanish to reach wider audiences. In the 2018 Excellence in Journalism Awards by the Inter American Press Association, 9 out of 13 award categories were given to collaborative teams (Sociedad Interamericana de Prensa, 2018). The collaborative project "Investiga Lava Jato", conducted by reporters from 15 countries in Latin America and Africa, obtained the 2018 Excellence in Journalism Award in the Data Journalism category.

Recent studies about collaborative journalism in the region found that collaborations are formed to enhance the impact of investigative projects, reach larger audiences, and yield comprehensive coverage (Cueva Chacón and Saldaña, 2019). Given that anti-press violence and limited support within legacy news organisations are the most common constraints for investigative reporters in Latin America (Saldaña and Mourao, 2018), working in conjunction with other news organisations – especially outlets in other countries – helps news

INVESTIGATIVE JOURNALISM IN LATIN AMERICA TODAY

organisations to reach the public even if the stories are shut down by political authorities or economic pressures. Yet collaborative work is not without drawbacks. Investigative teams struggle to meet deadlines, make good use of resources, and distribute labour and responsibilities properly when working with teams from other news outlets. Successful collaborations require editorial agreements early on in the project, as well as trust and good intentions among partners (Stonbely, 2017).

## Investigative journalism in digital native sites

Unquestionably, the coming of digital sites that prominently feature investigative stories has been a major development in Latin America in the past decade (Salaverría et al., 2019). Virtually every country in the region displays a small number of sites that exemplify this trend. These sites generally publish stories that are rigorous with facts, expose wrongdoing by powerful actors, put attention on urgent social problems and inequalities, bring out multileveled stories that include citizens' voices, and incorporate cutting-edge reporting techniques.

An incomplete list of these sites includes the following cases. Mexico's *Dromómanos* has documented problems such as violence, drug trafficking, and migration. It has used transmedia reporting and citizens' contributions to produce vivid, complex stories. It has partnered with civil society organisations to conduct policy advocacy to address those social problems. Mexico's *Animal Político* is widely known for its stellar reporting on social inequality, political corruption, migration, social programs, and human rights violations. In Venezuela, *Runrun.es* began as a Twitter account and blog in 2009, and it became an innovative investigative journalism site that works on exposing political wrongdoing in the country. Guatemala's *Nómada* and *Plaza Pública* produced several exposés that revealed collusion between the government and larger corporations in relation to a range of illicit behaviours, including tax evasion, fraud, and illegal campaign financing. They have offered in-depth coverage of sexual abuses and femicides implicating powerful actors, as well as the challenges of socially marginalised populations such as indigenous groups, LGBTIA, migrants, and women. Chile's Centre for Investigative Journalism (CIPER for the initials in Spanish) has exposed political corruption in the country and examined critical issues related to government and public policy. Launched in 2007, CIPER has made its goal to promote transparency and freedom of information. Colombia's *Cuestión Pública* and *La Silla Vacía* have regularly investigated government wrongdoing, shady dealings between politicians and corporations, and illegal public contracts. Paraguay's *El Surti* has featured fascinating, close-up investigations of the country's chronic problems: corruption, environmental degradation, and illegal economy. Also, it has reported on sexual violence, reproductive rights, and sexual rights. In Brazil, a host of news organisations, such as *Brasil de Fato, Agência Pública*, and *The Intercept Brasil*, have frequently published

233

investigations on government and corporate corruption, put the spotlight on social inequalities and human rights, and reported on citizens' struggles against power. Other investigative news sites include Peru's *IDL, Convoca,* and *Ojo Público;* Venezuela's *Efecto Cocuyo;* and Mexico's *Quinto Elemento Lab,* which have uncovered transnational networks of corruption involving powerful corporations and governments.

What are the distinctive aspects of these investigative sites? Compared to legacy news organisations, these sites have developed a novel, hybrid funding model that relies on philanthropic funding (mostly from international donors), subscriptions, and service provision – consulting, event organisation, data analysis (Requejo-Alemán and Lugo-Ocando, 2014). Such a funding model has allowed them to foreground investigative reporting, focus on public issues, and keep traditional public and private advertisers at a prudent distance. Equally important is the fact that they have become models of quality investigative reporting.

For instance, the Salvadoran site *El Faro* has become a sustainable project after years of not making any profit. According to the Knight Center for Journalism in the Americas, *El Faro* has four income channels: donations from international organisations (such as Open Society Foundations), advertising revenue, an annual crowdfunding campaign (#ExcavaciónCiudadana) where readers economically contribute to help sustain the project, and the sale of content to other news organisations (Nafría, 2018). Mexico's *Animal Político,* in contrast, depends on advertising to a larger extent than *El Faro,* but it uses its food vertical *Animal Gourmet* to sell ads and avoid government advertising. It also receives funding from consultancy, contributions from organisations such as Open Society Foundations and the Ford Foundation and crowdfunding campaigns (López Linares, 2018). A different case is Brazilian news site JOTA – which covers judicial issues – where it implemented an "a la carte service" for readers to cherry-pick products and services according to their needs: subscriptions, specialised newsletters, alert services, press clippings, and so on (Nafría, 2017).

## The irruption of data journalism

The generation of high volumes of information (so-called big data) in today's digital environment has contributed to the rise of data journalism as a tool for investigative reporting and storytelling. News organisations are increasingly demanding professionals with expertise in data analysis, visualisation tools, and statistics and mathematical skills. Many of the collaborative projects described earlier in this chapter applied data-analysis techniques or were conceived as data-driven projects. Moreover, the ability to analyze information collaboratively relies on the possibility of conducting data analysis in quantitative and replicable ways.

# INVESTIGATIVE JOURNALISM IN LATIN AMERICA TODAY

Research on data journalism conducted by teams at the *New York Times* and *Washington Post* indicates day-to-day data reporting in these outlets is neither transparent nor interactive, relies primarily on institutional sources (especially government sources), and offers little original data collection, which are supposed to be relevant features of data-journalism pieces (Zamith, 2019). In contrast, studies analysing data journalism in Latin America suggest this type of reporting is producing high-quality pieces and tracking more attention from the audience. Since the inaugural edition of the Data Journalism Awards in 2012 – a global event organised by the Global Editors Network – Latin American news organisations have obtained prizes at this competition every year. Transparency laws that guarantee access to official information in most of Latin American countries, in addition to the media's increasing demand for public information, are contributing to the development of data reporting for investigative journalism in the region (Palomo, Teruel, and Blanco-Castilla, 2019).

One of the most remarkable examples of data reporting in the region is *La Nación Data*, a project developed by Argentine newspaper *La Nación*, which uses data to tell stories and expand the use of data to activate demand for public information. It has become a major data journalism organisation in Latin America and has received a significant number of journalistic awards. While many news outlets are laying journalists off to reduce costs, *La Nación* has invested in a data journalism unit that has become "a data journalism powerhouse" in the region, according to NiemabLab (Mazotte, 2017).

Another example of the importance of data journalism in Latin America is the *Manual de Periodismo de Datos Iberoamericano*, an online, open-access handbook documenting the state of Ibero-American data reporting. Led by Chilean journalists Felipe Perry and Miguel Paz (2015), academics and practitioners from 16 countries (including Portugal and Spain) wrote entries for the handbook, covering topics such as information access, data routines, best practices, and digital tools.

Yet data reporting through computer-aided techniques has become a double-edged sword. On the one hand, data journalism is said to be a way to achieve a more systematic, accurate, and trustworthy journalism practice. On the other hand, organisations conducting data journalism are mostly elite news outlets, while the popular 'tabloid' journalism has not engaged with this practice. As such, "a new technologically adept and data-informed elite class might be on the rise, with important implications for democratic processes in advanced societies" (Felle, 2016; p. 85).

Despite universities increasingly including data journalism courses in their curriculum, it is still not common to find statistics courses in journalism programs (Nguyen and Lugo-Ocando, 2016). Undoubtedly, digital developments have brought benefits to investigative journalism in Latin America, but there is opportunity for growth in many aspects of the matter.

## Fact-checkers to fight misinformation

Fake news denotes "news articles that are intentionally and verifiably false, and could mislead readers" (Allcott and Gentzkow, 2017; p. 213). The so-called fake news became a buzzword during the 2016 US presidential election, when false political information was shared more frequently than correct, verifiable information (Silverman, 2016). Though fake news is not rare in the history of journalism, the current news media environment has shifted to digital and social media environments, where false information can spread at a faster rate, reaching wider audiences. Yet misinformation does not always come from false news stories or poor reporting – politicians and public figures can also mislead citizens through false claims or inaccurate statements. This is worrisome, as misinformation has the potential to become a real threat to democracy by affecting what people believe and how they make political decisions.

The spread of unverified information, rumours, and conspiracies has been a concern raised during several elections across the region, including Argentina, Brazil, Chile, Mexico, and Venezuela. In 2017, fake stories about several presidential candidates in Chile were spread on Facebook. Similarly, during the 2018 presidential election in Brazil, lies and rumours flood social media (particularly WhatsApp) to delegitimise traditional news outlets (Noel, 2009). In this context, Latin American countries have seen the emergence of fact-checking organisations where reporters and researchers work together to verify statements by public figures and debunk fake news, especially on social media.

The 2019 Duke Reporters' Lab identified 188 fact-checking organisations around the world, 39 more than what they counted in 2018 (Stencel, 2019). Latin America has not reached the numbers observed in North America and Europe, and yet, every year the number of fact checkers in the region increases substantially. Though this type of project usually emerges during election periods to verify candidates' claims, many outlets also work on debunking viral hoaxes and other forms of online misinformation. For instance, *El Polígrafo* (Chilean newspaper *El Mercurio's* fact-checking unit) verifies information every week, alternating between statements from political figures and rumours spread on platforms such as Facebook or WhatsApp.

Many of the fact-checking projects in the region belong to news organisations that also conduct investigative journalism: *El Sabueso*, from Mexico's *Animal Político*; *Detector de Mentiras*, from Colombia's *La Silla Vacía*; *Truco*, from Brazil's *Agência Pública*; *ConPruebas*, from Guatemala's *Plaza Pública*; or *Ojo Biónico*, from Perú's *Ojo Público*. By rating information from "true" to "false" (or even "ridiculous" in some cases), these websites contribute to improve the public debate while also educating audiences in data and media literacy.

But the pioneering case of Latin American fact-checking is *Chequeado*, an Argentina-based organisation launched in 2010. Inspired by US site FactCheck.org, *Chequeado* verifies statements of politicians and public figures and also trains journalists from other news organisations to conduct fact checking. Since

# INVESTIGATIVE JOURNALISM IN LATIN AMERICA TODAY

2014, *Chequeado* has organised the Latam Chequea conference, an event where reporters and editors from several countries discuss experiences and strategies to improve fact checking in the region.

Unlike the United States, where most of the fact-checking initiatives are associated with established media companies, Latin American fact checkers are more independent from traditional news companies. Half of them are not part of a large news outlet but work as a standalone website, belong to a non-profit organisation, are tied to independent news websites, or are affiliated with academic institutions. Such conditions are important for them to show new forms of practicing quality reporting.

## Obstacles and threats

The healthy situation of investigative journalism is remarkable, considering the persistence of formidable obstacles. Obstacles are not particularly related to journalists' beliefs about the importance of watchdog reporting or training opportunities; instead, they are grounded in a range of political and economic structures and dynamics that limit opportunities for in-depth examination and denunciation of wrongdoing.

One set of obstacles is the worsening of political conditions for investigative journalism, particularly in countries where elected governments evolved into authoritarian regimes, like Nicaragua's Daniel Ortega and Venezuela's Nicolás Maduro in the past decade. Reporters and news organisations that published exposés about human rights abuses and illegal activities by prominent government officials have suffered repression. Many reporters who authored critical investigations were thrown in jail without due process by the governments.

Elsewhere in the region, anti-press violence remains a critical deterrent. In a region with the highest rates of violence in the world, it is not uncommon that investigative reporters are targets of attacks, especially those covering illegal activities by intelligence and police services, human rights abuses by death squads, and drug trafficking. Investigative reporters outside metropolitan areas are particularly vulnerable to attacks, especially in countries such as Brazil, Colombia, and Mexico that annually record the highest numbers of anti-press violence.

Governments and illegal actors have been responsible. The state has often tried to squash critical reporting through verbal warnings, legal actions, physical violence, and direct pressure on news organisations and reporters. Frequently, the police and armed forces in collusion with politicians have threatened reporters and been responsible for the killing of journalists. Para-state actors such as drug traffickers and gangs, too, have threatened and murdered reporters. High levels of anti-press violence have continued amid impunity. Mechanisms to report attacks and protect reporters in Colombia and Mexico, the countries with the highest levels of anti-press violence in the past decades, have not been as efficient as they need to be.

Equally worrisome is the ubiquity of online harassment of investigative reporters. Not surprisingly, investigative reporters have been prime targets of online harassment, especially after stories get massive coverage and social media presence. Amid political polarisation, journalists publicly identified with ideological and political causes have experienced digital attacks by governments, armies of trolls, and ordinary citizens. Female reporters have been a common target of intimidations and attacks, including bullying, insults, doxing, stalking, and defamation (Lanza, 2018).

Another obstacle to investigative reporting is the uneven and arbitrary application of freedom of information legislation. Certainly, important progress has been made in this area with the passing of legislation granting access to public information in the past decades throughout the region. However, the persistence of several problems limits reporters' ability to scrutinise governments and other actors: weak traditions of compiling and managing public records, poor recordkeeping, insufficient staff and funds for government offices responsible for attending public requests for information, and erratic and unaccountable decisions in responding to petitions.

Finally, worsening work conditions negatively affect investigative reporting. By definition, investigative stories demand time and resources, which are both scarce for vast numbers of reporters. Holding two or more jobs isn't unusual, especially for reporters who live and work outside large metropolitan areas where salaries are considerably lower. Spending a substantial amount of time digging up facts, interviewing sources, analyzing documents, and producing stories seems a luxury.

## Why does investigative journalism matter?

An important issue to consider is the consequences of investigative journalism. Why does it matter? What difference does it make, especially when reporters continue to face significant obstacles and dangers? How do we understand the unique contributions of careful, fact-grounded, inquisitive reporting that reveals wrongdoing when groundless opinions massively circulate in the Internet and public attention is constantly pulled by myriad forms of content? Why are investigative stories, that generally take considerable time and resources and oftentimes quickly vanish in the digital atmosphere, important? Do they increase public knowledge and democratic accountability? These questions are particularly relevant in today's multileveled and noisy information ecologies, packed with all kinds of news, misinformation, rumours, spin and propaganda, and rapidly changing news cycles.

In the past, when journalism held a dominant position in public communication, understanding the importance of investigative journalism seemed straightforward. It was rarely disputed that investigative reporting made important contributions to the public good: hold the powerful accountable, document "invisible" social problems, inform citizens about behind-the-scenes

# INVESTIGATIVE JOURNALISM IN LATIN AMERICA TODAY

dealings that otherwise wouldn't have been known, deliver factual accounts that contradict official silence and lies, push the public to confront the dark side of capitalism and social miseries. In many cases, the publication of exposés single-handedly sparked judicial and congressional investigations, shamed government officials, triggered resignations, and caused public debates on important matters.

No doubt, many cases of investigative journalism by both legacy news organisations and digital native sites still have similar consequences. Certain stories sparked actions and contributed to effective policy change. Operação Lava Jato (Operation Car Wash), the biggest political corruption scandal in Brazil's history, is a good example. In January 2016, leading daily *Folha de São Paulo* reported that former President Luiz Inácio "Lula" da Silva benefited from the works that construction company Odebrecht made in a country house located in Atibaia, São Paulo, in exchange for favouring this company in contracts with state-owned oil giant Petrobras. The reporting process included data-journalism techniques and led to investigations that uncovered an unprecedented web of corruption in Brazil that ultimately extended to at least 12 countries, imprisoning company executives and public officials. At the same time, Peruvian non-profit investigative journalism organisation *IDL-Reporteros* revealed that Odebrecht also obtained contracts for public works in Peru. As such, the Lava Jato scandal is also an example of collaboration, where journalists from different countries joined forces to exchange sources and contacts but also to achieve a better global understanding of the case (López Linares, 2017).

Similar examples can be found in other Latin American countries. In Mexico, "El país de las 2 mil fosas" (The country of the 2 thousand graves) revealed how, between 2006 and 2016, the finding of clandestine graves in Mexico spread across the country. Using public documents, a group of independent journalists (sponsored by *Quinto Elemento Lab*) mapped the location of the graves and exposed the lack of organisation of Mexican authorities.

In 2018, an investigation led by *La Nación* journalist Diego Cabot uncovered years of briberies paid to Argentina's public officers by businessmen who benefited with large contracts. Known as "Los Cuadernos de la Corrupción" (The notebook scandal), this investigation had access to notebooks written by a driver of a public works official, who documented the times, value and even the weight of the bags of money he delivered around Buenos Aires. More than a dozen people have been arrested in Argentina due to the notebook scandal.

In 2012, Chilean President Sebastián Piñera promised to conduct the "best census ever" to know more about the Chilean population. However, a report by CIPER exposed serious methodological errors and manipulation of figures during the presentation of results. The director of the National Statistics Institute (in charge of the census) was forced to resign, and the census had to be conducted again in 2017, during Michelle Bachelet's second presidential term.

In Costa Rica, *La Nación* reporter Giannina Segnini uncovered political scandals that ended with two presidents prosecuted for corruption charges: Rafael

Ángel Calderón (Caja-Fischel case) and Miguel Ángel Rodríguez (ICE-Alcatel case). In Guatemala, investigative reporting that exposed a corruption network in the government had a crucial role in the resignation and subsequent detention of President Otto Pérez Molina in 2015. News outlets such as Guatemalan daily *elPeriódico*, magazine *ContraPoder*, and digital native *Nómada* led and strengthened the work of the International Commission against Impunity in Guatemala and the Public Prosecutor's Office (Higuera and Mioli, 2017).

We believe that investigate journalism matters for several reasons. It leaves public records of truth. It sheds light on social problems that otherwise wouldn't be widely known. It challenges factless, manipulative versions of reality.

## Questions for future research

The situation in Latin America raises questions we believe are significant for comparative studies of investigative journalism globally. What is remarkable is that despite well-known challenges in the news industry coupled with difficult conditions for critical reporting on power abuses and wrongdoing, investigative journalism has been resilient, innovative, and impactful. Reporters working in legacy news organisations and digital sites have continued to confront a range of obstacles, including the editorial positions of their own organisations. Yet they have managed to produce a steady stream of stories on important subjects that otherwise would not have been known. Many stories left an important record in terms of exposing wrongdoing and holding the powerful accountable, as described in the previous examples. However, cautious conclusions are warranted given the persistence of tough conditions for in-depth reporting on subjects affecting powerful interests, as well as intractable problems for political accountability in Latin American democracies.

Journalism scholars should refrain from piling up ambitious expectations about investigative journalism and address the feasibility of specific normative models in real contexts of practice. Any normative argument about the obligations of investigative journalism needs to be sensitive to political and economic circumstances. Important stories that bring transparency and accountability can drive broad changes only when other conditions are present (Waisbord, 2000). Also, we need to be mindful of the fact that investigative reporting, which generally takes up considerable human and monetary resources, might get easily lost amid information abundance and fast-moving news cycles. We need to understand better the lifespan of investigative stories and examine how stories affect public perceptions about political and social problems and collective action.

Journalism is one institution that, in its best moments, helps to address various informational challenges by injecting reason, facts, and voice in news ecologies and public life. What we need to learn from past waves of excessive optimism about journalistic innovations is that the reality of journalism and public communication is complex and chaotic, and the impact of investigative journalism is contingent on political factors beyond the reach of the press.

# References

Allcott, H., and Gentzkow, M. (2017) 'Social media and fake news in the 2016 election', *Journal of Economic Perspectives*, 31, 211–236. DOI: 10.3386/w23089

Cueva Cachón, L., and Saldaña, M. (2019) 'Stronger and safer together: The impact of digital technologies on (trans)national collaboration for investigative reporting in Latin America'. Paper presented at the ICA preconference Digital Journalism in Latin America, Journalism Studies Division (May 2019), Washington, DC.

Felle, T. (2016) 'Digital watchdogs? Data reporting and the news media's traditional "fourth estate" function', *Journalism*, 17(1), 85–96. DOI: 10.1177/1464884915593246

Higuera, S., and Mioli, T. (2017) *Journalism played a central role in the fall and arrest of the president of Guatemala* [Online]. The Knight Center for Journalism in the Americas. Available at: https://knightcenter.utexas.edu/blog/00-16284-journalism-played-central-role-fall-and-arrest-president-guatemala (Accessed: 01 August 2019).

Lanza, E. (2018) *Women journalists and freedom of expression: Discrimination and gender-based violence faced by women journalist in the exercise of their profession* [Online]. Organization of American States. Available at: www.oas.org/en/iachr/expression/docs/reports/Women-Journalists.pdf (Accessed: 15 July 2019).

López Linares, C. (2017) *Alliances help journalists tackle the Lava Jato case from a global perspective* [Online]. The Knight Center for Journalism in the Americas. Available at: https://knightcenter.utexas.edu/blog/00-18607-alliances-help-journalists-tackle-lava-jato-case-global-perspective (Accessed: 24 January 2020).

López Linares, C. (2018) *Animal Político shakes the Mexican political class with innovations in content, presentation and collaborative projects* [Online]. The Knight Center for Journalism in the Americas. Available at: https://knightcenter.utexas.edu/blog/00-19439-inno vations-content-presentation-and-collaborative-work-animal-politico-shakes-mexican (Accessed: 25 July 2019).

Mazotte, N. (2017) *How the Argentinian daily La Nación became a data journalism powerhouse in Latin America* [Online]. NiemanLab. Available at: www.niemanlab.org/2017/04/how-the-argentinian-daily-la-nacion-became-a-data-journalism-powerhouse-in-latin-amer ica/ (Accessed: 20 July 2019).

Nafría, I. (2017) *Brazilian reporters create profitable news site, JOTA, specializing in judicial issues* [Online]. The Knight Center for Journalism in the Americas. Available at: https://knight center.utexas.edu/blog/00-19067-brazilian-reporters-create-profitable-news-site-jota-specializing-judicial-issues (Accessed: 01 August 2019).

Nafría, I. (2018) *Lessons in innovation from Salvadoran site El Faro start with a focus on quality journalism* [Online]. The Knight Center for Journalism in the Americas. Available at: https://knightcenter.utexas.edu/blog/00-19217-el-salvador-lessons-innovation-el-faro-start-focus-quality-journalism (Accessed: 20 July 2019).

Nguyen, A., and Lugo-Ocando, J. (2016) 'The state of data and statistics in journalism and journalism education: Issues and debates', *Journalism*, 17(1) 3–17. DOI: 10.1177/1464884915593234

Noel, P. (2009) *How Fake News Conquered Brazil* [Online]. Medium. Available at: https://medium.com/news-to-table/how-fake-news-conquered-brazil-617ef6769ebc (Accessed: 01 August 2019).

Palomo, B., Teruel, L., and Blanco-Castilla, E. (2019) 'Data journalism projects based on user-generated content. How *La Nación* data transforms active audience into staff', *Digital Journalism*, [published online first]. DOI: 10.1080/21670811.2019.1626257

Perry, F., and Paz, M. (2015) *Manual de Periodismo de Datos Iberoamericano* [Online]. Santiago de Chile: Poderopedia and Universidad Alberto Hurtado. Available at: http://manual.periodismodedatos.org (Accessed: 20 July 2019).

Requejo-Alemán, J. L., and Lugo-Ocando, J. (2014) 'Assessing the sustainability of Latin American investigative non-profit journalism', *Journalism Studies*, 15(5), 522–532. DOI: 10.1080/1461670X.2014.885269

Salaverría, R., Sádaba, C., Breiner, J. G., and Warner, J. C. (2019) 'A brave new digital journalism in Latin America', in Túnez-Lopez, M., Martínez-Fernández, V.-A., López-García, X., Rúas-Araújo, X., and Campos-Freire, F. (eds.) *Communication: Innovation and Quality*. Cham: Springer, pp. 229–247.

Saldaña, M., and Mourao, R. R. (2018) 'Reporting in Latin America: Issues and perspectives on investigative journalism in the region', *The International Journal of Press/Politics*, 23(3), 299–323. DOI: 10.1177/1940161218782397

Silverman, C. (2016, Nov. 16) *Analysis shows how viral fake news outperformed real news on Facebook* [Online]. Buzzfeed. Available at: www.buzzfeed.com/craigsilverman/viral-fake-election-news-outperformed-real-news-on-facebook?utm_term=.ipYmZG024#.ol6m LXB57 (Accessed: 25 July 2019).

Sociedad Interamericana de Prensa. (2018) *SIP exalta la labor del periodismo nicaragüense al anunciar los Premios a la Excelencia Periodística 2018* [Online]. Sipiapa.org. Available at: www.sipiapa.org/notas/1212684-sip-exalta-la-labor-del-periodismo-nicaragense-al-anunciar-los-premios-la-excelencia-periodistica-2018 (Accessed: 01 August 2019).

Stencel, M. (2019) *Number of fact-checking outlets surges to 188 in more than 60 countries strong growth in Asia and Latin America helps fuel global increase* [Online]. ReportersLab. Available at: https://reporterslab.org/number-of-fact-checking-outlets-surges-to-188-in-more-than-60-countries/ (Accessed: 25 July 2019).

Stonbely, S. (2017) *Comparing Models of Collaborative Journalism*. Montclair, NJ: Center for Cooperative Media, Montclair State University.

Waisbord, S. (2000) *Watchdog Journalism in South America*. New York: Columbia University Press.

Waisbord, S. (2019) 'The vulnerabilities of journalism', *Journalism*, 20(1), 210–213. DOI: 10.1177/1464884918809283

Zamith, R. (2019) 'Transparency, interactivity, diversity, and information provenance in everyday data journalism', *Digital Journalism*, 7(4), 470–489. DOI: 10.1080/21670811.2018.1554409

# 18

# HOW THE UNITED KINGDOM'S TABLOIDS GO ABOUT IT

*Roy Greenslade*

## Introduction

The printed issues of Britain's most popular national newspapers, known as red-tops, have suffered substantial losses in circulation since the arrival of the internet. In the course of the 19 years after 2000, daily sales fell by 69%, while Sunday sales fell by 76%.[1] Although they have benefitted from significant rises in online readerships, the levels of revenue generated online have been but a fraction of those enjoyed from print. The combined losses of circulation and advertising income are serious.

In order to deal with the decline in profits, the newspapers' managers have instituted regular cuts in editorial budgets. Newsroom staffing has been severely reduced, and there has been a marked decrease in the resources allocated to journalism that does not produce copy on a daily, sometimes an hourly, basis. Investigative journalism is labour intensive. Publishers have therefore regarded investigative journalism as a luxury. Nevertheless, five red-tops – *The Sun, Daily Mirror, Sunday Mirror, Sun on Sunday* and *The People*[2] – have managed to carry out many investigations in the public interest. The *Daily Star* and *Daily Star Sunday* have not.

In the last edition of this book, in 2008, I identified Britain's largest-selling title, the *News of the World* (*NoW*), as 'the leading investigative newspaper' among the red-top titles. I pointed out that its reporters had taken 'full advantage of the developing technological advances' while pushing 'at the ethical boundaries'. In 2011, it was closed down because some of its staff had not only crossed those ethical boundaries but had crossed legal boundaries as well. Several of its journalists had routinely intercepted the mobile phone voicemail messages of many hundreds of people in what became known as the 'phone-hacking scandal'. After a series of criminal trials, four members of staff were imprisoned, with others receiving suspended jail sentences.

These incidents, and the resulting aftermath, notably the Leveson Inquiry, had a far-reaching impact on investigative journalism by the popular press, effectively reducing the frequency and potency of 'exposures' – usually involving celebrities – that had previously been meat and drink for Sunday red-tops and their daily stablemates. Nor was the hacking scandal the only problem facing editors. Changes to several laws – including the Regulation of Investigatory Powers Act, the Bribery Act and the Data Protection Act – inhibited tabloid-style journalism, as did interpretations of the right to privacy enshrined in the 1998 Human Rights Act. It brought English law into line with the European Convention on Human Rights. Despite these pressures, editors continued to encourage investigative work. This chapter will consider the history of red-top investigative journalism, the context in which phone-hacking occurred, a taxonomy of the methods used and a look at recent investigations.

## Pioneers of the 'dark arts'

Misbehaviour by popular newspaper journalists did not begin in 2006, when the phone-hacking phenomenon emerged in public. It was common from the Second World War onwards. The *News of the World* pushed way beyond boundaries regarded elsewhere as unacceptable.

### *'Fishing expeditions'*

There is no direct reference in the Editors' Code of Practice to fishing expeditions, the practice of going undercover or using subterfuge in the hope of finding something untoward. However, the regulatory bodies, the Press Complaints Commission (1995–2014) and the Independent Press Standards Organisation (2014 to date), have ruled against papers using last resort investigative methods on the off chance of landing a story. The precedent was set in 2001 when the PCC censured the *News of the World* for covertly filming a private Christmas party for the cast of the TV series, Emmerdale. The Commission ruled that it was an infringement of the party-goers' privacy because the paper had no prior knowledge of a transgression that it would be in the public interest to reveal. Guy (now Lord) Black, the PCC's director, said at the time: 'The code isn't there to stop legitimate investigation; it is there to stop fishing expeditions' ('News of the World censured for secret video', *The Guardian*, 17 April 2001; PCC Report 53. At http://www.pcc.org.uk/cases/adjudicated. html?article=MjAyOQ==&type=). That proved to be a landmark ruling, effectively closing the door on journalists setting off on investigations merely on a hunch or a whim.

### *'Blagging' information*

'Blagging', the custom of obtaining information over the phone through impersonation, is well known to journalists from their earliest days in the trade. It is unlikely that most refer to it as blagging or that they see much harm in the practice. It involves pretending to be someone you are not – a council official, perhaps, or hospital clerk or police officer – so that the person at the other end of the line can be persuaded to divulge confidential information. Down the years, many journalists, on local papers as well as nationals, have probably indulged in infrequent blagging, regarding it as a necessary way to obtain vital information in a society regarded as overly secret.

However, it is clearly an act of subterfuge and the Editors' Code of Practice (Clause 10ii) expressly forbids 'engaging in misrepresentation or subterfuge' to access material unless it can be justified 'in the public interest and then only when the material cannot be obtained by other means'. Nor should journalists think they can circumvent the rule by asking someone else to do it on their behalf because the same clause precludes the use of 'agents or intermediaries' to engage in subterfuge.

During the phone-hacking saga, it emerged that the *News of the World* used blagging persistently to obtain sensitive personal information about people in public life, particularly celebrities, in which there was no discernible public interest reason for doing so. They also out-sourced the work to freelance investigators, blagging specialists, with inside knowledge of the security vulnerabilities of certain institutions, notably mobile phone companies.

### Phone hacking

The phenomenon of phone hacking (the interception of mobile phone voicemail messages), first surfaced in public in August 2006 with the arrest of the *NoW*'s Royal Editor, Clive Goodman, and a freelance investigator and self-confessed blagger, Glenn Mulcaire. They were charged under the Regulation of Investigative Powers Act with accessing the voicemails of members of the Royal Household. In January 2007, both men pleaded guilty. Goodman was sentenced to four months in jail and Mulcaire, who faced extra charges relating to five other people, including Gordon Taylor, the chief executive of the Professional Footballers Association, got six months. It was revealed in court that the newspaper had paid Mulcaire more than £100,000 for his services (*The Guardian*, 26 January 2007. At www.theguardian.com/media/2007/jan/26/newsoftheworld.pressandpublishing1).

On the day of the hearing, the *NoW*'s editor, Andy Coulson, resigned but insisted he knew nothing of the crimes. Two months later, Les Hinton, the chief executive of the newspaper's publisher, Rupert Murdoch's News International, told a parliamentary committee that Goodman was the only reporter guilty of hacking. A 'full, rigorous internal investigation', he suggested, had found no evidence of other staff being involved (Davies, 2014: 17). Despite widespread scepticism across Fleet Street about that statement, proof of its falsity took years to emerge. The key which unlocked the truth was the discovery that Gordon Taylor, chief executive of the Professional Footballers' Association, had been paid £700,000 after he had launched a breach of privacy claim against News International. *The Guardian*'s Nick Davies wondered why Taylor's lawyer had managed to obtain such a disproportionately large settlement and why it had been paid so discreetly. Had the 'rogue reporter' defence concealed a wider use of hacking at the paper? A source contacted him suggesting it had, and Davies began a painstaking, lengthy investigation.

Meanwhile, the *NoW* found itself embroiled in a separate controversy which was to have far-reaching implications. On 30 March 2008, the paper carried a story which occupied almost the entire front page, headlined 'F1 Boss Has Sick Nazi Orgy With 5 Hookers'. It alleged that Max Mosley, president of the Paris-based motoring organisation responsible for licensing Formula One racing, had hired five women to indulge in sado-masochistic activities with a Nazi theme. Readers were reminded that Mosley's father, Oswald Mosley, had been the leader of a fascist party in Britain in the 1930s. The 'investigation' followed a familiar *NoW* pattern in the sense that it was a commercial deal. The paper was tipped off about the impending 'orgy' by the husband of one of the women. It was agreed that the couple would receive £25,000 in return for her filming the session with a pinhole camera concealed in the tie she wore as part of her costume. Some of the exchanges between Mosley and the women were in German.

On the day of publication, the paper posted video clips of the session on its website. But it had not translated the German dialogue, thereby wrongly assuming the Nazi element. This mistake was to prove costly when Mosley sued the paper on the grounds that it had invaded his privacy. The paper's second error was in deciding to halve the fee it had promised to the couple, which resulted in the woman refusing to give evidence at the high court hearing in July 2008 (Thurlbeck, 2015: 293). The judge ruled that the paper had failed to justify its Nazi claim and, without that, there was no public interest justification for the story. Mosley was awarded £60,000 and News International was required to pick up the costs. Mosley, however, outraged by the disclosure of his private life and the fact that the video clips were widely available across the internet, was anything but finished with the paper. He would go on to underwrite the legal costs of hacking victims (Davies, 2014: 261) and, following the Leveson Inquiry, would later fund a regulatory body in opposition to the one favoured by most newspaper publishers.

Davies, who sympathised with Mosley's plight, made headway with his hacking inquiries throughout 2008 and during the course of the next six months. They culminated, in July 2009, with his revelation in *The Guardian* of the secret payment to Taylor. In follow-up articles, he alleged that several *NoW* staff, including junior executives, had been guilty of hacking. Most of the victims he identified were celebrities or people who worked on their behalf. The police treated the stories with scorn and refused to investigate, even though hacking victims started to pursue civil claims against News International for breaches of privacy. Inside the *NoW*, however, the drip-drip-drip of Davies's exposures over the course of the following months was taken seriously, prompting the suspensions of some staff at the end of 2010.

It was in January 2011 that Scotland Yard finally launched a full-scale investigation into phone hacking, and the turning point came six months later with Davies's report in *The Guardian* that police had found evidence suggesting a mobile phone belonging to a missing, murdered teenager, Milly Dowler, had been hacked on behalf of the *NoW* (*The Guardian*, 11 April 2011). It was alleged that some messages had been deleted, thereby giving false hope to her family that she might still be alive.[3] This resulted in high-level resignations at News International and Scotland Yard and announcements by advertisers that they would withdraw their advertising from the *NoW*. Murdoch responded by closing the paper, and the last issue was published on 10 July 2011.

The closure made no difference to the clamour for an inquiry, and the prime minister, David Cameron, came under intense political pressure to act against the popular press, not least because he had appointed Coulson as the Tory party's director of communications in July 2007, just six months after Coulson's resignation as *News of the World* editor. Coulson continued in that role when Cameron became PM in May 2010. Publicity over hacking led him to resign from the post in January 2011. Cameron announced a judicial review into 'the culture, practices and ethics of the British press' to be chaired by Lord Justice Leveson. It was a landmark moment for newspapers, and its outcome has continued to be divisive.

## The Leveson Report: a chilling effect?

Evidence given at the public hearings during the Leveson Inquiry and the subsequent publication of the Leveson Report in November 2012 revealed a willingness to break rules, both ethical and legal, in order to maximise sales. Among the practices it highlighted were intrusions into privacy, the widespread use of blagging, impersonation, subterfuge, entrapment, harassment and surveillance, often connected to investigative journalism.

In its conclusion, the Report made only a single reference to investigative journalism, arguing that the press should be free 'to hold power to account, to conduct investigative journalism in the public interest', adding that it was necessary for the press 'to be accountable to the public in whose interests it claims to be acting and must show respect for the rights of others to such extent as legitimate public interest does not justify otherwise' (Leveson: 1459). This stress on 'public interest' as the justification for journalistic investigations underlined a clause in the existing Editors' Code of Practice, which was adopted in its entirety by the new self-regulatory body that emerged in the aftermath of the Report, the Independent Press Standards Organisation. It was similar in many respects to the previous regulator, the Press Complaints Commission, but with the availability to impose harsher penalties, including fines, for breaches of the Code. Despite the relatively tame compromise over the regulatory process, this proved an important moment for the popular press. Popular newspaper publishers and editors begrudgingly accepted that their culture had to change. They were not alone in complaining about supposed restrictions on their freedom. Some editors and journalists from the quality press were also concerned about the possible chilling effects on investigative journalism (Lashmar, 2013. At www.opendemocracy.net/en/opendemocracyuk/path-to-hell-investigative-journalists-view-of-leveson/; Ben Webster, *The Times*, 31 December 2012. At www.thetimes.co.uk/article/leveson-will-have-chilling-effect-on-journalism-bvwmzn52ghb).

Throughout the Leveson Inquiry, it was largely assumed that phone hacking was confined to the *NoW*, despite the screening on 24 July 2011 of a BBC2 *Newsnight* investigation which alleged that celebrities' voicemails had been hacked by the *Sunday Mirror*. This claim was rejected by Trinity Mirror's then-chief executive, Sly Bailey, as 'unsubstantiated' (Leveson: 169). She refused to hold an internal inquiry into the allegation, telling the Inquiry: 'I don't think it's a way to conduct a healthy organisation to go around conducting investigations when there's no evidence that our journalists have been involved in phone hacking' (*The Guardian* 24 September 2014. At www.theguardian.com/media/greenslade/2014/sep/24/trinity-mirror-sundaymirror).

Just days before the Leveson Report's publication, four phone-hacking claims were filed against Trinity Mirror (*The Guardian*, 23 October 2012). These turned out to be the tip of the iceberg. Over the following years, there were more than 100 civil claims of voicemail interception against the *Daily Mirror, Sunday Mirror* and *Sunday People* (*Press Gazette*, 25 February 2019. At www.pressgazette.co.uk/phone-hacking-pot-grows-by-12-5m-at-mirror-express-and-star-publisher-reach-full-2018-accounts/). By May 2019, Reach, the renamed Trinity Mirror company, had paid out £75 million to claimants, while the bill for News UK, publisher of the *NoW* and *The Sun*, was £400 million (BBC. At www.bbc.co.uk/news/business-48146162). Matters worsened for Reach in January 2020 with the news that the *Sunday People*, like the *NoW*, had targeted the mobile phone of murdered schoolgirl Milly Dowler in 2002 (*Byline Investigates*, 26 January 2020. At www.bylineinvestigates.com/mirror/2020/1/22/a6qgcu489qri8ui5okbddo1zez2q3s).

During the Leveson Inquiry, and in various parliamentary select committee hearings, it emerged that red-top story-gathering was motivated entirely by the desire of publishers, editors and their editorial staffs to maximise sales. There was too little oversight of editorial practices, a turning of a blind eye. The Leveson Report is sprinkled with references to the absence of internal governance at popular newspapers and a consequent failure to police journalistic ethics. It recommended that the problem should be addressed by publishers (Leveson, 2012). There was no industry-wide code of ethics until 1991. It was introduced when the Press Complaints Commission (PCC) replaced the Press Council. Editors and their journalists had previously tended to abide by a rough-and-ready application of 'custom and practice', with individual editors deciding what was fair and what was not. Many decisions were taken on an ad hoc basis. Public interest was sometimes sacrificed on the altar of circulation.

The formation of the Editors' Code of Practice, and its policing by the PCC, did change the culture, for a period at least, by underlining the public interest requirement for publication (Shannon, 2001). It was also agreed that editors would not openly criticise the PCC's adjudications, which were published in the offending paper without comment.

Investigative journalism, as practised by the red-tops, presented particular problems because of a lack of transparency about the reporting methods employed. While it was accepted that the confidentiality of sources had to be respected, other aspects of certain investigations remained impenetrable. If reporters had strayed across ethical boundaries, it proved difficult for those seeking to hold them to account to discover exactly how they had acted. What follows is a considered updating of the taxonomy of methods published in this book's previous edition.

### *Dark arts*

Surveillance technology has grown ever more sophisticated throughout the past 30 years, enabling the virtually undetectable use of covert recording and filming. It has been enthusiastically employed by red-top journalists engaged in one of the darkest of the dark arts: entrapment. Sometimes known as a 'sting operation', the method has often created controversy, with victims complaining that they were encouraged by journalists into committing illegal or unethical acts that they would not have done without being induced to do so. Most red-tops have entrapped people at some time and justified their use of deception by arguing it was in the public interest and thereby compliant with the Editors' Code of Practice and the law. However, it is not always easy to divine what is, and is not, entrapment. Subterfuge does not, of itself, equate to entrapment. Two high-profile cases involving Members of Parliament (MPs) illustrate the point. In 2014, the *Sunday Mirror* alleged that a Conservative minister, Brooks Newmark, had sent sexually explicit text messages, including an indecent picture of himself, to a young woman ('Tory minister quits over sex photo', *Sunday Mirror*, 28 September 2014). The 'woman' was an undercover journalist posing as a female party activist and using a fake Twitter account. He claimed he had been entrapped but, after further messages claim to light, he resigned his ministerial post. An inquiry by the Independent Press Standards Organisation cleared the paper of entrapment, but its use of subterfuge remained questionable ('Ipso's ruling on the Sunday Mirror over Brooks Newmark sting is flawed', *The Guardian*, 26 March 2015).

In 2016, the *Sunday Mirror* revealed that the prominent Labour MP Keith Vaz had cavorted with two male prostitutes and offered to buy them cocaine ('Labour MP Keith Vaz and the prostitutes at his flat', *Sunday Mirror* 4 September 2016). Although the two men were paid by the newspaper and agreed to film the encounter with Vaz, the newspaper denied that it was a case of entrapment. It had acted in the public interest. Vaz thought it 'deeply disturbing' that the pair were paid and argued that he had been entrapped ('MP to report Keith Vaz to Commons Standards watchdog', BBC, 5 September 2016. At www.bbc.co.uk/news/uk-politics-37274326). He resigned his chairmanship of the Home Affairs Select Committee, was later suspended from the Commons and did not stand for parliament in 2019. It is possible to argue that the Newmark story did involve entrapment, while the Vaz story did not. Both cases could be argued either way.

### Faking it . . . over and over again

The most frequent use of entrapment over recent decades was by *News of the World*, especially its investigations editor, Mazher Mahmood (see *Faking It*). His success encouraged reporters on rival red-tops to engage in similar tactics. Until his imprisonment in 2016, Mazher Mahmood was known for using disguises while carrying out undercover reporting, revelling in his nickname, 'the Fake Sheikh', which he gained due to his penchant for dressing up in Arab robes to fool his targets (Mahmood, 2008). The humour was not shared by scores of his victims, some of whom ended up in jail, nor by several judges and lawyers who condemned his methods on the grounds that most of his work depended on offering people inappropriate inducements to break the law and thus providing his papers – *News of the World* (1991–2011) and *Sun on Sunday* (2012–14) – with a public interest justification for publication.

Judicial concern at Mahmood's methods was aired first in 1999 at the trial of the Earl of Hardwicke on a charge of supplying cocaine. Mahmood posed as an Arab businessman who was prepared to spend £100,000 buying a substantial part of Hardwicke's scooter franchise. Mahmood coaxed the peer into buying cocaine to celebrate their deal. After listening to the evidence, the jury foreman handed a note to the judge on behalf of his fellow jurors saying they thought Hardwicke was a victim of entrapment and had acted under 'extreme provocation' (*The Independent*, 23 September 1999). The judge reflected his agreement by giving Hardwicke a lenient suspended jail sentence. At the time, TV actor John Alford was serving a nine-month prison sentence for supplying cannabis to Mahmood, who had posed as an Arab prince pledging to win him a Hollywood movie role. At his trial, the court heard Alford had been completely taken in by the 'elaborate . . . well-planned subterfuge' (BBC, 24 May 1999. At http://news.bbc.co.uk/1/hi/education/specials/drugs/351651.stm). Several of Mahmood's victims – all well-known people – who did not end up in court complained about being fooled by beguiling fake scenarios in which there were made tempting offers to misbehave or speak out of turn.

There were other cases that should have alerted the police and the Crown Prosecution Service to inquire into Mahmood's investigatory methods. One of the most contentious was the alleged plot to kidnap Victoria Beckham and hold her to ransom ('Posh kidnap: We stop crime of the century', *News of the World*, 3 November 2002). Five supposed culprits were arrested in a dramatic swoop by armed police following 'evidence' provided by Mahmood and held in custody for seven months before the start of their trial. At that hearing, an embarrassed prosecution lawyer announced that the case was being dropped because the main witness, who had several convictions to his name, had been paid £10,000 by the *News of the World* and his evidence would therefore be regarded as unreliable ('Truth behind the Beckham "kidnap" plot', *The Observer*, 8 June 2003. At www.theguardian.com/media/2003/jun/08/newsoftheworld. pressandpublishing).

After the closure of the *News of the World*, Mahmood joined the newly launched *Sun on Sunday*, where his first major contribution was yet another sting operation. But the moment of truth was around the corner. In June 2013, the *Sun on Sunday* boasted of a 'world exclusive' under Mahmood's byline. Tulisa Contostavlos, a singer and TV personality, had agreed to sell him a quantity of cocaine ('Tulisa's cocaine deal shame', *Sun on Sunday*, 2 June 2013). She was immediately arrested and later charged with supplying Class A drugs, which she denied. The following week, in an unusual move, the *Sunday People* detailed how Mahmood had pulled off his scoop in a piece sympathetic to Contostavlos's plight ('Tulisa £8m Bollywood deal sting: Tricksters posed as movie moguls in elaborate con', *Sunday People*, 9 June 2013). Her trial, in July 2014, collapsed when the judge said he thought there were 'strong grounds to believe' Mahmood had lied at an earlier hearing (BBC, 21 July 2014. At www.bbc.co.uk/news/uk-england-28403821). Mahmood was suspended by the *Sun on Sunday* while he and the paper waited to see whether the police would charge him. During that suspension, a Panorama investigation was screened, which alleged that Mahmood paid people to procure drugs that his targets would later be exposed as supplying. It also accused him of making offers to people with no recent history of drug misuse of scarcely believable career opportunities who were then pressured to obtain him cocaine (*The Fake Sheikh Exposed*, BBC1, 12 November 2014). Mahmood was finally charged with conspiracy to pervert the course of justice in September 2015 and went to trial the following year. He was found guilty of tampering with evidence and sentenced to 15 months in jail (*The Guardian*, 21 October 2016). He was formally dismissed by his newspaper.

## The reality: what the red-tops did investigate

It is noticeable that very few red-top investigations have appeared on awards shortlists in recent years. In October 2015, the chairman of the British Press Awards judging panel, Dominic Ponsford, spoke of it being 'particularly good to see so many entries this year from the tabloid end of the newspaper market, which does not always get the credit it deserves for campaigning and investigative journalism'. Yet, after the initial trawl through the entries, no red-top appeared on the shortlist for the investigation-of-the-year category. But Ponsford did have a point. Despite dwindling editorial budgets, and accepting the cavils mentioned previously, there has been investigative content. Here is a look at some examples.

### Daily Mirror: intruding into the Queen's privacy

The *Daily Mirror*'s reputation for high-quality investigative journalism was built around the work of two outstanding journalists: John Pilger, in the 1960s and 1970s, and Paul Foot, in the 1980s and early 1990s. Among Pilger's best work were his reports on social division within Britain and about war crimes in Vietnam, Cambodia and Biafra (Hagerty, 2003: 104; Seymour and Seymour, 2003). In Foot's weekly column, he exposed several miscarriages of justice cases (as previously). Foot was fired from the *Mirror* in 1993 after writing a column critical of the incoming management for making several of his colleagues redundant. A couple of years later, the *Mirror* launched a Foot-like column. Initially called *Sorted*, and written by Andrew Penman and Gary Jones, it concentrated on exposing fraudsters and rogue traders. Over the following years, with regular changes of Penman's partners and occasional changes of title, the column won an appreciative audience and garnered several awards. In July 2013, Penman went solo, and his 'Penman Investigates' column, despite its placement towards the back of the newspaper, is regarded as a key component of the *Mirror*'s content. Although somewhat disparagingly described in the industry trade magazine as an 'intrepid sleuth, who earns a living by doorstepping low-life conmen' (*Press Gazette*, 11 November 2006), there is a clear public service raison d'être for his column. For example, Penman's covert filming of a gang who preyed on unemployed people desperate to obtain heavy goods vehicle licences led to their conviction for fraud and prompted the judge to remark: 'It is not often that I get the chance to congratulate journalists, but this was a genuine piece of investigative journalism' (*Daily Mirror*, 26 February 2014).

Outside of Penman's column, there were other investigations, sometimes involving undercover reporting. By far the most controversial was the infiltration of Buckingham Palace in 2003 by reporter Ryan Parry, who spent two months working as a footman ('Buckingham Palace's extraordinary secrets revealed by fake footman', 19 November 2003. At www.mirror.co.uk/news/real-life-stories/buckingham-palace-queen-tupperware-philip-13663437). After the *Mirror* published details and pictures across more than 20 pages, Palace officials moved swiftly to prevent further revelations by going to court and winning a permanent injunction (*The Guardian*, 'Mirror reporter breached palace contract', 20 November 2003. At www.theguardian.com/media/2003/nov/20/pressandpublishing.mirror). The paper, having agreed to accept the injunction, contributed £25,000 to the Queen's legal costs (*Daily Telegraph*, 24 November 2003. At www.telegraph.co.uk/news/uknews/1447583/Mirror-agrees-to-Queens-injunction.html).

The following month, another *Mirror* reporter, Nick Sommerlad, revealed he had spent five weeks working as a security guard at Yarl's Wood, a refugee asylum centre. While there, he witnessed examples of racism and violence against detainees (*Daily Mirror*, 'Mirror reporter lands job as security guard at asylum centre . . . and discovers a culture of abuse, racism and violence that SHOULD appall us all', 8 December 2003). Sommerlad presented a 28-page dossier about his findings to an official inquiry headed by the prisons ombudsman, who recommended a set of remedial actions (At www.ppo. gov.uk/download/special-investigation-reports/special-yarls-wood-abuse-03. pdf). A search through the *Mirror's* files from 2008 to 2019 revealed a host of what could be termed low-level investigations. Among them were inquiries into racism among police officers, internet pornography, pension benefits for corporate managers, high railway fares, landlords demanding sex from female tenants and fire service cuts. Two stood out. In 2016, an investigation into unsafe tumble dryers earned Martin Bagot a place on the shortlist for investigative journalist of the year ('Killer in the kitchen: tumble dryer fires investigation', *Daily Mirror* 9 February, 2016. At www.mirror.co.uk/news/uk-news/ killer-tumble-dryers-alert-figures-7340981). And in 2018, Russell Myers filed several lengthy reports after spending eight days inside North Korea ('Inside Kim's Korea: Mirror spends eight days in the world's most secretive nation', *Daily Mirror* 14 September 2018. At www.mirror.co.uk/news/world-news/ inside-kim-jong-uns-north-13240416).

### *The Sun: a rapid turnover of low-level probes*

Unlike the *Mirror*, *The Sun* does not have a rich history of investigative journalism. Its editors have preferred to concentrate their resources on the rapid turnover of news stories rather than long-term projects. Although the paper has run many campaigns, usually on emotive subjects (*Help Our Heroes* in 2007 to raise money for wounded British servicemen; *Give Us Shelter* in 2015, which pressured the government to halt the closing of women's refuges and a 2014 partnership with breast cancer charity CoppaFeel), these have not been linked to investigations. In evidence to the Leveson Inquiry, a *Sun* executive listed four investigations as examples of its work (Leveson, 2012: 459–460). They included the exposure of a private detective who swindled money from the fund set up to find the missing girl Madeleine McCann ('Maddie fraudster nicked', *The Sun*, 25 November 2009) and the exposure of a court clerk who was taking money from drivers to delete convictions from their records ('Court in the act – clerk brags of £500 bribes to wipe records of dangerous drivers', *The Sun*, 4 and 19 August 2011). This was especially interesting because the reporter was given permission by the editor and legal manager to offer the clerk £500 and film the transaction, even though it contravened the Bribery Act 2010. But the public interest justification was obvious, and the clerk was eventually convicted under that same act and imprisoned for six years.

Most of *The Sun's* post-Leveson investigative content has not tended to involve lengthy reporting commitments. Much more significant was an investigation by the paper's consumer editor, Daniel Jones, into the link between Britain's biggest charity for pensioners and an energy company ('How Age UK pocketed £6m bung from E.ON and pushed expensive power deals to OAPs', 4 February 2016. At www.thesun.co.uk/archives/news/34227/revealed-how-age-uk-pocketed-6m-bung-from-e-on-and-pushed-expensive-power-deals-to-oaps/). It was given page one treatment and was one of the rare occasions in which a *Sun* investigation was shortlisted by the British Press Awards.

### Sunday Mirror: revelations of sex and dustbins

Although the Keith Vaz story was the *Sunday Mirror*'s most memorable exposure of a politician for his sexual peccadilloes, it published two somewhat similar tales. In 2014, the Conservative MP Mark Menzies resigned his post as a ministerial aide after the paper revealed his relationship with a man ('Tory MP quits in drugs & rent boy scandal', *Sunday Mirror*, 30 March 2014). And in 2018, a Conservative MP, Andrew Griffiths, stepped down as a junior minister the day the paper reported on his sending explicit text messages to two female constituents ('Married Tory minister quits over 2,000 sex texts', *Sunday Mirror*, 15 July 2018). These were conventional red-top 'investigations' in the sense that they relied on an informant tipping off the paper. An altogether different, and controversial, method was employed to reveal what kind of nappies were used in the household of the then-Conservative party leader, David Cameron. The *Sunday Mirror* trawled through his dustbin to discover, ostensibly, whether its contents matched his public commitment to recycling ('Tory Dave's nappy-gate: Cam's bin rumbled', *Sunday Mirror*, 18 March 2007). Yet two weeks earlier, when questioned at a select committee hearing about whether it was fair to rifle through people's bins, the paper's managing editor replied: 'We do not go through people's bins. We have never found much material there worth publishing' (DCMS. At https://publications.parliament.uk/pa/cm200607/cmselect/cmcumeds/uc375-i/uc37502.htm 6 March 2007). Aside from sex, politics and waste disposal, the *Sunday Mirror* has investigated further afield. In 2011, it carried a moving report from Somalia on the poverty and starvation suffered by people persecuted by 'Al Qaeda warlords'. Labelled as an investigation, it was carried across pages 16 and 17 (*Sunday Mirror*, 14 August 2011. At www.mirror.co.uk/news/uk-news/sunday-mirror-investigation-how-drought-147439).

### The People: trying to link royalty to sex

The sex-and-celebrity agenda of the *Sunday People*, preferably linked, even if tangentially, to royalty, played a large part in its choice of investigative content. One revelation involved a claim that a male Tory MP had sexually assaulted a male Labour MP ('Tory MP's sex attack on Labour MP in taxi', *Sunday People*, 5 November 2017), while another, looking into what it called 'a sex-predator culture' in parliament, recorded a researcher's claims about being sexually assaulted on more than one occasion by 'lusting male politicians' ('MP took Viagra pill, then groped me', *Sunday People*, 3 March 2013).

None of these stories, although tagged as investigations, merited the description. However, the paper produced photographic evidence to back up its undercover inquiry into human trafficking ('Busted: Nine held as we smash human smuggling gang', *Sunday People*, 20 May 2012). It also exposed Chinese laboratories producing the drug known as Spice ('Spice trail to China', *Sunday People*, 16 April 2017). Arguably its best investigation, which began by exploring the army's failure to hold an inquest into the death of one soldier, led to the discovery that six serving or former members of the same battalion had died from suspected suicide in seven years – more than any other regiment ('Mother's fury as six-year wait for military inquest of Afghan war hero', *Sunday People*, 25 November 2018).

If there is a disagreement over what constitutes 'investigative journalism' (Bernstein, 1977: 25; Hanna, 2005: 123) and even about the term's relevance (Pilger, 2014), then it is even harder to pin down its applicability when confronted with claims by red-tops that their stories should be regarded as investigations. Does a tip-off that X is up to no good and a rapid check that X is indeed misbehaving merit the description? Does ferreting in someone's dustbin and discovering something untoward amount to an investigation? Does paying someone to dish the dirt on a friend qualify? Editors often chose to append the term 'investigation' to stories that did not merit the description. Nevertheless, amid the celebrity kiss-and-tell dross, there has been some excellent public service work.

## Notes

1　July–Dec 2000, total average daily sale of *The Sun, Daily Mirror* and *Daily Star*: 6,400,991. July–Dec 2019 total: 1,978,729. July–Dec 2000, total average Sunday sale of *News of the World, Sunday Mirror* and *The People*: 7,432,523. July–Dec 2019, total average Sunday sale of *Sun on Sunday, Sunday Mirror, The People* and *Star on Sunday*: 1,755,806. Source: ABC

2　*The People* is generally known now as the *Sunday People*.

3　Milly Dowler, aged 13, vanished on 21 March 2002 on her way home from school in Weybridge, Surrey. Her remains were discovered on 18 September in Yateley, Hampshire. On 23 June 2001, a convicted murderer, Levi Bellfield, was found guilty of abducting and murdering Milly.

## References

Bernstein, C. (1977) 'Investigative journalism is simply a label', in Behrens, J.C. (ed.) *The Typewriter Guerrillas*. Chicago: Nelson-Hall.

Davies, N. (2014) *Hack Attack: How the Truth Caught Up with Rupert Murdoch*. London: Chatto & Windus.

Hagerty, B. (2003) *Read All About It! 100 Sensational Years of the Daily Mirror*. Lydney: First Stone Publishing.

Hanna, M. (2005) 'Sources', in Franklin, B., Hamer, M., Hanna, M., Kinsey, M. and Richardson, J. (eds.) *Key Concepts in Journalism Studies*. London: Sage.

Lashmar, P. (2013) 'The path to hell . . . an investigative journalist's view of Leveson', *Open Democracy*. 27 March 2013.

Leveson Report (2012) *An Inquiry into the Culture, Practices and Ethics of the Press*. London: TSO.

Mahmood, Mazher (2008) *Confessions of a Fake Sheik*. London: HarperCollins.

Pilger, J. (2014) *Tell Me No Lies*. London: Jonathan Cape.

Seymour, D. and Seymour, E. (eds.) (2003) *A Century of News*. London: Contender.

Shannon, R. (2001) *A Press Free and Responsible*. London: John Murray.

Thurlbeck, N. (2015) *Tabloid Secrets*. London: Biteback.

# 19

## UNITED KINGDOM

### Reporting of the far-right

*Paul Jackson*

This chapter aims to explore some of the ways investigative journalists have approached reporting on the British far-right in recent times. However, the far-right is not new and should not be presented as such by journalists; current activism is steeped in long traditions of extremism. It will examine some examples of standout investigative journalism that have led to significant impact in the past 20 years, showing how such reporting has been at the forefront of informing the public about this shadowy world. While far-right cultures are guarded about their inner workings, they are still political cultures that want to spread their messages more widely, no matter how offensive or taboo. As will be shown, the best investigative reporting has been able to move beyond such external messaging to explore the hidden spaces behind the far-right's public face. It will also explore some of the issues with reporting on this milieu. How can a balance be struck between reporting in the public interest and avoiding needlessly giving the far-right free publicity? How should journalists approach anti-fascists and others with expert knowledge on this complex milieu? And how can reporting avoid clichés and simplifications?

### History and key terms

The 'far-right' is a usefully ambiguous phrase. While leading academics have written many books and articles defining key terms,[1] to the wider public, the 'far-right' can signify anything from media-savvy radical politicians to extremists and terrorists. To understand the phenomenon of the far-right in the 20th century, as well as Cas Mudde (2007), Eatwell (2003),[2] Griffin (2018),[3] Jackson and Shekhovtsov (2014)[4] and Thurlow (1998)[5] are excellent primers.

In 2020, Britain's far-right space consists of a wide range of groups. Some are older and retain a small band of followers, such as the National Front, the British National Party and the Blood & Honour network. Accelerationist groups such as National Action and Sonnenkreig Division have also developed neo-Nazi youth culutres. Some are lone voices that inspire wider networks. Stephen Yaxley-Lennon/Tommy Robinson is the best example here. Some are imports from Europe, such as the Generation Identity (GE) movement, a small group that has grown in significance since around 2016. Newer anti-Muslim street marching groups linked to football networks, such as the Football Lads Alliance (FLA), have emerged. There are also new political parties, such as For Britain (FB), a largely Islamophobic party led Anne Marie Waters, which has picked up a range of activists from the wreckage of the BNP. The Brexit Party, founded in 2019, has largely superseded UKIP in the populist anti-establishment political space, and UKIP itself has become more overtly far-right, through its anti-Islam rhetoric in particular. In sum, while the far-right political fringe is small, it is certainly complicated. Careful use of language is important when reporting on it.

## The British National Party and reporting the far-right

There has been some truly excellent investigative journalism reporting on the far-right in recent years. The best of this reporting offers something deeper than merely highlighting the latest outrageous remarks from a leader seeking publicity. Rather, it penetrates deep into the inner workings of a far-right groups or network and draws out aspects of activism that are not designed to be seen by the public.

One response came from the National Union of Journalists (NUJ), which created a website called *Reporting the BNP: A Practical Guide for Journalists.* This was based around the NUJ's Code of Conduct, stating journalists should strive to report accurately and fairly, distinguish between fact and opinion and not produce material likely to lead to discrimination. Jeremy Dear, general secretary of the NUJ, explained the BNP was unlike any other political party due to their whites-only admission policy, Holocaust denial, high rates of criminal convictions and encouragement of attacks on journalists.[6] The website sought to provide context for journalists through a range of resources, including guides to the BNP's leaders, its key policies and its efforts to moderate its public image. It also included personal testimonies from two journalists with a long record of covering extreme right politics, the *Mirror*'s Tom Parry and the *Yorkshire Evening Post*'s Pete Lazenby. Parry warned of the issue of reporting leading to over-exposure; simply recounting the BNP's ongoing activities in the press risked giving it publicity that would help enlarge is appeal. Lazenby explained his strategy was two pronged: first, he sought to expose activists when they revealed their deeper extremist views. Second, he reported positively the experiences of people targeted by the party, such as minority groups, to help counter the racist narratives developed by the party itself. Lazenby also again warned of the threat of violence to journalists when investigating the party.[7]

## Anti-fascists and reporting the far-right

Anti-fascists have been central in putting swathes of information about the far-right into the public domain. Unsurprisingly, there has often been a close relationship between anti-fascist organisations and investigative journalism. The leading anti-fascist platform in Britain until the 2010s was *Searchlight*, a magazine founded in 1964 and which became a regular, monthly publication for the anti-fascist movement from 1975. *Searchlight* was an exemplar of grass-roots investigative journalism. Reliant on contributions and donations from wealthier organisations, it ran moles within many British far-right groups and worked to support those who became disillusioned with the movement, such as Ray Hill,[8] techniques it used to help secure a perspective few others were able to gain. *Searchlight's* activists have regularly worked with journalists and have developed a mutually beneficial relationship for the sharing knowledge. The magazine is still going, still edited by Gerry Gable, a founding member. In the 2000s, the then-editor of *Searchlight*, Nick Lowles, and Gable developed a new campaign to counter the BNP, *Hope not Hate* (HnH). In 2011, HnH became a standalone organisation, run by Lowles and others. It largely continues the investigative traditions of *Searchlight*, and its website and magazine feature regular stories about the ongoing dynamics of the far-right in Britain and internationally. While both *Searchlight* and HnH are left leaning, they have also operated in a pragmatic way, working with journalists of different political perspectives.

As well as these groups, organisations such as *Tell Mama* and the *Community Security Trust* also regularly monitor the far-right in Britain, primarily advocating for Muslim and Jewish communities, respectively, developing an array of data to influence the media and policymakers, among others. All these organisations can offer authoritative commentary and have helped many investigative reporters develop stories.

One standout example of the BBC working with *Searchlight* activists came in 1999, when *Panorama* devoted an edition to David Copeland. It was produced by Andy Bell, a long-standing supporter of *Searchlight* who also produced documentaries on C18 for World in Action earlier in the 1990s, while Lowles was assistant producer. The film included interviews with Gable and was presented by Graham McLagen, who went on to publish a book on Copeland with Lowles. In the episode, Gable explained how *Searchlight's* monitoring of the BNP allowed them to document Copeland's history of activism within the party before moving to more extreme neo-Nazi circles. Gable was also critical of the level of monitoring of the extreme right by the police and security services and stressed his group had superior intelligence. An interview with Assistant Commissioner of the Metropolitan Police David Veness recognised problems with the state's approach to far-right extremism and admitted there needed to be greater monitoring of it in the future. Reflecting on criticisms of police not doing enough to monitor the far-right, he stated: 'I hope I've made it clear that that was a commitment that we recognised was absolutely necessary and needed to be reinforced during the time of the nail bomb inquiry . . . and that is a very significant resource commitment, not only that we made, but we're going to keep up'.[9] Here, as well as investigating the far-right itself, journalists and anti-fascists were able to put pressure on the state to commit more resources to monitoring extreme right activity.

A benchmark for investigative practices was set in 2001 by a BBC *Panorama* documentary exploring the growth of the BNP under Nick Griffin's new, ostensibly more moderate, leadership. By this point, the party's fortunes were turning, and while it lacked electoral representation, it seemed to be gaining in popularity, especially in the wake of riots in northern towns in the summer of 2001, as well as capitalising on the impact of the 9/11 attacks. *BNP: Under The Skin* was the culmination of five months of investigations and was presented by Jane Corbin. It opened with undercover footage of the BNP's 2001 Red White and Blue Festival for its activists, which featured a speaker making crass jokes about Auschwitz to a receptive audience and members performing the Nazi salute. It also highlighted the party's links to the American white supremacist, and former Ku Klux Klan (KKK) leader, David Duke. More undercover footage at odds with the BNP's new image showed Griffin addressing a meeting in Texas, where he told the audience that his party's new focus on 'identity' rather than 'race' was simply a tactic to help sell BNP ideas to the public. Corbin interviewed Griffin, too, and he was confronted with this and other uncomfortable material, such as the criminal records of leading figures in his remodelled party. The report also examined Griffin's political roots, which included highlighting his longstanding racist views, such as advocating forced repatriation of non-white people and Holocaust denial. The programme contrasted Griffin's defence of the BNP with more honest disclosures of the party's inner workings from a leading organiser who had become disillusioned with the party, voiced by an actor.

As the BNP grew in stature in the 2000s, another piece of detailed investigative journalism came in October 2002, with the BAFTA award-winning *Young, Nazi and Proud* episode of Channel 4's *Dispatches*.[10] The programme focused on Mark Collett, then a leader of the Young BNP. The film was made by David Modell and was notable as Collett, a final-year student at Leeds University, had allowed cameras to follow him for several months as he developed BNP campaigns, organised fellow activists and met with key figures, including Griffin. With unprecedented access to a leading BNP member, it even explored Collett's relationship with his parents, who were conflicted as to how to regard their son's activism. The film concluded with Collett being confronted with his aggressive behaviour at an NF rally where neo-Nazi views and open racism were clearly on display. After months of recording Collett's more carefully guarded comments, Modell challenged him openly and recorded the results. He told Collett he had recordings of him making claims such that Hitler's Germany was a superior place to bring up children compared to modern Britain and that Nazism was good for Germany in the 1930s, leading to Collett suspending the interview, calling Griffin and resigning from the party. While the BNP quickly released a statement distancing itself from Collett's pro-Nazi views, he was soon reinstated and continued as a BNP activist. Nevertheless, like the 2001 *Panorama* documentary, the reporting was able successfully to penetrate beneath the surface gloss of the BNP and reveal deep continuities with an older, more extreme style of activism.

Such investigative documentaries could also lead to more problematic outcomes. *Panorama* returned to the topic in 2004. *The Secret Agent* was an episode that featured Andy Sykes, a BNP activist who was willing to go public and denounce the party. During filming, Sykes remained a party member and used his position to help BBC journalist Jason Gwynne gain unique access to the inner working of the party. This included attending a private meeting where Griffin made comments against Muslims, describing Islam as a 'wicked, vicious faith'. Griffin's speech was deemed by a barrister interviewed for the episode as criminal as it was designed to stir up racial hatred, illegal under the Public Order Act. The programme also again featured Collett, who described asylum seekers as 'a little bit like cockroaches' and also stated 'let's show these ethnics the door in 2004', implying a policy of racist repatriation. The programme's covert recordings led to the pair facing charges of stirring up racial hatred in April 2005 due to such remarks, but after two trials in 2006, they were acquitted of all charges. The fallout of the case included Gordon Brown, then Chancellor of the Exchequer, calling for a tightening of race legislation, demonstrating its high-profile impact.[11] However, the court case was also presented as a victory by the BNP itself. It used the trials to develop internal campaigning, including a blog for the 'Free Speech Two'. Its webpages explained the trials were an example of how a legitimate political party was being silenced by the media, the police and the political establishment.[12] While the documentary was successful in putting new information into the public domain, it also provided the BNP opportunities to turn this publicity to its advantage.

Interest in the BNP continued throughout the 2000s, as its electoral successes mounted. In 2009, Griffin's party gained two MEPs in the European elections, raising the issue of potential appearances on the BBC's flagship politics show *Question Time*. The programme's production company, Mentorn, decided it was appropriate to include a BNP voice for public scrutiny. Defenders of the BBC's decision included the BBC's director general, who argued that it was for Parliament to keep parties such as the BNP from the airwaves, not the BBC.[13] Griffin made clear he expected to be widely attacked but hoped to play the underdog and win sympathy. In the broadcast, he was widely considered to have come across poorly, though the BNP did record a small increase in public support. One YouGov poll after the broadcast highlighted 22% of people would consider voting for the party.[14] It was not at all clear that the broadcast had been a success in challenging Griffin's views or the BNP. Notwithstanding the high ratings, Griffin did not again appear on the show.

The following year, the BNP then returned to type and experienced a major rejection at the 2010 General Election, leading to terminal decline during the 2010s. Despite receiving over half a million votes, the party failed to gain a single MP. Griffin himself stood in Barking and Dagenham, a BNP stronghold, but was defeated by the Labour MP Margaret Hodge. This story was captured well by the More4 True Stories documentary *The Battle for Barking*, directed by Laura Fairrie, another standout piece of reporting as to how the BNP could be defeated through sustained activism by mainstream politicians and anti-fascists, who were both able to exploit the party's own failures.[15] The growth of the far-right often provokes a rise in anti-fascist activism, and by 2010, there were around 20,000 regular activists and 140,000 supporters working to stop any BNP breakthrough in the General Election. The party also faced internal issues, such as a BNP councillor being filmed brawling in the streets, alongside its publicity director publicly threatening to kill Griffin. The party's popular website was also offline for a period of time.[16] In other words, the BNP's inability to capitalise on its momentum in 2010 was not ultimately caused by the *Question Time* appearance but a consequence of these other factors. Those who simplistically cite Griffin's *Question Time* appearance as case of the BNP's decline should remember the phrase 'correlation is not causation'.

## The *Mirror*

As well as television, in the 2000s, Hope not Hate developed a close relationship with the *Mirror* as an outlet for campaigning. In April 2007, HnH and the *Mirror* started the first of a series of annual bus tours where celebrities and politicians would speak out against the far-right from regional locations, with the aim of stymieing the growth of the BNP.[17] Since this time, the relationship has become longstanding, and there have been a number of special sections of the *Mirror* devoted to the far-right created by HnH. For example in 2014, ahead of the local and European elections which saw UKIP break through, HnH published in the *Mirror* a special eight-page supplement, sponsored by Unison. It included articles by, among others, Lowles as well as Edie Izzard, a high-profile celebrity supporter of the HnH, alongside pieces by the *Sunday Mirror* editor Alison Phillips and *Mirror* columnist Brian Reade.

The decision to focus on UKIP as part of an anti-fascist campaign was controversial, as the party was increasingly seen as a respectable one, unlike the BNP. To justify such targeting, HnH included in the supplement a series of quotes from UKIP figures showing homophobia, misogyny, Islamophobia and racism, drawn from HnH's monitoring of the party.[18] The relationship between the HnH and Farage took a further turn in December 2016, when Farage accused the group of using violent and undemocratic means in an interview with presenter Nick Ferarri on his radio LBC radio programme. HnH responded with a crowd-funded legal campaign for defamation, leading to Farage making a public apology and retracting his accusation. However, both parties were forced to pay large legal costs, and Farage denied Hope not Hate's claims to have 'won'.[19]

The relationship between groups like HnH and the press has been fruitful in other ways, too, at least as an outlet for amplifying some of their more complex investigations. For example, in 2015 and 2016, HnH carried out undercover investigations into the US group the Loyal White Knights of the KKK. Reporting on the investigation included a lengthy feature in the *Guardian* from October 2016, which highlighted how HnH had exposed the KKK's extreme anti-Semitism, which included describing the Holocaust as a 'money making scam', and racism, including targeting back communities with extreme propaganda. In October 2018, the HnH material featured in another *Guardian* report, exploring the relationship between post-industrial deprived towns and support for the far-right.[20] Leading HnH figures, including Matthew Collins, a former activist in the NF, as well as Lowles, also regularly feature in press reports and broadcast media commentary on the state of the far-right. Meanwhile, in recent years, *Searchlight* has also helped the print media develop investigative journalism on the far-right. Notably, in May 2015, it aided a *Mail on Sunday* report on a major international gathering of Holocaust deniers at the Grosvenor Hotel in London. Gable worked on the investigation and was able to help provide context, identifying key figures such as Mark Weber, director of the leading US Holocaust denial organisation, the Institute for Historical Review (IHR), and Spanish figure Pedro Varela, another leading figure of the Holocaust denial scene.[21] The report was important, as it offered a major exposé of the continued activism promoting Holocaust denial themes, showing links between veteran British fascists and international networks.

As well as anti-fascists, over the past decade, there has also been a growth in the range of expertise that journalists can turn to. Think tanks such as the Institute for Strategic Dialogue and Quilliam have worked extensively on the far-right, though the latter also notoriously tried and failed to de-radicalise Yaxley-Lennon in 2013.[22] Moreover, many academics are often approached to offer comment or advice, and many are happy to do so. The recently formed Centre for the Analysis of the Radical Right (CARR), founded by Matthew Feldman, pools a wide range of such expertise. It has cultivated an extensive range of senior fellows; some are academics, and others are professionals, including leading Prevent Agenda coordinators such as William Baldét, who have a great deal of experience with working with journalists and challenging the far-right. In other countries, groups such as the Southern Poverty Law Center (SPLC) and the Anti-Defamation League (ADL) also monitor the extreme right and offer expertise to many journalists. Finally, regarding consulting academics and other experts, it is also important to highlight that one leading scholar in the field, Cas Mudde, has been critical of the media's tendency to focus only on male experts. He regularly tweets comprehensive lists of female specialists for the media to whom to turn.[23]

## Reporting on far-right extremism and responding to threats to journalists

A further area where investigative journalism has provided much-needed data on the far-right is lone actor terrorism. In recent years, cases such as Thomas

Mair and Darren Osborne have revealed that Britain is not immune from a growing trend of murderous violence that elsewhere has included Anders Breivik, Dylann Roof and Brenton Tarrent.

When investigating and reporting on such far-right violence, there are certainly clichés to avoid. This includes suggesting these politicised murderers are not really terrorists. Like Islamist attacks, far-right violence is terrorism, as it is violence carried out in the name of a political cause and seeks to use violence and the fear of violence to develop this agenda, which is the essence of terrorism. Another cliché is to suggest that such attackers have no connections to far-right groups, when often they are certainly profoundly inspired by them and often have been, or are, actively linked to them. Such far-right terrorists do tend to plan and carry out their acts alone, though, and so are often described by academics as lone actors, a better term than the sensationalist 'lone wolf'. Moreover, while often far-right terrorists have a mental health condition of some description, this should not be reported as the sole explanation for a turn to violence, another cliché to be avoided. Strikingly, a recent report by the Royal United Services Institute on lone actor terrorism noted that '35% of the perpetrators reportedly suffered from some kind of mental health disorder [while] the estimated percentage [of such disorders] for the general population is 27%'.[24] Moreover, leading expert on lone actor terrorism Paul Gill has argued mental health cases include a wide range of issues and are usually a 'cause of a cause' rather than something that alone explains extreme aggression. Mental health issues are often part of the background set of issues that lead a person to be socially isolated and frustrated rather than being something that removes from them culpability for their actions.[25]

Better reporting on far-right lone actor terrorists helps the wider public gain a detailed picture of a real person, which is often challenging due to reporting restrictions around a trial and limited access to the attacker. The investigative reporting into Thomas Mair in particular faced such challenges and has been very important in providing the public with a detailed picture of such a terrorist. In the hours after the attack, the SPLC was among the first to release relevant information on Mair, when it published material showing he had purchased materials from the American neo-Nazi group the National Alliance.[26] Other key information about his motivation was also quickly put into the public domain, revealing his links and sympathies with neo-Nazism. However, after being charged, reporting on the case became much more restrictive until Mair's conviction. Following his sentencing, a range of detailed profiles was then published in the press. These reports, gathered over several months and featuring detailed information from the trial, collated about as much factual information as any academic or think tank knows about Mair's background and reasons for carrying out the attack. Broadsheet accounts such as the *Guardian*'s 'The Slow-Burning Hatred That Led Thomas Mair to Murder Jo Cox',[27] the *Independent*'s 'Thomas Mair: The Far-Right Extremist Who Murdered MP Jo Cox',[28] and the *Financial Times*'s 'Thomas Mair: The Making of a Neo-Nazi

Killer',[29] among others, will remain important records for many who study the far-right. Similarly, the BBC2 documentary *Jo Cox: The Death of an MP* offered a carefully researched and detailed picture of both Mair and Cox. Its efforts to capture the impact of the killing on Cox's family, while also painting a complex picture of Mair himself, were particularly noteworthy.

Another recent case of a potential far-right lone actor terrorist was that of Jack Renshaw, a leading figure within the proscribed neo-Nazi group National Action (NA). Renshaw was a young activist who was also gay. While linked to the group, he also started to groom boys, which included making one 15-year-old take pictures of his genitals and sending them to Renshaw. He was convicted of child sexual offences in June 2018, but while under investigation, in the spring of 2017, he also hatched a plan to kill both the Labour MP Rosie Cooper as well as the police office investigating him for child sex offences. He disclosed this plan to another activist in July 2017, Robbie Mullen. However, Mullen had become disillusioned with the group and passed on details to HnH, which then informed the police. The plot was stymied, but the case underscores both the complex issues driving far-right activists who turn to violence and also helps reveal the serious nature of some of the information that may be disclosed to those who report on the far-right. HnH has published stories on the issue subsequently, especially after Renshaw's conviction, and gave its definitive account in the book *Nazi Terrorist: The Story of National Action* by Matthew Collins and Robbie Mullen.

Aside from anti-fascists themselves, some of the most useful investigative journalism on NA, one of the most extreme groups to operate in the United Kingdom in the past few years, has been carried out by the BBC's Daniel De Simone. As well as reporting on the group before its proscription in 2016, De Simone also followed its former members through their many trials since it was proscribed. His article on the Renshaw case, for example, 'The Neo-Nazi Paedophile Who Plotted to Kill', offers one of the most authoritative summaries of its many complexities.[30]

While NA has been at the forefront of re-branding British neo-Nazis, Stephen Yaxley-Lennon, or Tommy Robinson, has become the most high-profile figure of the far-right in recent times. Since leaving the EDL, he often claims to have become a journalist himself, for a time working for the Canadian far-right news site *The Rebel Media* before developing his own web presence. In 2018 and 2019, this has included a series of provocative live-streaming incidents. In May 2018, he was arrested after live-streaming outside a trial of a grooming gang, contravening reporting restrictions on the case. After a series of trials in 2018 and 2019, he was given a 9-month sentence on 11 July 2019 for being in contempt of court. Maintaining his innocence, he even wore a T-shirt with the slogan 'Convicted of Journalism' at his trial. This was a claim rejected by many professional journalists, including Society for Editors executive director Ian Murry, who described the idea of Yaxley-Lennon being a journalist as a 'dangerous distortion of the truth'.[31]

Yaxley-Lennon is reflective of a wider turn among far-right operators internationally to use the internet to create and disseminate their own media, other notable example being the news site *Breitbart News* and provocative figures such as Milo Yiannopoulos. While Robinson has now been removed from most social media sites, such as YouTube, Twitter and Facebook, he still has a large following on *Telegram Messenger*. His supporters also pose a threat to journalists. The BBC, ITV and Channel 4 journalists were reported to have hired private security firms to protect themselves at Robinson's trial in July 2019, while BBC reporter Dominic Casciani explained: 'At every hearing in this saga, journalists have been abused. People have been spat at, had cameras attacked. A cameraman was punched. . . . Lies have been told about us, our reports and events in court'.[32] Earlier in 2019, Yaxley-Lennon targeted another journalist, Mike Stuchbery, and live-streamed his actions. Yaxley-Lennon turned up at Stuchbery's home twice during one night and demanded to speak with him. His internet broadcast also gave Stuchbery's home address, and he stated of journalists in general: 'I'm going to make a documentary that exposes every single one of you, every single detail about every one of you. Where you live, where you work, everything about you is going to be exposed'.[33]

While the far-right has certainly changed in the 2000s and 2010s, gravitating less to larger groups and operating more as decentred networks of activists, the threat to journalists is, if anything, growing. Yaxley-Lennon's actions are not new, and there has often been a threat to journalists form the far-right. In the 1990s and 2000s, a publication linked to C18 called Redwatch, which later became a website, gave contact details of journalists who reported on the far-right, as well as anti-fascists and other critics. With the rise of the EDL and a return to reporting on street demonstrations resisted by the BNP in the 2000s under Griffin, the NUJ became vocal on the issue of defending journalists reporting on the far-right. In 2011, at the height of the EDL's growth, the NUJ submitted an emergency motion to the Trade Union Congress (TUC), calling for more support from the police to support journalists in their reporting. It argued journalists had been subject to a series of attacks at EDL rallies.[34] In 2013, the NUJ's Reporting the Far-right campaign praised the support of the TUC and spoke of the need for ethical journalism to respond to the 'international network of far-right organisations with a record of attacks on journalists'.[35] The issue of attacks on journalists has continued and sees no sign of resolution. Other recent cases include the far-right protestor James Goddard, who was found guilty of assaulting photographer Joel Goodman in June 2019. Goodman spoke afterwards about suffering 'verbal and physical abuse' on social media and in person for months.[36] In August 2019, NUJ general secretary Michelle Stanistreet called for police and others to do more to tackle what she identified as a 'coordinated surge in violent extremism against journalists and media workers'.[37] In sum, journalists who work in this area should be prepared to deal with aggressive responses by the far-right.

## Conclusions

This chapter has shown how reporting on the far-right can often be in the public interest. While merely sensationalised stories, especially those that give far-right leaders an uncritical mouthpiece, are unhelpful, the types of detailed investigations covered here hopefully offer some clear examples of how to develop well-researched, informative reporting. Journalism that goes beyond the public rhetoric has often been more successful in developing a richer and more complex assessment of the far-right. However, where to strike the balance between journalism that offers relevant new information and that which essentially offers free publicity to extremists who crave media attention always requires careful judgement. Good reporting on the far-right has a lasting impact as well, as it provides a detailed public record of activism that is returned to by many academic experts and analysts. Moreover, investigative journalists should always be careful of their own safety when engaging with the far-right. While far-right individuals and groups often court media attention, unpredictable activists can become frustrated when journalists explore the more uncomfortable aspects that they want to keep from the public's attention, leading to threats and even violence directed towards journalists. Be warned.

## Notes

1  Cas Mudde, *Populist Radical Right Parties in Europe* (Cambridge: Cambridge University Press, 2007); Jean-Yves Camus and Nicolas Lebourg, *Far-Right Politics in Europe* (Cambridge, MA: Harvard University Press, 2017).
2  Roger Eatwell, *Fascism: A History* (London: Pimlico, 2003).
3  Roger Griffin, *Fascism: An Introduction to Comparative Fascist Studies* (London: Polity, 2018).
4  Paul Jackson and Anton Shekhovtsov eds., *The Post-War Anglo-American Far-Right: A Special Relationship of Hate* (Basingstoke: Palgrave, 2014).
5  Richard Thurlow, *Fascism in Britain: From Oswald Mosley's Blackshirts to the National Front* (London: I. B. Tauris, 1998).
6  www.reportingthebnp.org [last accessed 23/08/2019].
7  www.reportingthebnp.org/index.php/personal-testimonies/ [last accessed 23/08/2019].
8  Ray Hill and Andy Bell, *The Other Face of Terror: Inside Europe's Neo-Nazi Network* (London: Grafton, 1988).
9  http://news.bbc.co.uk/hi/english/static/audio_video/programmes/panorama/transcripts/transcript_30_06_00.txt [last accessed 23/08/2019].
10  www.davidmodell.com/young-nazi-and-proud [last accessed 23/08/2019].
11  http://news.bbc.co.uk/1/hi/england/bradford/6135060.stm [last accessed 23/08/2019].
12  https://web.archive.org/web/20070313013814/www.bnp.org.uk/news_detail.php?newsId=731 [last accessed 23/08/2019].
13  http://news.bbc.co.uk/1/hi/8319136.stm [last accessed 23/08/2019].
14  www.theguardian.com/politics/2009/oct/23/bnp-poll-boost-question-time [last accessed 23/08/2019].
15  www.theguardian.com/tv-and-radio/video/2010/nov/30/documentary-documentary [last accessed 23/08/2019].

16  Matthew Goodwin, *New British Fascism* (Abingdon: Routledge, 2011), pp. 13–14.

17  www.mirror.co.uk/news/uk-news/magic-bus-464597 [last accessed 23/08/2019].

18  www.google.co.uk/url?sa=t&rct=j&q=&esrc=s&source=web&cd=13&ved=2ahU KEwiQ5L7fn5nkAhXPTxUIHdv3Ao04ChAWMAJ6BAgEEAE&url=https%3A %2F%2Fec.europa.eu%2Fmigrant-integration%2Findex.cfm%3Faction%3Dmedia. download%26uuid%3D2A5C6A7D-9C1E-480F-EFC1FAC43B318537&usg=AOvVa w2l1BmUdGW0jHbmY4flHbWe [last accessed 23/08/2019].

19  www.pressgazette.co.uk/nigel-farage-settles-libel-case-against-hope-not-hate-with-more-than-100k-in-court-costs/ [last accessed 23/08/2019].

20  www.theguardian.com/society/2018/oct/17/divided-britain-study-finds-huge-chasm-in-attitudes [last accessed 23/08/2019].

21  www.dailymail.co.uk/news/article-3045115/Nazi-invasion-London-EXPOSED-World-s-Holocaust-deniers-filmed-secret-race-hate-Jews-referred-enemy.html [last accessed 23/08/2019].

22  www.theguardian.com/uk-news/2013/oct/12/tommy-robinson-quilliam-foundation-questions-motivation [last accessed 23/08/2019].

23  https://twitter.com/CasMudde/status/1162063675764531201?s=20 [last accessed 23/08/2019].

24  Jeanine de Roy van Zuijdewijn and Edwin Bakker, *Personal Characteristics of Lone-Actor Terrorists* (London, Royal United Services Institute, 2016), 11 August 2017, www.strate-gicdialogue.org/wp-content/uploads/2016/03/CLAT-Series-5-Policy-Paper-1-ICCT. pdf [last accessed 23/08/2019].

25  Paul Gill and Emily Conner, 'There and back again: The study of mental disorder and terrorist involvement', *American Psychologist*, vol. 72, no. 3 (2017), 231–241.

26  SPLC, 'Alleged killer of British MP was a long-time supporter of the neo-Nazi national alliance', 16 June 2016, www.splcenter.org/hatewatch/2016/06/16/alleged-killer-brit-ish-mp-was-longtime-supporter-neo-nazi-national-alliance [last accessed 23/08/2019].

27  www.theguardian.com/uk-news/2016/nov/23/thomas-mair-slow-burning-hatred-led-to-jo-cox-murder [last accessed 23/08/2019].

28  www.independent.co.uk/news/uk/crime/thomas-mair-guilty-tommy-verdict-jo-cox-mp-murder-trial-court-latest-quiet-neighbour-a7434011.html [last accessed 23/08/2019].

29  www.ft.com/mair [last accessed 23/08/2019].

30  www.bbc.co.uk/news/stories-44798649 [last accessed 23/08/2019].

31  https://inews.co.uk/opinion/columnists/tommy-robinsons-pleas-to-journalism-are-a-dangerous-distortion-of-the-truth/ [last accessed 23/08/2019].

32  www.theguardian.com/media/2019/aug/19/uk-journalists-facing-growing-number-of-attacks-from-far-right [last accessed 23/08/2019].

33  www.theguardian.com/uk-news/2019/mar/05/journalist-makes-police-complaint-about-tommy-robinson [last accessed 23/08/2019].

34  www.pressgazette.co.uk/nuj-calls-for-support-against-far-right-groups/ [last accessed 23/08/2019].

35  www.nuj.org.uk/campaigns/far-right/ [last accessed 23/08/2019].

36  www.manchestereveningnews.co.uk/news/greater-manchester-news/james-goddard-guilty-assault-photographer-16487853 [last accessed 23/08/2019].

37  www.theguardian.com/media/2019/aug/19/uk-journalists-facing-growing-number-of-attacks-from-far-right [last accessed 23/08/2019].

# 20

# THE UNITED KINGDOM'S
# *PRIVATE EYE*

## The 'club' the powerful fear

*Patrick Ward*

The satirical magazine *Private Eye* is one of the best-known investigative publications in the United Kingdom, yet it feels somewhat anachronistic as we enter the third decade of the 21st century. Published fortnightly on low quality, unglossed paper, its stories are laid out across three or four columns per page in thick blocks of text. It is largely black and white, save for the occasional cartoon or column-width photograph. The front of the magazine is devoted to news and much of the back to spoof content, and even the most hard-hitting of its investigations will be punctuated with long-running in-jokes, such as references to its fictional proprietor, 'Lord Gnome', or its promise that stories will continue on 'p94' (the magazine is around half that length). However, while these conventions might risk alienating newer readers, they create an almost club-like atmosphere for its loyal readership.

Most prominently, the *Eye*'s front cover generally features a photograph from the news overlaid with speech bubbles mocking the great and the good. One controversial example, which followed the 11 September 2001 attacks on New York, featured a close-up of President George W Bush being informed of the incident. A member of Bush's detail is seen saying to the President, 'It's Armageddon, sir,' to which Bush declares, 'Armageddon [I'm a-getting] outahere!' (*Private Eye*, 2001). The *Eye* is often accused of employing 'schoolboy humour', somewhat fitting for a publication founded by four men who met in the early 1950s as teenagers at the private Shrewsbury School – Richard Ingrams, William Rushton, Christopher Brooker and Paul Foot (Macqueen, 2011a: 4). The first issue of *Private Eye*, containing nothing but jokes, was printed in 1961, with its first investigative journalism appearing in 1963 (Macqueen, 2011a: 4).

Perhaps most out of character in the modern age of journalism, *Private Eye* is almost entirely offline, with the very limited number of stories that do make it to the website being published contemporaneously with the print edition. There have been several notable attempts at reaching a digital audience, beginning with an ill-fated collaboration with Microsoft in the mid-1990s to produce an online version of the magazine (Thorpe, 1998; Mance,

2015). While the *Eye* has a presence on social media – 231,735 followers on Facebook and 417,129 on Twitter in September 2019 – this is largely used to tease print stories. Two of the few occasions on which the *Eye's* online content could truly be said to augment the print publication were its use of interactive maps showing the locations of properties in England and Wales owned by offshore companies (*Private Eye*, 2015) and local councillors who were late in paying their council tax (*Private Eye*, 2018). By and large, however, *Private Eye* is solidly a print publication, a strategy explained by its managing editor, Sheila Molnar: 'We can't find something that replicates the look and feel of *Private Eye*. Also, I've never known anyone who has been able to monetise it,' (Mance, 2015).

Despite all its apparent idiosyncrasies – or perhaps because of them – *Private Eye* is the best-selling current affairs magazine in the United Kingdom. In the six months leading up to June 2019, it sold an average of 233,565 copies per issue in the United Kingdom and Ireland, while its closest competitor, the *Economist*, sold 159,669 (Mayhew, 2019). As *Private Eye* editor Ian Hislop would say after the magazine's Christmas 2016 edition: 'This is our biggest sale ever, which is quite something given that print is meant to be dead' (Pons-ford, 2017). As of 2017, 57.1 per cent of *Eye* sales were through subscription (Gwynn, 2017).

*Private Eye* is a relatively small operation and since it employs fewer than 50 staff is not required to publish annual revenues and profits (Mance, 2015). It does carry advertising, usually at the very front and back of the magazine. The issue dated 9 August 2019 (*Private Eye*, 2019), for example, carries nine full pages of adverts out of a total page count of 48. However, in the past, the magazine appears to have made a point of its disregard for its advertisers' feelings. Hislop describes one occasion on which an ad for Virgin Atlantic was placed facing a page of copy (Steerpike, 2015): 'This was during [Rich-ard] Branson's hot air phase, and we did a picture of a balloon with Branson underneath it with the phrase "you've got to be careful putting pricks near balloons"'.

One notorious area of expenditure for *Private Eye* historically has been libel payments, and there is an enduring myth that Hislop is the most sued man in Britain (Macqueen, 2011b). Hislop claims to have 'fought 40 cases and won one, and we lost the costs on that' (Market Research Society, 2018). This noto-riety may have been bolstered by Hislop's sometimes defiant reactions to losing such actions, such as joking after losing a libel battle with Robert Maxwell, the late proprietor of the *Mirror*, in 1986: 'I've just given a fat cheque to a fat Czech' (Deedes, 2008).

Hislop's response to court rulings perhaps fits the overall tone of the *Eye*, and before we take a closer look at the investigative reporting, we will explore a little further the satirical edge of the magazine. This may seem like a distrac-tion, but it is the balance between these two types of content that gives the *Eye* its unique quality. Lockyer (2006) argues that both the investigative and the satirical journalist is in the business of unpicking the discrepancies between image and reality and goes on to quote Hislop:

> They are both basically doing the same job, which is questioning the official version. Either doing it with jokes or doing it with facts. After a bit if you are just doing jokes you're just taking the agenda from other people's newspapers. Whereas if you're breaking stories yourself then you can use both the satire and the journalism as a two-pronged attack.

At a more basic level, the *Eye*'s success might well be because people initially pick it up for the humour, but that then becomes a gateway to the journalism (Byrne, 2006).

Despite this jokey format, the *Eye*'s investigations have often exposed issues of great national and international importance. Paul Foot challenged the prevailing narrative of the 1988 Lockerbie bombing of a Pan Am jet over Scotland, which saw 270 people dead. Libya was blamed for the atrocity, but Foot, through working with the families of the victims, sitting through hearings and sifting through mountains of other evidence, concluded that the attack was in fact carried out by Iranian-hired terrorists from Syria. The official shift in blame to Libya coincided with attempts by the United States to secure the backing of Syria for the first Gulf War (Foot, 2001). Other high-profile *Eye* investigations have examined the contaminated blood scandal of the 1970s and 1980s, tax havens, the Private Finance Initiative and the phone hacking scandal.

Most *Eye* stories, however, are far shorter. They often highlight the hypocrisy of the press, politicians and business. Hislop notes: 'In the old days, *Private Eye* was there to break stories. . . . Nowadays, we're there to explain why stories are irrelevant or wrong and what the real story is' (Erlanger, 2015). While the more detailed investigations are to be found as part of the 'In the Back' section, the front-end news is a long way from the sort of 'churnalism' discussed by Davies (2009) that afflicts much of today's press.

We can briefly dissect one issue of the *Eye*, issue 1502 (*Private Eye*, 2019), to offer examples of its coverage. The opening news page features five stories, leading with an exposé of how hedge fund managers, one of whom was a donor to the Conservative Party leadership campaign of Boris Johnson, were short-selling the pound in anticipation of the economic damage expected from a so-called 'hard Brexit', a policy Johnson was at the time refusing to rule out. The following section is 'Street of Shame', which focuses on stories about the news media. Of the 13 stories in this section, 4 focus on the case of Carl Beech, whose fabricated allegations of a VIP paedophile network led to hundreds of press stories, a host of arrests and police raids of prominent politicians' homes. Much of this coverage reminds readers of what the news sources in question, including the *Daily Mail*, might prefer their audiences to forget: that despite their recent outrage that Beech's stories were believed by politicians and various state institutions, many of the now-indignant publications originally also printed his claims uncritically.

This is followed by a section devoted to stories about national politicians, 'HP Sauce', which in this issue features eight articles, one of which details the business links between incoming government security minister Brandon Lewis and Russian oligarchs connected to the Kremlin. Following sections include 'Rotten Boroughs' (about local authorities), 'Eye TV' (television) and 'Medicine Balls' (health).

Then, after the letters pages, come the jokes – nine full pages of cartoons and parodies, which in this issue include a spoof of P. G. Wodehouse's Jeeves and Wooster novels (here featuring the prime minister and his chief advisor as 'Leaves and Booster') and a 'diary' purporting to be by *Daily Telegraph* columnist Allison Pearson.

The magazine then enters its more detailed investigative section, 'In the Back', which in this issue hosts ten stories across four pages. They include investigations into tax evasion by central London souvenir shops, continuing coverage of a famous miscarriage of the justice involving the murder of private investigator Daniel Morgan in 1987 and a series of fires at waste incinerators run by the company Viridor (and attempts by its PR company to minimise negative publicity).

Many of the stories 'In the Back' are short updates on long-running investigations, as with the Daniel Morgan story. This carries on the tradition of Foot, the section's late editor, whose 'drip-drip-drip discovery and recording of evidence, over months and often years' (Greenslade, 2008: 336) ensures a story endures, with new evidence added, more sources coming forward and, in the best of examples, tangible victories along the way. *Eye* journalist Richard Brooks (2019) offers further insight:

> The great thing about doing things for Private Eye is that you don't just have to spend months on something before you print anything. . . . It takes a long time, but I think a way of doing these investigations, probably underrated now, is to keep coming back to them, develop them as stories, so that you often have new revelations month after month rather than having to do it all again in one go.

One key feature of all the news stories and deeper investigations throughout the magazine is their lack of bylines. With very few exceptions, no journalists or editors are named at any point in the magazine, although the occasional pseudonym is used for regular writers, such as TV reviewer 'Remote Controller' and health writer 'M. D.'. There are several reasons for this anonymity, which has been in place since 1967. Macqueen (2011a: 19), himself an *Eye* journalist, states that its editors 'have always been exemplary in absorbing legal fallout rather than allowing it to shower on junior staff'. Macqueen notes that the main reason was that 'by mid-1966 they were receiving regular leaks from newspaper offices, the BBC, Scotland Yard and the inner circle around prime minister Harold Wilson'. He goes on to quote Foot:

> The problem about the circulation of real information in our society is that people at all levels of it, especially at the top, do not disclose what they want to disclose. They are worried about their own position as discloser. . . . Only when they can be sure that they are safe does the information start to flow.

The importance of anonymity is highlighted in an anecdote by John McEntee (2011), reflecting on his time as a columnist for the *Daily Express* in the mid-1990s. He relates how his boss wanted a story printed in the *Eye*, which a colleague with links to the magazine then sent over to them by fax:

> Within minutes I was summoned to the managing editor's office, where a clearly embarrassed executive asked me if I provided *Private Eye* with stories. I said I did not and was informed that there had been two telephone calls and one fax message to the magazine's office from the Diary within the previous hour. It transpired that the switchboard was programmed to alert *Express* management to any contact with the Eye.

This anonymity is key when you consider the way in which the *Eye* sources many of its stories. Tim Minogue (2015), the editor of the *Eye*'s 'Rotten Boroughs' section since 1999, relates that each fortnight he receives 'perhaps 200 tips via email, plus more over the phone, via Twitter and in the post'. He adds, 'Sometimes the source works for the local paper, but can't get anything mildly controversial past their editor'.

As Hislop (Market Research Society, 2018) explains, again drawing on the idea of the *Eye* as a type of club:

> *Private Eye* is essentially a club, and it depends on people in specific industries . . . engaging with us and saying if something's going wrong, or you think something's bent or something isn't right, just letting us know, and that is how nearly every section of the *Eye* works. . . . The reason we tend to get our stories right is because we're told them by people in the middle of them.

Richard Brooks (2019), however, notes that these tip-offs are not the whole picture. 'A lot of people do come to us, but on really big stories, I think an interesting feature is that people tend not to. It may be the sort of online age and so on, but people with big stories are fine often to go elsewhere'. This was the case with his own investigations into corruption involving Saudi Arabia and Britain, which we will now examine in detail.

## Case study: 'Shady Arabia and the Desert Fix' (2014)

To offer an illustration of the way in which *Private Eye* conducts its investigations, we can look to a two-year investigation into the corrupt relationship between Britain's Ministry of Defence (MoD) and Saudi Arabia (Brooks and Bousfield, 2014). A six-page special report, 'Shady Arabia and the Desert Fix', was published by the *Eye* in 2014, expanding and updating its previous coverage of the issue. The two journalists leading the coverage, Brooks and Andrew Bousfield, won the coveted Paul Foot Award for investigative journalism in 2015 as a result. Two months after the publication of the first story in the *Eye* relating to the scandal (Private Eye, 2012), the Serious Fraud Office (SFO) opened an investigation, which, as of September 2019, is ongoing.

The investigation centred on what was known as the Saudi Arabia National Guard Communications (SANGCOM) contract, primarily between the Saudi Arabia National Guard (SANG) and the British MoD, which was used to supply multibillion-pound arms exports from the United Kingdom to the Saudis. In order to secure this lucrative market, the British relied on bribes, which were fed back to members of the Saudi royal family.

The story begins with revelations given by Ian Foxley, a former British army lieutenant-colonel, who was programme director on a contract worth £2 billion between the British government and SANG to supply the latter with telecommunications and electronic warfare equipment. Foxley, who was based in Riyadh, worked for the British company GPT Special Project Management Ltd and in 2010 discovered what he believed to be evidence of corrupt payments. He was alarmed to find that the most expensive elements of the contract were payments to offshore companies under the title 'bought-in services', which he soon found did not exist. He knew that a previous holder of his role, Mike Paterson, had informed EADS, parent company to GPT, about the problem before, but that nothing had come of it. Foxley took matters into his own hands:

> Before [Foxley's] colleagues arrived for their day's work, he located messages originally sent by Paterson to Pedro Montoya, the "group compliance officer" at Paradigm [the British-based EADS division], and forwarded them to his own GPT email address. He then strolled down the corridor to his own office, from where he forwarded the emails now sitting in his GPT inbox – complete with explosive attachments – to a personal email account and to one of [the SANGCOM chairman's] officials in the MoD's SANGCOM team.

Rather than investigating the claims, the MoD sent Foxley's information back to GPT, informing them of their employee's disclosure. Foxley was called into the office of Jeff Cook, GPT's managing director, where he was accused of theft and threatened with prison, a threat backed up by a member of the royal family who was also present at the meeting. Foxley left the office and escaped the country as quickly as possible.

These revelations were first published in the *Sunday Times* in October 2011 (Leppard, 2011), after Foxley was contacted by journalist David Leppard. The story was then picked up by *Private Eye* journalists Brooks and Bousfield, who wanted to further explore the issue. Brooks (2019) says that the *Sunday Times* reported what Foxley had told them 'but that clearly wasn't it by a long chalk, so we took it up and got in touch with him, got talking to him, explaining that we could do it in a bit more depth, we could stick with the story a bit longer . . . we would develop the story, follow up any consequences and so on'.

Foxley (2019), for his part, already respected *Private Eye*, so was happy for their involvement. 'They get to the bottom of things, they have their own credibility in terms of the quality of the investigative journalism. . . . I liken them to terriers; they'll get your ankle and they won't let go'. It is also worth noting that Foxley claims he was put under pressure by the SFO not to proactively speak to the media about the case but that he had refused to stay silent should the press contact him: '"No comment" is what villains do in police interviews when they don't want to incriminate themselves. . . . What I said to [the SFO] was that I will not go to the press'. This emphasises Brooks' earlier point about the importance of not simply awaiting tip-offs – it was proactive attempts by journalists that gave Foxley his platform.

The *Private Eye* report built on Foxley's revelations, linking them to broader sources of information, notably the offshore companies implicated in the contracts. The journalists wanted to understand how this bribery scheme was operating, who was involved and where the money was going. The article draws in the findings of former financial controller Mike Paterson, who had discovered that the mysterious payments were being sent to two companies based in the Cayman Islands: Simec International Ltd and Duranton International Ltd. Paterson had raised the alarm bell in 2007, taking his concerns to EADS. Despite this, the signoff of payments continued. Two years later, Paterson went to Philippe Troyas, the international compliance officer of Astrium, a division of EADS, who essentially admitted to the bribery: 'I am prepared to accept some corruption because I like my company better than ethics'. Usefully, Paterson recorded these conversations and kept details of the payments and gifts. This evidence revealed huge payments to Simec International. From July 2007 to July 2010, they amounted to around 15 per cent of the company's expenses, more than £14 million. All were signed off by the GPT managing director and other senior figures. Foxley took this wealth of information to the SFO in January 2011, and the *Eye* first provided coverage the following May (*Private Eye*, 2012). The SFO began a criminal investigation three months after the *Eye* published its revelations.

The investigation then goes back to look at the history of these arrangements, including their foundations in the early days of Western attempts to profit from Saudi oil wealth. Unearthed historical records reveal that the first SANGCOM contract was signed in the 1970s, with Cable & Wireless as the UK contractor, and that three companies were to receive commissions: Engineering and Trading Operations Company Beirut (led by Mahmoud Fustok, the brother-in-law to the then-head of the SANG and later king, Abdullah Al Saud), which would receive 10 per cent commission; Cable & Wireless Middle East, which received 2 per cent and Simec International (3 per cent). By the time of the investigation, all commissions were taken by Simec and Duranton. A contemporary memo uncovered by the investigation from the head of defence sales confirmed that these were indeed bribes. The *Eye* notes a story in the *Times* from 1978, which reveals that the United Kingdom had won the contract despite 'fierce foreign competition'. It was worth £400 million (around £2.3 billion in 2019).

This treasure trove of information was revealed with the help of Nicholas Gilby, an author specialising in the arms trade who had spent a huge amount of time sifting through documents at the National Archives. Brooks (2019) recalls that Gilby's assistance was vital: 'We would probably never have got that ourselves, so we relied on him giving us those documents. Why would he do that? Well, you've got to kind of develop those relationships really'. The journalists discovered that Simtec's origins were in Liechtenstein, a tax haven. Brooks (2019) recalls the relative ease with which they obtained information in this case: 'I wrote to the authorities in Lichtenstein, saying can I have some documents on this thing they'd set up in the 70s, and they actually did hand it over, which I was amazed by. You have to try'.

Simec had been created as a type of foundation in 1975, just as Cable & Wireless was preparing its proposal for a contract. Its formation documents revealed the names of Simec's two founders: Bryan Somerfield, a former diplomat, and a young engineer called Peter Austin. On the day Simec was founded, a separate company, which had strong links to the British political establishment, rebranded as Duranton Ltd. Five years later, Duranton was acquired by Simec, and Austin and Somerfield joined its board. Several years after that, Austin became sole owner of Simec and chair of Duranton. In 1982, Austin set up two companies in the Cayman Islands tax haven, which were also named Simec International Ltd and Duranton Ltd. These companies would continue to take SANGCOM payments until the scandal finally broke.

The investigation quotes an '*Eye* reader who worked on the project in the 1980s' who divulges that 'when the invoices were presented there was always a bottom line that said "administrative charge 3 per cent". That went to Mr Austin and he then disbursed it among a group of gentlemen known as The Club – and they were senior officers and princes of the royal family'. Using research by Gilby, the journalists pieced together the identities of 'The Club's' members. Brooks (2019) recalls being contacted by this unnamed source and the steps taken to verify their story:

> We checked [the source's information] with what we saw in historical documents, what seemed credible, with people who knew what

was going on at the time, and it all stood up really. . . . When people come to you with undocumented evidence or stories you've got to be pretty circumspect. We wouldn't really fly any kites, we'd have to be sure that it's true.

'Shady Arabia and the Desert Fix', at more than 7,400 words, provides far more detail and revelation than this brief summary gives justice. It also details the hunt for the elusive Austin, the connections between GPT and a senior government advisor, the 'blind eye' turned by GPT's high-profile auditors, and much more. It uses investigative techniques from checking LinkedIn profiles to doorstepping, poring over company records to checking newspaper archives. 'I did try to get a lot more on it from the MoD through freedom of information requests and I went to a tribunal, didn't really get anywhere, they were very secretive about the whole thing' (Brooks, 2019).

The story charts the eventual closure of the contract and notes that a new agreement was put in place, supposedly bribery-free, but for which there was very little information available. As to the investigation's impact, Brooks (2019) says:

The company involved is now shutting down, there may be prosecutions sitting on the Attorney General's desk. I think it's hard to say how much of that was our investigation and how much was the fact the case was referred to the SFO early on [and] it's just the outcome of their work. . . . There are a lot of cases where effect is claimed in journalism when it probably might have happened anyway, but . . . I would imagine it put pressure on investigators to look at the thing properly.

Could this investigation have been accomplished by another publication? Possibly, if they had the willingness to invest time and resources into doing so. However, unlike many news publications looking for quick returns, the *Eye* does seem well placed. Brooks (2019) again:

We will go back to stories, I think that's the thing. I think that does get you in deeper to other layers of the story . . . on what it means and why it's happening rather than just the quick headline. . . . I do think that other papers can be a bit fixated on the medium, the type of story. So, if it's a leak, for example, it's suddenly got this kudos and it's much more important than if the same information hadn't been a leak. So they'll splash stuff, we have this massive leak, look at the size of our database. We're still interested in what are the stories and how do you tell the story, which is a very fortunate position to be in for a journalist.

## Conclusion

At a time of continued cashflow shortfalls, digital-first one-upmanship and the clickbait headline, *Private Eye*'s continued insistence on remaining a fortnightly print magazine that dedicates a significant part of its coverage to longterm investigations makes it unique in the UK market. It has bucked conventional wisdom in its insistence to remain largely unchanged in format throughout its history. It is also a place to read stories you would not read elsewhere, away from the media's recycling industry of second-hand stories. Its famous respect for whistleblowers and anonymity for industry insiders means that it is still a trusted platform for contributors – part of its 'club'. As others scrabble for advertising revenue, *Private Eye*'s only apparent concession to the advertising industry was its relatively recent move to colour (Lockyer, 2006). Hislop (in Ponsford, 2017) puts the increasing success of the *Eye*, at a time of dwindling circulations across the newspaper industry, down to its combination of satirical and factual content: 'It's obviously to do with Brexit and Trump and people thinking where can I find something that might be true and something that might be funny? . . . I do think if people will pay £2.50 for a cup of coffee then they will pay [£1.80] for a copy of the *Eye*'.

## References

Brooks, R. (2019): Interview with Patrick Ward, London, 14 August 2019.

Brooks, R. and Bousfield, A. (2014): 'Shady Arabia and the desert fix'. *Private Eye* No. 1375, 5 September 2014. See www.private-eye.co.uk/special-reports/shady-arabia, accessed 29 September 2019.

Byrne, C. (2006): 'Ian Hislop: My 20 years at the eye'. *Independent* (online), 23 October 2006. See www.independent.co.uk/news/media/ian-hislop-my-20-years-at-the-eye-421312.html, accessed 29 September 2019.

Davies, N. (2009): *Flat Earth News*. London: Vintage.

Deedes, H. (2008): 'No fat Czech, or fat cheque, will persuade Hislop to see Captain Bob'. *Independent* (online), 7 August 2008. See www.independent.co.uk/news/people/pandora/no-fat-czech-or-fat-cheque-will-persuade-hislop-to-see-captain-bob-887120.html, accessed 29 September 2019.

Erlanger, S. (2015): 'An enduring and erudite court jester in Britain'. *New York Times* (online), 11 December 2015. See www.nytimes.com/2015/12/12/world/europe/britain-private-eye-ian-hislop.html, accessed 29 September 2019.

Foot, P. (2001): *Lockerbie: The Flight from Justice*. London: Press dram Ltd.

Foxley, I. (2019): Telephone interview with Patrick Ward, 23 September 2019.

Greenslade, R. (2008): 'Subterfuge, set-ups and stunts'. In de Burgh, H. (ed), *Investigative Journalism*. London: Routledge.

Gwynn, S. (2017): 'Private eye overtakes economist as UK's top current affairs magazine'. *Campaign* (online), 9 February 2017. See www.campaignlive.co.uk/article/private-eye-overtakes-economist-uks-top-current-affairs-magazine/1423821, accessed 29 September 2019.

Leppard, D. (2011): 'Whistleblower exposes Saudi Arabia royal "kickbacks"'. *Sunday Times* (online), 9 October 2011. See www.thetimes.co.uk/article/whistleblower-exposes-saudi-arabia-royal-kickbacks-rkwbhx82mgm?region=global, accessed 29 September 2019.

Lockyer, S. (2006): 'A two pronged attack? Exploring private eye's satirical humour and investigative reporting'. *Journalism Studies*, 7 (5), pp. 765–781.

Macqueen, A. (2011a): *Private Eye: The First 50 Years*. London: Private Eye Productions Ltd.

Macqueen, A. (2011b): 'The most sued man in Britain'. *Private Eye* (online), 2 March 2011. See www.private-eye.co.uk/blog/?p=165, accessed 29 September 2019.

Mance, H. (2015): 'Private eye bucks digital publishing trend'. *Financial Times* (online). See www.ft.com/content/6610cfd4-5dfa-11e5-a28b-50226830d644, accessed 29 September 2019.

Market Research Society (2018): 'Ian Hislop, private eye, on satire and censorship speaking at impact 2018'. *YouTube* (online), 14 March 2018. See https://youtu.be/h-AjiUkbuh8, accessed 29 September 2019.

Mayhew, F. (2019): 'News mags ABCs: *Private Eye* circulation holds firm year-on-year'. *Press Gazette* (online), 15 August 2019. See www.pressgazette.co.uk/abc-news-mags-private-eye-circulation-holds-firm-year-on-year/, accessed 29 September 2019.

McEntee, J. (2011): 'Staying in power, the eye has it'. *British Journalism Review*, 7 (5), pp. 7–10.

Minogue, T. (2015): 'The death of muckraking'. *British Journalism Review*, 26 (3), pp. 8–10.

Ponsford, D. (2017): '*Private Eye* hits highest circulation in 55-year history "which is quite something given that print is meant to be dead"'. *Press Gazette* (online), 9 February 2017. See www.pressgazette.co.uk/private-eye-hits-highest-circulation-in-55-year-history-which-is-quite-something-given-that-print-is-meant-to-be-dead/, accessed 29 September 2019.

Private Eye (2001): *Private Eye* No. 1037, 21 September 2001.

Private Eye (2012): *Private Eye* No. 1314, 18 May 2012.

Private Eye (2015): 'Selling England (and Wales) by the pound'. *Private Eye* (online). See www.private-eye.co.uk/tax-havens, accessed 29 September 2019.

Private Eye (2018): 'Those late paying councillors in full'. *Private Eye* (online). See www.private-eye.co.uk/councillors), accessed 29 September 2019.

Private Eye (2019): *Private Eye* No. 1502, 9 August 2019.

Steerpike (2015): 'Paul Foot award 2014: *Private Eye* wades in on HSBC scandal'. *Spectator* (online), 25 February 2015. See https://blogs.spectator.co.uk/2015/02/paul-foot-award-2014-private-eye-wades-in-on-hsbc-scandal/, accessed 29 September 2019.

Thorpe, V. (1998): 'Shurley shome mishtake?' *Independent* (online), 10 February 1988. See www.independent.co.uk/arts-entertainment/shurely-shome-mishtake-1143888.html, accessed 29 September 2019.

# AFTERWORD

## Manifesto for investigative journalism in the 21st century

*Paul Lashmar*

Investigative journalism is one sinew of a developed, healthy society. It connects those who run a state to their obligations – to the people; to fairness; to their duty, honesty and justice. At its best, it has set the innocent free, it has convicted the guilty and has made demagogues run. It uncovers material that the guilty want hidden, and it throws light into darkened corners of our societies; through its sunlight, it disinfects. Yet everywhere, across the globe, these ties are being loosened. Investigative journalism is under threat.

The situation is fragile. Leaders in many nations verbally support the Fourth Estate and investigative journalism, but when they come under its spotlight frequently counter it with exceptionalist arguments. President of the United States Donald Trump has undermined public confidence in journalists and journalism. Others have followed his lead of crying 'fake news' to divert attention from inconvenient truths. Investigative journalists are murdered in Russia and Malta, are arrested in the Philippines, are harassed in Turkey and Brazil and many other countries.

Since the war on terror was launched, with the consequential increase in the number of national security entities, it has become harder for journalists to undertake their Fourth Estate role. Organs of the state, including democratic states, snoop, surveil and seize. Documents released in 2013 by the former US National Security Agency (NSA) contractor Edward Snowden revealed that the Five Eyes electronic spying agencies and their partners now have extraordinary surveillance capability which they have used against almost anybody, including journalists. Many other countries have similar capabilities which they have used in order to repress freedom of expression and the freedom of the media.

Nor is it only the state about which we should be concerned. Individuals have used increasingly stringent privacy laws, brought into being by those with things to hide and the credulous, to hamstring investigations. Well-remunerated professional lawyers chill speech. Media proprietors and Editors misuse investigative journalism, deploying it as a marketing tool. Celebrities and business moguls make full use of the laws.

Social media companies have taken the lifeblood, in other words, the attention and the money that people will pay to be informed and entertained, from news publishers. They have left nothing in return. The news media of many countries, especially the press, have been further financially damaged by the Covid-19 pandemic and changes to the consumption of news. Due to the financial crisis in the media, great expanses of many nations no longer have professional news media.

Investigative journalism, notwithstanding the many upbeat stories previously, faces an existential threat because it pays its way only with great difficulty and ingenuity. What's to be done?

The way forward is to have the functions of investigative journalism understood and accepted in every society, not merely by the state but throughout the polity.

## States

The interests of the governors are not necessarily the same as the governed, nor the institutions that permit them to govern. Those in power must recognise that even if investigative journalism may harm them, it helps society.

Nations should openly recognise and espouse the value of ethically driven investigative journalism. This extends to recognising that the Fourth Estate has a role in monitoring the more secretive parts of the state, including the national security community and police.

Agencies of the state must protect investigative journalists. States and their agencies must not harass, provoke, unduly interfere with and harm investigative journalists. They should provide access to information and recognise the letter and spirit of laws that are designed to do just that.

The courts should respect and protect journalistic sources; laws must not permit bullies to hide behind legal actions and costs to chill investigative work and there must be sufficient public interest defences in criminal and civil law for public service investigative journalism.

All serious threats against journalists, including those on social media, should be prosecuted.

## Media companies and employers

It should be recognised as part of the contract of employment that investigative journalists have the right to chase a story wherever it leads, even if their proprietor, or the advertising desk, finds that uncomfortable.

Companies and employers must not have control over the public's attention. If they do, this stifles viewpoints and diversity. Publishers (electronic ISPs and other) should acknowledge this.

## Funding

Any negative rights and freedoms – against interference and restriction – granted to investigative journalists are nothing if there is not the positive power to exercise them. That is why investigative work needs to be properly funded:

- by media companies and employers, who should acknowledge a moral obligation to fund an activity that protects a well-functioning society, because that is the sort of society which allows them to do business successfully;
- by public service broadcasters, who have a moral obligation if they benefit from taxpayers' money to produce journalism of public benefit;
- by social media and information and technology companies, which have a moral obligation to ensure that the polemic and propaganda which makes up so much of social media is interrogated and exposed for what it is;
- through a levy on technological hardware for social media or broadband to feed back into the funding of quality, properly regulated and ethical journalism.

## The journalists themselves

Investigative journalists cannot expect their roles and status to be acknowledged in these ways, let alone valued, unless they prove their necessity and unless they fully acknowledge the responsibilities that justify these rights.

Investigative journalists should therefore be bound by an ethical code that balances freedom of the press with other rights in society. The code should be enforceable. If a journalist breaches that code, there must, as there are with other codes, be consequences. These consequences are to protect the public.

Investigative journalists should take every step to ensure that their training and abilities are as up to date as they can be: their education does not stop at the university door or with the granting of a professional certificate. Employers should guarantee retraining.

Investigative journalists should not investigate with the intention of only of protecting the commercial interests of their employers or of advancing the interests of lobbies.

Journalists should always act within the law wherever possible. If a journalist undertakes an illegal act, it can only be done in the overwhelming public interest.

Investigative journalists should not have dual roles where they are open to allegations of a conflict of interest, for example, working for corporate investigators or law firms.

Investigative journalism should never be subservient to political control, and journalists should reject allegiance to any political organisations in order to serve the wider public interest and be trusted by those of any politics and none.

Every effort should be made to encourage investigative journalism from diverse perspectives to ensure that all benefit from the safeguards that good journalism can bring.

# INDEX

17 Black (Dubai offshore company) 82
21st-century investigative journalism:
  Covid-19 pandemic and 281; funding
  and 282; intelligence agencies and 280;
  journalists and 282–283; manifesto for
  21st-century 280–283; media industry
  and 281; overview of 14; privacy issues
  and 280–281; social media companies and
  281; states and 281; threats to 280–281

Aabar (subsidiary company) 196, 198
Abedi, Salman 119
Abubakar Rimi Television (ART) 211
access journalists 31–32
accountability: Cairncross Review and 114;
  as core value of investigative journalism
  204; decline of news industry and 100;
  Latin-American investigative journalism
  and 231, 240; of intelligence agencies
  34, 40–41; local journalism in United
  Kingdom and 103; non-profit and
  mission-driven journalism and 103, 110;
  One Malaysia Development fund and
  196–197; Polish investigative journalism
  and 9; surveillance and 4, 94; Syrian
  investigative journalism and 140
Adamson, John 75
advertising revenue, decline in 100, 127,
  207–208, 278
'Africa Eye' (BBC documentary) 60, 65–66
*Akis* (Turkish magazine) 150–151
Aldrich, Richard 32–34
Alford, John 250
Alfter, Brigitte 11
Al Ghazzi, O. 66
Alibrahim, Ali 140
Al-Ibrahim, Mokhtar 141

Al Iqtisadi 141
Al Jazeera (AJ) 138
*All the President's Men* (film) 33
Al Noufal, Walid 143, 145–147
Altheide, D. L. 50
Altschall, J. H. 205
Al-Zoubi, Omran 139–140
Aman, Musa 188
Amnesty International 4–5, 44, 47–49,
  54, 65
'Anatomy of a Killing' (video) 65
Anglo-American investigative journalism
  1–3, 7–8
Anglo-American liberalism 2
Anglophone media 8
*Animal Politico* (Mexican digital native site)
  233–234
anonymity of journalists 211–212,
  272–273
anti-fascists 258–262, 265
Anwar Ibrahim 191–194
Arab Reporters for Investigative Journalism
  (ARIJ) 137–139, 142
Arab Spring 8, 138
*Arena* (Turkish TV programme) 155
Argentinian investigative journalism 239
Arizona Project 73–76, 79
Ascherson, Neal 34
Assange, Julian 4, 18
Association of Applied Journalism and
  Communication of China 129–130
Austin, Peter 276–277
authoritarianism 9, 188–191, 237

Babangida, Ibrahim Badamasi 207
Bachelot, Michelle 239
Baer, Bob 38

# INDEX

Bagot, Martin 253
Bailey, Sly 248
Baldét, William 263
Barisan Nasional Party 188
Bassiki, Mohamed 140
*Battle for Barking, The* (documentary) 262
BBC 3, 58, 67, 113, 119–120
BBC Media Action 158
Bebawi, Saba 8
Beech, Carl 271
Bell, Andy 259
Bellingcat Investigation Team 5–6, 61–63, 66–67, 109
Berger, Renata 164
Bevin, E. 6
Bhagalpur blindings of suspects awaiting trial 177–178, 180–182
big data 234
'Bihar's Computer Muddle' 183
Birney, Trevor 94–95
Black, Guy 244
Black Lives Matter protests 67
blagging information 244–245
Blaszczyk, Jacek 163–164
Bleasdale, Marcus 45
Bohai No. 2 oil-drilling ship sinking 125
Bojanowski, Wojciech 166–167, 171
Boland-Rudder, Hamish 3
Bolles, Don 73–76
Borg, J. 77
*Boston Globe* (US newspaper) 107
Boumelha, Jim 90
boundary work in journalism 52–53
Bousfield, A. 275
Brazilian Association of Investigative Journalism (ABRAJI) 5, 76
Brazilian digital native sites 233–234
Brazilian investigative journalism 233–234, 239
*Breitbart News* (website) 266
Breivik, Anders 264
Brexit Party 258
briberies paid to Argentinian public officers 239
Bribery Act 244
*Bristol Cable* (news cooperative) 103–104, 114–115, 119
British far-right journalism: anti-fascists and 258–262, 265; British National Party and 13, 258, 260–261; extremism and 263–266; historical perspective

of 25–258; *Mirror* and 262–263; neo-Nazism and 257, 259; overview of 13, 257, 267; public interest and 267; quality, impact of 267; Reporting the Far-right campaign 266; terminology, key 257; threats to journalism and 263–266; understanding far-right phenomenon and 257
British National Party (BNP) 13, 258, 260–261
British tabloids: background information 243; blagging information of 244–245; Buckingham Palace infiltration and 252; charity's link with energy company and 253; criminal trials of 243–244; decline in profits of 243; entrapment and 250–251; fishing expeditions by 244; investigative journalism of 12–13, 243, 251–255; legislation regulating 244; Leveson Inquiry and Report and 243, 247–251; low-level investigations by 253–254; misbehavior of 243–247; overview of 12–13; phone hacking by 243–248; sex-and-celebrity agenda of 254–255; sexual piccadilloes and 246, 254; 'sting operation' and 249–250; subterfuge and 249; surveillance and 249–250; term for 243; transparency and 249; Yarl's Wood refugee asylum centre and 252–253
Broersma, Marcel 222
Brooker, Christopher 269
Brooks, Richard 272–273, 275–277
Brown, Clare Rewcastle 10
Brown, Gordon 261
Bruns, A. 67
Brussels press corps 217
Bucak, Selin 9
Buhari, Salisu 203
Buk missile system 61
Bureau of Investigative Journalism 6, 94, 105, 108, 115–116, 118
Bureau Local project 7, 115–119
burn-out of journalists 110
Bush, George W. 269
'Byline Is Dead, The' (news feature) 184–185

Cabot, Diego 239
Cairncross, Dame Frances 113
Cairncross Review 113–114, 121

285

# INDEX

*Caixin* (Chinese magazine) 128
Calderón, Rafael Ángel 239–240
Cambridge Spy Ring 32, 34
Cameron, David 36, 39, 247, 254
Cameroon soldiers' murder of civilians 65–66
Campbell, Duncan 34
Cardona, Chris 81
Carroll, Albert 95
Casciani, Dominic 266
census scandal in Argentina 239
Center for Investigative Reporting (CIR) 103, 105
Central Investigative Office (CBŚ) 164
Centre for the Analysis of the Radical Right (CARR) 263
Centre for Investigative Journalism (CIPER) (Chile) 233, 239
Centre to Protect Journalists 73
Changchun Changsheng Biotechnology Co. Ltd. 129
Channels Television (Nigeria) 208–209
*Charlie Hebdo* (French magazine) 76
chemical warfare in Syria 3, 66–67
Chenzhou officials' corruption 125
Chepiga, Antoliy 63
*Chequeado* (Argentinian fact-checking project) 236–237
*Chicago Sun Times* (US newspaper) 171
child sexual abuse in Polish Catholic Church 163–164, 169–170
Chilean investigative journalism 233, 239
China: civic journalism in 131; condemnation of 2; conferences on journalistic work 129; economy of 7, 126–128; fake vaccine business in 129; harbinger of 7; human rights abuses and 60; media industry in 127–129; State Taxation Administration 134; Xi Jinping and 128–129; *see also* Chinese investigative journalism
China Central Television (CCTV) 129, 131, 133
China Internet Network Information Center (CNNIC) 126
Chinese investigative journalism: actors in 130; advertising revenue and, decline in 127; background information 125–126; Bohai No. 2 oil-drilling ship sinking 125; changes in 125–126; changing media environment and 126–129; Chenzhou officials' corruption 125; Cui Yongyuan's practices of 126, 131–135,

136n17; emergence of 125, 135; examples of 131–134; features of, main 129–131; genetically modified food and, safety of 126, 132–133, 136n17, 126; 'golden age' of 127–129, 131; historical perspective of 125–126; 'new era' of 126–129; overview of 7–8, 126; Sanlu Milk Scandal 125; on social media platforms 127, 130, 135; 'soft' versus 'hard' topics in 131; state and 128; Sun Zhigang's death 125, 135n1; tax scandal involving entertainment celebrities and 126, 133–134; technology in 'new era' of 126; transparency and 135
Chinese People's Political Consultative Conference (CPPCC) 132
Christian Aid 44, 46–47
CIA (Central Intelligence Agency) 30–31, 33
Cieśla, Wojciech 163
citizen journalism 66, 131
Civic Information Bill 121
civic journalism 66, 131
Civic Platform (PO) 165
civil liberties 30
clandestine graves in Mexico scandal 239
Clegg, Nick 91
clippings journalists 31–32
Cobbett, William 1
Code of Conduct (NUJ) 258
Çölaşan, Emin 153
collaborative journalism: awards for 232; Bureau Local project and 115–116; Daphne Project and 75; data journalism and 26–27; European Union investigative journalism and 11, 225–226; Latin-American investigative journalism and 232–233; local journalism in United Kingdom and 108, 115; *New York Times* and 75; non-profit and mission-driven journalism and 107–109; Panama Papers and 12, 24–25, 108, 232; power of 26–27
'Collateral Murder' (WikiLeaks video) 19
Collett, Mark 260–261
Collins, Matthew 263, 265
Collins, Valerie 116
Colombian digital native sites 233
commercial model of news, decline in 100–101
Commerzbank (Germany) 21
Communism 162, 168
Community Organiser of the Bureau Local Project 6–7

286

# INDEX

Community Security Trust (British organisation) 259

*Conservative Party Manifesto* 6, 93

content analysis technique 60

Cook, Jeff 274

cooperatives 114

Cooper, Glenda 4

Cooper, Rosie 265

Copeland, David 259

co-publishing model 106

Corbin, Jane 260

coronavirus pandemic 7, 100, 111, 121, 281

Corporate Affairs Commission (CAC) 212

*Correctiv* (German non-profit newsroom) 7, 116

Corrigan, Patrick 95

Coşkun, Alev 157

Costa Rican investigative journalism 239–240

Coulson, Andy 245, 247

Couper, Niall 51–52

Covid-19 pandemic 7, 100, 111, 121, 281

Cox, Jo 264–265

Crawshaw, Steve 45–46, 51, 53

Cresson case 223

cross-verification technique 59–60

*Cuestión Pública* (Colombian digital native site) 233

*Cui's Investigation of GMF in the United States* (investigative report) 132–133

Cui, Yongyuan 126, 131–135, 136n17

cultural differences in investigative journalism 2, 8, 11

*Cumhuriyet* (Turkish newspaper) 157

*Daily Maverick* (South African newspaper) 103

*Daily Mirror* (British tabloid) 252–253

*Daily Trust* (Nigerian newspaper) 204, 208

Dale Farm traveller site eviction (2011) 89

Danish Investigative Journalism Association 138

Daphne Project: agreed deadline and 80; challenges to 77–78; collaborative journalism and 75; development of 75–76; dilemmas of 81; division of labour in 80; follow-up 83; Forbidden Stories and 76–78; individual responsibility and 80; investigation 81–83; issues and problems of 80–81; legacy of 225; as model of inspiration 84; mutual trust and 80; principles of, key 79–80; stories published and 82;

technical infrastructure of 79; techniques and procedures in 78–81

Daraj Media 141

da Silva, Luiz Inácio 'Lula' 239

Dataharvest 225

data journalism: collaborative journalism and 26–27; current journalists and 32; digital sleuthing and 63; examples of 235; human source vs 194; Latin-American investigative journalism and 12, 234–235; new paradigm and 18–19; overview of 3; research on, by *New York Times* and *Washington Post* 235; technology and 23–24, 28; *see also* Panama Papers

data protection 95, 244

Data Protection Act 244

data retention 91

Data Retention and Investigatory Powers Bill (2014) 91

dataset 22; *see also* data journalism

David and Elaine Potter Foundation 103

Davies, Nick 245–247

Davis, David 96

Davison, John 44, 46–47, 53

Dear, Jeremy 258

*Death at the Police Station* (investigative report) 166–167

Degiorgio, Alfred 81

Demirel, Süleyman 151

Demirel, Yahya 152

democracy: decline of media industry and 100; 'democratic deficit' and 113; fake news label and 236; far-right and 13; freedom of information legislation and 221; Latin-American investigative journalism and 231, 236; Indian investigative reporting and 175, 184–185; investigative journalism and 203, 205; local journalism in United Kingdom and 113–114; Malaysian investigative journalism and 188, 198; media industry and 31, 41, 100, 103; Nigerian investigative journalism and 203–206, 212; Turkish investigative journalism and promise of 149

'democratic deficit' 113

*Der Spiegel* (German news website) 35

De Simone, Daniel 265

DiCaprio, Leonardo 192

digital native sites 233–234

# INDEX

digital sleuthing: 'Africa Eye' case study and 60, 65–66; Bellingcat case study and 61–63, 66–67; computer research versus on-the-ground fact-finding 66–67; data journalism and 63; development of 58–59; emergence of 57; establishment of 67; historical perspective of 57–58; methodology of 59–61; *New York Times* Visual Investigation case study 60, 64–65, 67; Nigerian investigative journalism 204, 210–213; overview of 5; potential of 67; results of 57; Storyful and 58–59; technology and 57–58; user-generated content and 58

Digital Verification Corps (DVU) (Amnesty International) 4–5, 44, 47–49, 54

*Dingxiangyisheng* (Chinese news source) 130

Dink, Hrant 156, 158

*Dispatches* (current affairs programme) 89

Doe, John 19, 21–22

Doğan, Aydin 153–154, 157

*Dollars for Docs* (*Propublica* series) 105

'Don't Spy on Us' campaign 93

Dorling, Phillip 35

Dowler, Milly 247–248

Draft Communications Data Bill (2012) 91

*Dromómanos* (Mexican digital native site) 233

Dubberley, Sam 51

Duke, David 260

Duke Reporters' Lab 236

Dündar, Uğur 155

Dunn, Tom Newton 92

Duranton International Ltd 275–276

Duterte, President 103

'Dying Homeless' (investigative report) 116–118

East Impact Hub (BBC) 119–120

Eatwell, Roger 257

economy 7, 20, 126–128

Editor's Code of Practice 244–245, 249

EDL 266

Egrant (company in Panama) 82

electronic devices, accessing 93; *see also* phone hacking

Elendu, Jonathan 210

Elendureports.com (Nigerian news platform) 210

*El Faro* (El Salvadoran news website) 232, 234

Ellsberg, Daniel 18

*El Surti* (Paraguayan digital native site) 233

Emergency (1975–1977) (India) 175

encryption 37

Energydesk (now Unearthed) (investigative unit) 47–48

engagement techniques 120

entrapment 250–251

'equipment interference' 93; *see also* phone hacking

'era of exposure' 32, 40

Erdoğan, Recep Tayyip 8–9, 149, 155–157

Ergenekon terrorist organisation investigation 156, 159n3

Essex police 89

ethical issues 27, 88–89; *see also* accountability; transparency

Ettema, J. S. 204

European Commission 217

European Convention on Human Rights 244

European Court of Human Rights (ECHR) 94, 223

European funds' flow investigative report 223–224

European Investigative Journalism Conference 225

European Union investigative journalism: collaborative journalism and 11, 225–226; context of 218; decision making and administration issues 224; European Commission power struggle and 217; European funds' flow 223–224; examples of 223–224; freedom of information requests and 221–222; general interest topics and 224–225; mapping, challenge of 218; overview of 11, 217; pesticide 224; research methods, varying 220–221, 226; resources for, further 225; storytelling and 222; subject matter in 219–220; transparency and 11, 217, 221; villains and, finding 218–219

Evans, Rob 38

Evans, Sir Harry 107

*Eye of Darkness, The* (documentary) 182

fact-checking 12, 109, 230, 236–237

fake news 3, 145–146, 236, 280

fake vaccine business in China 129

Fan, Bingbing 133–134

Fang, Zhouzi 132

Fan, Jichen 7–8

Farage 262

Farahi, Hamad 116

Farmsubsidy investigative report 223–224

# INDEX

far-right 13, 257–258, 263–264; *see also* British far-right journalism
FBC Media 193
Federal Security Bureau (FSB) 62
Feeney, L. 66–67
Feldman, Matthew 263
Ferarri, Nick 262
*Ferret, The* (news cooperative 114–115, 119
Fethullah Terrorist Organisation (FETO) 156–158
fictitious furniture export operation 151–152
*Financial Times* (British newspaper) 11
fishing expeditions of British tabloids 244
FitzGibbon, Will 3
Five Eyes Network 4, 36, 280
Football Lads Alliance (FLA) 258
Foot, Paul 13, 252, 269, 271, 273
Forbidden Stories 5, 76–78, 83
For Britain (FB) 258
Forensic Architecture (FA) 60, 67
Fourth Estate role 31–32, 37, 101, 205, 280
Foxley, Ian 274–275
Freedom of Information (FOI) Act 113, 205, 221, 223–224
Free Speech Two (British website) 261
Frost, Chris 87
Fu, Jianfeng 128
funding issues 4, 104, 106, 282; *see also* non-governmental organisations (NGOs) and investigative journalism
*Furniture File, The* (Mumcu and Öymen) 151–152
Fustok, Mahmoud 276

Gable, Gerry 259, 263
Gadowski, Witold 164
Galizia, Daphne Caruana 26, 73, 225; *see also* Daphne Project
Galizia, Matthew 75, 77–78
Gandhi, Indira 175, 177
Gandhi, Rajiv 183
Garside, Juliette 78
Gavin Millar OC 93
*Gazeta Wyborcza* (Polish newspaper) 162, 164, 168
Gellman, Barton 35
General Administration of Press and Publications (GAPP) 127
Generation Identity (GE) movement 257–258
genetically modified food (GMF) 126, 132–133, 136n17

*Ghost Plane* (Grey) 5, 38
Gilby, Nicholas 276
Gillmor, Dan 44–45, 50
Gill, Peter 34, 40
Give Us Shelter campaign 253
Giwa, Dele 206–207
Glasser, T. L. 204
Global Investigative Journalism Network (GIJN) 6, 101, 140
globalisation and investigative journalism 7
Global Witness 44, 47, 104
Goddard, James 266
Goenka, Ramnath 178
Goldman Sachs 195–197
Goodman, Clive 245
Goodman, Joel 266
Google 113
'Googletranslatish' 225
Gorzeliński, Maciej 162
Government Communications Headquarters (GCHQ) (UK) 31, 34, 39
GPT Special Project Management Ltd 274, 277
grassroots journalism *see* local journalism in United Kingdom
Great Recession (2008) 205
Green Blood Project 83
Greenpeace 44, 47–48, 50–51, 54
Greenslade, Roy 12–13
Greenwald, Glen 35
Grey, Stephen 5, 38
Grieve, Dominic 39
Griffin, Nick 260–262, 266
Griffin, Roger 257
Griffiths, Andrew 254
GRU (Russian secret service agency) 30, 62–63
Grzeszyk, T. 222
*Guardian, The* (British newspaper) 35–36, 39, 44, 48, 76, 87, 90, 247
Guatemalan digital native sites 233
Guatemalan investigative reporting 233, 240
Gülen, Fethullah 156, 159n2
Guterres, António 64–65
Gwynne, Jason 261

Hamada, Rachel 6
Hamdo, Ahmed Haj 140–141, 143–145
Hamilton, J. T. 45
hardware of journalism 185
Hardwicke, Earl of 250

INDEX

Harkin, J. 66–67
Harlukowicz, Jacek 168
Hassan, Majdoleen 140
*Hate Trap—The Anatomy of a Forgotten Assassination* (Şahin) 158
Heikal, Mohammad Hassanain 138
*Helsinki Watch Report* 154
Hermida, A. 59
Hersh, Seymour 3
Higgins, Eliot 61, 109
Hill, Ameila 87
Hill, Ray 259
Hinckle, Warren 33
Hinton, Les 245
Hird, Christopher 104
Hislop, Ian 270–271, 273
Hitler, Adolf 168
Hodge, Margaret 262
Holocaust denial 263
Home Affairs Parliamentary Committee 92
*Home of the Beast* (social media news platform) 130
Hope not Hate (HnH) (*Searchlight* subsidiary) 13, 262
Hosenball, Mark 34
Huazong Diule Jingubang 131
Hulnick, A. 31
human rights abuses 4, 47, 60, 66, 94–96
Human Rights Act 244
Human Rights Watch (HRW) 4, 47, 104
Hungarian farm subsidies investigative report 224

IDL-Reporteros (investigative journalism organisation) 239
*Imam's Army, The* (Şik) 156
Independent Press Standards Organisation 244, 247
*Indian Express* (Indian newspaper) 177–179, 182, 184
Indian investigative journalism: background information 175–176; blinding of suspects awaiting trial 177–178, 180–182; conundrum in India and 9, 175; decline in 9, 177; democracy and 175, 184–185; diversity of Indian press and 178; editor's role and 176; examples impacting India 178–184; historical perspective of 177–178; juveniles' deaths in Tihar Jail 178, 182–184; Modi and 185; Murdochization and 176; New Media

as focus of 184–185; online 184; overview of 9–10, 176–177; paid news and 176; reporters making impacts, list of 183–184; technology and 178; trafficking women 178–180
*India Today* (Indian newspaper) 184
infographics 105
Ingrams, Richard 269
innovation 109–110, 115, 120
insecticides in strawberry fields investigative report 105
*Inside Climate News* 103
Institute for Historical Review (IHR) 263
Institute for Strategic Dialogue (think tank) 263
intelligence agencies 30–32, 34, 40–41, 280; *see also specific name*
Intelligence and Security Committee (ISC) 39
interactives 105
International Centre for Investigative Reporting 211
International Commission against Impunity in Guatemala 240
International Consortium of Investigative Journalists (ICIJ) 3, 20, 23–27, 108, 175–176, 232
International Federation of Journalists (IFJ) 88
International Petroleum Investment Company (IPIC) 196
'Investiga Lava Jato' (collaborative project) 232
investigative journalism (IJ): belief in 14; changes in 3; complexities of 2; core values informing democratic potential of 204–205; corrupting influence of power and 204; as crime 96–97; as 'custodian of conscience' 135; functions of 7; normative arguments about 240; optimism about, learning from excessive 240; watchdog function of 135, 205–206; *see also* killing of journalists; *specific type*
investigative journalists 31–32; 282–283; *see also* killing of journalists; *specific name*
Investigative Reporters and Editors (IRE) 5, 74
Investigatory Powers Bill 6, 93–94, 96
Investigatory Powers Tribunal (IPT) 39
Ipeckçi, Abdi 151
Isakowicz-Zaleskj, Tadeusz 170

# INDEX

Islamist terrorism 30
Ismayilova, Khadija 5, 76
Ivannikov, Oleg Vladimirovich 62
Izzard, Edie 262

Jabrzyk, Jaroslaw 163
Jachowicz, Jerzy 162
Jackson, Paul 13, 257
Jerichow, Anders 139
Jho Low 192–193, 194–198
Jian Guangzhou 128
Jiang Xue 128
*Jo Cox* (BBC2 documentary) 265
Johnson, Boris 271
Johnson, Loch K. 40
Joint Investigation Team (JIT) 61
Jones, Daniel 254
Jones, Gary 252
Jordanian investigative reporting 138
Joseph, Josy 184–185
JOTA (Brazilian news site) 234
journalists *see* investigative journalists;
    killing of journalists
*Journal Media* (Irish newspaper) 120
Justice and Development Party (AKP) 149,
    155–157
Justo, Xavier 194–195, 197–198
juveniles' deaths in Tihar Jail (India) 178,
    182–184

Kącki, Marcin 164
Kaczyński, Jaroslaw 165
Kahya, Damian 48, 50
Kaźmierczak, Krysztof M. 165
Kamla, trafficking of 178–180
Kaplan, David 102
Kavanagh, Sarah 5–6
Khadem Al Qubaisi (KAW) 196
Khadija Project 5
Khanfar, Wadah 138
Khangoshvili, Zelimkhan 63
Khodorkovsky, Mikhail 83
killing of journalists: Arizona Project and
    73–76, 79; Green Blood Project and
    83; incidence of 73; overview of 5, 74;
    police investigations and 83–84; positive
    results coming from 73; Russian in
    Central African Republic 83; in Turkey
    154–155; *see also* Daphne Project
Kışlah, Ahmet Taner car bombing 154
Kittel, Bertold 166, 168–169
'knowledge controversy' 66

Kobre & Kim (law firm) 195
Kongar, Emre 149–150
Kopińska, Justyna 166
Kos, Alicja 163
Kovach, Bill 58, 162
Kuciak, Jan 73
Kuczek, Grzegorz 163

*La Nación* (Argentinian newspaper) 235
*La Nación Data* (Argentinian data
    journalism project) 235
Lashmar, Paul 1, 4, 14
*La Silla Vacía* (Colombian digital native
    site) 233
Latin America *see* Latin-American
    investigative journalism; *specific country*
Latin-American investigative journalism:
    accountability and 231, 240; background
    information 230–232; collaborative
    journalism and 232–233; data journalism
    and 12, 234–235; democracy and 231,
    236; in digital native sites 233–234;
    examples of 231–232; fact-checking
    and 236–237; forces hamstringing,
    political and economic 231; freedom of
    information legislation and 238; future
    research on 240; importance of 238–240;
    legacy media and 230–231; non-profit
    and mission-driven journalism and 45;
    obstacles to 237; online harassment of
    journalists and 238; overview of 12; rise
    in 231; threats to 238; totalitarianism and
    237; transparency and 233, 235, 240;
    violence against press and 237; work
    conditions and, worsening 238
Łazarewicz, Cezary 165
Lazenby, Pete 258
Lee-Wright, P. 44
legacy media 2, 4, 8, 119–120, 209–210,
    230–231; *see also specific name*
legal threats in United Kingdom: Bureau
    of Investigative Journalism and 94;
    *Conservative Party Manifesto* and 93; data
    retention and 91; Data Retention and
    Investigatory Powers Bill and 91; Draft
    Communications Data Bill and 91;
    European Court of Human Rights and
    94; government and 97; investigative
    journalism as crime and 96–97;
    Investigatory Powers Bill and 93–94, 96;
    National Union of Journalists and 88–89,
    93–94, 96; Northern Ireland human

291

# INDEX

rights abuses and 94–95; Official Secrets Act (1911) and 89; Official Secrets Act (1989) and 89, 94; overview of 5–6; phone records of journalists and 92–94; Police and Criminal Evidence Act and 89, 93, 96; Primary Disclosure and 89; Professionals for Information Privacy Coalition and 92; protection of sources and 87–88, 91; Regulation of Investigatory Powers Act and 89, 92; Secondary Disclosure and 89; 'shield law' and 93; surveillance 90; Terrorism Act and 89

Leigh, David 225–226
Leissner, Tim 196
Lemann, Nicholas 106
Lenfest, Gerry 100–101
Lepper, Andrzej 164
Leveson Inquiry and Report 243, 247–251
Leveson, Lord Justice 247–251
Lewis, Paul 38
libel 270–271
Lipinski, Adam 164
Liu Binglu 128
Local Democracy Reporters programme 113
Local Housing Allowance (UK) 118
local journalism in United Kingdom: access to information and 113; accountability and 103; BBC and 119–120; benefits to public and 120–121; Bureau Local project and 115–119; Cairncross Review and 113–114, 121; collaborative journalism and 108, 115; community influences and relationships and 115, 121; cooperatives and 114; coronavirus pandemic and 111, 121; crisis of 6; crossroads of 111; democracy and 113–114; 'Dying Homeless' investigative report 116–118; editorial judgement and 119; engagement techniques and 120; financial struggles and 112; funding for 121; future of 111–112, 121; innovation and 115, 120; investment in, call for 121; legacy media and 119–120; Locked Out investigation 118; National Union of Journalists and 111–112, 120–121; new models and 114; New Recovery Plan and 111–112; overview of 6–7; public interest and 119; *Searchlight* and 259; storytelling and 120; sustainability and 110, 114; technology and 113; traditional media models and 114; transparency and 115; Wales 121

Local News Matters 120–121
Locked Out investigation 118
Lockerbie bombing of Pan Am jet 271
Lockyer, S. 270–271
lone-act terrorism 264–265
Lopes, Tim 5, 76
'Los Cuadernos de la Corrupción' (The notebook scandal) 239
Love Cleans Up (charity organisation) 130
#LoveLocalNews 120–121
Lowles, Nick 259, 262–263
Lugo-Ocando, J. 45
Luminate Group 103
Luxembourg Leaks (LuxLeaks) 20
Lynch, Loretta 198

MI6 39
MacArthur Foundation 204
MacAskill, Ewen 35, 90
Macbridge (Dubai offshore company) 82
Macqueen, A. 272–273
Maduro, Nicolás 237
*Mafia Fuel* (investigative report) 164
Mahathir Mohamad 199
Mahmood, Mazher 250–251
*Mail on Sunday* (British newspaper) 13, 263
Mair, Thomas 263–266
Majeran, Miroslaw 163–164
Malaysia Airlines flight MH17 shootdown 61–63, 109
Malaysian investigative journalism: background information 187–190; democracy and 188, 198; election in 2018 and 199; land grabs and 187–190; Malaysian Anti-Corruption Commission and 191; New Media and totalitarian state in 190–191; One Malaysia Development (1MDB) fund and 191–198; overview of 10; power vs publicity and 197–199; pushback against journalists and 193–194; Sarawak Report and 10, 188, 190–193, 196; totalitarianism and 188–191; whistleblowers and 191, 194–195
Maltese investigative journalism 26; *see also* Daphne Project
Manchester Arena bomber 119
*Manchester Evening News* (British newspaper) 119
*Manchester Meteor* (British news cooperative) 114
Manning, Bradley (now Chelsea Manning) 19

## INDEX

*Manual de Periodism de Datos Iberoamericano*
(data journalism project) 235
Mao Zedong 1
Marley, Kemper 75
Marshall Project 103
Martinson, Jane 121
Mattausch, D. W. 31
Maxwell, Robert 270
McCaffrey, Barry 94–95
McCann, Madeleine 253
McEntee, John 273
McFadyen, G. 220
McLagen, Graham 259
McMahon, Félim 5
McPherson, E. 66
media industry: in China 126–129; decline
of 100; democracy and 31, 41, 100,
103; legacy media and 2, 4, 8, 119–120,
209–210, 230–231; New Media and 2,
8, 184–185, 190–191; print sales' decline
and 100; sustainability of 100, 103, 110,
114, 135; 21st-century investigative
journalism and 281; *see also specific
company name*
Media Lawyers Association 96
*Médor* (Belgian media cooperative) 120
Mellado, C. 205
Menderes, Adnan 151
*Metastaz* (Pehlivan and Terkoğlu) 158
Metropolitan Police (London) 87, 90
Mexican digital native sites 233–234
Mexican investigative journalism 233–234,
239
Meyer, G. 222–223
Michigan State University Vietnam
Advisory Group (MSUG) 33
Minogue, Tim 273
Mirage Tavern 171
*Mirror, The* (British newspaper) 13, 262–263
Mishkin, Alexander 63
mission-driven journalism *see* non-profit
and mission-driven journalism
*Mobilya Dosyasi* (The Furniture File)
(Mumcu and Öymen) 151–152
MoD (British company) 274, 277
Modell, David 260
Modi, Narendra 185
Molina, Otto Pérez 240
Molnar, Sheila 270
*Mordercy Dzieci* (*Murderers of Children*)
(investigative report) 163–164
More4 True Stories 13, 262

Morgan, Daniel 272
Morgan, Lord Chief Justice 96
Morozowski, Andrzej 164
Morris, Grahame 96
Mosley, Max 246
Mosley, Oswald 246
Mossack Fonseca 19, 21–22
Muddle, Cas 257, 263
Mulcaire, Glenn 245
Mullen, Robbie 265
Mumcu, Özge 152
Mumcu, Uğur 151–152, 154
Münir, Metin 158
Murdochization 176, 185
Murdoch, Rupert 176, 245, 247
Murray, Daragh 49
Murry, Ian 265
Muscat, Joseph 77, 82
Muscat, Vince 83
Museum of Homelessness 118
Myers, Russell 253

Najib Razak 191–193, 195, 197–199
Najsztub, Piotr 162
National Action (NA) (neo-Nazi
organisation) 265
National Alliance (American Nazi
organisation) 264
nationalism 11
National Propaganda and Ideological Work
Conference (2013) 129
National Public Prosecutor's Office 170
National Security Agency (NSA) 4, 18–19,
34–35, 280
national security issues: civil liberties
and 30; encryption and 37; 'era of
exposure' and 32, 40; historical context
of investigative journalism and 32–34;
intelligence agencies and 30–32;
overview of 4; rendition policy and 5,
38–40; security state and, rise of 41;
Snowden revelations and 2, 4, 18, 34–37,
39–41; Special Demonstration Squad and
37–38; surveillance and 4, 41; terrorism
and 30; in United Kingdom 32–34
National Union of Journalists (NUJ) 88–89,
93–94, 96, 111–112, 120–121, 258, 266
National Unity Committee 151
*Nation, The* (Nigerian newspaper) 208
Nazism 13, 166, 166–168, 260
*Nazi Terrorist* (Collins and Mullen) 265
Nehru, Jawaharlal 177

# INDEX

Neo-Nazism 166, 168–169, 257, 259, 264
netizens 126, 131
New Media 2, 8, 184–185, 190–191
New Recovery Plan 111–112
news industry *see* media industry; *specific company name*
News International 246–247
*News, The* (Nigerian magazine) 207
*Newswatch* (Nigerian magazine) 206–207
*News of the World* (*NoW*) (British tabloid) 243–247, 250–251
*New York Times* (US newspaper) 33, 75, 224, 235
*New York Times* Visual Investigation case study 60, 64–65, 67
*Next* (Nigerian newspaper) 203–204
*Next Edition* (Nigerian online news platform) 208, 212
Nigerian investigative journalism: advertising revenues' decline and 207–208; background information 203–204; decline in 203, 206–210; democracy and 203–206, 212; digital media's rise and 206–207; digital sleuthing and 204, 210–213; Freedom of Information Law and 205; in future 213; investigative units' depletion and 208–209; magazines' decline and 206–207; media and 205–206; online 204, 210–213; overview of 10–11, 203, 212; reputation of 206; 'roving' model of legacy media and 209–210; watchdog function and 205–206
*Nigerian Telegraph* (newspaper) 208
Nigerian Television Authority (NTA) 208
Niras 158
Nixon, Richard 33, 74
*Nómada* (Guatemalan digital native site) 233, 240
non-governmental organisations (NGOs) and investigative journalism: boundary work and 52–53; criticisms of 50–53; debate surrounding 44–45; examples of 44, 47–49, 54; expansion of 45–46, 53–54; funding 45–46; human rights abuses and 4, 47; as 'journalistic entities' 49–52, 104; mimicking journalists and 49–52; objectivity and, questions surrounding 50–54; overview of 4; Pergau Dam affair 47, 54n1; transparency and 54; *see also* non-profit and mission-driven journalism; *specific NGO name*

non-profit and mission-driven journalism: accountability and 103, 110; background information 100–101; burn-out and 110; collaborative journalism and 107–109; co-publishing model and 106; decline of news sector and 100–101; fact checking and 109; funding and 104, 106; governance and 104; growth in 101–103; Latin-American investigative journalism and 45; independence and 104; infographics and 105; innovation and 109–110; interactives and 105; overview of 6, 101; power of 106–107; public interest and 104–105; risk taking and 109–110; workings of 107
Nord, L. W. 204
Northern Ireland human rights abuses 94–96
Norton-Taylor, Richard 30–32, 40
*No Stone Unturned* (film) 94–95
Nycz, Cardinal Kazimierz 170

Obaid, Tarek 194
Obasanjo, Olusegun 206
Obermayer, Bastian 21, 77
Obermayer and Obermaier 21
Objective programme 158
objectivity 50–54, 81
Odebrecht (construction company) 239
Office for the Coordination of Humanitarian Affairs (OCHA) 64
Official Secrets Act (1911) 89
Official Secrets Act (1989) 89, 94
Offshore Leaks Database 27
Oldroyd, Rachel 6
Olojede, Dele 204
Omu, F. I. 206
Onanuga, Bayo 207
One Malaysia Development (1MDB) fund 191–198
online investigations *see* digital sleuthing
'Open Newsroom' project 59
Open Society Foundations 103
open source intelligence (OSINT) investigations 60–61, 65, 109
open-source journalism 5, 54
Operação Lava Jato (Operation Car Wash) scandal 239
optical character recognition (OCR) 23
*Optical Valley Guest* (social media news platform) 130
Organised Crime and Corruption Reporting Project (OCCRP) 5, 76–77, 79, 109

294

# INDEX

*Oriental Horizon* (news programme) 131
*Oriental Morning Post* (Chinese newspaper) 127
Ornacka, Ewa 165
Ortega, Daniel 237
Osborne, Darren 264
*Outlook* (Indian news magazine) 184
Öymen, Altan 151–152
Özal, Turgut 153
*Özgür Ülke* bombing 154

paedophilia in Polish Catholic Church 163–164, 169–170
Paetz, Archbishop Juliusz 170
paid news 176
Palczewski, Marek 9
Panama Papers: backlash against 26–27; collaborative journalism and 12, 24–25, 108, 232; data from offshore financial service providers and 19–21; dealing with data and 21–22; ethics and 27; format of data and 22–23; impact of 17–18, 28; International Consortium of Investigative Journalists and 3, 20, 23–24, 26–27, 108; John Doe and 19, 21–22; lessons learned 28; Obermayer and 77; Offshore Leaks Database and 27; overview of 3–4; publishing 26–27; research methodology of 221; shared responsibility for 12; stories within and without, finding 25–26; technology and 4, 23–24, 28
*Panorama* (British documentary) 13, 259–261
*Paper, The* (Chinese newspaper) 127, 130
Paradise Papers 156, 221, 232
Parashar, Amitabh 182
Parkinson, Jason 89
Parry, Ryan 252
Parry, Tom 258
Party's News and Public Opinion work Symposium, The (2016) 129
passenger name record (PNR) data 63
Paterson, Mike 274–275
Patora, Tomasz 164, 165
Payne, Kenneth 31–32
Paz, Miguel 235
Pearson, Allison 272
Pehlivan, Barış 158
Penman, Andrew 252
*People's Daily* 125, 129
Pergau Dam affair 47, 54n1
Perry, Felipe 235
pesticide investigative report 224

PetroSaudi International 194–198
Pew Research Center 45
*Philadelphia Inquirer* (US newspaper) 100–101
philanthropic support 6, 102–103; *see also* non-profit and mission-driven journalism
Philby, Kim 34
Phillips, Alison 262
phone hacking 244–248
phone records of journalists, accessing 92–94
Phythian, M. 40
Pilger, John 3, 13, 252
Piñera, Sebastián 243
'pitch and pay' for stories 120
*PLA Daily* 129
*Plaza Pública* (Guatemalan digital native site) 233
Poitras, Lauren 35
Police and Criminal Evidence Act (PACE) (1984) 89, 93, 96
police investigations 83–84, 93, 95
Police Service of Northern Ireland (PSNI) 95
Polish Communist Party (PZPR) 162
Polish investigative journalism: accountability and 9; awards for 166, 169–170; Communist Party and 162; crisis of 165; debate involving 172; examples of 163–170; explosives purchase from terrorist group at Okęcie Airport 162–163; methods of 163, 171; neo-Nazism 166, 168–169; original source reporting 171–172; overview of 9, 162; paedophilia in Polish Catholic Church 163–164, 169–170, 172; in past decade 165–170; post 1989 162–164; in present times 172; reconstructing events and 171; restraints on 165, 172; revival of 165–170, 172; Stachowicz's death 166–167; TNT purchase by *Super Express* reporter 163; in 21st century 164–165; undercover reporting and 171
*Polish Neo-Nazis* (investigative report) 166, 168–169
Polish People's Party (PSL) 165
Pompeo, Mike 30
Ponsford, Dominic 92, 251
Powers, M. 50
*Premium Times* (Nigerian online newspaper) 204
presentation technique 60
Press Club Polska 170

295

# INDEX

Press Complaints Commission (PCC) 244, 247–248
Press Council 247
Press Freedom Index 189
*Press Gazette* (British newspaper) 92
'presstitutes' 185
Price Waterhouse Cooper 20
Primary Disclosure 89
print sales, decline in 100
privacy issues 280–281
*Private Eye* (British satirical magazine): advertising revenue 270, 278; anonymous writers and 272–273; background information 269–270; bylines and, lack of 272–273; cartoons and parodies in 272; challenges facing 278; as club 273; employees 270; founders of 269; 'in the Back' section of 272; investigative journalism and 271–273; issue of, dissecting 271–272; libel payments by 270–271; Lockerbie bombing of Pan Am jet and 271; media distributing 269–270; overview of 13–14; sales of 270; schoolboy humour of 269; 'Shady Arabia and the Desert Fix' 13–14, 274–277; success of 271, 278; tip-offs 273
Professionals for Information Privacy Coalition 92
Project for Excellence in Journalism 45
*Propublica* (non-profit news source) 103–106
protection of sources 87–88, 91
Protess, D. 177
public interest 104–105, 119, 267
publicity 204
Public Order Act 261
Public Prosecutor's Office (Guatemala) 240
public relations 193
*Punch, The* (Nigerian newspaper) 208
Putin, Vladimir 24, 26, 30
Pytlakowski, Piotr 165

*Question Time* (British TV programme) 261
Quilliam (think tank) 263

Rachwani, Manar 142–143, 146
*Ramparts* (California-based monthly publication) 33
Ran, N. 183
*Rappler* (Philippine online newsroom) 103
Reach (British news company formerly Trinity Mirror) 248
Reade, Brian 262

*Rebel Media, The* (Canadian news website) 265
Red Granite Pictures 192
red-tops *see* British tabloids
*Redwatch* (British publication) 266
Red White and Blue Festival (2001) 260
Regulation of Investigatory Powers Act (RIPA) (2000) 89, 92, 244–245
remote sensing 60
rendition policy 5, 38–40
Renshaw, Jack 265
Reporters without Borders 189
Reporting the Far-right campaign (NUJ) 266
reputation management 193
Requejo-Aleman, J. L. 45
Reva and David Logan Foundation 103
Richard, Laurent 5, 73, 75–80
Riza Aziz 192
Robinson, Tommy 257, 265–266
Rodriguez, Miguel Ángel 240
Roof, Dylann 264
Rosenstiel, Tom 58, 162
Rosmah Mansor 192–194
royal families' investigative reports 225
Roy, Rammohun 177
*Runrun.es* (Venezuelan digital native site) 233
Rusbridger, Alan 36
Rushton, William 269
Russell, A. 52
Russian bombings in Syria 64–65
*Russian Insider, The* (news website) 62–63
Ryle, Gerard 18, 19–20

Sabbagh, Rana 137, 139
Sabuncu, Murat 157
*Sahara Reporters* (diaspora online platform) 204
Şahenk, Ayhan 154
Şahin, Haluk 150, 153, 155, 158
Saldaña, Magdalena 12
Salt Scandal 165
Sanlu Milk Scandal 125
Santer, Jacques 217
Sarawak Report 10, 188, 190–193, 196
Sarin, Ashwini 178–180
Saudi Arabia National Guard (SANG) 274
Saudi Arabia National Guard Communications (SANGCOM) 274–277
Sawers, Sir John 35–36
Scandinavian investigative journalism 221
Scotland Yard 247
*Searchlight* (grassroots news platform) 13, 259, 263
Secondary Disclosure 89

296

# INDEX

*Secret of Cups, The* (documentary) 131
Seglins, David 37
Segnini, Giannina 239–240
Sekielski, Marek 166, 169–172
Sekielski, Tomasz 164, 166, 169–172
Self-Defense Party 164
'self media' 127
self-publishing 54
Sen, A. 177–178
Şener, Nedim 156
Sergeev, Denis 63
'Shady Arabia and the Desert Fix'
    (investigative report) 13–14, 274–277
'Shame of It, The' (investigative feature) 182
Shane, Scott 37
Shared Data Unit (BBC) 119
Shearman & Sterling (law firm) 195
Sheehan, Neil 33
Sheinbaum, Stanley K. 33
Shekhovtsov, Anton 257
'shield law' 93
Shourie, Arun 176, 178–180
Şik, Ahmet 156, 158
Simec International Ltd 275–276
Singh, S. Nihal 178, 180
Sinha, Arun 177–178, 180–182
SITU Research 60
*Skin Hunters* (investigative report) 164
Skripal, Sergei 62
Smit, M. 218
Snowden, Edward 4, 34–35, 280
Snowden revelations 2, 4, 18, 34–37,
    39–41, 90, 280
Snow, R. P. 50
Sobolewska, Anna 166, 168–169
social media companies and future of
    investigative journalism 281; *see also
    specific media name*
software of journalism 185
*SoldFromUnderYou* (investigative report) 105
solidarity 204–205
Somerfield, Bryan 276
Sommerlad, Nick 252–253
Sonwalkar, Prasun 9–10
sources, protection of 87–88, 91
Southern Poverty Law Center (SPLC)
    263–264
Sowore, Omoyele 210
Special Demonstration Squad (SDS) 37–38
Spinwatch 1
Spotlight (*Boston Globe*) 107
Stachowiak, Igor 166–167, 171

Stachowiak, Maciej 167
Stanistreet, Michelle 91, 112, 266
Starkman, D. 205
states and investigative journalism 128, 281
*Statesman, The* (Indian newspaper) 184
State Taxation Administration (STA)
    (China) 134
Stead, WT 2
Steiger, Paul 103
Stelmasiak, Marcin 164
'sting operation' 249–250
Stockholm Center for Freedom 149
Storyful 58–59
storytelling 120, 222
Straw, Jack 38–39
Stuchbery, Mike 266
subterfuge 249
Suleiman, Suleiman A. 10–11
*Sunday Mirror* (British tabloid) 248–249, 254
*Sunday People* (British tabloid) 248, 254–255
*Sunday Times* (British newspaper) 34, 47,
    107, 195, 275
*Sun on Sunday* (British tabloid) 251
*Sun, The* (British tabloid) 248, 253–254
Sun Yat-sen University 130
Sun Zhigang 125, 135n1
*Superwizjer* (Polish TV programme) 168
Suri, Sanjay 178, 182–184
surveillance: accountability and 4, 94;
    British tabloids and 249–250; Bureau
    Local project and 7, 116; during
    coronavirus pandemic 7; fear of 67;
    investigative journalism and 41; legal
    threats in United Kingdom and 90;
    national security issues and 4, 41; state
    35, 90, 96; transparency and 41; *see also*
    Snowden revelations
sustainability of media industry 100, 103,
    110, 114, 135
Sykes, Andy 261
Syria 3, 64–67
Syria Direct 140–141
Syrian investigative journalism:
    accountability and 140; challenges
    of 142, 144–147; during civil war
    139–142; before civil war 137–139;
    in conflict zones 146–147; emergence
    of 137, 139; examples of 139–142;
    fake news and 145; Islamic factions'
    recruitment of children and 141; in
    non-conflict zones 143; overview of 8;
    passion and 144; practice of 144–147;

297

# INDEX

protection of journalists and 145; Sabbagh's articles and 137; society as hindrance to 146; Syria Direct and 140–141; Syrian Investigative Reporting for Accountability Journalism and 140; training in 142–144; war profiteers and 141

Syrian Investigative Reporting for Accountability Journalism (SIRAJ) 140

Szpala, Iwona 166

tabloids *see* British tabloids; *specific name*

Taib family 10, 190

Taib Mahmud Abdul 187–188, 191–193, 195

Talaga, Piotr 166

Tarbell, Ida 2

Tarrent, Brenton 264

tax avoidance investigative reports 21, 126, 133–134, 224–225

tax scandal involving entertainment Chinese celebrities 126, 133–134

Taylor, Gordon 245–246

team approach to reporting *see* collaborative journalism

technology: data journalism and 23–24, 28; developing 28; digital sleuthing and 57–58; in Indian investigative journalism 178; Investigatory Powers Bill and 93; journalism and 57–58; local journalism in United Kingdom and 113; in 'new era' of Chinese investigative journalism 126; Panama Papers and 4, 23–24, 28; surveillance 41, 249–250; Turkish investigative journalism and 154

*Tell* (Nigerian magazine) 207

*Tell It Like It Is* (news programme) 131

Tell Mama (British organisation) 259

*Tell No One* (film) 166, 169–170, 172

Terkoğlu, Barış 158

terrorism 30, 263–266, 271, 280

Terrorism Act (2000) 89

*Texas Tribune* 103

Theuma, Melvin 83

Thurlow, Richard 257

Tihar Jail (India) 178, 182–184

Tillack case 223

Tillack, Hans-Martin 11, 223

*Times of India, The* 183

Tkachev, N. 62

Today's Headlines 127

Toker, Metin 150

totalitarianism 9, 188–191, 237

*To Whom the Plot* (investigative feature) 166

Trade Union Congress (TUC) 266

traffic as king 113

trafficking women (India) investigative report 178–180

'transformational journalism' 101; *see also* non-profit and mission-driven journalism

transparency: British tabloids and 249; Chinese investigative journalism and 135; decline of news industry and 100; European Union investigative journalism and 11, 217, 221; Freedom of Information Act and 113, 115; Latin-American investigative journalism and 233, 235, 240; International Consortium of Investigative Journalists and 27; local journalism in United Kingdom and 115; non-governmental organisations and investigative journalism and 54; surveillance and 41; WikiLeaks and 18

Trevino, Josh 193

Trinity Mirror (British news company renamed Reach) 248

Troyas, Philippe 275

Trump, Donald 73, 280

truth-telling 52

Tsinghua University 127

Tunisian investigative reporting 138–139

Turkish investigative journalism: assassination of Turkish diplomats 158; book publishing and 149–150; challenges of 157–158; changes in media landscape and 152–154; conglomerates in media landscape and 154; democracy and, promise of 149; development of 150–151; emergence of 151, 159n1; Ergenekon terrorist organisation investigation 156, 159n3; FETO infiltration into government 156–158; fictitious furniture export operation 151–152; historical perspective of 149; Justice and Development Party and 149, 155–157; military coup and 152–153; overview of 8–9; repression of 149, 155–158; technology and 154; training 152, 158; violence against journalists and 150–151, 154–155

Uğur Mumcu Investigative Journalism Foundation 152, 158

Uighurs' human rights abuses 60

INDEX

UKIP 258
Umejei, Emeka 10–11
undercover reporting 171
Unearthed (investigative unit) 44, 47–48, 50–51, 54
UNESCO report (2017) 41
United Kingdom: Armed Forces sexual offences in 119; Bureau of Investigative Journalism 6, 94, 105, 108, 115–116, 118; Government Communications Headquarters 31, 34, 39; Local Housing Allowance and 118; M16 39; Manchester Arena bombing in 119; national security issues and 32–34; Queen's privacy and 252–253; restrictions on journalism and 5; tabloids in 12; *see also* British far-right journalism; British tabloids; legal threats in United Kingdom; local journalism in United Kingdom
United Nations Climate Summit (2011) 52–53
United Nations Educational, Scientific and Cultural Organization (UNESCO) 139
Ünker, Pelin 156
user-generated content (UGC) 49, 58, 130–131
US National Security Agency 4, 18–19, 34–35
US presidential election (2016) 236

van Eijk, D. 218–219
Varela, Pedro 263
Vaz, Keith 92, 249–250, 254
Veness, David 259
Venezuelan digital native sites 233
Verghese, B. G. 178
verification technique 59
Vine, Phil 52–53
visual investigation techniques 60; *see also* digital sleuthing
*Voice of San Diego* (non-profit news organisation) 103

Wacowski, Piotr 166, 168–169
Waisbord, Silvio 12, 50
*Wall Street Journal* (US newspaper) 67, 103, 197
Wang, Haiyan 7–8

Wang, Keqin 130
Wang, Lifen 128
Ward, Patrick 13–14
*Washington Post* (US newspaper) 33, 67, 74, 235
watchdog function 135, 205–206; *see also* investigative journalism
Watergate scandal 74
Waters, Anne Marie 258
Weber, Mark 263
Webster, Ben 248
WeChat (Chinese social media platform) 127, 129
Weibo (Chinese social media platform) 127
Welch, Dylan 37
'we media' 8, 127, 129–130
Wendland, Michael 74–75
whistleblowers 87, 191, 194–195
White & Case (London law firm) 195
WikiLeaks 2, 18–19
Wilson, Harold 273
Wojciechowski, Przemyslaw 164
*Workers' Daily* (Chinese newspaper) 125
*Work for Sex* (investigative report) 164
World Development Movement (now Global Justice UK) 47

Xi, Jinping 128–129
Xinhua News Agency 125, 129, 134

Yarl's Wood refugee asylum centre 252–253
Yaxley-Lennon, Stephen 257, 263, 265–266
yellow posters of *Médor* 120
Yeşil, Bilge 154, 157
Yiannopoulos, Milo 266
*Yimiao zhi Wang* (investigative feature) 129
yin-yang contracts 133
YouGov poll 261
*Young, Nazi and Proud* episode of *Dispatches* (British TV programme) 260

Zekman, Pamela 171
Zelizer, B. 52
Zieliński, Daniel 163
Ziobro, Zbigniew 169
Zubik, Malgorzata 166

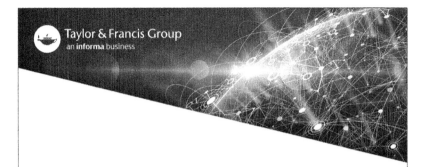